# Between Vision and Obedience— Rethinking Theological Epistemology

# Between Vision and Obedience— Rethinking Theological Epistemology

Theological Reflections on Rationality and Agency with
Special Reference to Paul Ricoeur and G. W. F. Hegel

George Ille

PICKWICK *Publications* · Eugene, Oregon

BETWEEN VISION AND OBEDIENCE—RETHINKING THEOLOGICAL
EPISTEMOLOGY
Theological Reflections on Rationality and Agency with Special Reference to Paul
Ricoeur and G. W. F. Hegel

Pickwick Publications
An Imprint of Wipf and Stock Publishers
199 W. 8th Ave., Suite 3
Eugene, OR 97401

www.wipfandstock.com

ISBN 13: 978-1-4982-6591-1

*Cataloguing-in-Publication data:*

Ille, George.

    Between vision and obedience—rethinking theological epistemology : theo-
logical reflections on rationality and agency with special reference to Paul Ricoeur
and G. W. F. Hegel / George Ille.

    xvi + 288 pp. ; 23 cm. Includes bibliographical references and index.

    1. Knowledge, Theory of (Religion) 2. Knowledge, Theory. 3. Ricœur, Paul. 4.
Hegel, Georg Wilhelm Friedrich, 1770–1831. I. Title.

BT50 .I45 2013

Manufactured in the U.S.A.

For my wife, Mihaela, and my three children,
Dorothea, Paul, and Michael . . .

# Contents

# Preface

THIS BOOK IS ABOUT rationality and knowledge, philosophical and theological . . .

I am aware, of course, that concern with knowledge and epistemology is still derided in some quarters today. I have been stubborn enough to pursue such a project over the years in spite of its bad press, at least in part, because I felt that there was some truth in the old Greek adage that "happiness consisted in the pursuit of knowledge." Beyond instrumentality and control, there is something profoundly meaningful about knowledge, which makes us who we are, humans created in the image of God, finite and fragile to be sure, yet always wanting to know more, always aspiring "to know the truth" or "trying to imitate the gods," as Aristotle had it.

I have also felt that although we presently have an unprecedented access to information, an immense amount of data available at our fingertips, just a "mouse click away," more often than not, that doesn't make us more knowledgeable but rather more confused . . . Information needs to be organized, evaluated, measured. We need rules and standards, intellectual and moral. Having information is not the same as having knowledge . . . And people are still being "destroyed from lack of knowledge" (of both God and the world, it should be added, as the two cannot be really separated). Whatever bad connotation epistemology may have, we still need to learn "to read the signs of the time." That is to say, the problem of rationality and knowledge must be restated and corrected rather than ignored or abandoned.

I am also aware that this is a peculiar subject, one that doesn't lend itself easily to direct analysis. Because of its elusive nature, our investigation is predominantly carried out in an "indirect" way. In other words, we will talk about a number of other things, about self and hermeneutics and about God and the world. Moving within such large spaces has its perils, of course, but also its rewards, as my analysis will hopefully indicate. Moreover, I seek guidance in this grand inquiry, lest my project would not spiral into an hopeless wandering into the "totality of the real." I follow Ricouer's hermeneutical journey in the first part, Hegel's speculative one in the second, in order to anchor my concerns historically and thematically. In the last part I engage a number of philosophers and theologians from both the continental and the analytical tradition and make use of theological insights from both the East and the West. My purpose is to bring hermeneutical philosophy/theology in direct confrontation with Trinitarian theology with the specific purpose of evaluating the present state of theological rationality. The result, as I hope it will become apparent, is a unique take at tracing the contours of a theological rationality freed from both modern and post-modern (hermeneutical) anxieties. The Christian knows, no doubt, that "the Lord is the Spirit," and that "where the Spirit of the Lord is, there is freedom." Of course, this is the same Lord "who gave himself for us to redeem us from all wickedness and to purify for himself a people that are his very own, eager to do what is good." That is why, as my friend Douglas Knight states in the preface of his book *The Eschatological Economy*, "the church must not take society's claims and description of itself with too much seriousness." In this respect, theological rationality can be genuinely free only to the extent it reconciles *philo-sophia* with Paul's reminder that it is in Christ that we witness "the manifold wisdom of God." From this perspective, reason always finds itself "under the sign of baptism," as "love of wisdom" entails an unwavering exercise of uncovering a rationality that also proclaims the "folly of the Cross." A Reason that comes against our consumerist society and its promises of well-being and success. But the church is also the place where "we rise" with Christ in order to embrace the world once again as God's good Creation, a world that is being remade, transformed and perfected in Christ and by the Spirit. Since "speaking rightly" about both God and the world, necessarily requires access to such a "high place," it necessarily entails not only knowledge but also virtues and intellectual duties. It requires vision but also obedience. Ultimately, as our analysis will show, when contemplated in its true theo-logical intention, epistemology is not really a human invention.

# Acknowledgments

THERE ARE MANY PEOPLE who made this project possible. I owe a great deal of gratitude to my PhD supervisor, the late Colin Gunton who introduced me to Trinitarian theology. During my studies at King's College London, I had the privilege to listen to and engage many of Gunton's colleagues, both theologians and philosophers who were regular contributors to the weekly seminars of the Research Institute in Systematic Theology. Among them, were Christoph Schwöbel, Francis Watson, Murray Rae, Alan Torrance, Paul Helm and Professor Zizioulas.

The years following the completion of my PhD thesis were eventful and tumultuous as my family and I relocated to the United States. A significant part of my initial project would be re-thought and re-written in the light of my new challenges and engagements as I gradually immersed myself again in theological reflection. I have to thank Professor Joel Green not only for encouragement and fruitful conversations but also for giving me the opportunity to teach Theology and Philosophy at Asbury Theological Seminary. I also owe a great deal of gratitude to my colleagues Larry Wood and Charles Gutenson for both their friendship and for conversations about modern/post-modern philosophy/ theology and about the challenges of teaching philosophy and theology and the role of such subjects in the life of the church.

There were many other people who, in one way or the other contributed to this project. I was blessed to get to know people like Anne Garrett, Charles Twombly and Paul Copan who not only that encouraged me in my work, but through conversations and theological exchanges kept my interest in such a peculiar subject alive. I am especially grateful to Paul Copan for reading and engaging parts of my manuscript. I had the privilege to get to know Paul, through another dear friend, Bill Smith, the director of the C.S. Lewis Institute of Atlanta. I am grateful to Bill for his friendship and support over the years. Our Wednesday meetings for lunch at Panera were always refreshing and theologically meaningful. Panera has also been the place for another meaningful (and regular, for a while) encounter, this time with Cristi Cocean, one of the pastors of the First Romanian Baptist Church from Lawrenceville, Georgia. I am thankful to Cristi for candid and practical theological conversations and for keeping me in touch with the daily concerns of the local church.

But this project could not have reached the present form if it weren't for the kind support and encouragement of both Professor John Webster and Professor William Abraham. I am immensely grateful for their willingness to read and engage parts of my manuscript.

I must also add that as an immigrant, I am condemned to inhabit (at least) two worlds and two cultures at the same time and I suppose the present project bears the mark of this double allegiance. In this sense, I must thank my Romanian friends who were studying with me (and put up with me); Daniel Bulzan, Danut Manastireanu, Dorin Axente and Silviu Rogobete among others. With many of them I have continued to exchange views and engage in (more or less friendly!) arguments over the years.

Finally, there were people closer to me, geographically and relationally, friends and family with whom I shared both the occasional burdens and sorrows and the little joys of daily life, (including perhaps the sweet delight of "small talk"!) Among them, Dan and Dorina Neiconi, Corneliu and Madalina Niculas, Emi and Ani Faur, Daniel and Dana Moraru, my dear sisters Ana and Eunice, my brother-in-law Traian, my nephews Beni and Eugen and my parents who never stop asking about that book that was supposed to come out . . . They all have been part of the "local church" for me, in more ways than they may have realized as we were tending to one another's needs and encouraging one another as "aliens in search for a better country" . . .

Finally, of course, my thanks go to my dear wife Mihaela who, not only that encouraged and supported me along the way, but provided "conditions of possibility" and concrete opportunities that made this project possible.

# Introduction

THE DISCUSSIONS ABOUT SUBJECT and validation in our late modernity tend to oscillate between the "weak" self of post-modernity ("empty" or "rhetorical") and neo-Cartesian versions trying, as they do, to recover a discredited foundation. Correspondingly, the solutions advanced range from calls for a new Enlightenment (in the face of the resurgence of myth and the irrational), to attempts to "re-enchant the world" (in the face of the growing threat of an impersonal instrumental Reason).

The present study seeks to respond theologically to such a situation from the perspective of God's action in and towards the world. Its aim is to trace a view of rationality that follows the drama of God's engagement with the world, thus involving dying and resurrection, ascesis and abundance, suffering witness and Eucharistic communion. Since, as Calvin notes, knowledge of God and knowledge of self are intimately bound together, this exercise of discerning the shape of a theological rationality in the present arena of competing promises of meaning and truth is carried out on two levels: the theo-logical and the anthropological.

As a theo-logical task, it engages with the concerns of the legitimacy of our God discourse. Following Barth, we want to hold to the task of theology as being the effort of the Church to clarify its own language about God. Such an effort takes place in the world (John 17:15) and in this respect has significant ethical overtones in its dependence upon God. This is why theology is fundamentally not a striving for relevance, as a genuinely "public discourse" is not born from such concerns. Yet, theology must take seriously the claim that the world is still God's world, as God's good Creation, despite the Fall. To affirm that is to allow for a certain intelligibility of both human experience and history, which in turn presupposes a reconsideration of the more ontological/universal claims (their nature and possibility in the light of Revelation). To paraphrase

Von Balthasar, it may be the case, indeed, that true philosophy cannot exist outside Christianity, or conversely that philosophical discourse is at bottom theology, albeit, more often than not, bad theology.

But this rather universalist perspective is counterbalanced by a parallel concern with the radical nature of Revelation as being not only *in* history, as we experience it, but actually *over against* it, and, indeed, as inaugurating a new history in the very midst of the present one. This latter claim challenges the "God's eye" perspective, uncovering the seriousness of our falleness and finitude and revealing both the gap between what we presently are and what we are called to be and also our utter dependence, as authors of discourse, upon God.

As an anthropological task, it situates the project in relation to modern philosophy by taking seriously a different, and yet related, set of opposing claims. First, the claim of description, manifest in a concern for ontology (as found in Heidegger and in some post-Heideggerian philosophy for instance), and second, the complaint of critical thought in regard to the implicit prescriptive dimension in any ontological claim. While this is usually rendered as the inevitable presence of human interests or subsumed under the more general category of desire, arguably such critique only reveals the same tension between "what is" and "what can or must be," or, spelled out in theological register, the invincible connection between ontology and soteriology.

Such claims are relevant not only in terms of how theology should address or respond to them but in the more general sense in which both the "descriptive" and the "critical" dimensions are inherently present in the kerygmatic and the prophetic aspect of the Gospel respectively. What is more, God's action in and towards the world not only mediates the tension between the two perspectives, between "is" and "ought," but enables us to situate the anthropological task itself within the same theo-logical endeavor, as God brings about his salvific acts through human beings in history and ultimately through the one man Jesus Christ.

*Our aim, therefore, is to restate the terms of theological rationality in the light of this mediatory role of agency, both divine and human.* A way back to properly epistemological questions may be opened up in this way, freed from the burden of the distinctions which set the agenda for the modern discussions about the self with their deep metaphysical assumptions (noumena/phenomena, transcendental subject / empirical subject, etc.). I shall only add that such an inquiry into human knowing, acting and being, from a theological perspective, is not (or at least not yet), a Christian anthropology, but fundamentally an investigation into the nature of the Christian claims to knowledge.

Formally, our analysis will emerge as a reply to a hermeneutical situation found to be pervasive in the present intellectual climate. In the first part, we shall attempt to trace the terms and problematic of this hermeneutical debate, in a critical engagement with Paul Ricoeur. Guided by his philosophical journey, we shall have the opportunity to assess theologically both the strengths and the weaknesses of the hermeneutical rejection of modernity. While a promising opening suggested by a mediation between a theology of the Word and a theology of Creation will be retained, Ricoeur's hermeneutical subject will be shown to remain ultimately inadequate from the perspective of God's relationship with his Creation. Such reflections will prompt us to turn to Hegel's bold self, to the philosopher who brought (or so he claimed), Revelation to the very heart of his philosophical system.

The appeal to Hegel, however, is prompted not only by the need for a more open engagement with ontological issues, but also because Ricoeur's own critical discourse uncovers a speculative dimension which needs to be further explored. Our engagement with Hegel is a battle on two fronts. On the one hand, I shall attempt to retain a "critical realist" reading of Hegel by reconsidering his profound engagement with history and historical questions, while, on the other, I shall use and pursue further Hegel's attempt to recast the meaning of history in Trinitarian categories.

In the light of our more general concerns, our engagement with Ricoeur and Hegel will help us to establish the problematic of our theological argument, to rethink what it means for theology to be faithful to its *Sache*, to carve out its own specific "realism" between "idealism" and critical approaches, to reimagine responsible theological speech that "looks forward to the day of God and hastens its coming." One may perhaps wonder whether we are trying to resuscitate an old debate about historical consciousness and the role of history in theological discourse. While we are neither directly engaging with this question here nor debating the starting point of theology, it must be said from the outset that this is in many ways true. As McCormack remarks at the end of his book on Barth, our relationship with nineteenth century theology is more complex than is usually thought. This must be thought through however not only in relation to Kant, but also to Hegel. The postmodern incapacity to renounce (Hegelian) speculation as well as the more recent neo-Marxist concomitant call for both "universality" and radical subjectivity (Alain Badiou, Slavoj Žižek) makes this task even more urgent.

If our engagement with Ricoeur and Hegel helped us to establish the principal coordinates of this problematic and to trace the lines of a theological reply it will have attained its goal.

In the last part, we shall reconsider "the ontological claim" (the "source" of our standards of rationality) in the light of contemporary Trinitarian thought. By engaging with a number of theological positions and recent proposals, we shall suggest that the basic grammar of the Trinitarian description, considered in its ontological intention (i.e., aiming at "the way things are"), calls for a "return to the world." This "return" is still "ontological talk" to be sure, yet it entails an invincible epistemological dimension which will be spelled out at the intersection between "Creation" and "Word" in a polemical disputation with both an idealism of "sense," and an idealism of "freedom."

Under the guidance of a Trinitarian view of agency, but specifically focusing on illumination, the emerging theological rationality will be conceived "under the sign of baptism," and articulated as *doxic obedience*, as a form of *holistic response* to God's redemptive acts, in and towards the world. Finally, by testing our proposal against a number of recent epistemological models, such response will be shown to trace the parameters of a theological rationality freed from both modern and post-modern (hermeneutical) anxieties.

By recasting reason in this new context, we hope to make a contribution to the present epistemological discussions in at least two ways. First, by clarifying the theological background of the collusion between ethics and epistemology (making thus a contribution to "virtue epistemology"), and second, by unveiling the dispute between "internalism" and "externalism" in a new (Trinitarian) light.

# Part I

## The Hermeneutical Self—
## From Meaning to Revelation

### *Reflections on Paul Ricoeur's Hermeneutical Project*

Higher than actuality stands possibility. We can understand phenomenology
only by seizing upon it as a possibility.

MARTIN HEIDEGGER, *BEING AND TIME*

### Introductory Remarks

THE WORK OF PAUL Ricoeur has inspired an impressive amount of literature. The formidable breadth of his philosophical compass, including as
it does, fields as diverse as literary criticism and analytic philosophy, psychoanalysis and biblical interpretation, not only recapitulates the battles
and aspirations of his own generation, but witnesses to the living tension
between reflection and action, past and present, academic vogues and
enduring truths.

Part I: The Hermeneutical Self

In a century of turmoil, marked by alternations of unprecedented bursts of hope for a reconciled humanity and unfathomable sources of disquiet, Ricoeur's writings display a specific alertness. Because the "world lieth in evil," responsible thought must prevent the enclosing of reason in a totality and point to its limits with Kant, yet, with Hegel, remain open to the human aspiration for the unity of being. But the inherent tension in this form of post-Hegelian Kantianism, as Ricoeur sometimes calls it,[1] takes up a unique character by virtue of a second and more fundamental tension, that between critique and conviction[2], that is, between the philosophical *logos* and his Christian commitment. It has been perhaps this distinctive standing that has continued to commend Ricoeur's work as an incessant source of insight for both philosophers and theologians.

In what follows, rather than offering an overview of Ricoeur's huge secondary literature, we shall limit ourselves to a brief recounting of a couple of relevant positions just by way of introducing our own engagement with Ricoeur. A number of theological treatments of Ricoeur seek to explore whether, and in what way, his hermeneutical insights are theologically warranted in a Christian reading of the Bible (Vanhoozer, Fodor[3]). Vanhoozer, for instance, insists that Ricoeur's hermeneutics must be understood in the larger context of his philosophical project. Thus, he traces Ricoeur's anthropological project back to Kant, via Heidegger. As a Heideggerian reading of Kant, the cardinal theological correction is a pneumatological one. Vanhoozer claims that it is in the light of the impossibility of a philosophical approximation of a doctrine of the Spirit, that Ricoeur's dealings with imagination and possibility become problematical. Other treatments focus specifically upon the hermeneutics of the subject in Ricoeur. Prominent among them remains Van Den Hengel's study. The long and intricate passage of the subject from dispossession to recovery uncovers a view of subject as "gift," enabled and sustained by a "schema of hope,"[4] attesting to Ricoeur, in Van Den Hengel's view, as a "philosopher of justification" and to a conception of

1. Ricoeur, *Conflict of Interpretations*, 412. See also Ricoeur, *Hermeneutics and the Human Sciences*, 193.

2. See Ricoeur's preference for this designation in one of his last books, *Critique and Conviction*, 139.

3. Vanhoozer, *Biblical Narrative in the Philosophy of Paul Ricoeur*. Fodor, *Christian Hermeneutics*.

4. Van Den Hengel, *Home of Meaning*, 247ff.

redemption specifically Pauline.[5] Albano's systematic study on the other hand, focuses upon the relationship between theology and philosophy in Ricoeur's philosophical anthropology.[6] Albano seems eventually to treat Ricoeur's work as a species of philosophical theology, which needs to be corrected with a full-fledged transcendental ontology. The more philosophical treatments try either to question or to correct various emphases, either his allegiance to Kant or Heidegger, or his unrelenting phenomenological or reflexive assumptions.[7] Some of them touch upon issues relevant to our study and occasional references will be made to such evaluations in the development of our argument.

This brief and undoubtedly highly selective survey brings together a number of concerns which nonetheless will here take on a quite specific form. We are interested in the Christian appropriation of Ricoeur's hermeneutics, and with Fodor,[8] we do acknowledge that the question of "use" must be consistently referred to the more primordial question of the referential intention of his discourse. Yet, we feel that a proper treatment of both truth and reference requires a more thorough referring to God's Trinitarian action. Similarly, we find Ricoeur's philosophical approximations problematical, and the doctrine of the Spirit vis-à-vis his paramount interest in imagination certainly needs theological clarification. We suggest however that under Trinitarian guidance, such a clarification receives a more comprehensive framework. Likewise, we do acknowledge Ricoeur's Reformed background and his unrelenting stress upon "losing oneself" as the precondition of genuine knowledge will receive special attention. Nonetheless, the speculative grammar of such a claim will be more critically referred to its philosophical roots. In the same vein, we consider Albano's concern for ontology and the more universal questions as legitimate concerns, even though the advent of such ontology is conceived differently.

Our engagement with Ricoeur may be situated perhaps at the crossroads of a systematic and narrative treatment. It will be systematic not

5. Ibid., 258.

6. Albano, *Freedom, Truth, and Hope*.

7. See, e.g., the collection of essays (with replies) contained in Ricoeur, *Philosophy of Paul Ricoeur*, ed. Lewis Edwin Hahn, or the collection of essays *Paul Ricoeur: The Hermeneutics of Action*, ed. Richard Kerney.

8. Fodor's stated aim is to "use and develop" Ricoeur. He deals extensively with Ricoeur's work on narrative being especially interested in the question of truth and the problem of reference.

so much in the sense of a clear-cut exposition of Ricoeur's position as opposed to similar treatments. Rather, the systematic aspect of our engagement will be reflected primarily in a coherent *"witness."* That is to say, the meaning of various terms and the coherence of various themes will be looked for within Ricoeur's own corpus of writings first. Ricoeur's use of various terms may perform different functions and receive slightly different meaning in his own writings. It is in the work itself as a whole, as a "witness" in its inseparable connection with its author, that we must look for the referential aim of a discourse.

But our engagement is also narrative. A synthesis circumscribed by an ultimate underlying intention (in its double hypostasis as "founding" in an author and "recovered" in a reader), if possible at all, remains abstract and fragile. There is more contingency to human intentions and decisions than first meets the eye. As we hope it will gradually become apparent, a narrative engagement presupposes a more complex structure of agency in history, which in turn raises the testimony of the "witness" beyond the contingent commitments of a human author.

We shall approach Ricoeur therefore not only in the light of his own intentions but sometimes against them. This is in fact in agreement with one of his hermeneutical convictions that the text must be allowed to speak for itself. Thus, while we shall listen to various themes as treated directly by Ricoeur, we shall also be attentive to incidental remarks made in different contexts, when both the subject matter and the point of view may be different, not only because this may throw some light upon silent assumptions, but also, more importantly, it may indicate potential openings towards a forever-anticipated unity of being.

In sum, a *kerygmatic-narrative* reading may be an apt term to describe our engagement with Ricoeur. We are aware that an attempt on our part to bring together the philosophical and the theological dimensions of Ricoeur's writings would go against his intention. Part of our purpose, however, is to show that Ricoeur's insistence on keeping them separate is ultimately untenable. As Findlay once said in regard to Hegel, the most rigorous musts, are perhaps also the most trivial and empty.[9]

But there is a second set of considerations which guides our engagement with Ricoeur, somewhat derived from the first. Many theological readings are, no doubt for good reasons, interested in Ricoeur's poetics. It is rightly felt that it is ultimately there that Ricoeur says "the essential."

9. Findlay, Foreword to *Hegel: The Essential Writings*, xi.

In material terms, that means less interest is devoted to a theological assessment of phenomenology or to Ricoeur's encounter with the masters of suspicion. Phenomenology raises perhaps less interest because it is, as Ricoeur himself acknowledges, inherently atheistic, while the encounter with Marx, Nietzsche and Freud marks only the problem, a dispossession and a loss, that which the poetics is supposed to address. The present study accords more space to both phenomenology and to the hermeneutics of suspicion (especially Ricoeur's response to Freud) precisely because part of our intention is to show their continuing relevance in the subsequent project. In other words, they are not mere signposts or symptoms expressing a need, but have a structural presence within the solution itself.

The first part focuses upon Ricoeur's hermeneutical journey. Following Heidegger, Ricoeur stresses repeatedly that understanding is always self-understanding. If the end point is seen to be a subject, as the only site where meaning can be fulfilled, the journey may be safely approximated as being fundamentally guided by an inquiry into meaning.

*1*

# The Search for Foundation

## From Reflexive Philosophy to Hermeneutics

### The Promise of a Project

As a beginning philosopher, Ricoeur found himself at the juncture of three major philosophical orientations: the French reflexive philosophy, the philosophy of existence of Gabriel Marcel and Karl Jaspers, and Husserl's descriptive phenomenology.[1] French reflexive philosophy appears in Ricoeur's own description as a way of thinking which can be traced back to the Cartesian *cogito*, through Kant and the French post-Kantianism, having Jean Nabert as its most prominent figure.[2] If preoccupation with epistemological issues, translated in the predominance of matters of justification and certitude, has been the overriding concern of such a line of thought, what Ricoeur retains from reflexive philosophy is its fundamental responsibility before reason. Ricoeur would often speak with unconcealed admiration of his first philosophy teacher, Roland Dalbiez.[3] His realist drive, manifest in his bold resistance to all idealist claims to immediacy or apodicticity, has remained a marked feature of his overall work.

---

1. Our brief historical survey is indebted to Ricoeur's own recounting of his intellectual journey. Cf. Ricoeur, "Intellectual Autobiography," 1–54, and Ricoeur, *Critique and Conviction*.

2. Ricoeur, "On Interpretation," 187–88.

3. Ricoeur, "Intellectual Autobiography," 4.

But this high regard for precision and intellectual integrity fully accepts the challenge of the existentialist concern for finitude, contingency and limit-experiences. Indeed, thought cannot be separated from life.[4] In this sense, Ricoeur's personal encounters with Gabriel Marcel and Emmanuel Mounier (the great Christian personalist) were destined to have discernible echoes in his own work.[5]

It is also true, however, that Ricoeur's encounter with existentialism took place within the more general context of the resurgence of the Hegelian studies in France after 1930.[6] Whilst the structure of Hegel's particular presence in Ricoeur's thought will be discussed in more detail later, it may be noted by way of anticipation, the undeniable Hegelian flavor of Ricoeur's untiring drive to mediate. In *Fallible Man*, he writes:

> Man is not intermediate because he is between angel and animal. He is intermediate within himself, within his selves. He is intermediate because he is a mixture, and a mixture because he brings about mediations.[7]

Ricoeur's mediations are never allowed, however, to lapse into facile amalgamations, skepticism or mere negativity.[8] As will become apparent, Ricoeur sees dialectic as being more than a mere "logic of appearance."[9] Mediation is both a given and a task. It always presupposes a tension which, rather than being exhausted in a final synthesis, opens the discourse to reality. An eloquent example here is Ricoeur's celebrated tension between faith and reason, described at times as an "internecine war," which had continued to haunt him in his later writings.[10]

4. See for instance the noting of the suicide of his fourth child. Ricoeur, "Intellectual Autobiography," 51.

5. Cf. ibid., 6–7.

6. See Descombes, *Modern French Philosophy*, 10ff. Under the influence of Kojeve's famous lectures on Hegel's *Phenomenology of Spirit*, a whole generation of intellectuals made use of a predominantly anthropological reading of Hegel.

7. Ricoeur, *Fallible Man*, 3.

8. Cf. Ricoeur, "Intellectual Autobiography," 11.

9. As Descombes notes, before 1930, "dialectic" had primarily a pejorative meaning. The neo-Kantians considered Hegel's philosophy as helplessly idealist, and consequently his dialectic simply a logic of appearance. Descombes, *Modern French Philosophy*, 10.

10. Ricoeur recounts the acute sense of conflict between faith and reason which has marked his intellectual life from the very beginning. On the one hand, his Protestant upbringing provided him with a strong sense of both religious experience (identified later with Schleiermacher's feeling of absolute dependence) and the preeminence

Nonetheless, it has been rightly maintained, I believe, that Ricoeur's first sketch of his grand project of a *Philosophy of the Will* bears the undeniable mark of Kantianism.[11] In his later years, Ricoeur labeled this "programming of his work" promised at the end of *Voluntary and the Involuntary* as "most imprudent."[12] Was this beginning of a system, subsequently abandoned? Is Ricoeur's own deploring of it an indication that perhaps a *kehre*, a reorientation, took place in the meantime? We suggest that a turn to the specific way in which Ricoeur engages with Husserl, and perhaps more importantly, the way in which some fundamental phenomenological concerns continued to inform his later works, may provide an answer to this question.

## Anthropology under the Aegis of Phenomenology[13]

Husserl's project aims to radicalize Descartes by establishing the *ego cogito* as the only foundation for science.[14] Descartes's long detour of anchoring the *cogito* in the divine perfection is rejected since, Husserl believes, such a move reinstates the gulf between exteriority and interiority, betraying thus Descartes's own radical intention.[15] If the outside is doubtful, one indeed has no choice other than to start with that which is immediately given.

---

of the Word of God (under the influence of Barth's theology, especially his famous commentary on Romans). Cf. Ricoeur, "Intellectual Autobiography," 5ff.

11. See for instance Vanhoozer, *Biblical Narrative*; Lowe, *Mystery of the Unconscious*; Bourgeois, *Extension of Ricoeur's Hermeneutic*; Anderson, *Ricoeur and Kant*; etc.

12. Ricoeur, "Intellectual Autobiography," 13.

13. In what follows, we shall not seek to present a neat description of Husserl's doctrine. Even if such an endeavour were shown to be unequivocal, it is doubtful that in the light of our concerns here that would be particularly illuminating. In fact, Ricoeur notes a certain incongruity between the phenomenological method described by Husserl and the concrete way in which he employed it. Cf. Ricoeur, *Husserl*. chapter 1. Note also the different interpretations of Husserl by his followers. Cf. Ricoeur, "Intellectual Autobiography," 11.

14. Ricoeur claims that an adequate description of Cartesian philosophy must acknowledge its two sources, God and the *Cogito*. (For a somewhat similar interpretation, see Pannenberg, *Systematic Theology*, 1:351.) In this light, Husserl does not radicalize but rather destroys the original sense of Cartesianism, asserts Ricoeur, which amounts to an implicit "atheism" structural to his phenomenological method. Cf. Ricoeur, *Husserl*, 84ff. See also Ricoeur, *Essays on Biblical Interpretation*, 109.

15. Husserl, *Cartesian Meditations*, 7ff. Husserl believed that doubt "should have put an end to all objective externality and should have disengaged a subjectivity

In this way, the access to reality, promised in the celebrated call "*Zu den Sachen!*," has as a necessary intermediate stage the "world-for-me." The most primitive reality is the reality of consciousness. The constitution of meaning in consciousness led to the famous distinction between acts of consciousness or intentions (the *noesis*), and their intentional correlates, the *this* or *that* of experience (the *noema*). The phenomenological analysis aims to describe the relationship between the *noesis* and the *noema* without posing questions of factuality. Phenomenology "brackets" the sensible reality (*epoché*) because its interest lies not in the *what*, but rather in the *how* of description. It is important to note that the phenomenological use of consciousness as "the consciousness of . . . something," is not connected with empirical consciousness; therefore, it is not the object of psychology.[16] In fact, Husserl took a great deal of effort in criticizing psychologism.[17] Rather than being concerned with "psychological facts," phenomenology is interested in what is "original," in enduring "essences." To know a thing is to know its meaning (what Husserl called *eidos* of a thing), its fundamental structure. How one can do this? By exploring its various appearances. Only after the "detour of imaginative variations" (*Abschattungen*, i.e., "profiles" or "sketches") can an adequate appropriation of the "objectification" (in the "realist" sense) be achieved. The call to "the things themselves" aims thus to go beyond the "naïve" realism of immediate self-perception, by promoting subjectivity to "the rank of a transcendental."[18] Husserl believed that in this way, self-certitude itself receives a more fundamental anchoring.

But it is important to note the kind of transcendentalism described in such a process. The ego is not endowed here with an Olympian perspective, since the actual perception is always situated in a point of view. The "appearing" as such, is always perspectival. There are always "horizons in need of clarification."[19] The "essence" of a thing is not immediately given,

---

without an absolute external world." See Ricoeur, *Husserl*, 83.

16. Husserl's transcendental ego cannot be objectified. Instead it serves as the foundation of psychology, in the same way as it serves as the foundation of all the other sciences. (This is why Ricoeur insists that Husserl's psycho-physical body has no connection with the incarnate body of the existentialists.) Cf. Ricoeur, *Husserl*, 35–48.

17. See Husserl, *Logical Investigations*, 1:90–196.

18. Ricoeur, *Hermeneutics and the Human Sciences*, 103.

19. "And in each actual experience it is surrounded—for essential reasons and not because of our weakness—with horizons in need of clarification." Husserl, *Cartesian Meditations*, 177, quoted in Ricoeur, *Husserl*, 141.

presupposing instead a conscious and oriented effort. Husserl often refers to it as the attempt to get beyond a mere "natural attitude." This is a gradual process, (assimilated at times as a special spiritual discipline) attained through the "imaginative variations" of the phenomenological reduction.

We should also stress in this connection the way in which Husserl thought he went beyond Kant. On the one hand, the things "as they appear to us," the world of phenomena, represent the "natural attitude" which must be overcome by ascending from the relativity of a particular positing of a concrete being, to its *eidos*. On the other hand, the being-in-itself, as an existence without me, is a false in-itself, a mere absolutisation of the ontic, of the "this" or "that" of "particular beings."[20] Hence, Husserl's transcendentalism is not secured by the category of *a priori* knowledge, but gained by the effort of gradual accumulations of the "profiles" of the object.

This insistence upon the grasping of the "essence" of a thing, as the necessary correlate of a genuine scientific endeavor, may appear to bring Husserl closer to Plato. Yet, the equal stress put upon the process of reduction, the attempt to reach a life-world, especially characteristic of his later works,[21] uncovers a different horizon of concern, indicating his allegiance to a concrete, intersubjective world. Husserl's radical pretension of establishing a "the third way," neither idealist nor materialist, neither objectivist nor psychological, was the main focus of Ricoeur's careful scrutiny. He writes:

> I attempted to dissociate what appeared to me the descriptive core of phenomenology from the idealist interpretation in which this core was wrapped. This led me to distinguish in Husserl's opaque presentation of the famous phenomenological reduction, the competition between two ways of approaching the phenomenality of the phenomenon. According to the first, ratified by Max Scheler, Ingarden and other phenomenologists of the time of the *Logical Investigations*, the reduction made the

20. Paraphrased from Ricoeur, *Husserl*, 177.

21. Ricoeur bases his interpretation here mainly on *Ideen I* and *Ideen II*. As in the case of Heidegger, he pleads for a fundamental continuity in Husserl. Such a narrative integration is, as it will become apparent, structural to Ricoeur's concept of narrative identity. In this light, Husserl's or Heidegger's *"kehre"* (and arguably Ricoeur's himself), is not based upon some language of decision or a radically immanent "conversion." All "conversions" must have a connection with the outside, an "exteriority" component. What arises from this is a vision which challenges the fundamentally "docetic" paradigms of both a transcendental knowing subject over against the world (the Cartesian epistemological picture), or an agent as a center of assertion (the Hobbesean "political" paradigm). We shall return to the meaning of such an interpretation below.

appearing as such of any phenomenon stand out more sharply; according to the second, adopted by Husserl himself and encouraged by Eugen Fink, the reduction made possible the quasi-Fichtean production of phenomenality by pure consciousness, which set itself up as the source of all appearing, more original than any externality. Carefully respecting the rights of the "realist" interpretation, I thought I could maintain the chances of an accord between a phenomenology that was neutral with respect to the choice between realism and idealism, and the existential tendency of the philosophy of Marcel and Jaspers.[22]

These concerns are already apparent in the first books of his *Philosophy of the Will*. In *The Voluntary and the Involuntary*, Ricoeur proceeds by an extension of Husserl's *eidetic* analysis to other spheres than that of perception, more precisely those of the will and affectivity. The cluster of themes introduced here, the phenomenological analysis of "project" (with its intentional correlate "the thing to be done by me"), the dialectic of acting and suffering and the nature of "character," will be developed in Ricoeur's later work (especially *Oneself as Another*). The next two volumes reunited under *Finitude and Guilt*, came as a correction of the "generic man" of the *Voluntary and the Involuntary*. The correction imposed itself because an analysis of "man's fundamental structure" tended to leave outside its zone of interest the empirical, the concrete aspect of human existence. The province of the "bad will," the mystery of the "fallenness of existence," has implicitly called for further ontological clarifications.

The first step in this direction is made in the *Fallible Man*. Ricoeur attempts here to ground the dialectic of the voluntary and the involuntary in an ontology of disproportion. Such an ontology, which takes its cue from an attempt to re-think human constitution as a finite-infinite polarity,[23] can account for a structural fragility of the finite will, but not for evil will as such. The analysis bears the mark of what Paul Ricoeur calls "the brilliant discovery of Kant," that is to say, it places the above endeavor in connection with the special place of transcendental imagination, as the third term in which reflection looks for its fulfillment

---

22. Ricoeur, "Intellectual Autobiography," 11.

23. Ricoeur believes that making finitude a global characteristic of human reality is an overstatement since "none of the philosophers of finitude have a simple and un-dialectical concept of finitude" (Ricoeur, *Fallible Man*, 3). In the same vein, he rejects absolute transcendentalism, a freedom over against nature, in the manner of Sartre's philosophy.

It is this special place of productive imagination, between sensibil-ity and understanding, as both determinative and determinable,[24] that sets the stage for Ricoeur's specific type of reflection. Genuine reflection is always "upon the object."[25] Correspondingly, the resulting "conscious-ness" of such an act is not yet self-consciousness but remains "purely intended, represented in the correlate."[26] It must be noted that in spite of a somewhat classical starting point as an infinite-finite polarity, Ricoeur does not re-iterate traditional anthropological subdivisions in terms of faculties.[27] The reality of the human invites a constant movement within the whole, unveiling itself as a dialectic of activity and passivity, openness and perspective. Whilst *Fallible Man* remains somewhat unique to the extent that an ontology is attempted here, such an ontology remains in many ways abstract. Fallibility, as Ricoeur himself recognizes, somewhat "slipped" between finitude and guilt.[28] A genuine account of the "evil will" will require a more radical methodological shift, which would enable an encounter with the historical and the contingent evil will.

This methodological decision will first make its way in *The Symbol-ism of Evil*. But this already prefigures Ricoeur's next step, the passage through symbolic thought, in other words, the beginning of hermeneu-tics. Before going further, however, it is instructive to chart two cardinal dimensions in this initial prefiguration of the self's journey.

## The Continuous Significance of Reflective Philosophy

Ricoeur's fundamental trust in the "power of knowing," coupled with his undeterred belief in the radical nature of reflection, appear to place him unequivocally in the reflective camp.

Indeed, it is noteworthy that in spite of his insistence upon the pri-ority of the world in the phenomenological analysis, Ricoeur insists at least in equal measure upon the early Husserl (from the *Logical Investiga-tions* to the *Cartesian Meditations*), where consciousness is defined more by its distance from the signified things. It is just such a distance that

24. See Kant, *Critique of Pure Reason*, 104 (SS 20; book 1, ch. 2).

25. Ricoeur, *Fallible Man*, 18.

26. Ibid., 18–19.

27. Ricoeur emphatically rejects for instance the Cartesian distinction between an infinite will and a finite understanding. Ibid., 25ff.

28. See Ricoeur, "Intellectual Autobiography," 16.

constitutes the power of signifying for Ricoeur.[29] This unveils an emancipatory dimension, grounded perhaps in Ricoeur's secret belief that in some way Descartes was, in his fundamental intention, closer to the truth than Husserl. Whilst Descartes transcends the *cogito* by means of God, Husserl transcends the ego by the *alter ego*.[30] Admittedly, Descartes's transcendence proved to be problematic. Yet Husserl's tacit acceptance of Kant's "transcendental illusion" has never seemed to question the immediacy of his own type of transcendence. Such considerations also anticipate the thought that perhaps the criterion of "reality" cannot be settled in a framework established within the confines of a self-world dualism.

We remember that part of Husserl's strategy has been precisely to set aside discussions about what is "real," and to concentrate upon the "experience" of knowledge *per se*. There is a sense in which, indeed, such an attitude is liberative, to the extent that it questions our categories and presuppositions, anticipating a phrase dear to Ricoeur, namely, the celebrated "return to the first naiveté." But this openness is also a barrier because such uncommitted attitude seems to suggest an ideal neutrality. Ricoeur was to comment later that in this sense phenomenology in its innermost intention "was condemned never to be completed and perhaps never genuinely to begin."[31] Or Ricoeur wants more. Not only a consciousness established in "stable unified significations,"[32] but the mystery behind its genius. As we shall see, this attempt at radical grounding opens the question of the nature of the speculative dimension in Ricoeur's writings. Nonetheless, the move itself rightly targets a different form of idealism inherent precisely in Husserl's descriptive aim.

---

29. Husserl seems here to treat perception only as a privileged mode of fulfillment. Of course, perception may be illusory or it may remain unfulfilled. In his last works, Husserl tends to ascribe a foundational role to perception depotentiating the claim of consciousness to constitute itself. See Ricoeur, *Husserl*, 204–5. Ricoeur's desire to preserve both horns of the dilemma (that is to say, a narrative integration of Husserl, which would retain in a radical way, both the early and the late Husserl), is telling in connection with his specific way of mediation.

30. For details, see Ricoeur, *Husserl*, 84ff.

31. Ricoeur, "Intellectual Autobiography," 11.

32. Ibid., 41.

## The Limitations of the Phenomenological Description

"The great discovery of phenomenology is intentionality,"[33] writes Ricoeur. The theme of intentionality (of consciousness as "consciousness of . . ." with its fundamental orientation towards the "outside") marks the break with the Cartesian identification between consciousness and self-consciousness. It is in this fundamental openness to the world, that the "de-centering" of the self is first anticipated. Phenomenology promises a better description of the connection between self and the world, precisely by focusing upon the dynamic of their interaction, rather than relying upon an abstract concept of knowledge. In such a scheme, the mind no longer opens unproblematically, in an *a priori* fashion, domains of objectivity. Nor is objectivity a mere product of the empirical verificationist principle. It rather appears as "a synthetic constitution . . . as a uniting of meaning to presence."[34]

Ricoeur felt however that Husserl's descriptive dimension, in spite of its attempt to go beyond a mere subject-object distinction is still too abstract, incapable of accounting for the richness of experience. His existential concern for concrete existence starts to question fundamentally the somewhat pejorative treatment of the "ontic" and contingent in Husserl. In fact, Ricoeur's own version of phenomenology (focusing as it does upon non-cognitive aspects (willing, motivation, action) as opposed to the more intellectualist versions of Levinas or Merleau-Ponty), can be seen as an attempt to dissociate his language of mediation from the idealistic tendency of Kant's practical positing. Intentionality discloses a structural thematization already at work in the consciousness itself. As fundamentally "outside-oriented," the meaning-bestowing consciousness, as the *noesis* of the *noema*, reflects a somewhat basic "spontaneity" of the soul, a pre-formed willing, revealing its fundamental connectedness with the world of objects. Genuine knowledge has its root in such fundamental dynamism, which connects the "inside" with the "outside." But this turn to a more ontological consideration of Kant starts to unfold

---

33. Ricoeur, "On Interpretation," 189.

34. Ricoeur, *Fallible Man*, 40. It is important to acknowledge therefore that Ricoeur, unlike Kant, does not subordinate knowledge to empirical criteria. Ricoeur insists that "the objectivity of the object is constituted on the object itself." Furthermore, "objectivity is neither in consciousness nor in the principles of science; it is rather the thing's mode of being." Ibid., 38–39. This opens up a potential theological elaboration of "objectivity" grounded in a conception of particularity.

a deeper problematic of the subject which would continue to haunt Husserl's project. Let us take a closer look at how this happens.

From a transcendental perspective Husserl's phenomenology may be seen as an attempt to extend Kant's inquiry from the possibility of science to the possibility of all experience. Kant's passage from a "successful science" to its conditions of possibility, tended to produce a narrow concept of knowledge (which the positivists took uncritically), and by implication, a narrow concept of the world (an intellectualist account in which the world is a mere idea of reason, necessary to unify our scientific experience). To extend the inquiry to the whole of experience is to question the status of Kant's transcendental subject with its unproblematic apperception. In this respect, Husserl's insight is essentially correct; we do need an "eidetic" reduction of all immanent life, which must be the correlate of the transcendental reduction (the bracketing of physical reality). Nevertheless, a number of problems remain. Ricoeur rightly asks: Is Husserl's radical ideal of scientificity sufficiently convincing?[35] Is not Husserl's "methodological conversion" also a metaphysical decision?[36] How can one distinguish adequately between a phenomenological and a psychological reduction? Seen from this perspective, Ricoeur's appeal to the masters of suspicion (especially to Freud in this context) can be understood as an effort to purge the eidetic reduction from its idealistic traits. A genuine description must put this "methodological conversion" to the test of reality.

Thus, Ricoeur expands the phenomenological project on two fronts: on the one hand, he pursues the fundamental constitution of the self in its objects, implied by its orientation towards the world (explored by strands of post-husserlian thought and particularly by Heidegger, in the concept of *Lebenswelt*), and on the other, he questions the very presupposition of such a process, to the extent to which it may draw its energy from a false consciousness, an unreliable intuition or perhaps a "false conversion." Both extensions seem to be prompted by an inner conflict which, Ricoeur believes, dominates all phenomenology, the requirement of reduction and the requirement of description.[37]

35. See Ricoeur, *Hermeneutics and the Social Sciences*, 102ff, where Ricoeur tries to uncover the main features of Husserl's idealism by showing that in fact such a claim to radical foundation remains in a very important sense at the level of intuition, therefore based in subjectivity.

36. See for instance Ricoeur, *Husserl*, 36; or his critique of Husserl via Kant, cf. Ricoeur, *Husserl*, 190ff.

37. Ultimately, the fifth meditation (cf. Husserl, *Cartesian Meditations*, 89–148)

In sum, Ricoeur wants to question both the idealism of consciousness and the idealism of "sense" implicit in Husserl's radical grounding.
This anticipates a dialectic of appropriation and distanciation, dialectic
which would become very much part of the fundamental grammar of
Ricoeur's philosophical style.

## The Impoverished Self: The Hermeneutics of Suspicion

### The Dispossession of the Self:
### The Guide of a Phenomenological Aporia

But phenomenology anticipates something else. As it is well known, Husserl believed that perception could be in principle fulfilled. But is such
potential of fulfillment always readily available to our experience? The
world confronts us with experiences which can hardly be "reduced," like
time and "negativity." Such experiences do not lend themselves to tidy
description. Can we always rely upon the integrity of the intellectual act
that guides the phenomenological analysis?

It is in this connection that the stark contrast between Husserl's phenomenology and that of Hegel is most apparent. Whilst the aim of both is
"to let experience appear and speak for itself," the great difference between
the two is that for Husserl, the negative remains foreign.[38] What is more,
this inexorable presence of the negative announces the end of phenomenology. This happens, paradoxically, notes Ricoeur, "at the very moment when
it promises an immense enrichment of the description, properly so-called,
of the human experience."[39] Genuine attentiveness to the "Other" must pay
serious attention to what, in Kantian language, remains inscrutable, that is

---

is unable to account properly for the existence of the other, and therefore to respond
adequately to the charge of solipsism, contends Ricoeur. The apperceptive transfer,
or "analogizing apperception" which "must at once respect the originality of the experience of the Other and root it in the experience of the owned body, . . . creates as
many problems as it solves because this is not a type of reasoning." It is rather a "pre-
reflective," "antepredicative" experience. Cf. Ricoeur, *Husserl*, 126.

38. It must be said that Ricoeur recognizes that Phenomenology itself begins with
a critique of the reflective consciousness. Thus "any investigation into 'constitution'
refers to something pregiven or preconstituted" (Ricoeur, *Conflict of Interpretations*,
102). But "Husserl's phenomenology is incapable of taking the failure of consciousness
all the way," concludes Ricoeur (ibid.).

39. Ricoeur, *Husserl*, 206. (See also Ricoeur, "Hegel and Husserl on Intersubjectiv-
ity," in *From Text to Action*, 227ff.)

to say, to the experience of evil and the irrational. Indeed, the world confronts the self with an ambiguous axiology, which profoundly questions the efficacy of a mere "methodological conversion." Is such a possibility readily available within the structure of the world? Moreover, can it be subsumed within a general logic of history of the Hegelian type? If it cannot, philosophy must not be content with establishing isles of rationality in an ocean of questionable meaning, or with reconciling the good with the evil in a single ontological principle. Such a challenge carries with it an equally radical methodological counterpart: Is the ideal of description itself sufficient, in a world which does not seem to offer too much hope? If the answer is no, Marx's adage, that the task of philosophy is not to describe the world but to change it, must be taken seriously.[40] In a similar fashion, if the transcendental reduction, as a smooth and linear recovery of the *eidos*, is interrupted by negativity, the inner reduction is itself confronted by the irreducible reality of the unconscious.

Is it not the case then that, in order to succeed, the phenomenological experience itself is in need of an absolute guarantor as in the Cartesian project? Is not perception, as a form of "unthematic spontaneity" or "not-yet-formed will," part of a more fundamental "enabling" which must guide the phenomenological reduction itself? Moreover, is Husserl's methodological conversion sufficient? Does not the structure of reality call for a more fundamental "healing" if phenomenological analysis is to be successful? For the theologian, such a direction of inquiry has soteriological intimations. In many ways, Ricoeur's interest in the will may be seen as a potential response to precisely such problems.[41]

As we have already noted, in Ricoeur's first books on the will, under the aegis of phenomenology, the structure of the will unveils itself in a dialectic of self and world. On the methodological plane, this gradually effects a passage from *eidetics* to *empirics*, that is to say, from a purely phenomenological and transcendental perspective to hermeneutics. From the perspective of content, this effort of reading the self in the world would raise, as we have just seen, not only questions about ontology and soteriology, but also about the enigma of evil. It will be this *aporia* of the bad will which will constitute the privileged field of exploration in the

---

40. See Marx's address to Feuerbach: "The philosophers have only interpreted the world . . . the point is to change it." Marx, "Theses on Feuerbach," 158.

41. Ricoeur will recall later that "it was with regard to a specific problem, that of bad will, that I had first become aware of the general condition for self-understanding." Ricoeur, "Intellectual Autobiography," 23.

encounter with the masters of suspicion. A different kind of terminology insinuates itself here that claims to unveil a more fundamental logic: the logic of desire.

## The Dispossession of the Self:
## Toward a New Foundational Science?

The "horizonal" characteristic of Husserl's "elusive ego," was only the beginning of the self's passion. The passage through Freud, Marx and Nietzsche would have to effect the real break down of its pretensions. Nevertheless, the mark of reflexivity, the meaning question, is still there guiding Ricoeur in his response to these challenges.

In what follows we shall take a closer look at this encounter. What all those masters of suspicion seem to have in common is their fundamental critique of the very premise of phenomenology, consciousness itself. To this extent, contends Ricoeur, Freud, Nietzsche and Marx confront phenomenology "on the same ground."[42] The fact that it is Freud who tends to occupy Ricoeur more than the other two is hardly surprising, for it was Freud who effected the final and perhaps most decisive humiliation of the human subject. Ricoeur writes:

> First there was the cosmological humiliation inflicted upon man by Copernicus, who destroyed the narcissistic illusion by which the home of man remained at rest in the centre of the universe. Then there came biological humiliation, when Darwin put an end to man's claim to be unconnected with the animal kingdom. Finally came psychological humiliation. Man, who already knew that he was lord of neither the cosmos nor all living things, discovers that he is not even lord of his own psyche.[43]

Freud's most disturbing claim is that consciousness cannot be trusted, that it lies to itself and that its true motivations are not immediately accessible. In the face of such a challenge Ricoeur wants to re-think and re-ground the concept of consciousness. Is reflexive philosophy still possible after psychoanalysis?

To this end, Ricoeur brings the claims of psychoanalysis under close scrutiny. A philosophical appropriation would imply an assessment of its claim to truth, its possibilities and its limits. But Ricoeur's ultimate

42. Ricoeur, *Conflict of Interpretations*, 99.

43. Ibid., 152.

concerns rest with his projected philosophical anthropology. He aims to attain a vision of humanity that would be able to integrate in itself the dialectic of consciousness and the unconscious. Freedom and dignity must pass through the bondage of the "economic" model, as he calls it, only to emerge again as a more truthful dialectic of fragility and responsibility. This latter claim also spells out the primary concerns of the present analysis. As in the case of phenomenology, even if a faithful description of the psychoanalytic theory and practice were possible, that would only be of secondary importance. What is important in the present context is the particular way in which Ricoeur appropriates it.

Ricoeur summarizes the principal claims of psychoanalysis under three headings. First, psychoanalysis is an analytical procedure for investigating the human psyche; secondly, it is a method or a therapy for the treatment of neurotic disorders, and thirdly, it is a doctrine connected to the previous two practices, which tries to indicate their theoretical foundation or establish psychoanalysis as a scientific discipline.[44] Let us analyze in turn the principal traits of this rather loose association.

To begin with, Ricoeur fully accepts the main challenge of psychoanalysis. The reflexive subject must acknowledge its own fragility. Ricoeur's reply to its crisis is to separate the Cartesian certainty from genuine self-knowledge. Self-adequation no longer precedes reflection. Self-consciousness is no longer a premise, but a task. The search for such adequation presupposes a labor, a travail.[45] Ricoeur is quick to point out that this is not a form of resignation. In fact, it is precisely this acceptance that opens the possibility of an inquiry into the scientific status of psychoanalysis itself. There are a number of ramifications to this problem which will be addressed in turn below.

We shall concentrate especially on the essay "The Question of Proof in Freud's Psychoanalytic Writings" not only because Ricoeur addresses the problem of truth in psychoanalysis and its claim to scientificity in a systematic fashion, but also because it pushes psychoanalysis to its limits. This latter treatment may be thus seen as a correction of a somewhat theoretical bias which characterized his earlier collection of essays on Freud (*De l'interprétation: Essai sur Freud.*)[46] By uncovering

---

44. Cf. Ricoeur, *Hermeneutics and the Human Sciences*, 255.

45. Ricoeur, *Conflict of Interpretations*, 101–2.

46. Ricoeur notes and seems to accept Gabriel Marcel's disavowal of the book as a lapse into abstraction. He writes: "I would reproach myself for having constructed everything on Freud's most theoretical texts . . . and not having sufficiently confronted

psychoanalysis's proximity to other points of view (theory of texts, theory
of history, natural sciences, ideology, etc.), Ricoeur displays once again
the same movement within the whole, so characteristic of his philosophical anthropology.

After noting psychoanalysis's filiation with the natural sciences
and its procedures of validation, Ricoeur dives into what he considers
to be a necessary preliminary analysis; an inquiry into the nature of the
psychoanalytic "facts." He identifies here the proper object of the psychoanalytic practice as being not desire as such, nor the realm of instincts,
but desire as meaning, desire in its interaction with the social institutions and the world of culture.[47] As we shall see below, if this leads to the
problematization of the "psychoanalytic facts," it nevertheless breaks its
initial narrowness ascribed to it by Freud himself, in his metapsychology.
Closely bound up with the notion of desire, Ricoeur enlists four traits of
the psychoanalytic practice.

First is its semantic aspect, that is to say, desire brought to speech,
told, confessed. Psychoanalysis is closer to a practice of interpretation
and deciphering, than to a report of facts of observable behavior. By connecting us with a universe of "motivation and meaning,"[48] psychoanalysis
uncovers its kinship with the practice of interpreting texts.

The second trait is its intersubjective character. By looking at the
patient-analyst relation, Ricoeur highlights the relevance of the "the
work" of the analyst.[49] The concept of transference, used in the struggle
against resistances, when the patient "repeats instead of remembering,"
uncovers, not only the semantic aspect of desire, but also its orientation
towards an "other." Psychoanalysis is more than mere "energetics," a mere
economy of desire, or a "mechanics" of instinctual forces.

The third trait is the "psychic reality" in the psychoanalytic practice.
Again, in apparent contrast to Freud's own positivistic intention, psychoanalysis does not operate in Ricoeur's opinion with a neat real/imaginary
distinction. The "work of mourning" (the reaction to the loss of an object) is of utmost importance at this juncture. In spite of the insistence to
confront the fantasies of desire with the reality principle, Ricoeur contends that the psychoanalytic cure does not actually vanquish the fantasy,

the experience of analysis as such." Ricoeur, *Critique and Conviction*, 24.

47. Ricoeur, *Conflict of Interpretations*, 163. See also Ricoeur, *Hermeneutics and the Human Sciences*, 248.

48. Ricoeur, *Hermeneutics and the Human Sciences*, 248.

49. Ricoeur, *Conflict of Interpretations*, 179.

but rather resituates it "at the level of the imaginary."[50] To the extent that, through sublimation, the psychoanalytic cure reorients our imagination, a subtle teleological dimension is revealed at the heart of an endeavor which draws its force from an archaeological model.

The last dimension, the narrative character of the psychoanalytic experience, anchors desire in a lived history performing a double function. The configuration of the case in the analytic practice articulates, first of all, a series of lived events into a meaningful whole. But the events themselves as recounted, receive a new efficiency. That is to say, the work of the analyst not only describes a past history, but *refigures* it; it somehow brings about the cure in the very process of recounting.

In the light of such observations, the claims of psychoanalysis need to be re-interpreted. First of all, perhaps unsurprisingly, Ricoeur contends that psychoanalysis remains interesting precisely by its praxis. The movement from misunderstanding to recognition designates a practice whose itinerary eventually transcends the theoretical corpus of metaphsychology. Yet, Ricoeur is reluctant to establish another theoretical starting point.[51] He concludes by spelling out the specific kind of truth corresponding to each dimension of desire listed above. The corresponding verification implied by such a description remains in this way fragmented, requiring the articulation of the entire network of the analytic practice (theory, hermeneutics, therapeutics and narration).[52] Ricoeur's only answer to the potential objection of circularity is to point to the relative autonomy of each domain. In other words, it is by virtue of the irreducible specificity of each sphere (which makes impossible its subsumption under a circumscribing totality) that the argument escapes a vicious circle, and a reciprocal reinforcement of the various fields is possible.

---

50. Ricoeur, *Hermeneutics and the Human Sciences*, 253.

51. In criticizing Freud's theoretical model of energy distribution Ricoeur stresses the social dimension of any theoretical paradigm by appealing to Kuhn (ibid., 271). That is to say, a theory is more than a mere noetic insight pursued under the guide of *Selbstreflexion*. On similar grounds, he rejects a pure phenomenological, linguistic or reflexive interpretation of psychoanalysis. Ricoeur identifies the same problem in all those attempts, namely, the rendering of the problem of the unconscious as a special case of consciousness. All those attempts carry with them an implicit idealism of consciousness (ibid., 262). See also Ricoeur, *De l'interprétation*, 337–446. As we shall see below, for Ricoeur the insertion of "an objectual" phase in the process is essential. The cycle of *Selbstreflexion* must come to an end if the challenge of Freud is to be taken seriously.

52. Ricoeur, *Hermeneutics and the Human Sciences*, 270.

## The Problematic of the "Real"—Redemptive Overtones

But how are we to understand it... it vances? How is reflexive philosophy
and philosophical anthropology instructed by it? Let us look in turn at
the nature of its truth claims, and at the way in which such claims im-
pinge upon the constitution of the Ricoeurian subject.

First, it should be recalled that Freud wanted to conceive psychoanalysis as a natural science. After all, he was an *Aufklärer*. Ricoeur's resistance to "reconstruct" experience on the basis of his theoretical models
is therefore understandable. But if Freud's metapsychology is problematical, where does the force of psychoanalysis's criticism lie?

What must be noted first is that psychoanalysis derives part of its
validity from its success. What the cure performs first is, in a first approximation, an extension of consciousness. It does that precisely by making
us aware of the mystification and the deceptions of the *id*, how consciousness lies to itself in its hidden aims of wish-fulfillment. It is this criticism
which establishes the condition for all genuine knowledge. But this does
not imply that psychoanalytic practice is a mere enlightenment, a kind
of cure through knowledge. If that were the case, the patient would be at
the complete disposal of the analyst, and psychoanalysis itself would be
no more than a technique of domination or manipulation. Rather, psychoanalysis draws its force from its practical dimension. It is within psychoanalysis as fundamentally *praxis*, a praxis that ultimately rests neither
upon a speculative construction nor upon a mere behavioral report, that
truth can emerge. That is to say, both diagnosis and the cure itself have a
concrete historical, empirical and social dimension. Desire as meaning is
always attached to an object of desire. Moreover, it is not enough for one
to know that he or she fits into a certain system of forces and motives.
One needs the power to break its spell. That is why the overcoming of
resistances is "a work," a struggle of an "other." Similarly, it is the work of
an "other" which breaks in the cycle of *Selbstreflexion*, announcing the
subject's self-delusion. This recognition of exteriority marks again the an-
teriority of the ontic plane to the reflective plane.[53] And this brings us to
another important implication which separates Ricoeur's appropriation
of psychoanalysis from other linguistic or phenomenological interpretations. It is precisely this bondage to the cycle of desire which prompts

<hr>

53. See also Ricoeur, "Question of the Subject: The Challenge of Semiology," in
*Conflict of Interpretations*, 244.

the insertion of the "objectual phase" in the analytic practice.[54] This testifies again to the double nature of "exteriority," as both empirical or "natural" and intersubjective. Ricoeur anticipates here the explanation-understanding dialectic which, as we shall see, lies at the very heart of his understanding of both texts and history. Explanation is required because "man's alienation from himself is such that mental functioning does actually resemble the functioning of a thing."[55] From an epistemological perspective, such a position prevents an idealism of consciousness. From a theological perspective, this speaks about a "fall" into the world of objects, a failure to be a human being. There is predictability and "control" because the "the subject" is no longer free. Even in Freud's own system this is more than a mere reflection of his own positivist and materialist position. Ricoeur discerns, in fact, a certain movement in the Freudian corpus, from a mere "mechanics" apparent in his first writings, towards an interpretation of culture, art and religion and finally to a re-interpretation of the previous edifice in the light of the eros-thanatos polarity.[56] This movement towards what Ricoeur calls "a romantic dramaturgy of life and death,"[57] betrays a certain tragic view of existence. Repetition, as the great law of the economy of desire, ends in death.

How then, does the psychoanalytic practice function as a work of truth? Can it possibly aspire to that comprehensive notion of truth that not only truthfully reveals a state of affairs but also brings about genuine healing? Is the psychoanalytic therapy a redemptive practice, able to transform and bring about freedom? At times, Ricoeur appears to suggest that . . . It is precisely by the enclosing into a genetic model, and a determinism of the past, that psychoanalysis is able to bring about a new problematic of freedom "no longer bound to the arbitrariness of free will but to determination which has been understood."[58] This seems to herald an idea of liberty specifically Christian and Pauline. Moreover, Ricoeur speaks further about the "re-education of our desire,"[59] and about "a new capacity to speak and to love"[60] opened by psychoanalysis. Is psychoanal-

54. Ibid., 185. Also Ricoeur, *Hermeneutics and the Human Sciences*, 261.

55. Ricoeur, *Hermeneutics and the Human Sciences*, 261.

56. Ricoeur, *Conflict of Interpretations*, 165.

57. Ibid.

58. Ibid., 192.

59. Ibid., 194.

60. Ibid., 192–93.

ysis a prophetic voice heralding both "judgment" and "salvation"? Over-all, Ricoeur seems to resist such a view. Indeed, according to Ricoeur, Freud remains more a tragic figure than a prophetic one.[61]

Nonetheless, psychoanalysis remains one of the most radical *possibilities* opened up to us.[62] Yet we may further wonder whether the ugly conspiracy of *thanatos* with the regressive principle can be contemplated from outside the perspective of freedom . . . Perhaps the "fall into nature," the bondage to the "object" can be genuinely seen only in the light of a symbol of resurrection that breaks the cycle of repetition. Perhaps the wandering nature of human desire and the difficulty of genuine loving, can be grasped only in the light of its overabundance. But Ricoeur would ultimately agree with that.[63] Was it not precisely such a problematic that prompted the insertion of other points of view? Indeed, in spite of its openings,[64] psychoanalysis remains fundamentally an archaeology. This is the reason why the regressive view of psychoanalysis must be confronted with Hegel's *Phenomenology of Spirit*. Freud's archaeology of the unconscious, burying as it does, the subject in a fate, must be complemented by a teleology of Spirit. It is only in such a light that the cycle of the "return of the repressed" is broken, and the phantasm may emerge as a symbol.[65] "Only a subject with a *telos* can have an *arche*."[66] Ricoeur's reading of Hegel's *Phenomenology* remains, however, overtly anthropological and historical. Whilst it undoubtedly enriches the picture by tracing the constitution of the subject in a dialectic of archaeology and teleology, for what Ricoeur calls "the vertical irruption of the Wholly Other,"[67] a different perspective is required. This different point of view is a philoso-

---

61. Ibid., 155.

62. Ibid., 192.

63. "Or, ce qui seul peut échapper à la critique de Freud, c'est la foi comme kérygme de l'amour: 'Dieu a tant aimé le monde'" (Ricoeur, *De l'intérpretation*, 515). Ultimately, Ricoeur seems to adopt the view (quite Reformed in character), that the symbols of evil can be only properly understood in the light of the symbols of the end. Thus, goodness and freedom are more primordial than evil and bondage. See also Ricoeur, *Symbolism of Evil*, 156. This theme shall be explored in more detail below.

64. See the implicit teleology in Freud, especially in his interpretation of art (cf. Ricoeur, *Conflict of Interpretations*, 174, 192–96). Freud naively believed that "only art is without danger" (ibid., 158).

65. Allusion to Ricoeur's application of this principle in his essay "Fatherhood: From Phantasm to Symbol." Cf. Ricoeur, *Conflict of Interpretations*, 468ff.

66. Ricoeur, *Conflict of Interpretations*, 161.

67. Ibid., 171.

phy of religion which is fundamentally "an interpretation of the divine names and the designations of God."[68] Since this latter endeavor remains distinct from concrete reflection, (which in fact, as Ricoeur notes, holds together regression and progression[69]), the criterion of "truth" remains in abeyance.

Perhaps we can now hint at why the status of psychoanalysis remains ambivalent in Ricoeur. The homology between Freud and Hegel reveals, among other things, their common rootedness in desire. Both regression and progression arise from a view of life as necessity and conflict. That is why a mere dialectic of archaeology and teleology remains insufficient. In such a case, however, we are left with an ambiguous "reality principle." On the one hand, the work of "truth" reveals only a tragic knowledge. Indeed, notes Ricoeur, Freud "turned to the language of tragic myth to say the essential."[70] Yet on the other hand, the "reality principle" as conflict and necessity, is mysteriously transfigured in the third term of the productive imagination, in a "sublimation" which breaks loose from the cycle of the "return of the repressed."

As a result, psychoanalysis as a work of truth tends to slip between two conceptions of the "real."[71] Such a situation may indeed help us to discern an opening between a romantic vision, expressed in hasty syntheses of freedom and nature, and a realism of cold descriptions which does nothing more than "accustom our eye to necessity." But how can we orient our love towards the right object? Ricoeur talks about imagination as a most sensitive zone, as a "blind point of knowledge,"[72] precisely because here is the field of competing "meaningful" projects. Imagination is indeed a frail territory.[73] We live in a culture which seems to appeal much more to imagination than to reason. Nonetheless, more must be said if such an opening is to become a viable alternative.

68. Ibid., 469. See also ibid., 22.

69. Ibid., 175.

70. Ibid., 158.

71. That is to say, in spite of Ricoeur's right refusal to associate psychoanalysis with "a technique of the night," dealing with the "dark side of humanity" (cf. Ricoeur, *Conflict of Interpretations*, 120), a genuine concern for "truth" cannot forever elude ethical categories. As we shall see below, without explicitly addressing this ambiguity a genuine re-enchantment of the world remains highly problematic.

72. Ricoeur, *Fallible Man*, 82.

73. See 1 John 2:15–17.

## Toward a Structure of Emancipation?

It is now time to draw together the main epistemological implications of Ricoeur's appropriation of psychoanalysis. It is significant to recall that Ricoeur insists in circumscribing psychoanalysis within its own specific point of view. The suggestion is made that, in fact, its strength lies precisely in its narrowness. This is why we must not be too bothered by its excessive claims. The ideal of unity is not given up, but genuine unity, it is claimed, is not possible without the recognition of such limits. Ricoeur fully accepts, for instance, the incapacity of phenomenology in the psychoanalytic practice. "A critique of Freudian meta-psychology must be completely non-phenomenological."[74] If consciousness is false-consciousness, I can no longer trust the *noema-noemata* relation. In this case, a transcendental analysis in the Kantian manner appears to be the only viable option. Under the guidance of Kant's distinction between the empirical and the transcendental subject, Ricoeur connects dialecti-cally empirical realism (meant to prevent a "fanciful metaphysics" of the unconscious),[75] with transcendental idealism, by dint of the inaccessibil-ity of the unconscious.[76] The unconscious, Ricoeur avers, is always medi-ated by interpretation. At first sight, this seems to be a mere application of a Kantian insight to the realm of the psyche. The facts of the psyche, like the things in the world, are both constructed and received. Ricoeur com-ments that seeking meaning is no longer "a spelling out a consciousness of meaning," but rather "a deciphering of its expressions."[77] In this context he also compares the counterfeit-manifest or revealed-concealed relation from such a scheme with the distinction between the things' appearance and their reality.[78] While such claims depotentiate the Cartesian certitude which set the stage for the modern epistemological discussions, they also seem to question the status of all transcendental approaches. A psychic event, is not less problematical than an event in the world. As meaningful events, both are on the threshold of realism and idealism. Now I am fully

74. Ricoeur, *Conflict of Interpretations*, 103.

75. Ibid., 108.

76. In fact this is a mere explicitation of Kant's transcendental idealism, which ac-cording to Kant, necessarily involves empirical realism. "The transcendental idealist is, therefore, an empirical realist, and allows to matter, as appearance, a reality which does not permit of being inferred, but is immediately perceived." Cf. Kant, *Critique of Pure Reason*, 347.

77. Ricoeur, *Conflict of Interpretations*, 148.

78. Ibid., 149.

aware that Ricoeur's transcendental idealism is a transcendentalism of consciousness (the reality of the unconscious as a diagnosed reality), and in this sense Kantian rather than Platonic. Yet, arguably, the Kantian idealism meets its Platonic counterpart precisely in the notion of the "real": what is genuinely real? In this sense, Ricoeur's refuge in Kant remains insufficient in the long run since epistemology must give an account of its ontological roots or its implicit theory of categories. Yet, we may well have in Ricoeur's analysis more than an application of a categorial discussion in a settled epistemology. The mediation by interpretation which qualifies the "object" of psychoanalysis as being more than instinct or desire (the semantic, intersubjective, "imaginative" and narrative character of desire), recalls Ricoeur's celebrated concrete reflection. In such a context what becomes important is not so much the limits, but the way in which the discourse opens towards the world, transgresses the limits. It is in such a light that the archaeological point of view points in fact to a teleological perspective. This is also the underlying reason for the homology Ricoeur draws between psychoanalysis, Hegel's *Phenomenology* and a philosophy of religion. This reasserts the old concern for "wholeness." It is in the same field that we are moving.

*But it is at this juncture that one can, in spite of Ricoeur's insistence upon the divergence of the points of view enumerated, identify the profile of a fundamental common structure of reflection.* Thus, psychoanalytic practice starts and ends in the analytical practice itself. Similarly, Hegel's phenomenology begins with the immediate and returns to it. As we shall see in more detail later, the interpretation of symbols and the hermeneutics of the texts follow the same pattern.

As we shall endeavor to show later in the project, within such a scheme, it becomes very difficult to distinguish between the Kantian "limit-idea" and the "otherness" of the third term in which imagination specifies and fulfils reflection as "concrete reflection." Moreover, the structure of what is genuinely "real" remains elusive if our starting and ending in experience is not theologically qualified. Critical thought may well contain an implicit promise of liberation. But how do we recognize genuine freedom? Is psychoanalysis able to bring about a true vision of reality or the advent of genuine healing? Or is it a mere postponement of pain by means of an utopian hope? This question must be retained not so much in its explicit epistemological guise, as in its ontological ramifications. Yet what psychoanalysis amply confirmed is at least the fact that the encounter with symbols, the deciphering of the signs, is more than a

mere epistemological exercise, touching as it does upon problems ontological and soteriological.

In conclusion, it is not as a new foundational science, or as a new
claim to totality that Ricoeur encounters psychoanalysis. Rather, it is as a
potential "redemptive technique," as a promise of freedom, able to resume
reflection beyond the dark aspects of experience, that it arouses his interest. As a parable of the passage from bondage to freedom, it performs
perhaps the most radical challenge to philosophic anthropology in epistemological guise. As we have seen, how "reflection survives" remains at
least undecided if not problematic. Nevertheless, the theological lesson is
that the question "What can I know?" needs a more original grounding.
Epistemology is not only about justification and warrant, but about freedom as well.[79] In this sense this encounter may well be the antechamber
of a poetics, anticipating perhaps its form if not its content, preparing the
ground for the passage from "what is" to "what can be," from actuality to
possibility. Only such a poetics may be able to obviate in a genuine sense
the logic of repetition and the cycle of death.

79. Ricoeur tends to use epistemology in the strict Kantian sense as a science of
justification and validation. It is criticism which tends to be accorded a richer semantic
content (critique of metaphysics, ideology, self . . . ). Part of our purpose is to substantiate a view of theological epistemology which would restore the rights of knowledge in a way which would invite rather than alienate ontological and soteriological
considerations.

*2*

# The Ontological Horizon

## *Preface to a Transcendental Poetics?*

But the greatest thing by far, is "to be metaphorical." This alone cannot be
imparted by another.

ARISTOTLE, *POETICS*, PART XXII

Everyone who drinks of this water will thirst again, but whoever drinks of
the water that I shall give him will never thirst; the water that I shall give him
will become in him a spring of water welling up to eternal life.

JOHN 4:13–14

IN HIS "INTELLECTUAL AUTOBIOGRAPHY," with a visible uneasiness,
Ricoeur attempts to explain the absence of the promised "Poetics of the
Will" from his anthropological project. He goes on to say, however, that

> I would not . . . say that nothing was accomplished of what I then
> termed a poetics. *The Symbolism of Evil, The Rule of Metaphor,
> Time and Narrative* do aspire in several ways to the title of poet-
> ics, less in the sense of a meditation on primordial creation than
> in that of an investigation of the multiple modalities of what
> I will later call an ordered creation, illustrated not only by the
> great myths on the origin of evil, but also by poetic metaphors
> and "narrative plots." In this sense, the idea of ordered creation
> still belongs to a philosophical anthropology in which the rela-
> tion to biblical faith and theology is held in abeyance.[1]

1. Ricoeur, "Intellectual Autobiography," 14.

We shall respect, for the time being, Ricoeur's desire of not mixing the genres, and postpone his more direct engagement with concrete theological themes for a later stage. Instead our purpose in this chapter is to follow the way in which Ricoeur extends a certain type of philosophizing, expressed by his indirect detour through signs, to language in general. In fact, the so-called "linguistic turn," as Ricoeur himself testifies, was less the result of either the ambition to "integrate" of a "later-day" Hegel, or the explicit desire to articulate a poetics. Rather, it was more the concrete outcome of "external polemics and internal wars,"[2] leveled against different positions within the vast linguistic current stemming from Saussure.

## The Challenge of Structuralism

The encounter with structuralism would further chasten the presuppositions of reflective philosophies, marking even more the departure from the philosophies of the "immediate" (Descartes, Hume, Bergson).[3] Nevertheless, as Ricoeur recollects, it was not as a hermeneutic of suspicion that he encountered structuralism.[4] Its particular questioning of the subject takes here a different form. In what follows, we shall examine the way in which Ricoeur meets the particular rationality which envelops the structuralist field. We shall try to show that the elements that make the encounter productive organize themselves again in a structure of emancipation, which eventually "sublates" the structuralist claim, yet retaining its "objectifying" insight.

With structuralism we witness, Ricoeur contends, "a reversal of the relation between system and history."[5] The traditional historical genetic method undergoes here a devaluing shift. While the move may be understood as a form of empiricism,[6] nonetheless, the interest in the particular and contingent recedes into the background as the systematic organization of the whole takes center stage.

Saussure's distinction between *langue* and *parole*, that is, between language as a system of signs or a set of conventions adopted by a social

2. Ibid., 18.

3. Ibid., 24.

4. Ibid., 22.

5. Ricoeur, *Conflict of Interpretations*, 31. I will incorporate page references into the text below.

6. See also Ricoeur, "Structure, Word, Event," in *Conflict of Interpretations*, 81.

body, and language as speech as the living activity of speaking subjects, will become the crucial contentious point in Ricoeur's dialogue with structuralism. This critical distinction is developed in three related directions which encapsulate three fundamental traits of the structuralist approach: the very idea of system itself, the relation between synchrony and diachrony and the structure of the linguistic laws.

In the first case, Ricoeur notes that the very system which brings about intelligibility eventually renders the particular signs arbitrary. As is well known, structuralism scoffs at the naïve idea that the sign stands for something else (82). The supremacy of the system inaugurates the reign of difference: "in language there are only differences"[7] or, "language is not a substance, but a form."[8] In the second case, although Ricoeur accepts that structuralism does not simply oppose synchrony to diachrony in a mere static scheme,[9] he nevertheless questions the particular type of dynamic obtained in the subordination of diachrony to synchrony.[10] The third trait touches more decisively upon Ricoeur's underlying concerns: structuralism claims that the ultimate abode of the linguistic laws is somewhat entrenched in the mind. This alleged deep-seated, "non-reflective" and "non-historical" power is, Ricoeur believes, closer to Kant's categories than to the Freudian unconscious (33). He dubs it (somewhat ironically) the "Kantian unconscious," because, of course, structuralism does not know and does not need a subject. It is ultimately this confident reliance upon an unproblematic categorial structure of understanding, that makes structuralism an abstract objectifying technique. Its "anti-idealist," "anti-phenomenological" and "anti-reflective" voice wants to be the voice of nature itself (33). Bound up with this is its hyperbolic scientific claim,

7. De Saussure, *Course in General Linguistics*, 120, quoted in Ricoeur, *Conflict of Interpretations*, 32. As in the case of phenomenology and psychoanalysis, Ricoeur's critique of various structuralists is more interested in the referential intention of their discourses than in their use of Saussure. It may be noted in passing that it has been argued that most structuralists "used" Saussure in a way Saussure himself never envisioned. See Thiselton, *New Horizons in Hermeneutics*, 8off.

8. De Saussure, *Course in General Linguistics*, 122, quoted in Ricoeur, *Conflict of Interpretations*, 82.

9. Ricoeur gives some credit here to Jakobson's famous article "Principles of Historical Phonetics." Ricoeur, *Conflict of Interpretations*, 33.

10. "Events are apprehended only when they have been realised in a system. . . . The dyachronic datum is the innovation which arises from speech" (Ricoeur, *Conflict of Interpretations*, 32). It is not so much the discrete logic that arises from such a move that is contested here, but its mechanistic grammar, its limited horizon and the reduction of "speech" to a mere event in the world.

which in point of fact marks its great dénouement: structuralism is not content with a description among others, but it credits itself *the* objective description. The price of this objectivity however is the closing of language upon itself.

Ricoeur sets out to rescue language from the structuralist cul-du-sac by following an already well-established strategy. First, as may have become apparent, he pushes the structuralist logic to its limits. This critical endeavor of pointing to internal *aporias* is then followed by the more constructive phase of inviting alternative perspectives. The resulting conflict of interpretation arises therefore as a productive and mutual interanimation which, on the one hand, challenges excessive and reductionist claims, whilst on the other, illuminates twilight zones and presses home emerging insights. Ricoeur's methodological credo is that "the consciousness of the validity of a method, . . . is inseparable from the consciousness of its limits" (44). Moreover, it is the awareness of those limits that deploys its true potential.

We may mention here briefly, by way of example, Ricoeur's reply to Levi-Strauss's structural anthropology.[11] What is remarkable in Ricoeur's account is not only the contrast he sets between Levi-Strauss's description of totemism ("where the arrangements are more important than the contents" [40]), and von Rad's theology of traditions (where the founding events dominate the scene, and where it is emphatically the content which determines the form), but the implicit openings identifiable in Levi-Strauss's own account. Once again, Ricoeur pays homage to his older conviction that genuine knowledge must feed in some sense upon the dynamism inherent in the reality under investigation. A detached configurational description of a cultural phenomenon at a given time, is incapable of answering his ardent desire to lay bare the rich texture of the event. Ultimately, the ambitious claim of structuralism remains abstract,[12] precisely because it too hastily encloses the event in a structure of explanation which minimizes the features pertaining to its configurative power.

Structuralism however, cannot be rejected altogether. If as philosophy it remains indeed unconvincing (51), it must be retained in the more modest form as a "tool of explication." In this way, the structuralist rejection of the primacy of subjectivity is integrated within Ricoeur's

---

11. See Ricoeur's analysis of *The Savage Mind* in *Conflict of Interpretations*, 44ff.

12. See also Ricoeur, "Intellectual Autobiography," 22.

more general anti-idealist concerns. The displacement of analysis from the level of the subject's intention to the level of linguistic and semiotic structures marks, Ricoeur believes, the passage of discourse through a necessary objective phase. Thus, Ricoeur "absorbs" the structuralist's moment of truth: Heidegger's "existentiell" dimension of deciphering meets Levi-Strauss's objective claim in the dialectic of explanation and understanding. Ricoeur concludes in Hegelian language, that structuralist thought remains a form of thought which does not think itself (51).

In sum, Ricoeur reconciles, once again, the invincible reflective stance of an enquiry into meaning with his never wavering sympathy for the anti-idealist and anti-reflective orientation of structuralism. Perhaps the structuralist's "would be" cosmology, which tends to level history in an undifferentiated concept of nature, may at least draw our attention to the fact that after all, we live in a universe where however "savage" life may be, the notion of order or of law is not entirely foreign. As in the case of the unconscious in Freud, language is itself an "unconscious instrument" (54), and it is only through the passage through its bounds that we may hope to capture the richness of the event. Even though the advent of novelty defies the "logic of structure," the "old" is not simply cast into a derisive "nature," but is recognized as having a constitutive "historicity." Room for founding events is left in this way. The advent of the new needs to be referred to a prior economy if it is to avoid a lapse into idle speculation. In fact, it is this economy, in its structural configuration that dispels the excessive or potentially mystifying claim of the symbol.[13]

*The claim of structuralism is thus retained in its critical function as contributing to the "new" rather than opposing it.*[14] Anticipating the language of the next section, we may even say that, somewhat paradoxically, structuralism becomes significant precisely at the point where it promises the least, that is to say, at the height of its totalizing claim to close language upon itself. It is upon "the ruins of the referring dimension" that

13. In "Structure and Hermeneutics" (*Conflict of Interpretations*, 79–96), Ricoeur suggests for instance that in the Middle Ages nature was always referred to the historical typology contained in the Bible. The "mirror" of nature therefore was not allowed to take a career of its own in an independent cosmology, but was always referred to the taxis of such an economy. Thus "natural symbolism is at once freed and ordered entirely in the light of the Word" (Ricoeur, *Conflict of Interpretations*, 60). In such a light, structuralism is "redeemed" as a "necessary intermediary between symbolic naivety and hermeneutic comprehension" (ibid., 61).

14. For this critical dimension, see especially Ricoeur, *Conflict of Interpretations*, 73–77.

one can say that "there is no mystery *in* language" . . . Nonetheless, there is a mystery *of* language, because indeed, "language speaks, . . . it says something about being" (78).

More has to be said however about this "reservoir of meaning ready to be used again in other structures" (47), if the conflict of interpretations itself is not to remain an idle confrontation. Will a more systematic inquiry into the full implications of the fundamental distinction between *langue* and *parole* be able to answer this challenge? Towards such concerns we shall now turn.

## Metaphor and the Creation of Meaning

Ricoeur's decision to offer a systematic treatment of metaphor grew out not only from the effort at a better articulation of his position vis-à-vis structuralism. The study of metaphor became the privileged place for exploring the more general problematic of the emergence of meaning in both its semantic and ontological implications. Nonetheless, it may not be an exaggeration to say that Ricoeur's cardinal contribution to the theory of metaphor draws its force from the crucial distinction which he takes from Emile Beneviste between the semantics of the word and the semantics of the statement, a distinction which he articulates as he parts ways with structuralism. As we shall see below, this distinction will ultimately connect Ricoeur's account of language with both his lifelong phenomenological interests in intentionality and with ontology and the problem of reference.

In what follows, we shall focus on *The Rule of Metaphor* not only because Ricoeur tackles here the contentious issue of the emergence of meaning in language "head on," but also because the structure of disclosure that emerges here will play a crucial role in his later works on narrative (the production of plots and narrative identity).[15] We shall attempt to show that the grammar of such a structure decisively consecrates the one theme Ricoeur has never tired of exploring: the Kantian productive imagination. In many ways, the theme may be taken as the touchstone of the whole study, fuelling as it does the unrelenting confrontation of two perspectives: the demand for totality and the irreducibility of the individual perspective.[16]

15. See Ricoeur's remark in this regard in, "Intellectual Autobiography," 27.

16. Even the form of the argument must comply with this sovereign rule. While the

The third study of the book, in which the semantics of the word are radically opposed to the semantics of the statement marks, in Ricoeur's own evaluation (4), the decisive step of the argument. But this radical opposition performs more than a polemical function: as we shall see, in the aftermath of the conflict, a new reconciliation becomes possible. We shall ask later what significance this move has for Ricoeur's theory of metaphor in particular, and the grammar of the structure of disclosure in general. Before that however, it seems fit to recall what is at stake in such an undertaking by sketching briefly the confines of the discussion as Ricoeur moves from rhetoric and Aristotle's theory of metaphor to semantics and finally to hermeneutics.

Ricoeur's point of departure in Aristotle, as will become apparent, is more than a critical recollection of a starting point irrevocably marked by a deplorable narrowness. Instead, it functions as a horizon of expectation, anticipating and enveloping Ricoeur's contribution to the theory of metaphor. Whilst the substitution theory, indeed, paved the way for the prevalence of the logic of "naming" in the subsequent Western tradition, nevertheless, Aristotle anticipated fully what is at stake here. By placing metaphor at the crossroad between *mythos* and *mimesis* he uncovered, Ricoeur believes, its hidden ontological traits. We shall return to this problem below.

Nevertheless, the main problem with the substitution theory, as it was appropriated by the West, is that it can only describe the present in terms of the past, the advent of the new, in terms of what has always been. It is this failure of the semantics of the word to transgress the closed "logic of the dictionary" that calls for the richer horizon of the interaction and fusion theories of metaphor enabled by the semantics of discourse. Ricoeur's contention here is that it is in discourse alone that the taxonomic view is overcome and the dynamism of speech unleashed. The concrete speech situation brings together event and meaning, identifying reference and predicative function, the noun and the verb. Discourse connects us with the world effecting the passage from sense to reference, and it is through discourse that language returns to the intersubjective world by its illocutionary and perlocutionary function (66–76).

---

book is devised as an undissimulated advance which enriches the discussion towards a forever anticipated unity of being, Ricoeur is quick to insist that the collection of studies does not conform to an unproblematic part-whole structure. Each study is marked by a unique point of view having thus an irreducibility proper to its specific field. See Ricoeur, *Rule of Metaphor*, 3. I will incorporate page references into the text above.

Such concerns guide Ricoeur in his dialogue with I.A. Richards, Max Black and Monroe Beardsley. Each of those authors uncovers the specific perspective of the field they represent (the philosophy of rhetoric, logical grammar, and literary criticism respectively), revealing complementary aspects of the process of disclosure. Ricoeur gradually traces a more comprehensive picture of what is at stake at the semantic level, not only by skillfully exploring their differences in the light of their specific perspective, but also by identifying a pattern common to all three: they all explore the tension between the "old" and the "new" by drawing upon the inter-animation between "subject and modifier," "tenor and vehicle" or "focus and frame."

It is against this background that Ricoeur starts to unfold the rich grammar of resemblance. First, Ricoeur resolves to show (against Jacobson), that his notion of resemblance does emphatically not force metaphor back into a substitution theory. Thanks to its semantic dimension, resemblance is no longer a substitution of a name, but a predicative operation. Ricoeur unpacks this "semantic proximity" expressed by resemblance as structurally grounded in the initial "distance" which in the process of the metaphorical predication is suddenly suppressed. Resemblance is therefore shown to be logically dependent upon such a distance. In this way, the operation of resemblance does not dissolve but rather preserves this distance within itself as a dialectic of identity and difference (196).

Ricoeur follows the trajectory of meaning further by working out the verbal and the sensible dimension of metaphor. Aided by the Kantian productive imagination, the mystery of the emergence of meaning is ultimately located in the concept of *seeing-as*. Resemblance itself is shown to be grounded in it. Ricoeur agrees with Wittgenstein that to see as . . . , is not a mere interpretation. It is not the case that we have a pre-determined meaning, an idea, into which we fit *this* image. Rather, "seeing as" is having *this* image (212). That is to say, it is not a resemblance between two ideas, not a mere noetic act. It is rather, Ricoeur claims, both act *and* experience.

Thus, "seeing as" quite precisely plays the role of the schema that unites the empty concept and the blind impression; thanks to its character as half thought and half experience, it joins the light of sense with the fullness of the image. In this way, the non-verbal and the verbal are firmly united at the core of the "image-ing" function of language (213).

The theory of interaction, with its stress upon transgression, and the fusion theory with its "iconized meaning," as fusion of sense and the imaginary, are thus thought together as the discussion reaches the limits of the semantic field. This further invites the question of reference. Ricoeur's more ontological concerns begin to emerge here, because in the passage from sense to reference the question of truth imposes itself.

To this end, Ricoeur undertakes a detour through the theory of models which he considers to be the decisive step towards the case for reference (239). Metaphor as a model, is a heuristic instrument, which re-describes reality. This process of re-description, whilst close to epistemology, is not inscribed in a logic of justification but in a logic of discovery. Such a logic does not rest upon a purely deductive procedure. Ricoeur agrees with the realist thesis of Mary Hesse that in a metaphorical experience both reality and rationality "are thrown open to question" (243). Rationality presupposes "the continuous adaptation of our language to our continually expanding world" (243). This insight is linked to properly poetical language under the guide of Aristotle's placing of the tragic *poiesis* at the intersection of *mythos* and *mimesis* (244). By taking Aristotle's dictum that "poetry is closer to the essence than is history" (245), Ricoeur concludes that "to see human life as that which the *muthos* displays is to reach its 'denotative' dimension" (245). The truth evoked by metaphor enables us *to see the world in its possibility*. Ricoeur clarifies further the concrete structure of metaphorical truth by depicting it in the form of a new mediation between ontological naiveté on the one hand and "mythified" metaphor on the other (249–54). The chief feature of metaphorical truth rests in its capacity to preserve the "is" and "is not" in an unresolved tension. Metaphorical truth, therefore, finds its final abode in the copula of the verb to be. "Being-as" is the correlate of the "seeing-as." The tensive theory of metaphor finds its correspondence in an equally tensive theory of truth.

The last study is reserved for the retrieval of this discovery in the language of philosophical speculation. Ricoeur attempts here to spell out some of the philosophical presuppositions of the previous move from sense to reference. He essentially pleads for "the relative plurality of forms and levels of discourse" (257–58). A new (and last) mediation is attempted at this juncture between a radical heterogeneity of discourse, of the form of Wittgenstein's language games, and the proposal of an unequivocal unity of being. In the well-known fashion, Ricoeur insists again that poetry and speculative discourse have an autonomy circumscribed by their own respective fields. His manifest concern is twofold. On the one hand, he resolves to show that there cannot be a direct transcription of the semantic workings of metaphor into speculative discourse. In this connection Ricoeur's test case is the doctrine of analogy. On the other, Ricoeur identifies the same tendency to level out discourse in a somewhat inverse move which does not suggest the absorption of metaphor into the concept but rather suggests the general metaphoricity of all language.

Here Ricoeur first challenges Heidegger's more restrained (if somewhat inconsistent) criticism of metaphor (280–84),[17] only to reject its subsequent deconstruction in Derrida's *White Mythology* (the theory of metaphor is merely the metaphor of theory [287]). Ricoeur denies, in this connection, that the distinction between literal and metaphorical is necessarily metaphysically loaded. Words do not have a primitive, natural, or original meaning in themselves. "Literal does not mean proper in the sense of originary, but simply current, usual" (290–91). Ricoeur is further keen to explain that such a distinction is based upon a conflict between two interpretations that characterize the advent of the new pertinence in language. The claim that the metaphorical and the metaphysical rise together on the one hand, and the alleged effectiveness of dead metaphors on the other, rests upon the prior decision of such an approach to level out discourse under the rubric of semiotics.[18] Ricoeur's reluctance to take for granted Heidegger's suggestion will turn out to have important theological implications opening as we shall see, the possibility of a mediation between a doctrine of the Word and a doctrine of Creation.[19]

17. Ricoeur considers Heidegger's claim to "have destroyed" metaphysics as hyperbolical supporting similarities with Hegel's totalizing claim to "have ended" history. As Peter Kemp shows (Kemp, "Ricoeur between Heidegger and Levinas," 48–49), Heidegger fails in this way to substantiate "a non-vulgar understanding of time" by implicitly assuming uncritical privilege to his own critical stance.

18.. Ricoeur substantiates in other places what separates him from Derrida's account of language. See for instance Ricoeur, *Figuring the Sacred*, 304. See also Ricoeur's response to Crossan, who claims that Ricoeur's theory of metaphor inevitably leads to that of Derrida (Ricoeur, "Response," 72ff.).

19. It may be noted here that Jüngel's theological elaboration of metaphor (cf. Jüngel, "Metaphorische Wahrheit," 71–122) remains in this sense too attached to Heidegger (and to Nietzsche for that matter), failing in my opinion to properly address the tension between a doctrine of Creation and a doctrine of the Word. More about that in chapter 8.

## The Structure of Disclosure between Being and Act

Let me summarize the main features of Ricoeur's analysis. Ricoeur appropriates the workings of metaphor as a paradigmatic case of an *ordered creation*.[20] Put simply, that would mean a conception which would be able to mediate between two forms of excess: structuralism, which assimilates the new under the rubric of the old, and the claim that the new emerges out of the void, that it defeats all paradigms.[21]

On the one hand, therefore, Ricoeur's dialectic between innovation and sedimentation defends a notion of deviance which is structurally dependent upon tradition (offering it the context of its very intelligibility as "deviance.") Imagination without rules cannot be thought, says Ricoeur, echoing Kant.[22] On the other hand, however, as we have already anticipated, the concept of "seeing-as" presupposes not only continuity but also an irreducible clash. Moreover, the new, insists Ricoeur, insinuates itself upon "the ruins" of the old. That is to say, no causal connection with the past can account for its emergence. Tradition is needed precisely in its difference and *as* difference. That is why the similar is seen "despite difference," "in spite of contradiction" (196). But how is such a mediation possible and what would be the principal upshot of such a radical reconciliation?

Let me take a closer look at the principal features of this relationship. Before proceeding, I must add that I shall not follow strictly the way in which Ricoeur develops his argument in *The Rule of Metaphor*. Instead (supported in fact by Ricoeur's own admission that the content and the form cannot be separated), I shall seek to explore a reciprocal interanimation between the semiotic, semantic and the hermeneutical levels in a dialectic which may be aptly called a dialectic of "revelation" and meaning.

## The Process of Disclosure: Metaphor as Event and Meaning

As we have seen, Ricoeur's departure from the substitution theory was prompted by the lack of perspective of a mere "logical" approach to language. It is the density of the event in both its semantic and referential

20. Ricoeur, "Intellectual Autobiography," 14, 27.

21 As in some forms of contemporary novel. See Ricoeur, "De l'interprétation," in *Du texte à l'action*, 16. There are differences between the article as it appears in this collection and the English translation of this volume *From Text to Action: Essays in Hermeneutics, II*.

22. Ricoeur, *Du texte à l'action*, 16.

perspective that really brings about the full scope of the metaphorical novelty. In this light, the appeal to tradition must be first questioned, whether that is expressed in terms of a "system of associated common places" (Black), or in terms of "the potential range of connotations" (Beardsley) (97). It is against tradition that metaphor first appears and it does so as a "clash," as "semantic impertinence" and as a "category mistake." The metaphorical occurrence does not inscribe itself at the end of a causal chain, or as the fulfillment either of an inductive or of a deductive argument. The crucial trait of resemblance, as Ricoeur conceives it, is therefore its insertion at the end, as *consequence* rather than as cause. Metaphor is an event of discourse and an event in the world. As semantic event, it brings together two previously unconnected fields: To say that "time is a beggar" for instance, is to humanize time, to bring its cosmic dimension in the proximity of our existential experience.[23]

But metaphor is more than a fleeting moment. The successful connection of the two domains is retained as *meaning*. The event fades away indeed, yet, thanks to its meaning inscription, the metaphor may be identified and re-identified over time. The event may be re-enacted in a new experience as long as its proposed "world" is in tension with the actual or "literal" world. Ricoeur insists that the metaphorical meaning "is not the enigma itself, . . . but the solution of the enigma" (214). This emphasis upon metaphor as *result* rather than as process uncovers Ricoeur's return to the "logical" aspect of metaphor. As enduring meaning, metaphor retains its tensive dimension as long as it remains "alive" (before becoming part of the lexical code). Thus, metaphor as process challenges logic only to re-capture it again. This is why Ricoeur returns to the semantics of the word and incorporates it into the semantics of the sentence. The "focus" (in Beardsley's vocabulary) becomes the *telos* of the metaphorical happening, the site of arrival of the new meaning. Its importance is an *a posteriori* importance, granted in the predicative operation which effects the transfiguration from the literal sense (the ordinary and the trivial), to the metaphorical meaning (the special and the extraordinary). Analogously, the emerging reference expressed by the metaphorical truth does not ultimately expel the literal reference but rather incorporates it in itself (albeit negatively). Truth as correspondence is therefore not denied but

23. "When Shakespeare speaks of time as a beggar he teaches us to . . . see time like a beggar. Two previously distant classes are here suddenly brought together and the work of resemblance consists precisely in this bringing together of what once was distant." Ricoeur, *Interpretation Theory*, 51.

"sublated." It is always included in a new perspective. Yet this new perspective never rests in full presence. Since after Hegel, absolute retrospection is no longer conceivable, this kind of retrospective correspondence always remains an "approximation."

Nonetheless, this tensive relation requires further explicitation. What is more, the complex structure of the event raises additional problems precisely at the intersection between sense and reference, between the subject and the world.

# The Form of Disclosure I:
## Metaphor between Act and Experience

Ricoeur insists that the metaphorical experience is an integral experience. It is not only "talking about one thing in terms of another," but also "perceiving, thinking and sensing one thing in terms of another" (83). This prompts a return to an older problematic: the irreducible tie between act and experience which, in turn, recalls another two sets of distinctions, that between "inside" and "outside" and between the verbal and the non-verbal. But the ambition to account for the intractable mystery of the moment of insight which includes this "affective" dimension into itself, becomes a dangerous venture. How can one do that without reiterating some of the romantic pitfalls? How can one avoid the trap of "reintroducing the philosophy of nature into the philosophy of spirit" (249)? Is Ricoeur ultimately able to resist the temptation of succumbing to the seduction of a philosophy of life?[24] The point is of significant importance not only from the perspective of Ricoeur's own project but in the more general sense in which the elusive tension between act and experience stands in need of a theological reply.

Before trying to address this contentious issue, allow me to summarize briefly the chief traits of this problematic mediation. We have seen

---

24. Van Den Hengel ultimately concludes that Ricoeur opts for a non-semantic theory. "It is ironic that eventually Ricoeur opts for a non-semantic theory," or "it is obvious that at this point the relationship of the verbal to the non-verbal is such that the non-verbal must be given priority." Van Den Hengel, *Home of Meaning*, 77, 79. Similarly, Vanhoozer contends that Ricoeur's proposal remains tributary to romantic conceptuality. Vanhoozer, *Biblical Narrative in the Philosophy of Paul Ricoeur*, 250–51. He also notes that the tension between invention and discovery is tilted in Ricoeur towards invention. Ibid., 65. It both cases, that would depotentiate Ricoeur's explicit effort to distance himself from the Romantic psychologism by giving uncritical priority to the noetic dimension.

that correspondence is in Ricoeur teleologically grounded, always conceived in an *a posteriori* fashion in which the last is the most real. We have
also suggested that the crucial ingredient at work in the voting perceiving
of "the similar in the dissimilar" is traced back to Kant's transcendental
imagination. But this tension between reception and construction, between understanding and sensibility which mysteriously finds fulfilment
in a third term, is for Ricoeur more than "an art hidden in the human
soul," being given a concrete linguistic and temporal articulation.

In the preface of *Fallible Man* Loewe rightly sees that "Ricoeur
would not yield to the Romantic tendency which would suggest that the
noetic, quasi-subjective pole is closer to the infinite while the noematic
is inherently limited. Rather, the structure provides a way of showing
that every experience has a certain limited, perspectival character, which
presents itself both noetically and noematically."[25] In the same book, on
the other hand, Kelbly opines that *Fallible Man* is more "constructed"
than, for example, the phenomenology of Merleau-Ponty revealing, in
Kelbly's opinion, a type of rationalism between Nabert and Husserl.[26]
While it is true that Ricoeur's interest in the will leads him to consider
even Kant as having been too intellectualist,[27] the insistence upon "the
thing's mode of being,"[28] in connection with his de-centering project,
testifies to an equal commitment to "exteriority." Even if we concede
that *Fallible Man* is the most Kantian book,[29] what is ultimately of import is not so much the Kantian dichotomies themselves, but rather how
Ricoeur's phenomenological mediations challenge their very presuppositions. Kelbly's questionable evaluation is due, in my opinion, to his failure adequately to account for Ricoeur's desire to retain the rights of both
horns of the dilemma in the *noema-noemata* disputation.[30]

In my opinion, Ricoeur remains consistent in his unrelenting
struggle against the subjectivist and the intellectualist dimension of
Kant's epistemology on the one hand,[31] and the idealist tendency of

25. Ricoeur, *Fallible Man*, xxi.

26. Ibid., xxxv.

27. Cf. Ricoeur, *Conflict of Interpretations*, 328.

28. See footnote 34 in chapter 1 above.

29. Cf. Anderson, *Ricoeur and Kant*, 10.

30. See also footnote 29 in chapter 1 above.

31. Ricoeur complains that in Kant the dimension of exteriority is blurred because
Kant lacked an authentic philosophy of religious imagination. Cf. Ricoeur, *Figuring
the Sacred*, 87.

Husserl's phenomenology on the other.[32] The novel is not disputed only between the rights of "the inside" versus "an outside," between creation and discovery, but also between "sense" and "non-sense." This heralds a different concern which bespeaks the advent of the new as a receding of chaos under the pressure of "sense," as "reality coming to speech," as laying bare a "meaningful" and "humanized" world.[33]

Moreover, the way in which Ricoeur imagines the specific tension between language and world, the notion of the "world of the text" as well as his specific appreciation of the "word discourse" explicitly calls for the treatment of imagination as a dimension of language.[34] Whereas it is true that "'Seeing-as' designates the non-verbal mediation of the metaphorical statement" (214 ), this aspect does not necessarily mark the recess to a non-verbal dimension. What we encounter here is rather the limit of semantics. "It is still the semantics of the poetic verb that is to be heard in these depths. . . . One would not be able to meditate in a zone that preceded language" (214–15).

*It is precisely because language refers to the world that one can neither give metaphor a total linguistic constitution nor unequivocally separate its non-linguistic aspects.* Language has an "other" and it is this tensive situation that ultimately grounds the advent of the new meaning. Yet, psycholinguistics still occurs within language. The density of the image/experience cannot be appropriated as such and eventually cannot be known as density, if it is not taken up by the verb.

The passage to reference occasions a further exploration of this theme. The phenomenology of feeling is aimed at de-psychologising mood: Feeling is not merely an emotional state of the subject. Instead, "it has an intentionality which attaches to things, persons and the world" (83). Thus "the joyous undulation of the waves," in Holderlin's poem for instance "is neither an objective reality in the positivist sense, nor a mood in the emotivist sense" (246). Ricoeur complains that such a polarization was the result of a previous objectification. In this way, the world opened up by the poetic discourse which feeds upon the tension between language and reality, between the verbal and the non-verbal expounded

32. As we shall see, such a position may be developed theologically and encourages a view of agency which is at work both in history and in consciousness.

33. A critique of this "meaningful world" (with its unmistakable Heideggerian traits) shall be offered in chapter 4.

34. See for instance "Metaphor and the Central Problem of Hermeneutics," in Ricoeur, *Hermeneutics and the Human Sciences*, 181.

at the semantic level, is somewhat transposed at the referential level into an "enchanted world" which brings nature and spirit together in a similar dynamic of *mythos* and *mimesis*.

I suggest therefore that Ricoeur's insistence upon the non-linguistic aspect of reality *does not necessarily need* to dispute the linguistic con-stitution of metaphor. As we shall see in more detail later, the claim that language "refers" cannot be grounded in a dialectic of language and world, but needs a more fundamental theological anchoring. Human language as created reality situates it at the same logical level with all created reality. Such a perspective discards a mere "metaphysical" view of language. Nonetheless, at the same time, language as mediator, must bear the mark of the mediated reality if mediation is to be in any way successful. Without entering here into the complex and heated debate of the analogy of being,[35] we may safely claim at least that language does need an ultimate guarantor of meaning, and in this sense, must bear the mark of this fundamental enabling. Language may thus be conceived as a fundamental covenantal relationship situated in some sense between creation and divine address.[36] We shall return to this aspect below.

## The Form of Disclosure II:
## Limit Idea and Autonomy—The Rise of the Concept

Ricoeur's plea for the autonomy of speculative thought may perhaps best be understood by returning once again to Aristotle. In the last chapter of the book, Ricoeur refers to Aristotle and to the speculative discourse he inaugurated by the analogical unity of the multiple meanings of be-ing as a counter-example for his own thesis of the irreducibility of the speculative and poetic discourses. Ricoeur's argument is essentially based upon the observation that the question "What is being?" breaks with both poetic discourse and ordinary discourse. In this way, the plurivocity which Aristotle establishes in *Metaphysics* in relation to the first term is no longer connected with "the multiplicity of meaning produced by the

35. See for instance the discussion in Torrance, *Persons in Communion*, 120ff.

36. Vanhoozer describes this covenantal relationship as a design plan for language that mediates God, the other (the intersubjective dimension) and the world. He identifies two dimensions here: the inter-subjective bond between speakers and the objective bond between language and reality, that is, the reality principle (mediation of the world) and social interaction (responsibility principle). Cf. Vanhoozer, *Is There a Meaning in This Text?*, 206–7.

metaphorical utterance" (260). In other words, particularity under the regime of the same is inexorably bound to the speculative question "that opened up the speculative field" (260). "The first term, *ousia*," Ricoeur claims, "places all the other terms in the realm of meaning outlined by the question: what is being" (260). The point is, therefore, that wherever the discourse is opened up by a speculative question, the entire grammar will bear the mark of this question. All later acts of predication are thus subsumed under the hegemony of this first category, being tied to this "substantial center" (261). The speculative discourse, alleges Ricoeur, follows this formal procedure of an undisturbed advance of meaning in contradistinction to the metaphorical expression.

Based on such remarks, Ricoeur suggests (in a somewhat Fichtean manner), that thought is capable of inaugurating out of itself new fields of intelligibility (which subsequently define their own rules and confines). The operation of thought needs to become a distinct operation. In fact the very success of the concept in fulfilling its semantic exigencies is crucially dependent upon the actual break with the metaphorical discourse (296). This break marks an unsurpassable limit: the gain in meaning is not unproblematically carried to the concept, remaining instead trapped in the conflict of "same" and "different" of the metaphorical expression (297).

Nonetheless, this celebrated autonomy of thought which endows the discourse with an inner necessity, "has its condition of possibility in the semantic dynamism of metaphorical utterance" (259, 296). Whereas a "direct causality" between the two forms of discourse is denied, a somewhat parallel interanimation of the two is necessary. The speculative discourse feeds upon the metaphorical. Yet Ricoeur seems to back off once again: "The speculative discourse can respond to the semantic potentialities of metaphor only by providing it with the resources of a domain of articulation that properly belongs to speculative discourse by reason of its very constitution" (259). This to and fro between metaphor and concept recalls a somewhat Heideggerian theme anticipated already in chapter 1, namely, Ricoeur's conviction that while an unproblematic advance from part to whole is not within the power of a finite subject, we nonetheless move within the same totality. The secret interanimation between various perspectives is grounded therefore in this profound ontological connection. This is the reason why Ricoeur can claim that "every gain in meaning is at one and the same time a gain in sense and a gain in reference" (297).

It is also interesting to note that Ricoeur makes recourse to phenomenology here. One can pass from one discourse to another only by
an epoché. This is not primarily a statement about the finitude of our perspective, but about the radical autonomy presupposed by the phenomenological *epoché*. Here Husserl's distinction between *Aufklärung* and
*Erklärung* is taken up to substantiate the radical opposition between the
logical space and the contingent world of perception and images (301).
But it is crucial to remark that this battle between concept and metaphor,
between construction and reception, between the rights of "interiority"
or the power of the mind and the demands of exteriority, seems to function as a paradigmatic case for a more general phenomenon which attests
to the irreducible plurality of all human discourses and forms of life.

Ricoeur emphatically believes that to account fully for the rights of
each mode of discourse demands a recognition of their difference. Only
such a strategic decision can break the cycle of the "same" and inaugurate
the autonomy characteristic to each individual field. Ricoeur seems to
suggest that an unproblematic passage from the "in-itself" to the "for-itself," from the implicit to the explicit is not opened to us. We cannot fully
inhabit the two perspectives at the same time. It is only when "we die" to
the one that the other truly opens to us. Later on, we shall ask whether
and to what extent such a perspective can function as an ultimate epistemic framework. Suffice to say for the moment that the nature of such
interanimation reveals again the configurative power of "discontinuity"
which acts as liberative and in a somewhat "enabling" way.

Ricoeur's refusal of an ontology of language appears now in an
even clearer light. If language and ontology are circumscribed by different *epochés*, the semantic perspective and the hermeneutical perspective
respectively, then no ultimate resolution is conceivable from the perspective of a reflecting subject. Ricoeur emphatically rejects a mere juxtaposi-
tion, a linear, unproblematic advance from sense to reference, from the
semantic point of view to hermeneutics. It is noteworthy that in Ricoeur's
conception, the transposition of the subject in linguistic idiom does not
seem to change decisively the situation of the philosopher.[37] As can be
inferred from more than one passage, Ricoeur understands the linguistic

---

37. While it is true that (after Heidegger and Gadamer), Ricoeur pleads for the
lingual condition—the *Sprachlichkeit*—of all experience (cf. *Wahrheit und Methode*,
367ff. quoted by Ricoeur, *Hermeneutics and the Human Sciences*, 115), as we have suggested, he rejects a linguistic "foundationalism."

constitution of the subject in phenomenological and Kantian terms.[38] Consequently, the "in-itself" of language, as a synthetic totality, as in the case of Kant's self, is refuted. "Language can be thought but not known" (304). The linguistic turn, therefore, does not bring about the final defeat of either the transcendental subject or the problem of meaning.

Yet in spite of these Kantian overtones, Ricoeur's account of the relationship between language and reality does not immediately mark a return to "interiority" nor does he intend to restore a romantic universality to feeling as the privileged place of the advent of the new. Instead, as we have seen, he wants to restore a view of the advent of novelty which would address the epistemological questions in the light of their ontological constitution, being thus able to get beyond the ontic-noetic distinction to a concept of "world," while nevertheless preserving the referential dimension of language. Would such a vision have the ambition if not to resolve, at least to articulate the enigma of a middle position which would be able to resist in equal measure both the hegemony of "the One" and the fragmentation of "the Many"?

## Towards What Content?

The advent of the new occasions more than an epistemological debate in its ontic-noetic or subject-world tension. It challenges, Ricoeur notes, our very understanding of "reality" and "truth." Metaphor can even function as a parable of the reconciliation between the One and the Many. Ricoeur claims with Berggren that "metaphor constitutes the indispensable principle for integrating diverse phenomena and perspectives without sacrificing their diversity."[39]

This plea for particularity aims to unfold a perspective in which each field is allowed to disclose its own criteria of "truth," so to say. Even clarity is not something that *we* bring to the discourse. In fact Aristotle's insight that "Being is said in many ways" is based precisely upon such a vision.[40] Reality coming to speech reveals different language games corresponding to different forms of life. Yet, language tends towards univocity,

---

38. Ricoeur, *Rule of Metaphor*, 304. Ricoeur, *Hermeneutics and the Human Sciences*, 101ff.

39. Ricoeur, *Rule of Metaphor*, 349n33.

40. Ricoeur ascribes this insight to Aristotle's *Nichomachean Ethics*. Cf. Ricoeur, *Hermeneutics and the Human Sciences*, 222.

bringing with it certain logical constraints. Resemblance remains indeed the call of the One. Interpretation as "the work of the concept" (302), relies precisely upon this concerted unifying effort. But this call is always a situated call, as we have seen, it is a call after the event. Observation comes too late to the scene says Ricoeur, recalling an old Hegelian theme (197).[41] A natural language (as opposed to a perfect system of signs), draws its vitality from its referring dimension. Accordingly, its coherence and internal consistency is the *consequence* of referring not its absolute presupposition.[42]

Yet, one must inquire sooner or later whether this promising dynamic is able to bring about concrete and material results. Perhaps one may rightly be skeptical that a systematic attempt of the *same* subject to describe the advent of the new can be ever successful. Is it not, in the very essence of the new to defy all formal considerations and to impose its agenda in terms of itself? We return in this way to the question of whether this incessant move between the One and the Many does not underwrite a more fundamental logic of emancipation. We shall only recount here the main features of this situation leaving a more theological evaluation for a later stage.

Ricoeur often insists that metaphor cannot be explicated without loss; to write a logical grammar of metaphor would mean, indeed, to defeat from the start the very structure of the new. A formal description can only say that the new defies our thought experiences, our noetic capabilities. Speculative thought retains it as a challenge, and "emulates" it or "approximates" it from its own resources. Indeed, the inter-animation of metaphor and concept remains elusive. When we think they are on the verge of a real encounter they turn out to be farthest away (313). Expressing it in phenomenological language, we may perhaps say that the elusiveness of Husserl's ego is here brought down from its abstraction and multiplied in a concrete plurality of selves corresponding to the successive *epochés*. Does this tantalizing dance before these fields of investigation ultimately trace the contour of a panoramic perspective? To be sure, Ricoeur is all too aware

41. I am referring to Hegel, as a philosopher of retrospection. As we shall see, Ricoeur rejects precisely this part of Hegel. Nevertheless, as will become apparent, what Ricoeur seems to have rejected is not the claim itself, but its dishonesty. The so called "restrospection" in Hegel eventually turns out to be a hyperbolic projection, as Feuerbach later complained.

42. As we have seen, this return to the "logical structure of metaphor" is intended to mediate between the absolute retrospection of a "meta-logic," on the one hand, and the nihilism of an irreducible metaphoricity of all reality on the other.

of both the presence of the reflective subject to itself, and the presupposition of meaning. But this only accentuates the dilemma.

On the one hand, the birth of the bold subject is forever deferred by the reminder of an all too present self which guides the inquiry at all times. In fairness to Ricoeur it must be said that such presence is no longer the unproblematic Kantian apperception but a subject oscillating between fragility and responsibility. Its constitution therefore, is no longer epistemic (in the Kantian sense) but gathers practical concerns (in an ethical framework which, as we shall see below, departs from the Kantian de-ontological point of view and attempts to recover the Hegelian *Sittlichkeit*, via Aristotle's concept of *phronesis*). On the other hand, however, "the death of the subject" remains a constant task. The philosopher forever finds himself in the situation of recognizing that after all, we always "rise up" with parts of ourselves. What really die are parts of the world . . . points of view . . . selves old and new configured by a plurivocity of signs with contradicting claims to truth.

Can we conclude, then, that what does not really die is the "dying" itself, the exercise which changes views and inhabits worlds, and gives up old prejudices only to take up new ones? We shall refrain from drawing such conclusions at the moment. If the "new" "speaks its own language," we shall remain faithful to our decision to postpone such conclusions for a later stage when we will treat Ricoeur's encounter with more concrete theological themes. Whatever the final outcome, the presence of a certain structure of emancipation is undeniable. As we will see in more detail later, even when the new is retained in its rich density of content, the "logical" structure in which it is inscribed tends to retain its inherent autonomous grammar. Moreover, the forever-deferred coincidence between "construction" and "reception" in the third term invites one, as in the case of Ricoeur's anterior mediations, to start from human experience and to return to it.

Nevertheless, Ricoeur's insistence upon the concrete experience of the new, its historical character and its *a posteriori* interrogation creates a number of openings that invite further theological exploration. Underscoring the bringing together of "the clarity of the concept" and "the dynamism of meaning" (303). Ricoeur appeals to the Kantian productive imagination, recalling a famous passage from Kant's *Critique of Judgment* in which Kant talks about the spirit (*Geist*) in an aesthetic sense, as "the life-giving principle of mind" (303).[43] "This struggle to think more guided by [this] 'vivifying principle,' is the soul of interpretation" (303). A post-Hegelian appropriation of this mediation of exteriority encourages a less psychological and more inter-subjective account of such a "life-giving principle." Of equal significance is Ricoeur's rejection of an ontology of language which attests to his resistance to all types of foundationalism. We are neither configured by mere objects[44] nor are we addressed by an impersonal or tautological call as in Heidegger. The invincibility of the verbal dimension calls for an author of discourse. Language is indeed spoken *to us* before being spoken *by us*. Similarly, the dimension of feeling in its objective correlate of an interior may perhaps attest to the beauty of Creation in its teleological orientation and its openness towards its Creator.

But these are not really the concerns of Ricoeur. Rather his main source of disquiet after the finishing of *The Rule of Metaphor* was the too strong ontological claim of the concluding chapter. In his "Intellectual Autobiography" Ricoeur adds that such a claim can be taken with the somewhat cautionary note that it must be fulfilled concretely, that is to say, in a reader. Ricoeur may have wanted to give more specificity to "the world" opened up by the metaphor. Such a world, if it is not to remain either abstract or mythological, must find fulfillment in a concrete human experience. Ricoeur feels perhaps that without this qualification, such a claim remains hopelessly general, too close to Heidegger's panoramic ontology, too prone to being suspected of dishonesty.

Nevertheless, this is not to say that Ricoeur wants anything less. The nostalgia for the bold claim has not been tempered. Indeed, the greatest thing, by far, is to be master of metaphor (*metaphorikon einai*), to *be* metaphorical (23)! The profound ontological denouement of situating novelty at the intersection between act and experience consists therefore in unveiling its paradoxical constitution: To experience the advent of the novel would be both to find oneself as a source or a "living spring" and yet to discover it as exterior: to "invent" it in a primary affirmation and yet to see it (to see the "similarity in dissimilars"),[45] to receive it as "revelation."

Was it not, in the last analysis, this "gain in being" that was in view, in the light of Ricoeur's anthropological project? As we have seen, Ricoeur

---

43. Cf. Kant, *Critique of Judgment*, 156–57.

44. As in many postmodern proposals: e.g., Baudrillard, *Système des objets*.

45. Aristotle, *Poetics*, 1459-a 3–8.

attaches to this advent of the new (following Bachelard, but more fundamentally Heidegger) an ontological weight. It is this new being in our language that expresses us "by making us what it expresses" (214–15). It is this more primordial event that subsequently becomes a noetic presence, "an increment to consciousness." How are we to talk then about identity in the light of this enigmatic conjoining of act and experience if human being can no longer be conceived as "a stable essence," an undisputed source of insight? Ricoeur's turn to narrative and temporality paves the way for such elucidation.

## The Promised Land of Ontology

### Narrative Identity

The insistence that ontology must be fulfilled in a subject enables us to see the entire structure of disclosure as a parable of identity. If the ontological reference marks ultimately "an increase in being," the advent of the new is the correlate of an ontological happening whose site is the subject. But this final appropriation needed to undergo a number of additional clarifications related to time, historicity and narrativity. This task is undertaken in *Time and Narrative*, where the rich kinship between metaphor and narrative is further clarified. The Kantian productive imagination continues to guide Ricoeur's analysis in outlining the structure of the plot with its capacity to configure in a united "whole" disparate intentions, causes and chance.

But what is the content of the resulting narrative identity? Before answering this question Ricoeur tries to elucidate the problem of reference, in the new context of the narrative statements. The end result is a modified version of the same aim, that of redescribing reality (congenial to metaphor), in its both uncovering and transforming function. Both history and fiction configure human life. But whereas "fiction [refigures] the experience of the reader by means of its very irreality, history [remodels] experience by the reconstruction of the past on the basis of traces left behind."[46] Through this double allegiance to both actuality and possibility narrative, very much like metaphor, is another instantiation of *ordered creation* situated between *mythos* and *mimesis*, between history and fiction. Fiction opens human projects towards possibility, effecting the passage from what "is" to what "can be." History, on the other hand,

---

46. Ricoeur, "Intellectual Autobiography," 48.

introduces an ethical dimension into the equation by uncovering our indebtedness to the past. Both, affirms Ricoeur, are equally important. Together, they constitute an amalgam of action. Narrative identity comes to expression at the very intersection of history and fiction, being "an unstable product" of memory and expectation, founding event and eschatology. The concept of narrative identity is developed and further clarified, however, after the finishing of *Time and Narrative*.[47]

In an article published in *Esprit*[48] Ricoeur distinguishes between two uses of the self: self as sameness (*idem*) and self as "ipseity" (*ipse*). Sameness, maintains constancy of the self with itself, assuring its permanence in time and enabling us to recognise people with the passage of time. Ricoeur will call this *character* in *Oneself as Another*.[49] *Ipseity*, on the other hand, expresses the teleological aspect of the self, projecting it into the future, in Heideggerian terms, "placing the self before itself." This dimension is also temporal in character in so far as it finds itself in a constant process of change. Nonetheless, this transformation does not imply a radical swerving from any notion of continuity. Even here, one may identify a "what" at the very heart of the "who," which would find its model in what Ricoeur would later call *"keeping one's word."* Ricoeur attempts here to unpack the equivocalness of "sameness," more precisely, to disentangle the problem of identity from the substantialist tradition which ascribed to it an immutable substructure or an unchanging core. It has been this underlying ontology which has ultimately rendered the problem of identity in terms of "whatness." Ricoeur starts to trace the contours of his groundbreaking ontology of ipseity, suggesting that the "same" identity should be subordinated to the question "who?." A full account of the ontological implications of these distinctions will be offered in *Oneself as Another*.

## The Return to the Philosophical Discourse—Attestation

*Oneself as Another* constitutes Ricoeur's first systematic attempt to thematize the self in the light of his long hermeneutical detours. The book starts

47. Ricoeur acknowledges that in *Time and Narrative* the discourse is too preoccupied with the constitution of human time in narrative, for being able to identify clearly "what is at stake in the very question of identity applied to persons and communities." Cf. Ricoeur, *Oneself as Another*, 114.

48. Ricoeur, "L'Identite Narrative," 295–304.

49. Ricoeur, *Oneself as Another*, 121.

with the explicit aim of mediating between a Cartesian "exalted" self and the "empty subject" of Nietzsche. However, as Jean Greisch rightly notes, this is more than a mediation. Ricoeur's desire is rather to leave such opposing alternatives behind.[50]

To this end, the language developed earlier is further expanded by identifying three different features in the ordinary use of the language of the self: the reflective use, the *idem/ipse* distinction mentioned above and the correlation between the self and the other than self. Those features enable three separate articulations of the hermeneutics of the self: "reflection by way of analysis," "the dialectic of selfhood and sameness," and "the dialectic of selfhood and otherness."[51] The recourse to this plurivocity of meanings inscribed into the very structure of language, seems appropriate for a necessarily indirect exploration of the self.

In dialogue with the analytic philosophy of ordinary language Ricoeur addresses first the problem of the self at the semantic level, as it is discussed in semantics and in pragmatics. This analytic moment recalls the well-known dialectic of explanation and understanding. While Ricoeur acknowledges the validity of the questions "what?" and "why?," it is eventually the question "who?" which captures his interest, calling each time for fresh perspectives of investigation. Thus, from transcendental analysis, Ricoeur moves to the pragmatics of language, then to the semantics of action and narrativity, and finally to ethics. The passage through narrativity effects the transition from the descriptive part of the study to the prescriptive one. The dialectic sameness-selfhood at work in narrative identity is here pressed further into the realm of action. It is possible, suggests Ricoeur, to transfer the operation of emplotment from the action to the character (characters are themselves plots). In this way, a dialectic internal to the character results. As the narrative follows a concordance-discordance sequence, yet, as a whole it preserves its unity, so it is with the character. A parallel constitution of both action and self is thus indicated. This dialectic of acting and suffering occasions the passage to ethics. Ricoeur attempts now to give an account of the ethical and the moral dimension of the self, in this new narrative context. The guiding question here is "who is the moral subject of imputation." The critique of "the moral vision of the world," present in his previous works, here takes on a more systematic form.

50. Greisch, "Testimony and Attestation," 84–85. Cf. Ricoeur, *Oneself as Another*, 16.

51. Ricoeur, *Oneself as Another*, 16.

Ricoeur's "little ethics" takes its cue from the crucial distinction between ethics and morality; ethics designating the aim of an accomplished life, morality the articulation of this aim in norms. By opposing the aim to the *norm*, Ricoeur opposes Aristotle (the teleological perspective), to Kant (the deontological point of view), suggesting the primacy of ethics over morality. Their corresponding "figures" within the perimeter of the self are *self-esteem* and *self-respect*, respectively. Self-esteem is therefore more fundamental than self-respect. Whilst the ethical aim needs to undergo the test of the norm, "practical wisdom" in conflictual situations marks the return to the tutelage of ethics.

After completing this detour of reflection on "who," by the analysis of what, why, and how, in the last study, Ricoeur is prepared to reflect upon the ontological implications of this intricate philosophical analysis. Alongside the other two dialectics mentioned at the beginning of this section, the last one (the dialectic between selfhood and otherness) is given the largest space. A correlative polysemy of "otherness" (corresponding to that of the self) comes into view in this dialectic. Within the larger framework, the fundamental triad describe-narrate-prescribe, and correlatively, the growing vehemence of the question "who?" (developed gradually in the series of questions, "who is speaking?," "who is narrating?," "who is the agent of action?"), seems to lead to the centrality of praxis as the locus of the constitution of human identity, designating action as the thematic unity of the book[52]. Ricoeur has indeed been careful to guard himself against totalizations, only being prepared to affirm an "analogical unity of action." Acting and suffering as a fundamental mode of being, seem to replace the metaphysical tradition, so caught-up by the concept of Being as substance. In the wake of Heidegger, Ricoeur may perhaps be seen as proposing, in Van Den Hengel's words, "a new ontology of action and passion,"[53] which would amount to devising a practical philosophy in the manner of Manfred Riedl.[54] Is this to say that Ricoeur breaks from the metaphysical tradition?[55] Ricoeur seems to resist such an interpretation! "My major concern," he states in his reply to G. B. Madi-

---

52. Ibid., 19.

53. Van Den Hengel, "Paul Ricoeur's *Oneself as Another* and Practical Theology," 471.

54. Riedel, *Für eine zweite Philosophie, Vorträge und Abhandlungen*; cf. Ricoeur, *Oneself as Another*, 19.

55. See also Madison, "Ricoeur and the Hermeneutics of the Subject," in Ricoeur, *Philosophy of Paul Ricoeur*, 72.

son, "is to do metaphysics in another manner, on the basis, precisely, of a hermeneutic phenomenology."[56]

Let us examine briefly this "other way" of doing metaphysics, which is both hermeneutic and phenomenological. One notion becomes particularly important as Ricoeur's ontological proposal unfolds, namely, the notion of attestation. Jean Greisch is profoundly right, I believe, not only in ascribing it a foundational role in Ricoeur's ontological proposal, but in connecting it with its famous correlate, the concept of testimony.

In what follows, following Jean Greisch,[57] I shall summarize Ricoeur's ontological proposal from the perspective of attestation. The figure of attestation appears in Ricoeur as the reply to a type of validation and certitude, which has dominated philosophy since Descartes. The renunciation of the claim to foundation has gradually uncovered a mode of being which no longer relies upon the Aristotelian being-true being-false distinction.[58] This *aletheic* or veritative mode of being, which, Ricoeur avers, gathers in itself both ontological and epistemological concerns, does not claim and does not need an absolute guarantee to truth. Thus, the new *vis-à-vis* of attestation is suspicion rather than falsehood. This new mode of being, which attempts to ground the "what?" question in the "who?" question, the "believe that" in the "believe in," is neither mere belief (opinion), in the doxic sense, nor a mere psychological condition.

The pressing question which arises at this juncture, however, is whether and how, such a proposal can be ontologically grounded. We have already noted Ricoeur's insistence upon the "objective" aspects implied by the analytic detour ("Objectification" with its "realist" twist is the right counterbalance for the idealist and phenomenalist tendencies). Overall, the dialectic of explanation-understanding reiterates Ricoeur's allegiance to a world, by further spelling out the ontological bearings of experience as finite and inter-subjective (the experiences of passivity corresponding to the "otherness" of selfhood—one's own body, the "foreign" and consciousness).

Attestation is tested each time against such a background. It is important to note that attestation recalls the structure of disclosure depicted earlier. The rise of the capable agent at each level (the power of speaking, the power of doing, the power to recognize oneself as a character in a

---

56. Ricoeur, "Reply to G. B. Madison," in *Philosophy of Paul Ricoeur*, 95.

57. Greish, "Testimony and Attestation," 81–98.

58. Ricoeur, *Oneself as Another*, 302.

narrative, the power to assume ethical responsibility), is contemporaneous with the advent of the "new" which accompanies human action in
all of these fields. But this commitment to the world wants to express
something more than self as "care" (Heidegger) and perhaps something
more than an ontology of action and passion. The resources for this
ontology are located in Aristotle, more precisely, in the ambiguous field
delimited by the relation between *energeia* and *dunamis*.

The challenging thesis of a ground of being "at once potentiality
and actuality" is advanced here,[59] which is further substantiated with the
help of Heidegger's use of Aristotle. Ricoeur questions, however, the reap-
propriation of Aristotle's *energeia* and *entelekheia* in the direction of the
Heideggerian facticity.[60] Instead an appeal is made to Spinoza's *conatus*,[61]
which, in Ricoeur's opinion, brings power and act together, as "the effort to
exist and the power to be." Such a view may account not only for becoming
but also for the presence of "otherness" in the constitution of the self. It is
in this latter direction that Ricoeur attempts to overcome the "abstractness"
of Spinoza's particularity and dispel the suspicion of determinism. If the
*demarché* of activity in this enlarged view of ethics (which would include
the sum total of human actions), is to be more than mere "mechanics," a
more adequate account of particularity must be given. It is at this point that
attestation must receive the decisive reply of testimony.

It is noteworthy that, as Greisch remarks,[62] Ricoeur does not ab-
solutize the notion of narrative identity. This is why the capable subject
remains fragile in a precarious balance between possession and dispos-
sesion. "In a philosophy of ipseity like my own, one must be able to say
that ownership is not what matters."[63] This fragility of the self betrays
not only its radical dependence on "otherness," but also the configuring
force of contingency. It is also noteworthy that in the dispute between
universalist and contextualist ethics, between universality and historicity,
Ricoeur attempts to go beyond a mere dichotomy between argumentation (a universalism of the ethics of discussion, as found in Habermas
and Karl Otto Apel) and convention. An equilibrium is sought between

59. Ibid., 308.

60. Ibid., 314.

61. Ibid., 315.

62. "Narrative identity does not exhaust the question of the ipseity of the subject."
Ricoeur, *Time and Narrative*, 3:249. Cf. Greisch, "Testimony and Attestation," 92.

63. Ricoeur, *Oneself as Another*, 168; cf. Greisch, "Testimony and Attestation," 91.

argumentation and conviction.[64] We may safely claim, I believe, that this "considered conviction" is but the correlate of testimony.

Ricoeur concludes his last study by leaving "otherness" in abeyance. In commenting on the source of the "injunction" Ricoeur contends that "one does not and cannot say whether this Other . . . is another person whom I can look in the face or who can stare at me, or my ancestors for whom there is no representation, . . . or God—living God, absent God— or an empty place."[65] Genuinely to indicate the grounds of this otherness, a different discourse is required if we are not to subsume this very "otherness" to the category of the "same." Ricoeur is perhaps implicitly suggesting that the relationship between attestation and testimony needs a theological elaboration. His later distrust in the "sufficient openness" of Aristotelian ontology to the proposal advanced at the end of *Oneself as Another*,[66] may be further interpreted indeed as a fear that such an ontology may still remain abstract.

It may well be that philosophy reaches its limits here. But can the philosopher reflect by forever bracketing out what is essential? The notion of testimony has brought us closer than ever before to a threshold which in fact feeds the very philosophical quest: a view of disclosure that would bring meaning and truth together, an ontological vision in which the right desire would be reconciled with the right idea in a genuine *polis*. If we are genuinely to fulfill our thirst we must step beyond this threshold . . .

---

64. Ricoeur, *Oneself as Another*, 291;334. Cf. Greisch, "Testimony and Attestation," 96.

65. Ricoeur, *Oneself as Another*, 355.

66. Ricoeur, "Intellectual Autobiography," 50–54.

*3*

# Hermeneutics, Creation, and the "Re-enchantment" of the World

This attempt to introduce a complete revolution in the procedure of meta-physics, after the example of Geometricians and the Natural Philosophers, constitutes the aim of *The Critique of Pure Speculative Reason*. It is a treatise on the method to be followed, not a system of the sciences itself. But at the same time, it marks out and defines both, the external boundaries and the internal structure of this science.

IMMANUEL KANT, *THE CRITIQUE OF PURE REASON*

I do not crush the world's corolla of wonders . . .
My mind does not kill the mysteries I meet on my way
In flowers, eyes, on lips or in tombs . . .

LUCIAN BLAGA, *POEMS OF LIGHT*

DOES RICOEUR'S PROPOSAL ENABLE us to experience the world as "Creation"? Can we, following the indication of his thought, not only "think" the truth but know it? With these questions we have reached a turning point. Our investigation so far, while mainly "descriptive," has already raised a number of theological questions in an effort to ground theologically our experience of the world in general, Ricoeur's philo-sophical undertaking in particular. Since, in the Apostle Paul's words, it is indeed in God that "we live, and move, and have our being" (Acts 17:28), no serious concern for experience and meaning can genuinely bracket out the question of God. Nonetheless, a more radical step is required. One of our working hypotheses has been that neither a universal and unproblematic access to the truth of reality grounded in the datum of Creation nor the privileged perspective of the "ecclesial being" can be simply taken for granted. We cannot forever remain in an attitude of "generic" faithfulness to the truth without critically inquiring into our ethical stance before the summons of the Word. The implicit and unrelenting inquiry into meaning in the light of the adventures of the subject must be therefore referred to the more radical question of how the reality of what we believe to be genuine and true impinges upon our conception of the world, history, and ultimately upon our epistemic practice.

But let me first anchor this evaluation of Ricoeur into our more general concerns. There have been various attempts to go beyond the Kantian dual framework from Fichte onwards conducted from various angles: reflective philosophy, phenomenology, philosophy of science, etc. We do not want to rehearse here the nature of the various attempts but rather to draw attention to what is arguably, part of their fundamental problematic: the figure of a "subject" over against a "world." The hermeneutical quest was born in the tension between these two terms or, more precisely, after the loss of confidence in an unproblematic correspondence between the two. The fading away of the belief in the mind as the mirror of the world brought about a crisis of knowledge, at least in the form traditionally conceived. From a theological perspective, this situation may be referred back to the more general problem of God's relationship with the world. In other words, to talk about Hermeneutics and Creation together may be seen as an attempt to devise a modality of re-thinking the relation between God and the world after Descartes and Kant. We shall explore this relation in a single step by conducting the discussion on two levels: on the one hand, I shall seek to show that the Kantian grammar of Ricoeur's attempt to "re-enchant" the world, and more specifically his way of "listening" to Revelation, reveals a number of problems which stand in need of a theological address. On the other hand, however, I shall try to indicate along the way a number of openings which would lead me to suggest that the tension between "what is" and what "can be," the structure of novelty or the emergence of the new, the very substance from which hermeneutics lives, can be successfully addressed by appeal to the Trinitarian grammar of God's relationship with the world (creation categories, providence, illumination, divine action). Moreover, thinking Hermeneutics and Creation together may uncover a prejudice ingrained in some modern theological replies to the Cartesian subject, which may be seen best in their suspicion towards "nature." The prejudice, in its crude form, goes something like this: if to the "fallen subject" corresponds an equally "fallen world," what is really needed is "redemption" rather than knowledge. While "naturalism" in its modern guise, must be, obviously, left behind, my claim is that more often than not such suspicion reveals a structural dependence upon the paradigm it wants to contest. The redeemed subject as a "transfiguration" of the autonomous subject arguably took shape in the shadow of the adventures of the modern self, that is to say, following its rise and fall. I shall attempt to show later in the project that theology may gain a relative independence[1] from such conceptuality which tends to situate redemption and knowledge in radical opposition, by looking again at God's relationship with the world conceived in its Trinitarian dimension. In the process, the concept of "nature" will receive a distinctive theological flavor and certain aspects of the doctrine of Creation may receive a better intelligibility.

## Reason and Revelation in Conflict:
## The "Kantian" Ricoeur

Having discussed the persistence of an emancipatory dimension in Ricoeur, and having seen his undeterred belief in the creative capacity of the mind, how and to what extent can we talk about Ricoeur as a neo-Enlightenment figure as Lewis Mudge suggests in passing?[2] Part of the aim of this chapter is both to follow this dimension in Ricoeur's more exegetical and theological writings and to integrate such findings in Ricoeur's larger philosophical concerns.

Perhaps the most common criticism of Ricoeur has been his reliance upon Kant.[3] It appears at times, indeed, that Ricoeur's "Poetics of the Will," as it can be inferred from his theological essays, constitutes an expression of a hope "within the limits of Kant alone."[4] That Kant has constituted an unrelenting source of insight for Ricoeur is undeniable. Ricoeur frankly acknowledges, in fact, his own indebtedness to Kant, and

---

1. I used the term "relative" to point to two aspects: First, there is the formal consideration that no reply can be absolutely independent of that to which the reply is intended, and second, the redeemed self in opposition to the autonomous self is arguably a genuine biblical theme. (e.g., Rom 3:5; Gal 2:20, etc.)

2. Ricoeur, *Essays on Biblical Interpretation*, 1.

3. E.g., the studies of Anderson, Vanhoozer, Burgeois, etc.

4. I allude to Vanhoozer's expression in Vanhoozer, *Biblical Narrative in the Philosophy of Paul Ricoeur*, 38ff.

at times specifically refers to the kind of Kantian limits he employs in his philosophy. However, he is equally eager to spell out the kind of "extension" (*Erweiterung*) he applies to Kant, "extension" seen as more important than the "limit." Ricoeur claims to have pursued the movement of extension further than Kant, without repudiating though his critique of the *noumenal* absolute.[5]

To be sure, one can easily identify a traditional Kantian vocabulary in Ricoeur's writings, distinguishing as it does between the rational self and the empirical self, between freedom and nature, activity and passivity, reception and construction. Our interest, however, lies not so much in the identification of dualities *per se*,[6] as in the concrete career of this terminology and the extent to which it perpetuates the theological problems Kant more or less inaugurated.[7] Let us look briefly at the concrete Kantian problematic Ricoeur wants to preserve.

Ricoeur engages explicitly with Kant's doctrines in a number of places.[8] In a very sympathetic reading of *Religion Within the Limits of Reason Alone*, we discover in fact not only the roots of Ricoeur's own philosophical interests but also the source of his own determination to keep theology and philosophy separate. An attempt is made here to appropriate the book as a philosophical hermeneutic of religion. Ricoeur claims that the study of religion (as in fact the title suggests) does not really "extend" Kant's perimeter of discussion. It adds nothing to what we already know from his other works.[9] Religion stands in relation to philosophy as an outsider, at the edge, separating the transcendental realm of philosophy from the historical terrain of religion. Ricoeur further notes that the whole study is put in motion not by freedom as related to the rational structure of the will (*Wille*), but by the "factual situation" of human freedom torn apart as it is between desire and duty. It is the peculiar situation of free will understood in this sense (*Wilkur*), as a bound free

---

5. See Ricoeur, "Reply to Patrick Burgeois," in *Philosophy of Paul Ricoeur*, 566ff.

6. As in some postmodern critiques like those of Anderson (*Ricoeur and Kant*) or Milbank (*Theology and Social Theory*, 263–68).

7. For a criticism of Kant from a theological perspective, see Barth, *Protestant Theology in the Nineteenth Century*, 266–312.

8. E.g., Ricoeur, "Philosophical Hermeneutics of Religion: Kant," in, *Figuring the Sacred*, 75–92; Ricoeur, "Biblical Hermeneutics"; Ricoeur, "Freedom in the Light of Hope," in *Conflict of Interpretations*, 402–24, etc.

9. Ricoeur, *Figuring the Sacred*, 75. I will incorporate page references into the text above.

will or servile will that prompts the reflection on religion. This mysterious bondage which cripples human action is inextricably bound with the
problem of radical evil. Moreover, it is the historical existence of evil that
calls for a type of reflection which cannot be other than hermeneutical.
We learn here that a familiar theme from Ricoeur's theological essays,[10]
his celebrated "logic of superabundance," had been long anticipated in
Kant: it was Kant who first maintained that the reply of religion appears
as a schema of hope constituted in the form of "in spite of," or "even
though" (76). In the same vein, the Kantian insight that "the disposition towards the good . . . is more originary than evil is radical" (77) is
implicitly connected with Ricoeur's famous wager that meaning is more
fundamental than non-sense. In such a light, one may undoubtedly see
Ricoeur's concern for the will from *Freedom and Nature* to *The Symbolism of Evil*, as grounded in a Kantian problematic. Nevertheless, we must
remember that such a problematic is Christian before being Kantian and,
after all, Kant's own undertaking may be seen as an effort to be faithful to
the Christian tradition.[11]

This is not to say that Ricoeur fully condones Kant's implicit Christology. In many ways, he is aware of its shortcomings. Nonetheless, before addressing its problems, Ricoeur is extremely detailed in indicating
Kant's effort to retain the orthodox intention of the tradition. There are in
Kant, anticipations of more than mere exemplarism in Ricoeur's reading.
Christ "is not only an example of duty," claims Ricoeur, "in which case
it would not exceed the Analytic, but an ideal exemplar of the highest
good . . . Christ is an archetype, . . . because he symbolises this fulfilment.
He is the figure of the End."[12] Consequently, Christ is more than an idea:
"this archetype is irreducible as an idea to a moral intention . . . it has established itself in [humankind] without our comprehending how human
nature could have been capable of receiving it."[13] What is more, in the
tradition of Augustine, Kant seeks to present a conception of evil, able to
avoid the pitfalls of both Pelagianism and Manicheism.[14] As a result, both

---

10. See for instance Ricoeur, "Logic of Jesus, the Logic of God," in *Figuring the
Sacred*, 271ff.; see also "Hope and the Structure of Philosophical Systems," in ibid.,
206–7.

11. See also Gunton, *Actuality of Atonement*, 3–8.

12. Ricoeur, *Essays on Biblical Interpretation*, 182.

13. Ibid., 181n6.

14. Ricoeur claims that Kant's view of the will constitutes a significant advance in
regard to that of Augustine who did not have the conceptuality to mediate between

radical evil and regeneration remain ultimately "inscrutable" to us: "How it is possible for a naturally evil man to make himself a good man wholly surpasses our comprehension."[15] Despite the disastrous tendency of displacing the historical Christ with human moral reason, Kant was at least able to glimpse beneath the theme of the fall through seduction a more original innocence. The affirmation of such innocence rescues Creation from an original guilt and, in Ricoeur's opinion, opens the schema of hope. Even Kant's ecclesiology offers something commendable: Ricoeur believes that in spite of Kant's harsh criticism of institutional religion he nevertheless attempts to disentangle "the true figure of the church from its historical caricature."[16]

But if Ricoeur admires and partly re-iterates Kant's philosophical approximations of Christianity, he disavows Kant's neglect of particularity in general and the historicity of Christ in particular. This is part of a larger picture that involves, in fact, the rejection of a whole ethical view which, Ricoeur thinks, is the dead part of Kant's system. In doing so, a whole methodological style which separates form from content (duty from desire, coherence from life, universality from historicity, legality from effectiveness, rationality from reality) is called into question.[17] It was in fact the framework created by those distinctions that crippled his vision of regeneration. Most important of all, Kant really missed the passivity and alterity specific to the experience of conversion, failing to realize that "the element of alterity [must be] bound not just to the presence of the archetype [a humanity well pleasing to God—the Christological principle] at the heart of reason, but more importantly, to the efficacy of this representation which is the very efficacy of faith."[18] This latter reference to the efficacy of representation may perhaps suggest Ricoeur's concern to ground Christology ontologically (to overcome the suspicion of exemplarism in a more decisive way) and to connect it with a doctrine of the Spirit. We may perhaps further infer that failing to see Christology in its historical context and in its relation to the Spirit inevitably leads to its "interiorization" in a rational principle.

Pelagianism and Manicheism. Cf. Ricoeur, *Conflict of Interpretations*, 269ff.; 302.

15. Ricoeur, *Figuring the Sacred*, 82.

16. Ibid., 90.

17. Ibid., 209.

18. Ibid., 87.

Nonetheless, like Kant, Ricoeur is not really interested in developing a full-fledged Christology His only hope is to produce a better approximation within the strict confines of reason. But even anticipates in
the following passage what may be seen as his own attempt at a better articulation of such a problematic. An adequate description was prevented
in Kant because he lacked, Ricoeur believes, a philosophy of the religious
imagination.[19] But this observation is followed by a most intriguing remark: Ricoeur comments that such a "mythopoetics of the imagination
would violate the contract of agreement, of congruence, of mutual fit that
Kant attempts to establish and to preserve between philosophy and religion, on the frontier of reason alone."[20]

Must we not ask in such a light, whether Ricoeur's own effort to "extend" Kant and his lifelong interest in imagination does not itself, whether
implicitly or explicitly, trespass across the frontier between the two "language games"? How are we to understand Ricoeur's "extension" of Kant,
as an explicit effort to explore precisely this dimension of imagination?[21]
But before unpacking further this latter question, we need both to anchor
this conflict within the larger framework of his philosophical concerns,
and to see it at work in the interpretative practice.

## The Concept of Distanciation

I shall attempt here to explore in a more systematic fashion what I consider to be a key concept in Ricoeur's work, philosophical and theological
alike, the concept of distanciation. The investigation, which will recall,
and attempt to thematize, a number of now familiar themes touched upon
in the previous chapters, will concentrate especially upon the capacity of
the concept of distanciation to limit, to mark external boundaries and

19. Ibid., 87.

20. Ibid., 88.

21. For a treatment of Ricoeur's extension of Kant, see Burgeois, *Extension of
Ricoeur's Hermeneutics*. See also Burgeois, "Limits of Ricoeur's Hermeneutics of Existence," in Ricoeur, *Philosophy of Paul Ricoeur*, 549–66. The "correction" Burgeois applies to Ricoeur is situated however within the same "transcendental" space with the
difference that he considers fit to reject the Kantian notion of radical evil. Thus, Ricoeur
"remaining too Kantian" (562) must be really read as remaining faithful to one of the
fundamental intentions of the Christian dogma. (Of course, how successful Ricoeur had
been in doing so is another question). This is why Burgeois's call for "a neutral place for
the possibility of evil and of good in the existential possibilities of *Dasein*" (564) is of little
relevance for the present analysis and perhaps for theology in general.

yet to "extend," to configure the "internal structure" of emancipation, by incorporating into itself both epistemological and ontological concerns. We shall conduct our inquiry from two directions: on the one hand, from the perspective of Ricoeur's own position in the larger hermeneutical debate, and on the other, from the perspective of Ricoeur's own philosophical project.

## From Exegesis to the Structure of Understanding

The hermeneutical problem is far from being new. Ricoeur identifies exegesis as its initial context. Exegesis, as a method of deciphering a text begins "with its intention, on the basis of what it attempts to say."[22] This effort to reach a univocal meaning, to bring into dialogue communities separated by space and time marked the birth of the exegetical debates.

But the very appearance of the exegetical debates signals, according to Ricoeur, the subsequent philosophical interest in it. That is so, because the effort to make contemporaneous communities by means of a written text raises additional questions related to meaning, language and history, which go beyond questions of method or technique. Two tendencies must be noted at this point. Both have their roots in the Romantic period, more precisely in Schleiermacher, who, in Ricoeur's appreciation, brought to hermeneutics the Kantian Copernican revolution. The first trait of this revolution is its move from regional hermeneutics to general hermeneutics. The key to reach univocal meaning in the interpretations of texts is based upon our ability to understand language, or our linguistic skills. One must rise above the particularity of the individual texts and even above the particularity of various exegetical strategies and reach the general conditions of understanding any text. Such a move, Ricoeur thinks, established a Kantian horizon to hermeneutics, instituting it as a general method irrespective of content.[23] The development and importance attached to classical philology must be understood in this context.

The other move was Romantic in character. A genuine understanding of a text gives access to the individuality of its author. The text is an expression of his or her unique personality. The understanding of a particular text is different from grasping some general characteristics pertaining to a historical period. Genuine understanding must accede to

22. Ricoeur, *Conflict of Interpretations*, 3.
23. Ricoeur, *Hermeneutics and the Human Sciences*, 46.

that which makes the text unique and unrepeatable. Somewhat ironically, this second move, which in Schleiermacher's opinion really effects the interpretative task, ultimately confirms the first by rendering language as a mere tool for conveying the subjectivity of the author.

Subsequently, Dilthey expanded the enquiry by bringing history into the discussion. Yet, his famous distinction between understanding and explanation, between nature and history, Ricoeur thinks, forces understanding back into psychological intuition.[24] Nevertheless, his contribution to hermeneutics is significant. To begin with, he prompted the necessity for an enquiry into the ontological roots of historical understanding. Moreover, he unveiled the crux of the problem: "That life grasps life only by the mediation of units of meaning which rise above the historical flux."[25] It was this insight which suggested a genuine alternative to Hegel's absolute knowledge.

But the main dissatisfaction with both Schleiermacher and Dilthey remains their ultimate failure to transgress the epistemological confines of the discussion. Historical knowledge involves what Ricoeur calls "the paradoxes of historicity." Neither a psychological account of meaning, of being transported into another psyche, nor life as the "bearer of meaning" can explain how "a historical being [can] understand being historically," or "how can life objectify itself."[26] It is at this point that Ricoeur appeals to phenomenology.

In fact the explicit appeal to phenomenology is based upon an implicit and reciprocal connection. One the one hand, hermeneutics itself starts with the presupposition of meaning.[27] Ultimately this is its great wager. On the other hand, phenomenology, as the late Husserl testifies, must conceive its method as an *Auslegung*, an interpretation.[28] As we have anticipated, the question in need of an answer is now how understanding in general is possible for a historical being. It is Heidegger's ontology of understanding that guides Ricoeur's further investigation. Heidegger insists that the historicality of both subject and object is in need of explicitation. The discourse which brings that to language is prior to any methodology. The question of truth therefore, is removed from

24. Ibid., 49.

25. Ibid., 53.

26. Ricoeur, *Conflict of Interpretations*, 5.

27. Ricoeur, *Hermeneutics and the Human Sciences*, 114ff.

28. Ibid., 120ff.

the epistemological constraints of a Kantian theory of knowledge. But Ricoeur's main dissatisfaction with Heidegger's proposal is not so much its apparent circularity,[29] but rather its ultimate incapacity to return to properly epistemological questions, to show in what way such fundamental ontology can enter into dialogue with the human sciences.[30]

Gadamer's further exploration of the Heideggerian ontology, in spite of its partial success, uncovers, according to Ricoeur, another apparent irreconcilable conflict: the conflict between what Gadamer dubbed the *alienating distanciation* and the *experience of belonging*. The price hermeneutics pays for its claim to universality is "the destruction of the primordial relation of belonging."[31] Gadamer seems to be saying that as soon as hermeneutics rises above the historical flux, the ontological hope is shattered. Its own reliance upon its transcendental capability is, in actual fact, an alienating experience.

It is at this end of the spectrum that Ricoeur situates his own hermeneutical contribution. He is determined not to choose between truth and method. If the experience of belonging does not allow a critical instance, we are forever caught up in tradition. Such fundamental ontology is still incapable of orienting our practical living. What is required, Ricoeur suggests, is not merely to repudiate distanciation but to assume it. Without such dialectic of proximity and distance we are unable responsibly to situate ourselves in what Gadamer called *Wirkungsgeschichtliches Bewusstsein* (the consciousness of the history of effects).[32] Such dialectic sets the stage for Ricoeur's concept of "the world of the text." Nevertheless, the concept gathers more fundamental concerns, related to Ricoeur's philosophical project.

29. Ricoeur, *Conflict of Interpretations*, 10. Heidegger denies the circularity of reasoning insisting rather upon "a remarkable relatedness backward and forward." Cf. Ricoeur, "Heidegger and the Question of the Subject," in *Conflict of Interpretations*, 223ff.

30. Ricoeur, *Hermeneutics and the Human Sciences*, 59. Ricoeur, *Conflict of Interpretations*, 10–11.

31. Ricoeur, *Hermeneutics and the Human Sciences*, 60.

32. Gadamer, *Truth and Method*, 267–68, 300ff.

## The De-centering of the Self:
## From Symbol to Text

Ricoeur's philosophy is also an anthropological project. We have followed in the previous chapters the migration of this project from its initial framework of reflexive philosophy to phenomenology and finally to hermeneutics. As has been shown above, the principal upshot of this move was the radical questioning of the indubitable transparent ego of Descartes.

Ricoeur often notes that hermeneutics is conditioned phenomenologically by its presupposition of meaning. Now the fundamental problem of the phenomenological account of meaning is that the bearer of meaning is the subject.[33] Ricoeur points out that it was precisely Husserl's failure to find the Ego at the end of his *Logical Investigations*, that inaugurated the hermeneutical task. As we have seen, since the *cogito* can no longer function as foundation, both self and meaning must be recovered from the world.[34] In such a light, the task of reflection itself is redefined. It becomes what Ricoeur calls "concrete reflection." This concrete reflection is not intuition, but rather the effort to "re-comprehend the ego in the mirror of its objects, its works and ultimately its acts."[35] Ricoeur inaugurates the search for the self by a hermeneutic of symbolic expressions. He recognizes that those symbolic expressions, from cosmic symbols to dreams and religious symbols can be organized around various methodologies and rules, depending on their nature. Yet it is precisely this conflict of interpretation that anticipates a better understanding of the world. How is this so? First of all, by the symbol's very structure of signification. Ricoeur defines the symbol by distinguishing between a hidden and a literal meaning.[36] Interpretation consists precisely in arriving at the surplus of meaning promised by this structure of double or multiple meaning. What is important to note is that this interpretative undertaking dislocates the reflective effort to ground interpretation upon itself.

In his early writings on symbol, Ricoeur seems to treat the various symbolic interpretative strategies on the same footing, from the Freudian analysis and Nietzsche's hermeneutics of suspicion to religious phenomenology, claiming that each strategy is valid within the limits of its

---

33. Ricoeur, *Conflict of Interpretations*, 246.

34. "The constitution of the self is contemporaneous with the constitution of meaning." Ricoeur, "What Is a Text?," in *Hermeneutics and the Human Sciences*, 159.

35. Ricoeur, *Conflict of Interpretations*, 327.

36. See for instance Ricoeur, *De l'interprétation*, 19–28.

own theoretical circumscription.[37] However, later in his career Ricoeur is less prepared to do so.[38] Without denying their critical function, it must be admitted that some hermeneutic strategies are indeed reductive. The travail of meaning must traverse the hermeneutics of suspicion towards a hermeneutic of faith, towards "the richest, the fullest and the most elevated meaning." In fact, as he later confesses, his very interest in the symbolic expression, which he took from Mircea Eliade,[39] was promoted by the promise of wholeness and unity of being.

Two structural, if interrelated, features of Ricoeur's undertaking must be noted. First, is his effort to identify not only the plurivocity of meanings but also the signs of their unity. As we have seen, Ricoeur believes with Aristotle that "being is said in many ways," yet the symbol conjures up wholeness and its surplus of meaning is the first sign of such anticipation. And second, the peculiar position of the symbolic expression, on the threshold of language marks its potential capacity to explore the real, to open the world for language. As we have indicated in the previous chapters, such considerations will assist Ricoeur further in his treatment of both metaphor and narrative.

In his later writings Ricoeur extends his hermeneutical compass generally to texts. The concentration upon texts wins in profundity Ricoeur claims, to the extent that a text is able to "speak" in a way the symbol cannot.[40] This move also gives more credibility to his de-centering project. Due both to its compass and to what Ricoeur calls "its ability to project a world," the self is in this way confronted with a more articulated ontological promise. In the light of Ricoeur's more general philosophical concerns, we are now in a better position to assess the concept of the world of the text, and how the dialectic of understanding and explanation features here.

---

37. Ricoeur, *Conflict of Interpretations*, 15.

38. Ricoeur, "On Interpretation," 192. Ricoeur, "Intellectual Autobiography," 19.

39. Ricoeur, "Intellectual Autobiography," 19. Ricoeur's attitude towards Eliade's work has been however significantly critical in spite of "a deep and faithful friendship" (cf. Ricoeur, *Critique and Conviction*, 32). See his review of Eliade's first volume, *History of Religions*, in *Religious Studies Review* 2 (1976) 1–4. "There is a polarity of proclamation and manifestation which Mircea Eliade does not recognize in his homogenous concept of manifestation, epiphany and so forth" (Ricoeur, *Figuring the Sacred*, 71).

40. Ricoeur, *Interpreation Theory*, 78.

## The Structure of the World of the Text

The task of hermeneutics consists in projecting in front of the text a world which I could inhabit.[41] What remains to be interpreted? "I shall say: to interpret is to explicate the type of being-in-the-world unfolded in front of the text."[42] A cardinal feature of the concept is its triple autonomy, not only in regard to the intention of the author, but equally in regard to its initial audience and the history of its production. Let us look briefly at the cluster of concerns gathered in this expression.

First of all, Ricoeur talks about a "world." The primary aim of interpretation is neither the restoration of the someone of discourse (its author), nor its direct reference to the world (its objectifying reference). In fact, Ricoeur remarks, the aim of most literary fiction is to destroy the actual world. Nevertheless, the text depicts its own world whose reference is not the immediate empirical reality at the level of what Ricoeur calls "manipulable objects," but rather a possible world, a world in which I can project "my ownmost possibilities." The capacity of the text to project a world responds to our condition of belonging by a structure of anticipation. Yet, the positing of the *Dasein* in front of the text is also a reminder that interpretation mediates a distance.[43] As we have seen, the question Ricoeur asks is how to reinstate the dialogue with the sciences, yet without returning to the reflective subject. The answer, Ricoeur believes, is suggested by the very nature of the text. Indeed, it is the text itself which invites us to assume distanciation at the very heart of the experience of belonging. Ricoeur conducts his argument by exploring in detail the rich phenomena of textuality, appealing in turn to linguistics, semantics, theory of speech-acts and theory of action. In each case, distanciation is shown to occupy a central place.

The initial situation of discourse confronts us with a passage from event to meaning. "Discourse, by entering the process of understanding, surpasses itself as event and becomes meaning."[44] Here we have, Ricoeur

41. Ricoeur, "On Interpretation," 194.

42. Ricoeur, *Hermeneutics and the Human Sciences*, 141.

43. This is not a version of reader-response approach. In fact, such a suggestion would go against the innermost intentions of Ricoeur's de-centering project. This world is situated in front of the text because the text anticipates, in Hegel's terms, a richer figure of the Spirit, a better world, the kingdom which is coming and which alone is able to give a self to the ego. "There is no point in replacing an intentional fallacy with an affective fallacy," writes Ricoeur. ("De l'interprétation," 31, my translation).

44. Ricoeur, *Hermeneutics and the Human Sciences*, 134.

notes, the first distanciation, the distanciation of the saying in the said. But the text as a finite totality confronts us with the notion of work which has a literary genre and a particular style. This step enables Ricoeur to recall another mediation necessitated by the disjunction effected by Dilthey between Understanding (*Verstehen*) and Explanation (*Auslegung*).[45] Since the work has "structure and form," it is fitted for a semiological analysis. This process proves, against Dilthey, that not all explanation is necessarily causal or "naturalistic." Thus explanation is placed at the very heart of understanding. The reconstruction of the discourse in the work is connected back to the event precisely by the notion of style. Somehow, it is the style which refers the text back to the author of discourse. This announces the second distanciation implicit in the text, namely the "objectification" of the author in his work. Ultimately, interpretation is a form of *reply* on the part of the reader to this fundamental distanciation.

But the most important distanciation occurs in the paramount changes the text undergoes in the passage from speaking to writing. In such a passage, the text becomes autonomous. It follows a new career leaving behind the intention of its author. "Textual meaning and psychological meaning have different destinies."[46] The crucial remark to be made, therefore, is that the concept of distanciation is not something *we* bring to the text by our "objectifying" enquiry. "Distanciation is not the product of methodology and hence something superfluous and parasitical; rather it is constitutive of the phenomenon of the text as writing."[47]

## The Problem of Criteria

In what follows we shall try to show that the concept of distanciation is not only constitutive for both Ricoeur's concept of the world of the text and the explanation-understanding dialectic, but also that its basic grammar reveals an underlying concern of his philosophical project.

In *"De l"interpretation"* Ricoeur claims that the first task of hermeneutics is to reveal the internal dynamic which governs the structure of the text. Such reconstruction, as we have seen, is the condition of the possibility of the world of the text. But this internal dynamic reveals a filial connection with the dialectic between explanation and understanding.

45. Ibid., 92.
46. Ibid., 91, 139.
47. Ibid., 139–40.

Moreover, a somewhat similar tension can be found at various levels, in every interpretative experience from signs and symbols to texts, and finally in the very structure of human action. Let us briefly recount what happens at each of these levels.

As we have seen in chapter 2, at the level of metaphor, the concept of semantic innovation presupposes a background distance between the two terms which, by the act of the metaphorical predication, are brought together. Similarly, at the level of narrative, the singularity of the plot brings about a new pertinence in the emplotment. Again, this goes back to the dynamic between a certain narrative typology and the singularity of a particular plot. The restructuring of the internal norms of a certain narrative typology in the light of those new inventions reflects the appropriation of an initial distance. Even the theory of action and history itself requires a distancing of action from its agent, in the sense in which its meaning is no longer dependent upon the initial intention of the agent. Ricoeur reiterates similar concerns when he addresses the relationship between hermeneutics and ideology. Since in principle "hermeneutical experience discourages the recognition of any critical instance,"[48] the text can emancipate itself only by recognizing distanciation as part of the mediation itself.[49] What is remarkable to notice is that a similar structure of distanciation is present at every level where emancipation or a logic of discovery is insinuated.

In his hermeneutics of symbols, in the attempt to unify various hermeneutical strategies, Ricoeur aimed to find a logic of double meaning based upon this symbolic expression. Such a logic would be transcendental rather than formal, revealing, Ricoeur says, "not the conditions of the possibility of a nature, but the conditions of the appropriation of our desire to be."[50] As it started to become apparent, this logic of double meaning, which had continued to haunt Ricoeur in his later writings, raises an enigmatic tension at the very heart of his de-centering project. Ricoeur is well aware that one cannot establish an epistemological stance no longer reliant upon the subject, without indicating first its ontological structure. This is why the appeal to Heidegger's ontology is not optional. At first sight, Ricoeur's long detour seems to be an attempt to effect a gradual reading of the signs of such ontology. Is it not better, Ricoeur

---

48. Ibid., 90.

49. Ibid., 91.

50. Ricoeur, *Conflict of Interpretations*, 19.

asks, "to begin with the derived forms of understanding, and to show in them, the signs of their derivation?" From a theological perspective, this may be seen as a form of natural theology. Yet, Ricoeur is confronted from the very beginning with a difficulty Hegel anticipated more than a century earlier: we cannot even begin to show a single sign, without having the sign already. We cannot show the truth, without being in the truth. Such is the difficulty of the problem of criterion: it must be both ontological and epistemological, or perhaps better, it may perform an epistemological function only by virtue of its ontological novelty.

To sum up, in an impressive detour, Ricoeur sees his contribution to the hermeneutical debate, precisely in this conception of the world of the text which, as we have seen, on the one hand, mediates between understanding and explanation, and on the other, heralds the fulfillment of his anthropological project, by giving a self to the ego. Central to such a process, the feature which distances Ricoeur from Gadamer, is the insertion of distanciation at the very heart of the experience of belonging.[51] From his earliest work on symbols to his late work work on narrative, Ricoeur's effort had been to show that such distanciation is not the product of reflective consciousness, but rather part of the text itself, and more generally, part of our experience of the world. To discover this inner dynamic of the text, which alone is able to anticipate being, is, according to Ricoeur, to add to the ontological project an analytical precision which is lacking in both Heidegger and Gadamer.[52] Thus, a way is opened for the dialogue with the human sciences. Such emancipation of hermeneutics means more than an unveiling of our fundamental belonging, which would leave us caught up in tradition. It is instead able to adopt a critical stance, to account for the structure of novelty, and ultimately for the dynamic of history itself.

Yet, despite its promises, this "analytical precision" does not seem to produce an immediate effective criterion in the way described above. If Heidegger asks, "How is understanding in general possible?" Ricoeur asks: "How is a critical control possible in the light of such fundamental ontology?" As we have seen at the end of chapter 2 above, this "return" to epistemology retains a strong transcendental flavor. What we have, therefore, are only the conditions of the possibility of such a criterion whose structure, Ricoeur claims, takes refuge in neither subject nor tradition

51. For an explicit critique of Gadamer, see also Ricoeur, *Hermeneutics and the Human Sciences*, 63ff.

52. Ricoeur, "De l'interprétation," 34.

(even though both are somehow included). We learn that distanciation is not the product of our "objectifying" tendency, but rather structural to our existence in time. But there are a number of indications that Ricoeur wants to say more. A turn to his theological essays will enable us to see whether, and in what way the biblical text may throw further light upon the above issues.

Ricoeur acknowledges that the biblical text confronts us with a special case. Since it is the text which brings forth its own truth, it must also produce its own rules of deciphering it. Hence, we cannot employ classical categories in establishing the rules of interpretation for such a discourse. We must enter the circle of form and content, contends Ricoeur, by following "the most primitive dialectics of exteriorization and objectification on which the different modes of discourse will build the autonomy of the corresponding literary forms."[53] Thus each mode of discourse (narrative, parable, hymn) has its own rules of interpretation. Ricoeur's longing for a transcendental logic surfaces here again when he calls for a generative poetics, at the level of the taxis of discourse (which would somewhat be a correlate of Chomsky's generative grammar). The triple autonomy of the text is re-affirmed here in the same way, and distanciation plays the same function as both obstacle and instrument.[54] The implication is that once the modes of discourse have been established, "a structural approach is not only possible, it is necessary."[55] Ricoeur insists that "this is not to submit the text to an alien law, but to restore it to itself."[56] Thus, his celebrated motto, "To explain more, is to understand better,"[57] is somehow intended to reinforce the old Protestant adage that Scripture interprets itself.

The insistence upon the fundamental importance of the non-speculative, pre-philosophical language as the prime material for naming God leads to the conclusion that the Bible has a polyphonic voice.[58] The Bible confronts us with different ways of naming God. Yet, such differences have a creative function. "Not only does each form of discourse give rise to a style of confession of faith, but also the confrontation of these forms

53. Ricoeur, *Figuring the Sacred*, 37.

54. Ibid., 38.

55. Ricoeur, "Biblical Hermeneutics," 68–69.

56. Ricoeur, *Figuring the Sacred*, 43.

57. See, for instance, Ricoeur, "Intellectual Autobiography," 31.

58. Ricoeur, *Figuring the Sacred*, 224.

of discourse gives rise to tensions and contrasts, within the confession of faith itself, that are theologically significant."[59] The relationship between general and special hermeneutics remains thus somewhat ambiguous. Whilst it is the Scripture which establishes its own rules, once the modes of discourse have been decided, general rules apply.

On the one hand, therefore, Ricoeur seems to hold a radical synchronic approach. The Bible has a polyphonic voice, and the various modes of discourse cannot be reduced to one another according to some more fundamental logic of being. Ultimately, naming God remains plural. On the other hand, however, Ricoeur insists equally upon the diachronic aspect of the text. The biblical text is primarily historical and narrative.[60] What is more, the insistence upon the internal dynamic of the text, which ultimately initiates the interpretation, allowing Ricoeur to claim that "the text interprets itself," appears to make such a diachronic claim radical.[61] It is easy to see that in their extreme versions, both approaches prevent an ontological happening. The synchronic approach ends up in a broken text (*texte eclatée*), while the diachronic approach in a constant deferral of meaning.

I suggest that this paradoxical situation is the implication of the very concept of distanciation as both obstacle and tool. Ricoeur's rejection of psychologism reflects his agreement with Kant that we cannot deduce the self from the world processes. Yet, the series of objectifications, of the "saying in the said" and of the subject in the work, suddenly opens history to critical inquiry. How? By producing traces which can be now "explained." This is how understanding starts. Thus, history becomes a "text" to be read. The tendency to subsume the historical mediation to the textual mediation, however, is resisted. Ricoeur is quick to stress that the *aporia* of time and the fundamental historicity of experience endow the text with a special dimension. Ultimately, the text is grounded in the event, reflecting as it does an irreducible experience or "form of life." Are we then to conclude that "the advent of truth," the very content of the promising "world of the text" mediated by this concept of distanciation remains enclosed in a Kantian problematic, trapped between an elusive causality of freedom and an indifferent "cosmic process"?

---

59. Ricoeur, *Figuring the Sacred*, 39.

60. Ibid., 225; Ricoeur, *Essays on Biblical Interpretation*, 79. We shall return to this aspect below.

61. See especially Ricoeur, *Essays on Biblical Interpretation*, 49ff.

We may remember that in explaining the antithetic of pure reason, that is to say, the application of the principles of the understanding be yond the boundaries of experience Kant writes:

> This dialectical doctrine will not relate to the unity of under-
> standing in empirical conceptions, but to the unity of reason in
> pure ideas. The conditions of this doctrine are—inasmuch as it
> must, as a synthesis according to rules, be conformable to the
> understanding, and at the same time as the absolute unity of
> the synthesis, to the reason- that, if it is adequate to the unity of
> reason, it is too great for the understanding, if according with
> the understanding, it is too small for the reason. Hence arises a
> mutual opposition, which cannot be avoided, do what we will.[62]

Is Ricoeur eventually forced to choose between saying either too much or too little in spite of the promising opening of the concept of the world of the text? Having summarized the structure of distanciation in Ricoeur's hermeneutics, we need further to explore the concrete content of the speculative dimension entailed by distanciation. To this end, we shall turn to Ricoeur's own "approximation" of Revelation. That will enable us both to look at history at the critical point of its intersection with a concrete ontological option, and to rehearse once again the problematic of the structure of disclosure but guided this time by the specific concerns of the Christian idea of Revelation.

## Revelation and Manifestation

Ricoeur's essay "Toward a Hermeneutic of the Idea of Revelation" is para-digmatic in more than one respect.[63] It is not only the fact that Revelation is approached frontally, but also the way in which the theme itself gathers most of his lifetime intellectual concerns. In this sense, the endeavor may be seen as a big systematic case occasioning the deployment of all the weaponry of Ricoeur's intellectual armory.

The hermeneutic quest proceeds, as always, by learning to discern the real question. Such question takes contour, thinks Ricoeur, in the mislead-ing conflict between two excessive claims: "an authoritarian and opaque concept of revelation and a concept of reason which claims to be its own

---

62. Kant, *Critique of Pure Reason*, 258.

63. Ricoeur, "Toward a Hermeneutic of the Idea of Revelation," in *Essays on Biblical Interpretation*. I will incorporate page references to this essay into the text above.

master and transparent to itself" (73). The problem of Revelation is indeed formidable because the task of the interpreter is not to establish the right relation between two foreseeable realities, but to uncover the realities themselves. Thus the undertaking has the ambition to recover both "a conception of revelation and a conception of reason" (73).

The problem with the traditional concept of revelation lies, suggests Ricoeur, in an amalgamation of three levels of language: the level of the confession of faith, the level of the ecclesial dogma and the level of the magisterium (the rule of orthodoxy) (73). Such amalgamation obscures Revelation's original dynamism present in both the confessing community and living preaching, making the concept not only opaque but also authoritarian. Ricoeur's problem, therefore, is the rising specter of an illegitimate authority reflected in the emancipation of dogma from its subordinate or derivative position. To address this problem, "we must carry the notion of revelation back to its most originary level" (74).

By analyzing in turn the main expressions of biblical literature, Ricoeur tries to indicate in each case how the particular way of addressing moulds our understanding of Revelation. In the end, a "pluralistic" and *"polysemic"* concept of Revelation emerges which is, Ricoeur thinks, "at most *analogical* in form" (75). In the second part, Ricoeur deploys what he calls the response of a hermeneutical philosophy. Such a response aims to uncover the false scandal between faith and reason by undertaking this time a critique of philosophy's reliance upon a concept of transparent reason and autonomous subjectivity. The concept of truth as manifestation emerges eventually as a more apt contender for resonating with a non-heteronomous view of Revelation. In what follows, we shall take a closer look at Ricoeur's moves.

Ricoeur takes his cue from the prophetic discourse which functions as "the basic axis of inquiry," by virtue of being the most challenging. Expressions like, "Thus says the Lord" bring the idea of Revelation, Ricoeur believes, closest to the idea of a double author. "Revelation is the speech of another behind the speech of the prophet" (75). But in spite of its central place, the prophetic discourse by itself produces too narrow a concept of Revelation, Ricoeur opines, linking it too tightly to the concept of Inspiration as "one voice behind another" (76). This qualification of Revelation is necessary especially in the light of its unfortunate consequences in the history of thought. Ricoeur has two particular concepts in mind here: God's plan and the end of history. God's speech has all too often been enclosed in conceptual form, thus taking precedence over the event of speaking and in this way condemning history to irrelevancy.

It is, first, the narrative discourse which tempers the voice of the prophet. What narrative brings on the scene is "a world" and "events." The meaning of the narrative is connected not with an immediate voice but with the significance of the events. The notion of "foundational event" is born here. Revelation is perceived as a break, as a discontinuity, bringing about a new reality. From the perspective of a theory of history, such a position fundamentally pleads for the non-transparent character of the event. The event, as Revelation, does not complete any previous development, nor is it apprehensible in terms of a previous conceptuality.[64] We recognize here the specific idiosyncrasy of novelty discussed in the last chapter. There is primacy of event over text. "God's mark is in history, before being in speech" (79). The structure of the narrative discourse therefore awakens us to the "narrowness of the theologies which attend only to word events"—a position which Ricoeur (referring perhaps to some of the excesses of the New Hermeneutics—Fuchs, Ebeling, Frei) labels as an "idealism of Word-Events."

Ricoeur's treatments of Law, wisdom and hymnic literature have a somewhat similar function. Each in its specific way challenges categories usually associated with the idea of Revelation. Thus, he points to the misleading rendering of the Torah as law, with the consequent association with a divine law and heteronomy. Instead Torah, as the expression of the Covenant, represents "a much more concrete and encompassing relation," being fundamentally a response to grace and consequently foreign to any idea of heteronomy. It was precisely this transformative dimension and Torah's orientation towards holiness that gave rise to the proclamation of a New Covenant, that transcends a mere set of precepts towards "a new relational quality." Accordingly, Revelation means not only founding events and the end of history, but also a dynamic orientation of our practical actions and of our institutions.

If Torah challenges the idea of submission understood as heteronomy, wisdom literature addresses the idea of autonomy. Wisdom is not a private possession. To be wise is to participate in wisdom. Correlatively, human wisdom by itself, materialized in right action can never reconcile "ethos" and "cosmos." This is perhaps best expressed in the unjust suffering of the righteous. The active quality of suffering forbids a facile

---

64 As for instance in a causal understanding of history. See Ricoeur, *Contribution of French Historiography to a Theory of History*, 1.

dialectic of "world" and human action as a solution of bringing ethos and cosmos together. Ricoeur implicitly points here to the Christological and soteriological ramifications of Revelation as wisdom. A re-enchantment of the world (prefigured in the reconciliation of ethos and cosmos) is more than a puzzle of knowledge calling for a more complex understanding of agency.

Ricoeur ends his detour with the hymnic literature. The prayers and songs addressed to God are not simply an expression of human feelings. They become revelatory in the very process of expressing them in an I—Thou situation. Revelation here is intimately connected with the idea of transformation, of conformity to a higher reality.

In the second hermeneutic detour, an attempt is made to challenge philosophy's refusal of revelation by pointing to the ground of this refusal, namely, its assumption of a transparent truth and the boastful autonomy of the thinking subject. This ground proves to be equally problematical mirroring somewhat the heteronomy of the magisterium. In fact this is the idea of rationality which finds itself in conflict with Revelation. Ricoeur proposes instead the concept of truth as manifestation.

The preparatory concepts of writing, work and the notion of the world of the text build towards the idea of the revelatory function of poetic texts. By Poetics, Ricoeur, of course, is not referring to a specific genre but rather to the "totality of these genres inasmuch as they exercise a referential function that differs from the descriptive referential function of ordinary language and above all of scientific discourse" (100). As noted above, this poetic function resides in the capacity of a text to open new possibilities of living over and against the world of actuality (by which Ricoeur means "the world of manipulable objects.") We recall the familiar theme of the radical character of disclosure in Ricoeur's insistence that this new possibility arises upon "the ruins of the descriptive discourse" (101). It is in this revelatory function that we see the promissory signs of the re-enchantment of the world:

> My deepest conviction is that poetic language alone restores to us that participation-in or belonging-to an order of things which precedes our capacity to oppose ourselves to things taken as objects opposed to a subject. (101)

According to Ricoeur, this capacity of a text (and particularly of fictitious texts) to "redescribe" reality can give us an idea of revelation as a non-violent appeal. The idea of revelation understood in this "nonreligious, nontheistic and nonbiblical sense of the word" is capable "of entering into resonance with one or the other of the aspects of biblical revelation" (100).

## On the Content of the Form: The Bible between the Experience of the World and the World of Experience

How are we to characterize this confrontation between Ricoeur's impressive tour de force of biblical theology and his hermeneutic philosophy? We shall first try to point to the potential problems the concept of Revelation so described raises.

It is noteworthy that Ricoeur does not only present various forms of discourse in their diversity, but he is careful to draw what he perhaps considers to be the legitimate conclusions of such a presentation (90–95). At a formal level this tends to establish itself as a regulative grid starting to shape an epistemological position insofar as the various modes of discourse concur in uncovering Revelation's *modus operandi*.

The immediate implication in terms of content, is that the diversity of genres appears to be threatened by formalization under the pressure of an overarching category of experience on the one hand, and by the original concern to uncover a non-heteronomous concept of revelation on the other. Each time, the "what" of Revelation is retained in its significance in relation to the "how" of Revelation. In other words, the content, the "what" tends to be retained as the meaning of the "how." Now this is arguably a necessary exercise, a legitimate way of relating "form" to "content." Moreover, there is little doubt that Ricoeur's criticism of an overly psychologized view of inspiration which tends to subsume the diversity of biblical texts under a single model is justified. Nonetheless, equally legitimate is the question of whether, and to what extent, Ricoeur's alternative proposal is better suited in preserving the integrity and irreducibility of the content. We have seen that, for Ricoeur, interpretation remains the invincible mediatory practice. His unrelenting struggle against immediacy has convinced him that neither the "inside" nor the "outside" can be simply taken for granted. Such a view tends to be skeptical of the "immediacy" of speech or direct address (whether this takes the form of an "other" or of an "inner voice"). Even in the case of the dialogical situation, *it is the dialogue itself,* which becomes revelatory. As we have seen, Revelation as non-heteronomous must bring the ontic and the noetic dimensions together. Thus, in spite of prophecy functioning as the axis of inquiry, Ricoeur tends to include the above forms of revelation under the more general category of manifestation.

I agree, therefore, with Wolterstorff's criticism that in Ricoeur's hands the notion of divine discourse tends to be absorbed by manifestation. He rightly calls our attention to the centrality of God's speech in an adequate concept of Revelation.[65] Indeed, had God not spoken, we would have been left "with our own thoughts and self-deceptions."[66] Revelation as manifestation may well entail a more appealing concept of non-heteronomy. Nevertheless, we cannot allow it to function as a transcendental for all types of revelation. Again, Wolterstorff is right in pointing to the irreducible normative dimension of divine discourse.[67]

But it would be equally wrong to remain at a merely normative stance. I can see Wolterstorff's point in his argument that speaking is not revealing.[68] Yet, to apply that to God unproblematically is hardly acceptable.[69] Are not all God's acts redemptive and loving acts? Even in the case of direct commands like, "Get thee out of thy country, and from thy kindred" (Gen 12:1), we may suspect that speaking was in some mysterious way also revealing. Does not the famous "hall of faith" from Hebrews 11 tell us that those people were able to "see" the aim of a good life to which the command pointed, beyond and above a terrestrial country, and above and beyond their experience of welfare? It is because our faith is never empty, never attached to a naked will or an irrational inner or outward impulse that we can "see" things that cannot be seen. A normative view of discourse is not really

65. More than twenty years ago, in attacking the concept of revelation as history, James Barr wrote: "Far from representing the divine acts as the basis of all knowledge of God and all communication with him the O.T. texts represent God as communicating freely with men, and particularly with Moses, before, during and after these events. Far from the incident at the burning bush being an interpretation of the divine acts, it is a direct communication from God to Moses of his purposes and intentions. This conversation instead of being an interpretation of the divine act is a precondition of it" (James Barr "Revelation through History and in Modern Theology." *Interpretation* 17 [1963] 197, quoted by Wolterstorff, *Divine Discourse*, 30).

66. Torrance, *Theological Science*, 31.

67. Wolterstorff, *Divine Discourse*, 75–93.

68. Ibid., 19–36.

69. Jüngel is right when he notes that "the New Testament usage . . . (John 1:1; Heb 1:2) makes clear that God, according to this tradition's understanding, not only speaks in order to communicate something; rather, he speaks in order to communicate himself and thus to make possible fellowship with himself and to provide a way to participate in his own being" (*God as the Mystery of the World*, 12–13).

able to answer these questions. Wolterstorff claims that it is in the light of this normative view of discourse that "we take the material world into our service"[70] But it is enough to note the means of of truth in Habermass theory of communicative action, to realize that such a triumphant claim is simply not immediately true. The experience of discourse is not only a "given" but also a scandal. Our discourse is "distorted" and our claims do not situate us in an unproblematic ethical order. And we should do well neither to minimize this scandal nor regulate it prematurely. The success of the Word in our world (Isa 55:10) is precisely in spite of its fallen condition and it is emphatically not based upon a given, universally accessible normative stance (Rom 5:8). Yet, as it turns out, Wolterstorff would probably agree with many of the above points.[71] Moreover, at closer scrutiny, the differences between his own proposal and that of Ricoeur, considered really in their ultimate implications, are probably less dramatic than he appears to portray them.[72] Ricoeur's insistence upon this non-heteronomous view of Revelation, in connection with his stress upon imagination, in spite of its problems, uncovers I believe a profound theological insight which is really missed by Wolterstorff. As I shall argue in more detail later, theological

---

70. Wolterstorff, *Divine Discourse*, 93.

71. See especially his discussion of doxastic practices (Wolterstorff, *Divine Discourse*, 169–272) where he talks about justification and belief as active obedience indicating that the connection between disposition and will is moulded by a certain concern for truth and meaning.

72. One of the ironies of Wolterstorff's otherwise very competent treatment of divine discourse is his plea for the recovery of intentionality against the background of his own sovereign disinterest in the "intentions" of his interlocutors. In his criticism of Ricoeur, Wolterstorff never mentions for instance that Ricoeur allows in fact for the retrieval of the intention of the author. He also fails to indicate that Ricoeur is not primarily interested in criteria of competence but in the historicality of understanding, more specifically the finite and contextual character of discourse and the concrete historical career the discourse takes. In fact, Wolterstorff himself deals with this dimension of discourse as an event in the world in his discussion of doxastic practices. He acknowledges for instance a difference between what a speaker wants to say and what he actually says (*Divine Discourse*, 201). He also distinguishes between human and divine intention and implicitly appeals to a tradition and a community of interpretation (ibid., 218–21). And I would obviously agree with his final comment that in order to interpret God's discourse more reliably we must know him better (ibid., 239). However, our whole effort is to attempt to give a theological dimension to this "worldly event" as a fundamental enabling which does not (whether implicitly or explicitly) relapse into the well known habit of introducing the God language *ad extra* in a world which may be accounted for without recourse to God.

epistemology cannot afford to be either too "internalist" (as in Ricouer's depiction) or too "externalist" (as Wolterstorff's position seems to suggest).

In the concluding part of the essay Ricoeur complains that "we too often and too quickly think in terms of a will that submits and not enough of an imagination that opens itself" (117). I believe that Ricoeur is right to question an entire voluntarist tradition (whose main traits are well expressed in what Ricoeur often calls "the ethical view of the world") which finds its chief expression in Kant's moral philosophy. However, I think he is wrong to oppose obedience to imagination especially in the light of his plea for a reconciliation between revelation and reason.[73] Assessed in the more general context of Ricoeur's concerns however, the claim has clearly a polemical tone. Nonetheless, I would venture to say that if we are not to claim either too much or too little, something more must be said about God's relationship with the world as it appears concretely expressed not only in its general historical dimension, but also in a special community without which, in a fallen world like ours, the two are indeed doomed to remain in conflict.

In sum, whilst a non-heteronomous view of Revelation that would bring will and imagination together is not only desirable, but most importantly, perhaps truer to the nature of Revelation itself,[74] it is doubtful that the subsumption of Revelation under a general hermeneutics of experience can adequately affirm this. In fairness to Ricoeur it must be said that he is careful to add that the corrective value of revelation as manifestation cannot be directly connected with the religious meaning of Revelation. The specific Christian content cannot be deduced from the general features of the poetic language (104). Nonetheless, as in the case of metaphor, Ricoeur affirms that in spite of this radical disjunction, a homology between the two can, in actual fact, be established. What remains to be done, therefore, is to confront more consistently the implicit ground of this homology, together with the alleged corrective value of manifestation to a number of theological themes that arise (whether

73. "For what are the poem of the Exodus and the poem of the resurrection . . . addressed to if not to our imagination rather than our obedience?" Ricoeur, *Essays on Biblical Interpretation*, 117.

74. The very notion of the bound will with its associated metaphor of captivity implying as it does elements of seduction and appeal to reason as the old story of the Fall testifies, promotes an image of the will in inextricable relation to both reason and imagination. The power of the Gospel consists precisely in its capacity to come to us as Good News. More often than not, God encounters us with a "still small voice," as he once encountered Elijah (1 Kgs 19:12).

implicitly or explicitly) in Ricoeur's treatment of history. In doing so, we hope to be able both to gradually uncover the nature of the speculative dimension in Ricoeur's hermeneutics and to point to a number of openings that may be further explored theologically.

## Creation Overtures: The "Weight" of History

Ricoeur manifested a sustained interest in history discernible from his earliest writings. Ward rightly identifies a slight shift and gain in profundity in his thought from his early *Histoire et Vérité* to his opus magnum *Temps et Récit*.[75] Let us look at Ricoeur's interest in history in the light of this development.

Ricoeur's dealings with history in his early writings bear an undeniable Kantian and existential flavor. The interpreter of history finds himself caught up between cosmic history and existential history, between the unity of history and its fragmentary character.[76] Our concrete experience of history remains ambiguous in Ricoeur's view. This existential plane of ambiguity is placed between the rational (and abstract) plane of progress and the "supra-rational" plane of hope.[77] As such readings of history remain ultimately incommensurable, we must face the "risk" of being human, since we can never know for sure whether our cultural acts edify rather than destroy.[78] Ricoeur talks freely about both a lord of history in a schema where a theology of love coincides with a theology of history, and the irreducible constructive dimension of history, a history that remains ambiguous, whose ultimate meaning remains hidden. For the Christian there is, indeed, only one history a history that will be "recapitulated in Christ." But this ultimate sense is not the object of reason but of faith.[79] It

---

75. Graham Ward notes that Ricoeur's early views of history were deeply influenced by the Annales School, particularly by Raymond Aron, Lucien Febre, and Marc Bloch (cf. Ward, *Theology and Contemporary Critical Theory*, 51ff.) While reacting against the positivism of earlier French historiography, the Annales School, however, effected what Ricoeur later called "the eclipse of the event in French historiography" (*Time and Narrative*, 1:95–120). Ricoeur's defense of narrative (*Time and Narrative*, 1:121–74) comes as a response to his dissatisfaction with the anti-event and anti-narrative stance of this approach.

76. See especially Ricoeur, *Histoire et Vérité*, 81–98.

77. Ibid., 96–97.

78. Ibid., 130–31.

79. Ibid., 95–96.

is noteworthy that Ricoeur conceives his discussion at three levels: transcendental, existential and theological. The theological dimension, therefore, is not called to address either the rationalist and totalizing claim, or the broken existentialist plight. Rather, it remains somewhat distinct and exterior, albeit parallel to both discourses. Ricoeur's later interest in narrative would focus precisely upon the specific structure of this middle ground which would bring the transcendental and the existential perspectives together. Can we not, in such a light, contemplate this latter task as feeding upon the profound theological insight that, after all, there is just one history, that themes like eschatology, freedom and the end of history are irreducible features of a meaningful history? Can we not further say that genuine responsibility before reason would require us further to substantiate the nature of this elusive territory of interranimation between various perspectives?[80] But as we know, Ricoeur does not want to mix theology with philosophy. An account that would preserve its neutrality in regard to religion would satisfy Ricoeur's belief in the relative autonomy of the philosophical discourse.

Seen in this light, Ricoeur's sympathy for Heidegger is not surprising. Heidegger's "world" not only insinuates itself as a mediating term between abstract or instrumental reason and existential plight, between cosmic time and existential time, but promises an ontological horizon that claims to remain neutral in regard to the question of God. There is no need to insist too much on the fact that Ricoeur's language, in what he calls the response of a hermenutical philosophy, is significantly tributary to Heidegger.[81] It is true that Ricoeur insists that the reply of the hermeneutic philosophy takes its cue from the Scriptural texts, rather than from either a general experience of being-in-the-world or a phenomenology of care or preoccupation. Nonetheless, the acceptance of this contingency only confirms the presuppositions of a general hermeneutics of experience. Such a hermeneutics is finite and perspectival.

80. As we shall see in more detail below, the concept of testimony may be seen in such a light as contributing precisely to the rationality of this middle ground. In this way, Ricoeur's growing interest in the event does not ultimately change the terms of the discussion preserving as it does the tensive relation between philosophy and theology.

81. I am especially referring to Ricoeur's use of the Heideggerian view of truth as disclosure, the concept of the "worldhood" of the world (*Weltlichkeit*), one's ownmost potentiality-for-Being, as well as his critique of the modern technological project. See Heidegger, *Being and Time*, 63ff., 181ff. Of course Ricoeur criticizes Heidegger's concrete deployment of this conceptuality as we shall see below. Nonetheless, these are undoubtedly Heideggerian concerns.

More often than not, we are called not to choose our starting point but rather to acknowledge it.

There are a number of aspects worth considering here in the light of our previous considerations. To begin with, Ricoeur notes that the biblical text belongs to the same historical reality, functioning exactly in the same way as any other text. That is to say, there is a certain non-coincidence between what happened back there and our appropriation of the text today. The past cannot be simply accounted for in terms of the category of the "same." History is not a grand hall in which we can "talk" to one another. But the past is not radically different either. The "weight" of the past in the present may be seen in an analogical way as a dialectic of "same" and "other." Between the "eternal present" of the "same" and the abstract character of history as "other," we must find a way to talk about history which would bring past, present and future together within the same ontological horizon.[82] This retrospective view is however, never "conclusive," remaining narrative and immanent. Our interpretation is finite and "all thought about thought has presuppositions that it can never master."[83]

Now it is important to remark that the objectification of the text, the "death" of the author and her inscription in the work are articulated along such lines. A text always actualizes new and unfulfilled possibilities of a past history in a schema which defies a mere logic of correspondence in an inscription-appropriation duality where an appeal is always made to a transcendental criterion beyond and above the historical flux. With Heidegger Ricoeur rejects the traditional substance ontology, insisting that the ontological horizon is to be deciphered in its temporal structure which avoids subsuming the process of becoming within either a purely logical or a teleological framework.

I take, therefore, Ricoeur's insistence upon this view of manifestation as being a-religious as basically signifying his allegiance to Heidegger's "world" as a humanized, meaningful world, in which the attempt to account for "being" is made "in time," without recourse to any "external" criteria or meta-physical reality.[84] It has been argued however

---

82. For details, see Ricoeur, *Reality of the Historical Past*, esp. 36; Ricoeur, *Time and Narrative*, 3:142–56.

83. Ricoeur, *Time and Narrative*, 3:206.

84. See also Gadamer's comment: "For Heidegger, the existential analytic of *Dasein* implies no particular historical ideal of existence. Hence with regard to any theological statement about man and his existence in faith, it claims an *a priori*, neutral validity" (Gadamer, *Truth and Method*, 262). Gadamer himself defends this neutrality even

that Heidegger's world fails to rely consistently upon a merely immanent temporality. The a-historical tendency manifest in his insistence upon an "original" disclosure of Being in Greek thought, rendered by Gadamer as a "teleology in reverse,"[85] betrays non-hermeneutical elements at work in his ontology of disclosure.[86]

In such a light we may further ask whether Rioceur's criticism of Heidegger may not be better understood precisely against the background of a more fundamental anchoring of such a world.[87] Relevant for our argument here is Ricoeur's succinct and systematic evaluation of Heidegger that can be found in "Emmanuel Levinas Thinker of Testimony," where he places Nabert between Levinas and Heidegger. We have here a subtle critique of Heidegger's ordinary meaning (compared with Nietzsche's genealogy of morals) and of his manifest incredulity towards the world of the "they."[88] Are we not to understand Ricoeur's concern for alterity, for the fate of the "ontic" in the light of his expressed belief not in Revelation in general but in God's Revelation as historical? Is not Ricoeur's dissatisfaction with Heidegger's "indeterminate" call in his concept of *Gewissen* an indication that, if not qualified, the proposed "world" of Heidegger remains most suspicious?[89] If Heidegger's break with the

though he acknowledges that such a claim is problematical for the understanding of faith (ibid., 331ff.).

85. Ibid., 256.

86. E.g., DiCenso, *Hermeneutics and the Disclosure of Truth*, 77. See also Marion, *God without Being*, xxii (and 38ff., for an exposition of Heidegger's gnostic tendencies).

87. I am not referring here to Ricoeur's critique of Heidegger's "short route" to being. I am rather inferring that Heidegger's failure to return to epistemological questions (discussed above) may be connected to his failure to return to ethical questions. Ricoeur alludes to this second failure in "Heidegger between Nabert and Levinas" (cf. Ricoeur, *Figuring the Sacred*, 112), without connecting it however with the former criticism. This double criticism may be well interpreted as an expression of a fundamental incredulity about the ontological option itself.

88. According to Ricoeur this ultimately leads to a "height without transcendence" and an "exteriority without otherness." Cf. Ricoeur, *Figuring the Sacred*, 110.

89. Ricoeur's attitude towards Heidegger has been notoriously ambiguous. For a succinct evaluation, see Kemp, "Ricoeur between Heidegger and Levinas," 44–46. Kemp notes that the late Ricoeur "has shown a certain regret for having abandoned Jaspers, for whom 'in a broad sense the whole of philosophy is ethics,' in favor of Heidegger, whose analytic of *Dasein* 'did not permit him to have moral and political criteria' to judge his own time" (quotation from *Le Monde*, 27 June 1987, in Kemp, "Ricoeur between Heidegger and Levinas," 46). Even in his early assessment of Heidegger, Ricoeur is cautious in regard to the ontological promise of Heidegger's option. "On this path the theologian must not be in a hurry to know whether being

Greek philosophy which identifies world with nature[90] must be undeniably welcomed, we have every right to question a "re enchantment" of the world with it seems to owe more to Taoism than to a Christian view of Creation.[91]

*We have reasons to believe therefore that rather than being a-religious Ricoeur's concept of Revelation calls for an explicitation of what eventually remains an irreducible presupposition of any discourse of revelation namely, Creation. When this presupposition is not spelt out within the confines of the referential intention of Revelation itself, it does not necessarily become less religious, but rather attached (whether implicitly or explicitly) to a different (and more or less ideal) referent.[92]*

Perhaps we should not be afraid to speak again about general revelation and about a theology of nature in spite of the unfortunate career of naturalism. Recently Gunton has advanced the challenging proposal of a recovery of a doctrine of Creation at the very heart of the doctrine of Revelation.[93] The proposal merits our attention as it points to a theological resolution of a situation which exhibits a number of similarities

---

for Heidegger is the God of the Bible. . . . To think the expression 'word of God' is to agree to be engaged on paths which may become lost" (Ricoeur, *Essays on Biblical Interpretation*, 72).

90. Cf. Remi Brague, *Aristotele et la Question du Monde* (Paris: PUF, 1988, ch. 1), quoted by Kemp, "Ricoeur between Heidegger and Levinas," 44.

91. It has been Tomonobu Imamichi who suggested that Heidegger's "world" has close similarities with Okakura's *Book of Tea*, which speaks of Taoism as "the art of being in the world" (Imamichi, *Betrachtungen uber das Eine*, 89, 154. Cf. Kemp, "Ricoeur between Heidegger and Levinas," 44). For a detailed criticism of Heidegger's mythologizing tendency, see Caputo, *Demythologizing Heidegger*. Caputo sees Heidegger's later works essentially as a secularization of the biblical conception of the history of salvation. For a critique of Heidegger from the perspective of biblical theology, see Ingraffia, *Postmodern Theory and Biblical Theology*, 101–64.

92. In his more theological/exegetical essays, Ricoeur *does* talk about Revelation and Creation within a schema of Redemption, but, arguably, his philosophical conceptuality continues to inform his exegesis. See for instance the collection of essays written with Andre LaCocque. Ricoeur accuses theologians of philosophical speculation (LaCocque and Ricoeur, *Thinking Biblically*, xv) but his focusing more on the breaks between Creation, Revelation, and Redemption than upon their unity within the context of God's Trinitarian action—which leads him to talk about the "always-already-there" of Creation and the "perpetual futurity" of Redemption—betrays once again his indebtedness to Kant, i.e., a "naturalized" reading of both texts and history. (See Ricoeur, "Thinking Creation," in *Thinking Biblically*, 67).

93. Gunton, *Brief Theology of Revelation*. I will incorporate page references to this book into the text above. I see this direction of investigation as the only viable response to the problematic concept of Revelation as history.

with Ricoeur's concerns. Indeed, it is suggested, a genuine theology of revelation does not need to choose "between autonomy and authority" (22). In fact, in a number of senses Revelation is "integral to our being in the world" (22). By drawing a distinction between natural theology and a theology of nature, Gunton attempts to correct an imbalance he sees in Barth, who failed to do justice to the ontological status of the world in his theology of Creation (41–42). The problem of modern naturalism (and by implication of the modern theology's distrust in a theology of nature) is located "in the history of the doctrine of creation and its fate in the medieval world" (42).

In sum, because the theology of creation was so strongly dependent upon a certain view of reason (defined within the confines of a particular philosophy) the defeat of that particular philosophical vision effectively meant the defeat of the doctrine of Creation as well (42). More precisely, Gunton suggests that both Plato and Aristotle made their presence felt in the medieval synthesis. He emphasizes especially the transference of the Platonic forms to the mind of God (prominent in the theologies of Philo, Augustine and to a certain extent in Maximus), which effectively erased the Trinitarian mediation of Creation and particularly the Christological one which is so prominent in the New Testament (Hebrews 1; John 1; Colossians 1). This situation led to an excessive stress upon the human mind and to a divorce between Creation and Redemption. Barth's emphatic rejection of natural theology must be seen in this context. But, Gunton contends, Barth was not entirely successful in connecting the two. The subordination of both Creation and Redemption to covenant and election has led to the subordination of Creation to a soteriological (and perhaps more worrying) to a protological, rather than eschatological principle (46).[94]

Thus, while a theology of nature is the gift of biblical revelation (59), Gunton is eager to add that general revelation and natural theology are two quite distinct categories, and should not therefore be confused. God may be revealed in the things that have been made, but it does not follow that the discernment of this truth is achievable by unaided reason" (55). Gunton pointedly concludes that "not the patterns of Platonic formality or Aristotelian causality but Trinitarian relationality offer possibilities for drawing analogies between the being of God and that of the world" (62).

---

94 This indirectly confirms our plea for a balance between "internalism" and "externalism." I shall return to this point later on.

It is perhaps worth recalling in this context the heated debate gathered around Ricoeur's confessed faithfulness to Anselm and Barth, if only because Gunton's critique of Barth may perhaps offer a valuable indication that a mere evaluation in terms of one's allegiance to Barth's understanding of God's preeminence is not in itself sufficient.

Much ink has been spilled in this controversy. I shall briefly rehearse here the main terms of the discussion by referring primarily to Frei's version of Barthianism, alluding however to some other modern exponents of narrative or non-foundational theologies.[95] Frei believes that genuinely to affirm the primacy of Revelation and the concept of God's prevenient grace is to affirm the irreducible identity and particularity of Jesus of Nazareth as depicted by the Gospels. Frei's suspicion is that in an account in which the concern for meaning prevails, justice cannot be done to this irreducible particularity. No attempt can be made to base the particular history of Jesus upon either a general human experience, a universal history or religious experience for that matter.[96] We must maintain, with Barth, that history is a predicate of God rather than God being a predicate of history.[97] In the same vein, Thiemann, a proponent of non-foundationalist theology and an admirer of Frei, holds that in fact no argument for the divine prevenience can be produced. As soon as one does that, it inevitably "founds" the very preeminence he/she wants to defend upon a prior principle.[98] Thus, in spite of Ricoeur's formal allegiance to Barth, he may be suspected of doing precisely that.[99]

95. There are three names to which Frei acknowledges his debt in the preface to his famous book *Eclipse of Biblical Narrative*: Eric Auerbach, Karl Barth, and Gilbert Ryle. In relation to Barth, Frei writes: "He distinguishes historical from realistic reading of the theologically most significant biblical narratives, without falling into the trap of instantly making history the test of the *meaning* of the realistic form of the stories" (italics his). Frei, *Eclipse of Biblical Narrative*, viii.

96. For a criticism of the hermeneutics stemming from Schleiermacher, see especially Frei, *Eclipse of Biblical Narrative*, 307ff.

97. Frei, *Types of Christian Theology*, 19–27. For Frei's version of Barthianism, see esp. 38–46.

98. Thiemann, *Revelation and Theology*, 9ff.

99. Frei maintains that Ricoeur's hermeneutics either reverts to a type of theology which subsumes the specificity of Christ under a general meaning or ends in hermeneutical incoherence. Cf. Frei, *Type of Christian Theology*, 6–7, 30–34. With similar implications, Lindbeck renders Ricoeur's hermeneutics as experiential-expressive. Lindbeck, *Nature of Doctrine*, 136. For a more recent attempt to somewhat reconcile Frei and Ricoeur on their view of narrative, see Loughlin, *Telling God's Story*, 139–61. Loughlin fails to indicate, however, the full ramifications of Ricoeur's dialectic between

My purpose here is not to offer a direct criticism of either Frei's or Thiemann's version of non-foundationalism, nor to defend Ricouer's alleged Barthianism. Rather my intention is to relate the claim of God's prevenience (which I consider legitimate and important) to its referential intention and to point to a number of problems inherent in the very terms of the controversy.

At first sight, there are indeed a number of themes which may commend Ricoeur as being closer to Barth. At a formal level we have seen that Ricoeur appeared to be prepared to talk about general hermeneutics in the light of biblical hermeneutics. It may also be pointed out that Ricoeur's implied Christology in *The Symbolism of Evil* emphatically affirms Christ as the epistemological key for both freedom and duty. Captivity is understood in the light of deliverance and sin in the light of redemption.[100] The Old Testament figures are understood only retrospectively in the light of Christ's actual life, death and resurrection. The "how much more" of grace of Romans 5 implies not simply the restoration of an old order but the gift of New Creation.[101] Walter Lowe was in principle right to connect the tendency of thought to be enclosed within itself, (tendency that constituted the target of Ricoeur's unrelenting critique) to Luther's *homo incurvatus in se*.[102] Is not Ricoeur's very project of de-centering the preliminary task of any talk about preeminence? At the end of *The Symbolism of Evil*, Ricoeur affirms that the first task of the philosopher is not to begin, but to remember. And this hermeneutical remembering "follows essentially an Anselmian schema."[103] It is also noteworthy that Ricoeur opposes both the project of a rational theology, and that of an existentialist theology.[104] Immediacy must be fought in all its expressions, whether it takes the form of an immediacy of reason or an immediacy of experience. Apologetics is rejected as well, precisely because we cannot "justify" our experience of God by appeal to some other foundation. Ricoeur affirms that "the philosopher does not have to

---

history and fiction. As we shall see below, there is more to it than affirming that "the Bible has a double intention of recognition and of possibility" (Loughlin, *Telling God's Story*, 152).

100. Ricoeur, *Symbolism of Evil*, 270–75.

101. Ibid., 269–72.

102. Ricoeur, *Fallible Man*, xv.

103. Ricoeur, *Symbolism of Evil*, 357.

104. Ricoeur, *Essays on Biblical Interpretation*, 96–97.

justify the word of God," but rather "to set up the horizon of significance where it may be heard."[105]

But the source of concern lies perhaps in the fact that it is felt that a mere dialectic of universal and particular can never be successful in safeguarding God's preeminence. Genuine theological discourse can never be based upon a prior philosophical conceptuality of whatever kind. Instead, it must be faithful to its own object. Now of course all depends on how this faithfulness is conceived in the light of God's self revelation. Two things may be said in this context.

First of all, such concerns do not necessarily go back to a unique theological position that can unproblematically be ascribed to Barth. Indeed, as we have seen, Ricoeur's "anti-naturalism," the stress upon finitude and the fragility of humanity, the perspectival character of knowledge and the rejection of foundationalism, may be traced back, via Heidegger, to Kant (at least to a certain interpretation of Kant). An adequate theological evaluation should not therefore be content to remain at a negative, and in this sense still abstract defense of God's preeminence as a form of anti-naturalism, but must further inquire into the material and concrete form this affirmation takes. But neither can we claim that only because Ricoeur insists that his listening to faith is clothed in a certain philosophical language, is the particularity of the Christ event necessarily subsumed to a general philosophical theory. In fact, perhaps few philosophers would believe today that philosophy has the monopoly of universality. As we have tried to show, Ricoeur's attempt to "extend" Kant by his famous mediation in the third term may be seen as an effort to anchor the universalizing tendency of the concept in the particular. If not only Revelation in the narrow sense but the concept of revelation in general calls for an "after the fact" discourse, then no theory of categories can be simply and unproblematically assumed, *a priori*.[106] Rather the question of

---

105. Ibid., 97.

106. In such a light, to claim that Frei moves from particular to general while Ricoeur moves in the opposite direction, as Vanhoozer suggests, is mistaken (Vanhoozer, *Biblical Narrative in the Philosophy of Paul Ricoeur*, 156) simply because the very notion of a general theory of meaning is highly problematic. It is significant, perhaps, to quote Ricoeur's motto to one of his essays on history: *Quo magis res singulares intelligimus, eo magis Deum intelligimus* (Ricoeur, *Histoire et Vérité*, 45.) This quotation from Spinoza reveals not only Ricoeur's belief in the configurative force of particularity but his unrelenting struggle against solipsism in all its forms. Far from suggesting that Ricoeur's implicit Christology is without problems, we simply want to point out that such formal distinctions and generalizations must be referred to their

how successful Ricoeur has been in preserving the preeminence of God must be debated in the context of his concrete engagement with material aspects. And this brings us to the second point.

We should be prepared to question the assumption that a formal allegiance to Barth immediately and adequately asserts God's preeminence. Perhaps the discussion itself conducted in terms of "Barth or non-Barth," must be referred once again to its referential aim and to its concrete theological performance. McCormack's recent exploration of the Kantian philosophical roots of Barth's own theological thought has at least confirmed that a mere discussion in terms of Barth's anti-naturalism does not yet touch upon Barth's genuine theological contribution.[107]

In this sense it must be said that Ricoeur rightly attempts to correct an excessive intratextuality professed by many exponents of the New Hermeneutics by calling attention to the referential aspects of the biblical discourse, to its "aboutness." In many ways this meant, indeed, a reopening of the problematic of history. Revelation happened in history and our texts have a historical dimension. The problem with Ricoeur is the restrictive space he accords to this "aboutness," molded as it is by his view of manifestation. To call attention to this dimension therefore does not necessarily mean to depotentiate God's being in his revelation, or to transform God's act into a static datum. Barth was undoubtedly right to maintain a *diastasis* between God and the world against the idealist or existential tendency of co-positing God and human agency together. *It*

---

concrete theological performance. A thorough analysis must make more consistent recourse, I believe, to the more general concerns of the nineteenth-century theology in general and Schleiermacher in particular. As we shall see below, the problem with Ricoeur's attempt to mediate manifestation and proclamation is not so much his preference for manifestation as his post-Hegelian Kantianism which prevents an adequate description of both.

107. McCormack contends that "to the extent that Barth concerned himself with philosophical epistemology at all, he was an idealist (and more specifically a Kantian)." McCormack, *Karl Barth's Critically Dialectical Theology*, 465. McCormack does not seem to have many problems with Barth's allegiance to Kant (reflected especially in the dialectic of veiling and unveiling). We may however legitimately ask whether, and to what extent, the Kantian grammar is not at the root of his problematic theology of Creation or perhaps even at the root of his Christomonism. His view of the subject as reiteration arguably shows his continual dependence upon a philosophy of consciousness, confirming thus that Barth's attempt "to overcome Kant through Kant," in McCormack's words, is after all problematic. We shall return to this problem below.

rather means to attempt to understand the *"scandal of the cross" in its full historical implications.*[108]

A truly *a posteriori* theology and genuine concern with "material" aspects" starts with the recognition of Jesus' uniqueness in his concrete relation to the Creator Father and the transforming Spirit. It is the movement in *this* totality that unpacks the full dimension of the theological task. This awakens us to the fact that the distinction between a genuine "theological" treatment and the lapsing into a "principle" is by no means evident, reflecting more often than not a task rather than an achievement. In many ways, post-Barthian theology rightly understood this task to consist in referring such epistemological discussions to the rich Trinitarian grammar which underwrites God's relationship with the world. As we already anticipated, this exercise uncovered a number of imbalances in Barth's own writings. His oft quoted christomonism for instance, harshly sanctioned by Jenson's well known claim that Barth's dogmatic writings may be seen as an "inversed" metaphysical system, cannot be easily dismissed.[109] The drive of systematization situates the theologian in constant danger of reducing God's relationship to the world or God's self-giving in Christ to an all-encompassing concept or an abstract principle. The right insistence upon the particularity of Christ can lapse into a tautological exercise and lose precisely the treasured concrete particularity. As Hegel showed in the famous introduction of his *Phenomenology of Spirit*, particularity can become very abstract indeed . . .

In sum, I do not mean to suggest that Ricoeur's allegiance to Barth is wholly justified or that his implicit Christology is unproblematical. *Rather my suggestion is that we can never escape the universal—particular dialectic unless we adopt a more modest stance in this debate.* To say that is to affirm that a final verdict to such a dilemma can never be given in terms of logical *aporias* of the kind Kierkegaard invites in his discussion about the possibility of something new.[110] There is no doubt that Barth was supremely aware of this in spite of the shortcomings of his own per-

108. The tendency to oppose "noetic" rationality to "ontic" rationality as the ultimate framework of discussion can be arguably traced back to some of the assumptions of the philosophy of consciousness. It must be said in this context that noetic rationality is part of a wider order, which is created, historical and ecclesial.

109. Jenson, "Karl Barth," 21–35.

110. Cf. Kierkegaard, *Philosophical Fragments*, 11ff. I do not deny the value of the critical exercise which forever forces us to distinguish between divine and human agency. I simply suggest that to remain at this formal level is to expose oneself to subtler forms of self-deception.

formance. This is the main reason why he did not linger for too long on abstract discussions about hermeneutics. As Busch remarks, Barth cast derision on what he considered to be "the short-lived talk about hermeneutics."[111] Saying that however, we should be aware that we must never be too emphatic in this latter rejection lest the rejection itself take up a foundational role.[112] Barth, indeed, rejects both general and special hermeneutics.[113] Ricoeur on the other hand, like Bultmann, somehow wanted to accept both. While, as has been remarked, it is perhaps more difficult to express coherently Bultmann's construal,[114] as we have attempted to show thus far, Ricoeur's dialectic between universal and particular in connection with his insistence on the separation of philosophy from theology, uncovered an emerging structure of emancipation which renders history problematical from a theological perspective. It is now time to relate this structure of emancipation to what appears to be the ultimate test-case, the concept of testimony.

## Testimony: A Poetic Summons?

In more than one respect, the concept of testimony remains one of the most promising concepts from Ricoeur's work. In the light of Ricoeur's famous mediation in the third term, it may even be considered as the touchstone of Ricoeur's hermeneutic philosophy. Testimony not only challenges the autonomy of the subject but orients philosophy towards a different source. Indeed, Ricoeur admits that "testimony is a problem for a philosophy for which the question of the absolute is a proper question."[115] We may further say that Ricoeur's whole insistence upon "the economy of the gift," "the hyper-ethical," upon "a power which precedes us," reflects his belief that the rejection of the principle of identity from the traditional metaphysical constructions based as it was upon the foundational position of the reflecting subject, is not in itself sufficient. Moreover, he

111. Busch, *Karl Barth*, 466.

112. This ultimately amounts to a defense of criticism or meta-discourse. There is no such a thing as concern with "pure" content.

113. "But this must not confuse us into thinking that the very opposite way is the right one. There is no such thing as a special biblical hermeneutics." Barth, *Church Dogmatics* I/2, 466.

114. See for instance Ogden, *Christ without Myth*, 130–47. See also Ricoeur's criticism of Bultmann in "Preface to Bultmann," in *Essays on Biblical Interpretation*, 49–72.

115. Ricoeur, *Essays on Biblical Interpretation*, 119.

appears to make this "economy of the gift" which he sees encapsulated in Paul's phrase "how much more" from Romans 5 the principal mark of his theological contribution. (He even compares it with Schleiermacher's "feeling of absolute dependence," Tillich's ultimate concern and Barth and Bultmann's "trust in spite of ").[116] But the concept of testimony promises to address a more specific question. Can one not only relate, but also differentiate, between Revelation and history if all historical knowledge presupposes an invincible noetic mediation?[117]

In the last section of his Revelation essay, Ricoeur reminds us that the world of the text has been conceived as "deliberately a-historical or trans-historical."[118] In a first approximation, therefore, the concept of testimony performs essentially a critical function, further dismantling the potentially constructive dimension of this latter world. It is testimony which introduces contingency.[119] Ricoeur thus acknowledges that the "transcendentality" of the "world of the text" raises serious problems. At a more superficial level we may certainly affirm that Ricoeur's critique of the world of the text attempts to honor the work of the historians and critical thinkers. Do we not have abundant historical reasons to welcome a critique which so often uncovered abusive and manipulative uses of the Bible? But it is important to remark that there is a more fundamental reason involved here, pertaining to Ricoeur's very effort to de-center the subject. We have seen that Ricoeur's anti-idealist convictions make him suspicious towards all kinds of transcendentalism, but more importantly, all transcendentalism for Ricoeur necessarily involves a transcendentalism of consciousness. It is always a subject that makes a claim. In other words, the "transcendentality" of the text cannot be easily separated from either the subjective experience of their human authors or the immanent causality of the text's history of effects. Is this to say that the biblical text

116. Cf. Ricoeur, "Expérience et langage dans le discours religieux," 15–16.

117. Our aim here is not to engage fully in the debate of revelation as history, but rather to pursue further the question of the "weight" of history in the light of our previous considerations. (For a statement of the debate, see Pannenberg, *Anthropology in Theological Perspective*, 485ff.; Pannenberg, *Systematic Theology*, 1:230–57.)

118. Ricoeur, *Essays on Biblical Interpretation*, 109;151.

119. It may be noted in this connection that a world of the Bible which remains "transcendental" in this sense is not really a world of the Bible but, as Ricoeur's Yale's critics were eager to remark, a poetic text which is "applied" to the Bible, delimiting thus, as Kant honestly pointed out "both the outer limits and the internal structure" of this world.

remains fundamentally incapable of affirming its referential "height"? Let us listen more closely to what Ricoeur has to say.

We must first remark that Ricoeur approaches the problem of testimony by explicitly stating that testimony occupies a place "comparable to that of poetic discourse in relation to the objective aspect of philosophical discourse."[120] In this way the critical work of testimony takes in fact the form of a "poetic sanction." In spelling out the meaning of testimony, Ricoeur uses here, in a similar fashion, three preparatory concepts: the concept of the *cogito* mediated by a universe of signs, the Gadamerian concept of "belonging to" and the concept of appropriation. What Ricoeur attempts to do is basically to retrieve a concept of reflection no longer based upon a subject transparent to himself but rather "mediated" by experience. As we have already seen, this includes a dialectic of appropriation and distanciation. This "second order reflection" which makes distanciation the necessary step in the realisation of the very experience of belonging is, Ricoeur claims, not an *a priori* given, a constitutive foundation, but is itself a form of experience, arriving "unexpectedly like a crisis."[121]

Ricoeur wants to say that appropriation is not a mere noetic exercise, being instead fundamentally grounded in the concrete and objective mediation of "writing" and of "work." In other words, understanding does not belong to a different order which would be able to respond and approximate from its own resources the genius of the author but is mediated in the same objective world of experience. Ricoeur sees the benefit of this conceptuality within the fact that it is able to bring about the dethronement of the consciousness's claim to constitute itself, at the very heart of an epistemological inquiry. Thus, a view of appropriation becomes possible situated at an equal distance from both a subjectivist romantic hermeneutics and an objectivist epistemological perspective. As we shall see later in our study, assessed in the more general framework of a doctrine of Creation, this view of appropriation will have important theological implications.

But of course what interests us is not only the de-centering of consciousness but also the nature of this "otherness" that comes from the text ("otherness" which is able to give us, as Ricoeur says, "a larger self").[122] Now it is precisely testimony that marks both the final blow to autonomy and the

---

120. Ricoeur, *Essays on Biblical Interpretation*, 105.

121. Ibid., 107.

122. Ibid., 108.

advent of otherness. Ricoeur recalls Nabert's question: "Do we have the right to invest one moment of history with an absolute characteristic"[123] To accept contingency is to go beyond the Kantian example or symbol. The path toward originary affirmation can be opened only by "those events, acts and persons that attest that the unjustifiable is overcome here and now." Testimony "confers the sanction of reality on ideas, ideals and ways of being that the symbol depicts to us."[124] The transcendental world of the text thus stands under the criterion of "reality" uncovered by testimony. Here Ricoeur is effecting the inversion alluded to above: the world of the text is no longer seen as an unproblematic poetic world. It is rather testimony which is seen as a "poetic" correction of what remains basically a transcendental concept. This non-historical or trans-historical world must purge its idealistic traits by "feeding" upon testimony.

Testimony is, however, in need of interpretation in its own right because the absolute character of testimony, encapsulated in the founding event as event and meaning at the same time, fades away. Ricoeur summarizes this grand trial of truth in a three-fold dialectic of testimony: event and meaning, the trial of false testimony and testimony about what is seen and of a life. The first sign of the "height" engendered by testimony is noted in the dialectic of event and meaning. "The event is our master"[125] concedes Ricoeur, signaling the radical break with a purely immanent temporality. The event receives a foundational role by virtue of its capacity to transform the accidental into a destiny. The second dialectic describes the reply of reflection to the critique of testimony. The knowledge enabled by testimony cannot be either immediate intuition or a form of absolute knowledge. "For a finite existence like ours appropriation can only be a critical act."[126] Ricoeur follows Nabert once again by appealing to his criteriology of the divine: This criteriology is according to Ricoeur just a reiteration of the medieval "way of eminence": "in forming predicates of the divine we disqualify the false witness; in recognizing the true witnesses we identify the predicates of the divine."[127] But the most important dialectic is that of a life. It is here that consciousness confesses the profound inequality with its correlate, the "outside." Here

123. Ibid., 116.
124. Ibid., 111.
125. Ibid., 114.
126. Ibid.
127. Ibid., 115.

Ricoeur concedes that the self must undergo a radical denial. "Reflection cannot produce this renouncing of the sovereign consciousness out of itself. . . . Who would save his life must lose it."[128] Against Nabert, who imagines a correspondence between the historical affirmation of the absolute and the inner affirmation of consciousness, Ricoeur affirms the priority of historical testimony.

Yet, in spite of this seemingly promising development, Ricoeur concludes the Revelation essay by referring this priority of historical testimony to Kant's productive imagination. In this light, the image of testimony as "presentation" of what for reflection remains an "idea,"[129] casts a shadow of doubt upon both the divestment of the subject and the "truth" of testimony, recalling as it does the already familiar theme of the irreducibility between "interiority" and exteriority," between concept and metaphor, between philosophy and poetics. Thus historical testimony never really "meets" its "aesthetic" presentation. The event, mediated by its "history of effects," has indeed a "weight," but this weight presupposes an ambiguous history in which "human constructions" inevitably contribute to its richness. This is why history is always understood as a dialectic of reception and construction, history and fiction. In this way, the dimension of "height" is recast once again in the unrelenting struggle between "exteriority" and "interiority," between representation and concept, between faith and reason.[130]

We may therefore conclude that the concept of testimony shares the fate of Ricoeur's assessment of Aquinas's analogy,[131] sealing an agreement with Heidegger voiced at the end of *The Rule of Metaphor*. We must choose between thinking and poetry,[132] between saying either too much or too little. The poetic world, the Kingdom of God, the New Covenant or the New Creation are always mediated "worlds" manifesting thus an irreducible non-identity between idea and representation, perception and construction. Ricoeur has been faithful to his decision not to dissolve the *noumenon* in relation to God. That is why he consistently avoids

128. Ibid.

129. Ibid., 116.

130. See also Ricoeur, "Hermeneutics of Testimony," in *Essays on Biblical Interpretation*, 153.

131. In Ricoeur's reading of Aquinas the descending order of signification and the ascending order of being converge but never actually meet. See Ricoeur, *Rule of Metaphor*, 272–80.

132. Ricoeur, *Rule of Metaphor*, 313.

talking about God or Jesus Christ as the "reference"[133] of the biblical text. Nonetheless, at least two things have become abundantly clear. First, the Ricoeurian "world" or "enchanted world" needs a more fundamental anchoring, and second, Ricoeur's fulfillment of the ontological horizon in the subject of appropriation remains fundamentally in want.

We may recall that Ricoeur asked for a de-psychologized doctrine of the Spirit and, against Nabert, pleaded for the priority of "exteriority." That may have sounded like a step in the right direction, towards the recovery of the "ontic." But in an account in which testimony, the experience of community and the actualization of freedom are consistently referred to an immanent temporality the only possible correlate of a "psychologized" Spirit is its "objective" counterpart. We may conclude therefore that testimony appears to have overcome "interiority" but has been incapable of adequately addressing the problem of "height." Both "the world of the text" and testimony have had to pass through the defile of interpretation. And interpretation is always a reflective exercise, always the work of the concept. Reflection has undoubtedly been de-centered by indicating its radical dependence upon its "outside." Nonetheless, its "coming to life" in ever-new "aesthetic" presentations of "otherness" betrays an irreducible affirmation of itself at the very heart of its dependence on the other. The "old" is always present in the "new." Of course, it must be said that Ricoeur warns us once again that as in the case of the world of the text, his use of testimony can only offer a philosophical approximation of the biblical experience of revelation. But as we have tried to show, a mere reiteration of (abstract) "anti-naturalism" does not really help the theologian. The theologian wants to know whether this last recasting of testimony in the endless process of interpretation does not mark a return to noetics, thus condemning the theological discourse to a structural inadequacy. A way to inquire into this latter problem would be to attempt to grasp the exact meaning of Ricoeur's "return" to "dialogue" after the encounter with poetics. What is the agent capable of "saying" after visiting the lofty world of "possibility"? Is there "proclamation" after "manifestation"? We shall conclude our assessment of Ricoeur by confronting his hermeneutical project with this final question.

---

133. E.g., Ricoeur, "Biblical Hermeneutics," 33, where he claims that the ultimate referent of the parables is human experience.

## The Hermeneutical Self and the Struggle
## between the "One" and the "Many"

The principal upshot of our critique of Ricoeur's view of Revelation was not so much the concept of truth as manifestation itself but the alien conceptuality attached to it. We should welcome, among other things, his critique of the modern technological project, of instrumentalist rationality which divides reality into subjects and a world of objects organized as a structure of order discernible *a priori* and upon which we are to exercise control. Nonetheless, as has been shown, Heidegger's ontological project onto which the concept of manifestation has been grafted, remains fundamentally in want. An alternative between a "sacramental view," in which the world is seen as a mere temporal expression of an eternal form and a detached objectivist perspective, can hardly be conceived outside of God's concrete relationship with the world. The insight that the advent of truth is possible in time must eventually be referred to its source. A re-enchanted world cannot be articulated apart from its dynamic relationship with its Creator. If manifestation means essentially "listening" the inevitable question is: listen to what? Or perhaps more importantly: listen to whom? What has started to become apparent is that the consistent effort of avoiding a direct confrontation with these questions inevitably takes upon itself an alien structure of emancipation.

We are now better equipped for a more systematic evaluation of Ricoeur's post-Hegelian Kantianism and its theological significance in the light of his view of revelation. We shall make a start by addressing the question left unanswered at the end of the last section. To this end, we shall confront one more time the two dimensions that have never stopped haunting Ricoeur's hermeneutical project: manifestation and proclamation. Our task is once again eased as Ricoeur engages directly with precisely this problematic.

In "Manifestation and Proclamation,"[134] Ricoeur attempts both to confront and relate what he calls a phenomenology of manifestation with a hermeneutics of proclamation. The first thing to be noted is that manifestation is ascribed here a slightly different semantic content, being thematized under a phenomenology of the sacred.[135] Its logic of meaning is

---

134 Ricoeur, *Figuring the Sacred*, 48–67. I will incorporate page references in the text above.

135. This is an important remark as in such a light we cannot simply say that Ricoeur has an unproblematic view of an always-already "graced" world.

inscribed this time in a law of correspondences (e.g., the true temple always conforms to some celestial model, the correspondence between the micro-cosm and the macrocosm, etc. [54]). Ricoeur draws here upon the work of the comparative historians of religions, more specifically upon the work of Mircea Eliade. This synchronic, a-temporal approach is confronted with the hermeneutical and historical approach of the religions that based their existence upon the word of God and upon a collection of texts. Ricoeur's plea for proclamation recapitulates the whole force of the Old Testament's unceasing combat against the sacredness of nature and the rituals of Baal and Astartees (55). Hearing the word takes precedence over the vision of signs in a general tendency which remains "fundamentally ethical and not aesthetic" (55). Moreover, this turn against idols takes on radical forms. The prophet's word announces a total disruption of the cosmos. One may even go so far as to say that "prophecy unmakes the cosmos that ritual is em-ployed to make sacred" (57). Jesus himself does not attenuate this tension but further radicalizes it. The "new" always disrupts the "old." "Whoever wants to save his life must lose it." The new logic which emerges is there-fore no longer a logic of correspondences but a logic of limit-expressions. Terms like the Kingdom of God, the New Covenant, the New Creation emphatically challenge the cosmic symbolism in an experience which, as the correlate of the limit expression, becomes a limit-experience. While the language of those limit expressions is no doubt special, Ricoeur reiter-ates his belief that it is the experience itself that constitutes "the ultimate referent of our modes of speaking" (61). Can in such a light, the "virtually antisacral" dimension of kerygma be reconciled with the nostalgia for a re-enchanted world?[136]

The first step towards a reconciliation is made by accepting the validity of the critique of modern technological culture as expressed in the writings of Heidegger, Habermas and others (62–63). Against icono-clasm in general and Bultmann's demythologizing program in particular, Ricoeur maintains that desacralization of the world is neither a "fact" nor our destiny (63).[137] This may be "an incipient re-evaluation of the sacred" which is based "on the very re-evaluation of values" (63). Such

---

136. Ricoeur seems to give at least partial credit to Bultmann's view that Christian-ity is inherently antisacral and demythologization is in fact part of the task of faith initiated as it was by the strong iconoclastic orientation of the Old Testament and Early Christianity itself.

137. Ricoeur implicitly suggests that Bultmann was unable to see the strong ideo-logical string attached to modern secularization.

a re-evaluation, whose principal critical task is to connect a "degenerate sacred" with the scientific-technological ideology, has a parabolic significance, crying out that our culture is nihilistic, that our world is not possible without the sacred. Ricoeur asks rhetorically:

> Can we live without some originary orientation? Is it simply a residual pheneomenon, or an existential protest arising out of the depths of our being, that sends us in search of privileged places, be they our birthplace, the scene of our first love, or the theatre of some important historical occurrence . . . ? Can we abolish the symbolism of the threshold, the door, and the entrance, along with every ritual of entrance and of welcome? Can we completely desacralize birth (our coming into the world) and death (our passing to the place of rest)? (64).

The genuine task of faith is not "secularization" but the re-enchantment of the world:

> The Word we said, breaks away from the numinous. And this is true. But is it not so to the extent that the Word takes for itself the function of the numinous? There would be no hermeneutic if there were no proclamation. But there would be no proclamation if the Word too were not powerful; that is, if it did not have the power to set forth the new being it proclaims. A Word that is addressed to us rather than our speaking it, a Word that constitutes us rather than our articulating it—a Word that speaks—does not such a Word reaffirm the sacred just as much as abolish it? (65).

This may seem to announce a dialectic of Word and Spirit that would re-trace the contours of a theology of Creation. It is noteworthy that an appeal to John's prologue is made to fathom this new reconciliation between word and manifestation: "The Word became flesh and dwelt among us. . ." (65). It is further acknowledged that in fact this synthesis provided the basis for the concept of Revelation from the Greek Fathers to Hegel. Ricoeur devises this re-affirmation of Creation as an internalization of manifestation. The cosmic symbolism does not die, but is rather re-interpreted. This invincibility of the sacred is in fact evident in the history of the Church in the dialectic of preaching and sacraments (67). The most powerful metaphor that capitalizes this superior re-evaluation of the sacred is the symbolism of death and resurrection. This new vision does not need therefore to oppose ethics to aesthetics, history to nature. Ricoeur may well see this infusion with the "Spirit" of the austere world of the *logos* as a return to a Romantic theme. Indeed, he confesses that he cannot conceive a religious attitude that does not proceed from a feeling of absolute dependence (85.)

Is this to say that Ricoeur reiterates the concerns of a type of theology stemming from Schleiermacher as his Yale critics have suggested? Indeed many of Ricoeur's devout followers seem to belong to this camp. But perhaps such an assessment would be simplistic. It is worth taking a brief look at a modern defense of Schleiermacher by an author who does not conceal his admiration for Ricoeur.[138]

Williams's principal aim in his article "Hegel and Schleiermacher" is to bring to light the true dimension of Schleiermacher's "feeling of absolute dependence" against Hegel's sarcastic caricature of it.[139] Schleiermacher's concept of feeling, Williams maintains, is in fact not different from Hegel's concept of general perceptual consciousness. He further argues that "like the later Husserl, Heidegger and Merleau-Ponty, Schleiermacher breaks with the Cartesian version of consciousness as purely rational, self-transparent and cut off from the world and embodiment."[140] Schleiermacher's modalizations of *Gefühl* (the feeling of freedom and the feeling of dependence) are, in Williams's opinion, irreducibly social and intersubjective being articulated in a life-world. To be sure, Williams may be fighting quite a specific battle here, that of dispelling the "myth" which has become so influential in the West, allegedly perpetrated by Feuerbach and Barth, that the theological tradition influenced by Schleiermacher remains a form of natural theology encouraging immediacy and subjectivism.[141] Moreover, it may be perhaps further suspected that such a phenomenological reading of Schleiermacher remains largely anachronistic. Whatever the case, Williams's study rightly points, I believe, to some interesting (and often overlooked) connections between Hegel and Schleiermacher. In spite of their different emphases as to the essence of Christianity (the self-consciousness of a particular form of life

---

138. Williams, "Hegel and Schleiermacher on Theological Truth," 52–69. It is enough to note that the concluding section of Williams's essay is entitled "How Does the Symbol Give Rise to Thought."

139. "If religion in man is based only on a feeling, then the nature of that feeling can be none other than the feeling of his dependence, and so a dog would be the best Christian, for it possesses this [feeling] in the highest degree." Cf. Williams, "Hegel and Schleiermacher," 52.

140. Ibid., 56.

141. Cf. Ibid., 53.

in Schleiermacher versus the development of the historical doctrines in Hegel), they were both concerned with the historical and hermeneutical ramifications of the concept of experience and the relationship between theory and praxis.

We must admit, therefore, that the concerns of the Romantic synthesis, even in its excesses, are more complex than is often assumed. We return in this way to an earlier point. A doctrine of Creation must do more than to refer itself to a polemic concept of natural theology. If we are to talk adequately about hermeneutics and history we cannot avoid the complex concerns raised by the concept of experience and the ever subtler forms the very concept of mediation takes.

That such problems preoccupy Ricoeur is hardly deniable. Like Williams, Ricoeur would envisage a common field of concerns which would bring Schleiermacher and Hegel together. What is more, Ricoeur acknowledges, in principle, the perennial value of Schleiermacher's hermeneutical program as both Romantic and critical. "Perhaps hermeneutics is forever marked by this double filiation,"[142] Ricoeur writes. But, as we have indicated, Ricoeur does not want to remain at this feeling of absolute dependence. The philosopher must do more than that. A philosophical reflection upon religion is indeed more indebted to Hegel than to Schleiermacher.[143] In the light of his view of the relationship between philosophy and theology, it is not difficult to see that an appropriation of Hegel's hermeneutics may well cohabitate with Schleiermacher's "religious extension" of Kant. It is significant to note that Ricoeur's summary of what he calls a modern hermeneutics of religious representation, which would be consonant with Hegel's philosophy of religion, betrays striking similarities with Ricoeur's own more general hermeneutical program. Three aspects are mentioned here.

First, there is the moment of immediacy, by which he refers to Hegel's non-hermeneutical moment (the Absolute becoming immediately present in the incarnation of Christ). It has been this moment which inaugurated the process of interpretation. Second, there is the figurative mediation. Because Christ is no longer present "disappearance and negativity are the conditions of the appropriation of the meaning of the

---

142. Ricoeur, *Hermeneutics and the Human Sciences*, 46.

143. Ricoeur, following Gadamer, endorses a hermeneutics that follows Hegel rather than Schleiermacher. Ricoeur, "Status of *Vorstellung* in Hegel's Philosophy of Religion," 88.

event."[144] Moreover the religious appropriation of this process takes narrative and symbolic form being carried out by the confessing community which re-enacts the initial presence in remembrance and interiorization. And thirdly, there is the task of conceptualization. "The concept, Ricoeur avers, is the endless death of the representation,"[145] attempting to reproduce in itself its inner dynamism. Ricoeur closes the hermeneutical circle by pointing to the fact that Hegel's philosophy remains a circular process: it starts and returns to religious immediacy, whether this is religious experience, Word-event or kerygmatic moment.

This, I believe, summarizes best a hermeneutical procedure which we have seen at work in Ricoeur's writings. As the previous chapters have amply attested, Ricoeur's hermeneutical detours always start and end in experience. It is perhaps ironic to see in Ricoeur an almost universal application of Hegel's hermeneutics of religion, especially in the light of Ricoeur's emphatic refusal to connect philosophy and theology.[146] Is this not an unanticipated confirmation that the concept of experience and the question of meaning have indeed an irreducible theological dimension?

Ricoeur concludes "Manifestation and Proclamation" significantly by asking: "Must we not confess that the end of the word is bound to some new birth of the sacred and its symbolism beyond its death?[147] In the light of our previous considerations, this "end of the word," undoubtedly highly problematical for the theologian, may well endorse Hegel's view that the age of the Spirit "sublates" that of the Son, or may join perhaps in the ambiguous suggestion made at the end of *Phenomenology* that it is in the essence of the Spirit to "return" to the world . . .

We have seen however that Ricoeur repeatedly denies the Hegelian *Aufhebung*.[148] Are we to conclude then that Ricoeur's speculative

144. Ibid., 87.

145. Ibid.

146. This is not to say that there are not differences. In opposition to Hegel, Ricoeur writes that "I tend to interpret absolute thought less as a final stage than as the process thanks to which all shapes and all stages remain thoughtful" (87). But as we anticipated, what is rejected is not so much Hegel's *a posteriori* recollection, but its totalizing claim. It is true that, with Gadamer, Ricoeur believes that Hegel should be abandoned rather than conquered through criticism (cf. Ricoeur, *Time and Narrative*, 3:202–6, esp. 206n14). Nonetheless, this renunciation to a first order mediation of history and truth can be arguably conceived as a second order reflection on its conditions of possibility.

147. Ricoeur, *Figuring the Sacred*, 69.

148. In his early writings Ricoeur seemed to have been more sympathetic to Hegel

grammar returns decisively to Kant, in what fundamentally remains a broken dialectic? It may seem, indeed, that the perpetual rise from, and return to, experience gradually configures a structure of emancipation which remains torn apart in a double allegiance: the symbol is bound to the configuration of the cosmos while metaphor remains a free invention of discourse.[149]

But what is remarkable to note at this juncture is that even here Ricoeur's mediation between Kant and Hegel is not a "mere construction." One more time, Ricoeur anchors his mediation in "exteriority," carefully indicating a speculative field common to both Kant and Hegel. We may remember that towards the end of *The Rule of Metaphor*, Ricoeur contests Derrida's proposal of a collusion between metaphor and *Aufhebung* (with the consequent instrumentalization of dead metaphors). Ricoeur insists there that the operation that constitutes the "suppression-preservation" which Hegel calls *Aufhebung* is distinct from, and subsequent to, the operation of transfer. The second operation, Ricoeur insists, "creates a proper sense in the spiritual order out of an improper sense coming from the sensible order." "This pair of operations," it is further suggested, "is not fundamentally different from what Kant considers to be the production of the concept in its schema."[150] It is this point of contact that grounds Ricoeur's double allegiance, both to the power of the mind and to the world, to language and to experience.[151] As has started to become apparent, this gave rise to a speculative grammar, marking decisively the

---

(see his essay "Return to Hegel (Jean Hyppolite)," in *Lectures II: La Contrée des philosophes*). Later on, he becomes more critical and concerned about Hegel's totalizing claim (Ricoeur, *Time and Narrative*, 3:193–206). See also Ricoeur, "Intellectual Autobiography," 23.

149. Ricoeur, *Figuring the Sacred*, 53. Even the way in which Ricoeur qualifies the linguisticallity of the symbol (54) recalls the same metaphorical structure described in chapter 2. The phenomenology of manifestation would thus appear to be just a "structural" moment which needs to be overcome. This confirms the thesis that both proclamation and manifestation are included in the larger category of experience.

150. Ricoeur, *Rule of Metaphor*, 292.

151. Von Balthasar notes that, in Hegel, "the whole of the metaphysics of Spirit and Being is developed within the framework of the Kantian opposition between concept and intuition, and thus ultimately between the general and the particular." Balthasar, *Glory of the Lord*, 588. It is Ricoeur's ultimate dependence upon such a grammar that often leads him to a false either/or: "Religion is constituted less by faith than by hope" (*Conflict of Interpretations*, 481); or between will and imagination (see *Essays on Biblical Interpretation*, 117).

emancipatory dimension in Ricoeur's structure of disclosure. Let us summarize the main theological implications of this situation.

## The Poverty of Exteriority

We have noted Ricoeur's unrelenting fight against the idealism of consciousness and its deceptions. The "outside" must be given priority over the "inside," the "world" over the self. It was in this context that Ricoeur called for a de-psychologized doctrine of the Spirit. Ricoeur was certainly right to go against an "interiorist" tradition which collapsed the "height" in "interiority," reducing God to the immanent structure of the human soul. But we have further seen that the "outside" is not immediately given, but is itself in need of interpretation. The biblical text cannot function as an unproblematic transcendental as it does for most narrative theologians. Even testimony as "the sanction of reality upon ideas," cannot escape the defile of interpretation. We have further seen that the receding of "exteriority" under the "pressure" of interpretation leaves the very concept of "otherness" in peril. A theological reply to a psychologized understanding of the Spirit must do more than point to its "objective" counterpart in an immanent temporality (an "objective" Spirit whose totalizing claim has been questioned). Moreover, I suggest that the silencing of the transcendental dimension of the Spirit is the first step towards a new return to "interiority." Thus, calls to acknowledge this transcendental dimension, such as we find in Zizioulas[152] for instance, are essentially anti-monistic and anti-modalistic in character, fighting against a tendency in the modern period (especially since the Enlightenment) to "secularize" it whether as a historical principle or a principle of imagination or creativity. It is not so much therefore that Ricoeur favors or is tilted towards the noetic dimension. It is rather the case that in a situation in which the Ultimate subject remains elusive and incomprehensible, rationality always "returns" and finds expression in the finite subject.

Ricoeur seems to oscillate between a Hegelian view of concrete freedom actualizable in community, where "what is rational is real," and a "practical" mediation which would understand being not only as "desire to be" but also "as effort to exist." I would venture to suggest further that only a theological elaboration of this community of freedom, as a community that is "in the world, yet not of the world" (John 17) can enable

152. E.g., Zizioulas, *Being As Communion*, 130.

us to "rescue" the dimension of "height" without falling into historicism. If the witness is genuinely to attest to God's presence in the world,[153] his concrete presence needs to be affirmed and spelled out not only Christologically but also pneumatologically and ecclesiologically. Indeed, God in Christ and through the Spirit is at work in a concrete historical community of redeemed believers which exists at the same time as an eschatological community in which God's promise that he would live amongst his people (Jer 31:31–34) is fulfilled *hic et nunc*. In other words, to account for this transcendental dimension of the Spirit, is to point to the fact that to affirm God's promise and live in the light of hope as in fact Ricoeur would want to do, means to affirm that God has fulfilled his promise in Christ through the power of the creative and transforming Spirit in the reality of the Church. That is to say, truth and "fullness of life" is possible in our world. Indeed, in the Spirit, meaning is no longer endlessly deferred. We are instead given critical discernment and guided into all truth (John 16:13). Can we not, in the light of this community, better understand Ricoeur's ambiguous recourse to "the sanction of reality"? Can we not better conceive the relation between ethics and "aesthetics," between call and response? If the reality of the Church is enabled and brought about by *this* Spirit, we do not have to choose between a prophetic spirit and the spirit of *koinonia*, the spirit who actualizes freedom and the call to obedience.[154] In this way, this ethical community becomes a space of communion, the place where liberty meets obedience and freedom reveals itself as freedom for the other (1 Cor 4:8).[155]

As we shall see in more detail later, this vision does not necessarily amount to another totalizing claim. There is no suggestion here of a return to an unproblematic concept of participation, nor are we saying that we must employ an undifferentiated view of "presence." It is simply to spell out the implicit rationality of God's action in Christ and through the Spirit. When this Trinitarian grammar is left out, as we have seen, "exteriority" itself takes on a different speculative path which rather than

153. See Ricoeur, *Essays on Biblical Interpretation*, 111.

154. It is significant to note that when inquiring into the epistemological stance of the critique in a generalized theory of ideology, Ricoeur admits that such a place does not exist. Ricoeur, *Hermeneutics and the Human Sciences*, 240ff.

155. It may be remarked that the discussion of community has arisen as an answer to an historical aporia and it was not inserted as a transcendental concept. This is in line with our effort to uncover a theological dimension of history and to conceive the theological task as both a concrete and descriptive activity, and yet transformative and redemptive.

solving the *aporias* of history renders the whole enterprise highly problematical from a theological perspective (the emergence of an "objective"
Spirit, the implicit adoption of a modalist Trinity).

## The Invincibility of Autonomous Freedom

This brings us to the more general idea of freedom. In his early writings, Ricoeur connects the idea of freedom with the "developmental"
paradigm. He believes that it was St. Paul who "opened the way to all
the 'progressivist' theologies of history which . . . are manifestly prolon-
gations of his 'how much more' and his 'in order that.'"[156] In the same
context, Ricoeur commends the efforts of German idealism *contra* a mere
paradigm of return to an earlier paradise. Ricoeur's appeal to Irenaeus
in discussing freedom in connection with maturity must be understood
along the same lines. Freedom as emancipation has always had historical
and cosmological ramifications.[157]

Indeed, the theme of "maturity," of coming to adulthood is writ
large in Ricoeur's view of freedom. He talks not only of the risk of being human but also about the risk God assumed in creating man.[158] This
recourse to Irenaeus seems to suggest a homology between Ricoeur's own
hermeneutical project and a theological view of history that takes temporality seriously. We attempted to show earlier that the hermeneutical developments in the wake of Hegel have opened up this appreciation of the
richness of history and that there is probably more to German idealism
than an immediacy of reason or an immediacy of experience. The fact
that the significance of history has been intimately connected with the
messianic and eschatological orientation of the biblical revelation cannot
be ignored. Ricoeur rightly maintains that while it is true that the idea
of the continuous progress of humanity has been an unfortunate rationalist secularization of eschatology, the conflict itself between Christian

---

156. Ricoeur, *Symbolism of Evil*, 273.

157. Mark Wallace suggests that Ricoeur's hermeneutical position may be characterized as "Arminian" (as opposed to Barth's "Calvinist" position). Wallace, "World of
the Text," 152. While this may be formally true, we have tried to show, however, that
Ricoeur's view of freedom gathers profound historical concerns attempting to bring
together human desire and divine command. This is what is ultimately at stake in a
non-heteronomous view of Revelation for Ricoeur.

158. Ricoeur, *Histoire et Vérité*, 131.

eschatology and progress is a false conflict.[159] But Ricoeur has consistently refused to go further into what he has always seen to grow into unacceptable panoramic syntheses. Yet, as we have seen, this constant exorcism of *Aufhebung* tends to make growing (and perhaps impossible) demands upon its constitutive terms.

Ricoeur touches upon this idea of freedom much later when he attempts to trace the contours of a theology of conscience.[160] It is significant to note that in Ricoeur's view, the responding self (i.e., the self which listens to the Word), must not contest the Enlightenment idea of autonomy held by both Kant and Hegel. On the contrary, such a view, Ricoeur maintains, "opens new possibilities of interpretation for the dialogic structure of Christian existence."[161] Ricoeur returns here to the Heideggerian concept of *Gewissen* as a dialogue of the self with itself and attempts to graft the correlative prophetic and Christomorphic self upon this irreducible anthropological presupposition. What happens in such a process in Ricoeur's description is a reciprocal move: on the one hand the call of the self is intensified, on the other, the transcendent figure is internalized into an inner voice.[162]

Ricoeur concludes, following Bultmann, that the concept of *suneidesis* in the Apostle Paul constitutes an inalienable structure of existence. Perhaps unsurprisingly, we discover here an argument similar to the one developed in the Revelation essay: a theology of conscience requires a simultaneous reinterpretation of the phenomenon of conscience and of the Christian kerygma.[163] Ultimately, as in the case of Revelation, the voice

159. See "Le Christianisme et le sens de L'histoire," in Ricoeur, *Histoire et Vérité*, 81ff. Ricoeur argues here that progress and mystery or progress versus hope do not meet at the same level and that the idea of progress in the rationalist sense grew as a consequence out of the instrumentalization of history, history as "successful history," in which the notion of success shares the presuppositions of the modern idea of the domination of nature.

160. Ricoeur, "Summoned Subject," in *Figuring the Sacred*, 262–75. This essay constitutes Ricoeur's final lecture of his 1986 Gifford lectures (left out of *Oneself as Another*). Originally published under the title "Le sujet convoqué: A l'école des récits de vocations prophétique," 83–99.

161. Ricoeur, *Figuring the Sacred*, 271.

162. Ibid.

163. Ricoeur pleads for a mediation between the autonomy of conscience (in the spirit of the Enlightenment) and the symbolics of faith. "The Christian is someone who discerns 'conformity to the image of Christ' in the call of conscience. This discernment is an interpretation" (ibid., 274). No synthesis between the verdict of conscience and the Christomorphism of faith is imaginable.

of the interpreter remains invincible. This leads us to wonder whether Ricoeur's proposal is not a mere variation of the Hegelian idea of freedom which grows out at the interaction between an autonomous mind and the historical advance of Christianity (the full dimension of autonomy coinciding with the ultimate intention of historic Christianity). In spite of Ricoeur's rejection of this ultimate synthesis, the concrete expression of freedom cannot defeat this demand. If responsibility is to be more than mere idle talk, the "capable" subject must presuppose such a "momentary and provisional approximation."[164] But this parallel advance brings us to the most important feature of Ricoeur's structure of emancipation.

## The Power of Negativity

We remember that Ricoeur's decision to develop a philosophy of the will carried with it a certain anti-intellectualist concern expressed mainly in his unrelenting effort to de-center the subject. Yet we have also noted Ricoeur's anti-voluntarist stance in his equally undeterred effort to restore the power of imagination as an inexhaustible source of forever fresh transcendental worlds. We have further seen that it was ultimately this tension which left us with the *aporia* of a voice from "nowhere," to which was ascribed the criterion of "reality" becoming the "judge" of imagination. Perhaps, at the limit, the "judge" becomes also the "seducer." But such a synthesis remains always at the horizon, always torn apart between philosophy and poetry. We noted above that the absence of "height" marked the withdrawal of "otherness" under the critical pressure of interpretation. We also noted that it was not the "return" of "rationality" in itself which was in question. As it became apparent, genuine ontology must include such a "return." The problem was rather that in the absence of God language the significance of the return itself tended to be misconstrued.

Ricoeur's faithfulness in separating the work of the theologian from the work of the philosopher[165] has led him to distinguish between the

164. I alluded to one of Ricoeur's expressions in *Oneself as Another* where he attempts to trace the contours of attestation in the framework of "good life": "The certainty of being the author of one's own discourse and of one's own acts becomes the conviction of judging well and acting well in a momentary and provisional approximation of living well." Ricoeur, *Oneself as Another*, 180.

165. Ricoeur claims that he did that under the influence of Barth. The claim appears less surprising when we realize that the Barth Ricoeur is talking about is probably the early Barth (strongly voluntarist and anti-intellectualist), the Barth of *Romans.*

"power of obeying" and the "power of daring."[166] To be sure, he is prepared to admit that this "power of daring" does not take shape in abstraction from what is essential.[167] Nonetheless, it must ineluctably follow the internal rules of the order to which it belongs. This leads the philosopher to speak about "the autonomy of responsible thought."[168] "If there is only one Logos, the logos of Christ requires of me as a philosopher nothing else than a more complete and a more perfect activation of reason; not more than reason but *whole* reason" (his italics).[169] I would wholeheartedly agree with Ricoeur if this Christological insight would be placed in the larger scheme of God's engagement with the world. But such a claim remains necessarily "internalist." It does not speak so much about the implicit integrity of Creation or about its relative independence, but rather about the power of expression of the human mind as the correlate of an "aesthetics" which remains beyond our grasp. As we have seen, this "power of daring" emerges time and again, at the very heart of dispossession itself.

In fact Ricoeur admits that this "mini-death of reason,"[170] this "letting go" of the self, is still part of the reflective order. It is both "an ethical and a speculative act." Ricoeur's appeal to Nabert's originary affirmation reveals filiations not only with Fichte but also with Hegel's dialectic of negativity. Nabert maintains that it is by deepening solitude and by "negating others" that we discover that we are not alone.[171] Original affirmation "as desire to be and as effort to exist" appears thus to be a form of "negating the negative." This is why Ricoeur insists that the "*depouillement*" of the self presupposes a renunciation of both "the empirical objects and the transcendental objects of metaphysics." But this "losing of the world" becomes part of the grammar of the "advent" of the Word. As early as *Histoire et Vérité* Ricoeur writes:

> La Parole de création et de re-création n'est pas un langage de science, n'est pas une cosmologie, n'est pas même une étique ni une esthétique. Elle est d'une autre ordre. Ce départage ne peut être,

---

Ricoeur, *Critique and Conviction*, 150.

166. "Le philosophe et le théologien annoncent chacun quelque chose d'essentiel, l'un l'audace de la vérité et l'autre l'obéissance à la Vérité." Ricoeur, *Histoire et Vérité*, 182.

167. Ricoeur, *Conflict of Interpretations*, 403.

168. Ibid., 403.

169. Ibid.

170. I alluded to Von Balthasar's expression used to designate the speculative Good Friday.

171. See Nabert, *Éléments pour une Étique*, 48–57.

dans notre économie passionnelle, qu'un cruel apprentissage de
la rupture, qu'une dure école de déception où la déchirure est la
seule chance de la suture.[172]

Ricoeur manifests a fascination for the metaphors of absence; the
empty tomb, dying to oneself, the irreducible hiatus between Christ's
death and His resurrection.[173] This wager on negativity raises the question as to where the dispossession ends and the affirmation begins and
whether the underlying continuity in the very discontinuity does not
secretly undermine both endeavors.[174] Does Ricoeur resist the temptation of "regulating the scandal of the cross"? Is he able to succeed where
Bultmann failed, namely, in genuinely carrying such a scandal to its full
historical and anthropological implications?

In one of his late interviews, Ricoeur acknowledges that his oscil-
lation between theology and philosophy, this constant struggle between
two allegiances, has escaped him. "I do not believe that I am the master
of this game, or the master of meaning," he confesses.[175] Nonetheless, it
is also here that we can see, perhaps in a most clear way, the austerity of
his post-Hegelian Kantianism. The suggestion made here is that genuine
de-centering presupposes the application of the biblical requirement of
dying to oneself in a most radical way. Ricoeur believes that the consciousness's renunciation of both the transcendental and the empirical
objects forbids a projection of meaning beyond one's physical death.
In fact the meaning of resurrection itself can be better understood as
"resurrection" in the Christian community. The Church as the "body"

172. Ricoeur, *Histoire et Vérité*, 182–83.

173. Cf. Ricoeur, *Conflict of Interpretations*, 409; Ricoeur, *Essays on Biblical Interpretation*, 145.

174. It must be said here that Ricoeur does take (and emphatically so) Kierkegaard's
critique of Hegel's negativity. Cf. Ricoeur, *Conflict of Interpretations*, 313. See also the
two articles dedicated to Kierkegaard: "Kierkegaard et le mal" and "Philosopher après
Kierkegaard," 292–316. Nonetheless, in spite of Ricoeur's recognition that evil remains
irrational and hope exists "in spite of" evil, the philosophical approximation of hope
still feeds upon what essentially remains a "tragic" dimension of experience. Again,
what Ricoeur seems to contest is not so much the configurative power of negativity
but rather the undifferentiated way in which Hegel used it. See also Ricoeur's plea for
the religious significance of atheism. Ricoeur, *Conflict of Interpretations*, 440–67. The
significance of Detmer's critique consists not so much in pointing to the genetic fallacy
Ricoeur commits, but rather in implicitly unveiling the limits of the Kantian's critique
of the transcendental illusions. Cf. Detmer, "Ricoeur on Atheism: A Critique," 477–93.

175. Ricoeur, *Critique and Conviction*, 150. I will incorporate the references to this
interview in the text above.

of Christ is Christ's resurrected body. Resurrection means acquiring a body which is other than physical. And other than physical can only be historical . . .[176] Ricoeur is well aware that the speculative grammar of such a "resurrection" (or perhaps "survival") in the memory of God is closer to Whitehead and Hartshorne (158). Yet, like Hegel, Ricoeur manifests sympathy for the mystics and particularly for Meister Eckhart, who bracketed the concern for personal resurrection (156). The exercise of "detachment" and the work of mourning (the place where Eckhart meets Freud), is more meaningful in Ricoeur's opinion than the "affirmative vigor" of the resurrection narratives (152). Such a Promethean view of radical negativity which severs any hope for an afterlife, does not want to remain at a tragic view, however, and neither does it think of itself as re-iterating Heidegger's being-towards-death (156).[177] Instead, it seeks to affirm that "joy is still possible when everything has been given up" (157). This is perhaps the ultimate ambition of speculation: to transform death, in Paul's words, the last enemy to be destroyed (1 Cor 15:26), in the affirmation of life *hic et nunc*, in a "meaning" which does not rest upon the "positive" and "mythological" view of a "parallel time," but entirely upon the "transfiguration" of something which remains forever finite and insufficient. It is perhaps surprising to find such Gnostic overtones in a philosopher who has devoted so much effort in fighting against intellectualism. But this extreme *ascesis* also reveals how fragile our conceptions of mediation are. Is not this radical mediation of the self by its "other" as a "negation of the negative" a relapse into immediacy? Cannot one suspect it to be a restatement of the Husserlian solipsism in a new guise (where the ultimate disruption of the immanent meaning is just the prelude of a more fundamental re-affirmation)? As we have seen, Ricoeur wants, indeed, to bring will and imagination together, to speak of an "enchanted world," to think, perhaps, vision and obedience within the same conceptual space. . . . But can one do that while still making recourse to

176. It is interesting to note that Ricoeur finds support for his Hegelian understanding of resurrection in John, where elevation begins at the cross (Ricoeur, *Critique and Conviction*, 152). But this affirmative "power of death" implicitly affirms a "modalist" view of God where the death of Jesus "is" (literally) the death of God with its Gnostic overtones.

177. As we shall see later, this radical "theology of death" and celebration of finitude is part of the "anti-metaphysic" orientation of a good many modern theologies (e.g., Jenson, *Systematic Theology*, 196ff). Similarly, Jenson argues that the Church is the risen body of Christ. For a criticism, see Molnar, Review of *Systematic Theology*, 117–31.

such an abstract "rational/ethical" demand? Can one genuinely do that by offectively refusing the rich configurative power of God's revelation of Himself in three persons? The life span, God's speech and actions may appear scandalous at times. But we may rightly ask, as once the Apostle Peter did,[178] whether there are better alternatives out there . . .

We may perhaps press home Ricoeur's "logic of superabundance" by saying that the grace of "accepting meaning" is more fundamental than both the virtue and the logic of renouncing it.

## Concluding Remarks

Allow me to conclude by saying that from a theological perspective, Ricoeur's hermeneutical self, in spite of its promise, falls short on more than one count of responding to the metaphysical malaise it so rightly describes. The mediatory practice of interpretation appears to be fraught with transcendental *aporias* caught up between reception and construction and haunted by the struggle between the one and the many.[179] Due to his determination to preserve the *noumenon* in relation to God, Ricoeur's "return" to the subject remains circumscribed within a reflective exercise, saying either too much or too little, posing a false choice between "an affirmative noetics of God" and a logic of naming whose meaning is constantly deferred.[180] As a result, the emerging structure of emancipation has been shown to bear the mark of the philosophy of consciousness which begot it. In the end, in spite of Ricoeur's subtle mediations and

---

178. Allusion to Peter's words in John 6:67: "Lord, to whom shall we go? Thou hast the words of eternal life."

179. It is important to note here that a mere criticism of historicism does not really address the theological issues involved in a genuine theology of history. It is not enough to say therefore, as Ward does, that "the subject matter is investigated, connections are made and its findings given meaning by considerations which are themselves non-historical and abstract" (Ward, *Theology and Critical Theory*, 48). The mere criticism that such a position "is dependent upon metaphysical convictions" is itself abstract. Ricoeur is well aware of this dilemma when he points to the limitations of narrative in general and narrative theology in particular. In *Critique and Conviction*, for instance, Ricoeur admits that time cannot be held "captive in the nets of narrative. . . . World time, cosmic time, is structured after the manner of the very production of the world and not after that of the production of the narrative." Ricoeur sees this admission as a final homage paid to Heidegger. Cf. Ricoeur, *Critique and Conviction*, 88. See also Ricoeur, *Figuring the Sacred*, 236ff. We shall return to this problem below.

180. Cf. Ricoeur, *Essays on Biblical Interpretation*, 94. In the next section we shall attempt to lay bare the false ideal of an affirmative noetics of God.

promising openings, the reflective subject is still trapped in a "naturalistic" reading of both texts and history.[181] In other words, Ricoeur's "return to Kant" doesn't really solve the problem. Instead, it seems to complicate things further. As in Kant, Ricoeur's "anti-naturalism" becomes the mirror-image of the paradigm it wanted to contest, thus rendering it as abstract and ultimately, ineffectual. As in Kant,[182] will and imagination, obedience and vision, don't really meet. As a consequence, a theologically meaningful "extension" of Kant doesn't really happen as the world does not sufficiently open up to God. And without a proper vision of God, a genuine "re-enchantment" of the world remains unconvincing. . . . Moreover, since the "duties of the mind," are still configured within the tight constraints of Kant's "rational Law" (with its "negative logic" and austere vision), the "hermeneutical self" remains somewhat anxious and fragile. Yet, somewhat paradoxically, proudly assuming such stance, boldly dwelling on this dialectic of saying either too much or too little. . . . Later on, we shall explore in detail how, in an authentic "theo-logical" epistemology, such "duties of the mind" have to be radically informed by God's Trinitarian action in and towards the world.

I must also point out that it is not so much Ricoeur's alleged entrapment in "modern" conceptuality (apparent in terms and distinctions like "distanciation," "objectification," "explanation vs. understanding," etc.) that is the problem, but rather his (explicit and implicit) refusal to allow the rich language of God's Trinitarian action to correct and, when necessary, to transform this conceptuality.

181. Such "naturalization" of both self (its reflective capacity) and "world" (with its implicit "tragic" overtones), is somewhat apparent, as we have seen, in Ricoeur's concept of distanciation and in his talk about the alleged "autonomy" of both self and texts. And as already noted, the concept of "productive imagination" won't solve the problem by itself. While appeals to the doctrine of the Spirit may seem appropriate in this context and a step in the right direction, as we shall see in more detail in later chapters, if we are truly to avoid naturalism in general, a relapse into a mere psychological understanding of Spirit in particular, with its plethora of problems, a full re-evaluation of Illumination must be undertaken, which, as we shall see, needs to be conducted in the larger context of God's action as Father, Son and Spirit in and towards the world. John Webster is thus right to complain about the implicit "naturalism" of many hermeneutical proposals. I will return to both, his critique and his re-evaluation of the doctrine of illumination in the last chapter.

182. While still defending Kant against the view that he banished God from his ethical theory, John E. Hare nonetheless remarks that while in Duns Scotus, obedience is a route to union with God, there is no such union in Kant where "Rational law" (obedience, respect for the law) remains an end in itself. Hare, *God's Call*, 90.

Is this to say that our engagement with Ricoeur remains significant only through its failure? Not at all! I have implicitly distanced myself from attempts to evaluate Ricoeur's work in a genetic way (reducing it to an "arche" whether this be Kant, Husserl or Heidegger), or as a mere "cultural" performance as a mediation between already established categories, and have insisted instead upon the dynamism and the semantic aim of his discourse (both with and against Ricoeur's own intention). Such an insistence has revealed along the way a number of openings.

We cannot but retain Ricoeur's effort to restore the realism of the event of history against the excesses of Fuchs and Ebeling. It is significant to note that in the *Revelation* essay he commends Pannenberg's effort implying that without a genuine encounter with history and experience the question of God remains largely subjective.[183] Yet, in the same essay, Ricoeur re-iterates his attachment to the Word. It is as "Word" that the new logic of meaning comes to us. "All theology is theology of the Word," says Ricoeur.[184] It is in the light of such claims that we may discern an incipient and promising mediation between a theology of the Word and a theology of Creation. It is noteworthy that by pointing to the resistance to revelation of a whole philosophical tradition in general and to Feuerbach's idealism of consciousness in particular, Ricoeur echoes Pannenberg's criticism of Barth's rejection of natural theology.[185] In Pannenberg's view, Barth took too much from Feuerbach's criticism of religion.[186] It

183. Ricoeur, *Essays on Biblical Interpretation*, 80.

184. Ricoeur, "Theologie de la parole," 302, in *Exégèse et Herméneutique*, 301–20. See also the link Ricoeur makes between his ontological proposal and Jüngel's theology. Ricoeur, *Oneself as Another*, 25.

185. Ricoeur may seem indeed close to Pannenberg's view of Revelation as history. Pannenberg insists in the same way that "ideas of the Word and of a God who speaks stand in great need of interpretation" (Pannenberg, *Systematic Theology*, 1:242). We find in Pannenberg a somewhat parallel flattening (albeit conceived differently) of the dynamic of God's speech in the suggestion that God always speaks within the "agreed consensus of the Church's discourse" (ibid.). This panoramic perspective may be understood as presupposing that God always speaks what the Church likes or is prepared to hear implicitly subsuming Christology and Ecclesiology under a hermeneutics of history. As in the case of Ricoeur, the insistence upon Revelation as non-heteronomous does not seem to leave sufficient space between the addressed and the addressee. In this connection it may be noted that Schwöbel is right to say that we are left in Pannenberg with a manifest difficulty (as in Hegel, it may be added) of distinguishing between divine and human agency. Cf. Schwöbel, "Rational Theology in Trinitarian Perspective," 527.

186. In spite of its problems (noted above) Pannenberg is right, I think, to stress that Barth had a different view of religion from that of Schleiermacher and Hegel. Cf.

appears now in an even clearer light that the hermeneutic which brings about such a displacement of consciousness, being as Ricoeur claims, "the reverse of Feuerbach's critique of alienation,"[187] plays the function of a theology of nature, as the implicit and necessary ground of revelation.

Richard Kerney is right to situate Ricoeur's hermeneutical effort between ethics and poetics.[188] We often find in Ricoeur appeals to Spinoza's enlarged view of ethics, ethics as the space of human action. To take this semantic aim in its full theological dimension means to look again at God's relationship with the world as a dynamic of divine and human action, to see God's story as our story. It is also to see once again *theoria* as irreducibly anchored in *praxis*, to conceive human action (our theological task included) as a form of response to God's grace. I see this as one of the most promising theological developments of Ricoeur's hermeneutical theory.

If a full blown theology of imagination still remains the task of Trinitarian theology, part of the remainder of this book is to substantiate and to build upon a way of thinking ethics and imagination together, in a view that neither opposes desire or reason to will under the aegis of an anthropological model of faculties, nor reiterates a romantic synthesis between the human and the divine (in more or less subtle forms).[189] It is against such

---

Pannenberg, *Systematic Theology*, 1:104–5. It may be also added here that in spite of Barth's radical rejection of natural religion (or perhaps precisely because of that), his position remains still too close to the consciousness model, a tendency which surfaces either in excessive epistemological concerns or in a view of God as a re-iterating subject. We shall return to these problems below.

187. Ricoeur, *Essays in Biblical Interpretation*, 109.

188. Ricoeur, *Hermeneutics of Action*, 173ff.

189. It may be said in this context that a view which opposes either metaphor or imagination to the work of the Spirit as Vanhoozer seems to suggest, remains inadequate. Cf. Vanhoozer, *Biblical Narrative*, 257, 265. Apart from the fact that such a view relapses into a psychological understanding of the Spirit as a subjective principle, it implicitly entails a problematic view of Creation. As we have seen, Ricoeur rightly draws attention to the need for a de-psychologized doctrine of the Spirit. Yet, he tends to relapse back precisely into such a vision by refusing the support of God language in general and of Trinitarian theology in particular. In his autobiography Ricoeur writes: "My primary concern, which has never wavered, not to mix *genres* together has instead drawn me closer to the notion of a philosophy without any absolute, a philosophy I saw defended by my deeply regretted friend, Pierre Thevanez, who held it to be the typical expression of a Protestant philosophy" (Ricoeur, "Intellectual Autobiography," 13). Perhaps a Protestant philosophy wanting to keep the absolute at bay, if it is to avoid a "mythologization" of either world or language (Heidegger may be suspected of doing a bit of both), can never really go beyond the interiorist tradition inaugurated by Augustine.

a background that a theological view of epistemology that does not oppose subject to object, creation to redemption, may be substantiated.

I should like to summarize these openings by suggesting two principal directions of inquiry that will be further explored theologically:

If Ricoeur's correction of Heidegger as a "return" to epistemology and ethics is to become theologically viable, we need not only a break with the ambiguities of Heidegger's "world," but also a more thorough elucidation of the "who" question. Ricoeur acknowledges that "if the universe is not originally meaningful, understanding is forever impossible."[190] It is only in the light of this ultimate Author that the "who" question may break away from the shackles of a philosophy of consciousness. In such a light, we may perhaps take Ricoeur's call to undertake again the task assumed by Hegel in the last century, in all its seriousness.[191] This would imply, however, more than a mere concern for historicality. We need instead to consider the hermeneutical task in the light of Hegel's radical claim that God can be known truly as in history we have the full revelation of God, with all the risks that this claim involves. To return to Hegel would mean to reconsider, in Barth's words, both its great promise and its great problems; it would require us to follow not only its concrete historical mediation, but also its transcendental anchoring and its dependence upon the rationalist tradition which marked its failure. The task raised before us would then be to attempt to ground the emancipatory dimension of our "descent" from ontology neither in language nor in the power of the mind, but in God's concrete relationship with the world as Father, Son and Spirit. And this brings us to our second point.

Ricoeur's claim to return from ontology to epistemological questions, contemplated as we have seen from Ricoeur's own positioning between ethics and poetics, suggested the need to devise such a return at the intersection between a doctrine of the Word and a doctrine of Creation. It moreover suggested that such a return is fundamentally an "ethical return": that is to say, on the one hand it may be assimilated as a practice, a "doxastic" practice, we may say, while on the other, that it appeals to and affects both will and imagination. Thus, to devise theological epistemology between creation and re-creation, between "is" and "ought" or between what we presently are and what we are called to be, can be fundamentally conceived as a response to God's action in and toward the

---

190. Ricoeur, *Conflict of Interpretations*, 5.
191. Cf. Ibid., 497.

world, response which by virtue of devising will and imagination together remains "free" and "rational" within the bounds of createdness.[192] Such a response therefore can never be conceived within the narrow limits of an inquiry guided by the question of meaning. Instead, it must be fully referred to the reality on which it fundamentally depends and to that which is called to return.

In one of his more recent essays[193] Ricoeur talks about the "self-complacency of hermeneutics," which he sees manifest in two opposing tendencies: hermeneutics as foundational science, as discourse about discourse, and the hermeneutical fragmentation, the infinite proliferation of "the hermeneutics of." It is extremely significant to note that Ricoeur claims that one cannot fight both battles at the same time. He believes that to do so is to engage oneself in a totalizing task. Nonetheless, as we have seen, this has effectively lead to a tendency "to move either too quick or too slow" between the one and the many.[194]

Perhaps this is the inevitable fate of any critical discourse. It is true that after Hegel it became clearer than ever before that a mediation between the two does not appear to be open to a finite, human perspective. That is why Ricoeur remains skeptical of Trinitarian language in general and of Hegel's Trinitarian speculation in particular. Ricoeur might have a point here. Nevertheless, I propose to leave such a possibility open, to give such a mediation one more chance. But before that, let us hear again Hegel's seductive voice . . .

192. This is, in fact, the potential, more often than not left unexamined, of narrative theology. The appeal of narrative rests indeed in the fact that will and imagination are addressed together. We have good reasons to hope for more than a "world of the text" as a possible world I can inhabit. As I have already suggested, the Church as an actual intersubjective reality fulfils God's promise that He would live in the midst of his people. We are addressed as persons, and in being so addressed, we may contemplate an already existing community. It is because this experience of participation precedes the dialogical experience enabling us to hear the call as Good News not as a mere summons that a theological view of rationality which is truly *a posteriori* is possible. More about that in chapter 6.

193. Ricoeur, *Figuring the Sacred*, 304.

194. Plato's famous remark "the wise men of our time are either too quick or too slow, in conceiving plurality in unity" (Plato, *Philebus*, 161) is still highly relevant for our own age . . . A proper criterion for such a dialectic is only conceivable within a Trinitarian framework.

# Part II

## The Absolute Self—Hegel's Journey from Revelation to Meaning[1]

He who would speak to another of this
Though he spoke with angel tongues
Would feel the poverty of words.

HEGEL, *ELEUSIS*

SO TYPICALLY ROMANTIC WERE those verses that few could have guessed that Hegel would be able to turn this hopeless feeling of the "poverty of words" into the bliss of Absolute knowledge. Indeed, Hegel's philosophy appears to be no less than an initiatory ascent, confident that it can break the silence, and make us hear the Truth again, or perhaps even more, stare it in the face and dwell in its presence.

1. I am aware that it is Hegel's ascent from untruth to truth in the *Phenomenology* that can be read as the precursor of all inquires into meaning where the question of truth is subordinated to that of meaning. In such a case, Hegel's effort would remain under the auspices of a move "from meaning to Revelation." Nonetheless, if a certain continuity is allowed to Hegel's works, then there is an important sense in which a theological reading is suggested to offer the condition of possibility of such an endeavor in the first place. Such an ascent is possible for Hegel because the truth has been revealed. Hegel's problem, as we shall see below, is precisely the way in which this truth is conceived.

Part II: The Absolute Self

We were left, at the end of the previous section with a rather nostalgic subject. A subject in desperate need for Revelation, "ready to receive it with joy" yet, incapable of an adequate reconciliation with his/her own concept of Reason, lying fatally, as it did, in the shadow of the transcendental inquiry. Such a subject appeared to propel a type of rationality which claimed both too little and too much at the same time. There has been a longing for a different type of encounter, and indeed a growing hope for a "promised land" at the end of the journey. Yet, the longing prevailed, since like Moses, we may at best contemplate it from afar, but never enjoy it.[2] Criticism tends to live from its own substance, and the promissory tone of Ricoeur's radical disruption of meaning at the very heart of meaning was no exception.

Now to be sure, this necessary passage through "the valley of the shadow of death" made a notorious career in Hegel. And as has been already anticipated, it was precisely the totalizing claim of the logic in which this passage was wrapped, that overshadowed the Hegelian proposal. Yet, as our analysis has shown, a mere return to Kant had the equally unhealthy tendency to render belief in revelation itself as idolatrous. Let us engage once again with the Hegel who "departs" from Kant, the philosopher who makes Revelation the very presupposition and possibility of truth. A closer examination of Hegel's thought might be beneficial in more than one respect.

Hegel, like no other, powerfully pleads for the need of ontology. "One cannot remain forever in the square before the temple. . . . Nor is there love for the truth which is not possession of the truth."[3] This bold invitation called for a radical approach and for an equally radical method. And here, Hegel is incredibly modern in more than one aspect. He argued like no other, against most of his contemporaries and long before modern reaction to positive epistemologies (Kuhn, Polanyi), that scientific knowledge requires one to leave oneself entirely within the possession of the object.

More importantly however, Hegel appreciated perhaps better than many theologians of his day the explanatory power of Christian Revelation. His philosophical approximations of many theological themes exerted a long lasting fascination. The spell of the phenomenological and existentialist search for mediations (self-other, Subject-object,

2. Allusion to Ricoeur's own words, in Ricoeur, *Conflict of Interpretations*, 24.
3. Hyppolite, *Genesis and Structure of Hegel's Phenomenology of Spirit*, 5.

Universal-particular, knowledge and being) fades when one realizes not only that Hegel was there long before them, but that the grand horizon of his philosophical compass makes the latter appear as no more than a regional philosophical exercise. Merleau-Ponty captures well this insight when he writes: "Hegel is at the origin of all the great philosophical ideas of the past century—for example Marxism, the philosophy of Nietzsche, phenomenology, German existentialism, psychoanalysis; it was Hegel who started the attempt to explore the irrational and integrate it into an expanded reason, which remains the task of our century."[4]

But this latter remark brings to the center not only the promise but also the problem of the Hegelian enterprise, that is, his idea of Reason. It was in fact the idea of rationality itself, in its various forms that has come under the critique of today's postmodern discourse. To ascertain a standard of reason, it is suggested, is to reiterate an emphatic Cartesian self. The recourse to Revelation does not really solve the problem, but rather radicalizes it, since no epistemic practice can effectively separate metaphysical claims from subjectivity. Moreover, the Revelational claims are perhaps especially under the suspicion of what Habermas called "systematically distorted communication." An examination of Hegel's project would enable an enquiry into the roots and nature of this suspicion. Whilst such investigation might perhaps reinforce some of Ricoeur's fears hinted at in the first part, we also hope that a careful evaluation of Hegel's conceptuality might point to viable ways to overcome the problem. The "reversed" detour through Hegel (Revelation, History, Meaning) suggesting as we shall try to argue, a fundamental feature of the basic grammar of his project, would enable us to assess both the force and the weakness of such an approach. More specifically, by focusing upon a number of problems of the Hegelian "middle" we hope to indicate the contours and the proper framework of a genuinely "theo-logical" concept of knowledge.

4. Merleau-Ponty, *Sens et Non-Sens*, 109.

*4*

# Hegel the Philosopher of Revelation

THE PURPOSE OF THIS chapter is to set Hegel in context. I shall formally adopt a historical-systematic approach without delving too deeply into the details of Hegel's conceptual intricacies. Nonetheless, some general clarifications will be attempted about both content and method, the nature of the subject matter, and the nature of the approach itself. By looking at the kind of claims Hegel makes within both the overall perspective of his philosophy and the general intellectual climate of his day, a particular interpretative position will come to view, pleading for the centrality of the theological framework of interpretation, if a holistic understanding of his claims is to be obtained.

Let me say a few words about the more specific ramifications of this working hypothesis. In regard to the Hegelian text itself, a "synthetic" reading will be preferred. A holistic rhetoric may admittedly be used as a subterfuge for dealing with the concrete text. Yet, the analytical work, which explains the details without illuminating the whole, or points to the contradiction (playing one passage against another), without seeing its resolution is, as Hegel would say, the poor and empty work of *Verstand*. Hegel's philosophical style forbids a too tight and peaceful advance from one topic to the next. Understanding Hegel requires somewhat of a movement in circles, coming back and forth, in the hope that the result will illuminate the start and vice versa.

With regard to Hegel's famous terms, as has been often remarked, it is notoriously difficult to remain faithful to Hegel's categorial development by using a different terminology than his. One of Hegel's fundamental beliefs was that the part and the whole do reflect each other being organically related. Altering a small part requires the reinterpretation of the whole. Establishing one center or main theme refashions the grammar of the entire system. And if one is to avoid saying either much less, or saying something else, as both Fackenheim and Findlay suggest, faithfulness to Hegel's own language and structure is essential, especially when systematic judgments are made. Attentiveness to both the "historical" Hegel and Hegel the "logician" or the "category theorist" is thus required. The basic presupposition is that Hegel deals with real problems in real history, which still are, more or less, our problems. Against the view that Hegel is helplessly caught up in a historical period whose *Weltbild* is fundamentally *passé* and therefore by and large irrelevant to us, we tend to side with Findlay ("Hegel deals with problems of permanent philosophical interest and importance"[1]), and, having a still fresh memory of the long (and disastrous) historical career of a particular Hegelian ideology, not ignore Kojeve ("It is possible that in reality the future of the world, and thus the meaning of the present and that of the past, depend, in the last analysis, on the way in which the Hegelian writings are interpreted today."[2]) In such an approach, biography and historical questions are important but not central. In fact, Hegel's own concept of truth aims at transcending both a sociology and a psychology of knowledge.

Yet, saying that, it must be pointed out that this "faithfulness" to Hegel's terminology or to "Hegel's spirit," is emphatically not our ultimate criterion. Indeed, in the light of our theological concerns, a balanced hermeneutical method would not only carefully consider and assess alternative readings of Hegel[3] but would further inquire into the reasons for such a situation in the light of the referential intention of Hegel's own discourse.

## Enlightenment, Romanticism, and Beyond

If we were to concentrate in a statement the most general feature of Romanticism, we would probably follow Craig, in pointing towards an

---

1. Findlay, *Hegel: A Re-examination*, 11.

2. Kojeve, *Hegel, Marx et le Christianisme*, 339–66, quoted by Hyppolite, *Genesis and Structure of Hegel's Phenomenology of Spirit*, xxviii.

3. Iwan Iljin argues for a complementarity of hermeneutic schemes, maintaining that Hegel's logic can support three different readings, i.e., a scientific systematic, a theological-religious, and a cosmological. Cf. Iljin, *Die Philosophie Hegels*, 208, quoted by O'Regan, *Heterodox Hegel*, 92. My analysis of Hegel is indebted to O'Regan's competent study.

overwhelming emphasis on wholeness and unity.[4] Yet this stress upon unity is more specific both in its origin and its proposals. In regard to its source, it may be noted in passing that it took shape as a revolt, a reaction, and in this sense it has to be referred back to *Aufklärung*, its opponent. As to its proposals, in the context of the celebrated nostalgia for the ancient world, a revival of the old mythical, "spirit-filled" epochs has been sought, over against the dry, austere, rational utopias of the Enlightenment.

Hence, it is not that the theme of unity and reconciliation appeared as a new thematic for thought for the Romantics. There is a sense in which, of course, such a theme is as old as the tacit sadness induced by the puzzling sense of the "fallenness of existence" with its consequent longing for Redemption. Rather it had been the acuity of such perception in the light of the disruption effected by the Enlightenment, which has made the response more dramatic and urgent. The stable metaphysical structure and worldview of the medieval period were far behind. With the dawn of Renaissance first, and Enlightenment afterwards, along with a growing awareness of the human ability to investigate and discover the secret laws of nature, we witness a shaking of the medieval equilibrium. The development of science within the shape of the emerging Newtonian paradigm, raised notions like autonomy, certitude and scientific proof to the status of the highest virtues of the age. It almost seems that starting from himself, man might eventually be able to climb the staircase up to God himself. The intellectual climate is gradually penetrated by this causal and mechanistic construal. That such has been the confidence of the *Aufklärer* is vividly exemplified by the focus of their intellectual concerns. The essay question presented for a contest under the auspices of The Royal Academy of Science from Berlin in 1762 is telling in this respect. "Whether metaphysical judgements generally, and in particular the fundamental principles of natural theology and morals, are capable of proofs as evident as those of geometry?" Ironically, Kant had been the great defeated in this contest . . .[5]

In fact, it was precisely Kant who, whilst still advocating the Enlightenment stress upon autonomy, tempered somewhat its exaggerated hopes. His series of distinctions (between practical and theoretical reason, between the thing-in-itself and the thing-as-it-appears-to-us), establish limits for Reason while allowing, as he was convinced, room

4. Craig, *Mind of God and the Works of Man*, 136.
5. Solomon and Higgins, *Age of German Idealism*, 9–10.

for faith. We can investigate the physical world *ad infinitum*, says Kant, yet, we shall never be able to know reality as it is in itself, since there are some problems inherent in our very exercise of knowledge. The problem is not in reality but in us. Kant's "Copernican Revolution" enjoyed a wide appreciation in a relatively short time. Whereas in the medieval world-view it was somewhat felt that despite our limitations, being in the state of grace we are made partakers of the divine reality, which consequently reconciles us with creation, Kant left no hope for anything similar.

Such was the nature and magnitude of fragmentation by the time the Romantics launched their attack against the Enlightenment. In a spiritless age, the yearning of the Romantics was for the recovery of life and concrete relations, broken by their predecessors, between man, nature and God.

Yet, Hegel's own relationship to both Enlightenment and Romanticism is more complex. Let us engage ourselves in a closer examination by considering first his departure from Kant. In his *Critique of Pure Reason*, Kant reconfirms in many ways what has been increasingly felt as being the major problem of the Enlightenment heritage, namely, the sovereignty of instrumentalist rationality. Indeed, while turning a skeptical eye to the naïve optimism of the Enlightenment,[6] Kant remains faithful to the celebrated adage *sapere aude*, the Enlightenment autonomy principle.[7] Yet, an important qualification is made: we cannot know the things in themselves, we know them only as they appear to us. Thus, Kant opens the way for the critique of such a rationality. But Kant's proposal would soon dissatisfy both the theologian and the scientist. It is not surprising therefore to find in the philosophy after Kant an increasing concern for some kind of a unified perspective able to heal the Kantian divide. A single self-evident principle, or a reliable starting point was to be sought, which might enable the kind of certainty and foundation required by a systematic science. It was felt that the series of distinctions effected by Kant (intellect-sensibility, theoretical-practical, subject-object) must originate in such a fundamental, most primitive principle. The radicalization of enquiry radicalized in turn the approach to the nature of the "I." Hence we witness a rather "mythological" self in Fichte,[8] as a result of a somewhat inward grounding of the transcendental Ego, or a shift

6. See Kant, *Religion within the Limits of Reason Alone*, 15–50.

7. "Have courage to use your own mind." Kant, "Beantwortung der Frage," 481–94.

8. I used Findlay's designation. See Findlay, *Hegel: A Re-examination*, 50ff. For Fichte the positing of the Ego is primordially a free act, an ethical gesture which divides reality in self and non-self.

of emphasis from inwardness to outwardness in Schelling's positing of a final coincidence between Ego and Nature, the subjective and the objective principles.[9]

Hegel is dissatisfied with both solutions. It is certainly not only the problem of a starting point. It is the very nature of the positing of the problem, which is at stake. To be sure, Hegel started as an enthusiastic Kantian (i.e., his "Lives of Jesus" where Jesus is portrayed merely as a moral teacher), to continue with a Romantic note of protest against institutionalised religion (i.e., his *Early Theological Writings*). Yet, already in his early notes Hegel writes:

> Either the ideal is within me, in which case it is not an ideal, or it is outside of me, in which case I can never attain it.[10]

It has been this dilemma that called for an option able to transcend both a mere choice between inwardness or outwardness, and a facile mediation between the two. By laying bare the *aporia* of the starting point, Hegel's proposal unveils the need for ontology. A number of things may be said in this context.

First, to reinstate the primacy of "content" is to reopen the concern for totality. The subject matter of Philosophy is the Whole. That is why everything is important for Hegel, and nothing can be ignored. But there is more. Every movement of thought is a movement of Being as well. The pair *an sich* (thing-in-itself) and *für sich* (thing-for-itself) for instance is employed to suggest that both subject and object are but moments of the same process, which lose coherence precisely when separated. Consequently, "what is rational is real and what is real is rational."[11] The ultimate truth must be expressed "not as substance but as subject as well."[12] This anti-substantialist insight further radicalizes Kant. Since the claims of knowledge are ontological claims, it follows that Kant's limit is an anthropological limit. Whereas there is a sense in which Hegel recognizes such limitation, he points out that there is no reason why the lack should not be in reality as a whole, as well. Why should the Kantian antinomies be restricted just to a limited set? Is not the puzzling picture of history

---

9. See for instance the introductory comments from his transcendental system. Cf. Schelling, *System of Transcendental Idealism*, 1–6.

10. Quoted by Hyppolite, *Genesis and Structure of Hegel's Phenomenology of Spirit*, 198.

11. Hegel, *Philosophy of Right*, 17.

12. Hegel, *Phenomenology*, 80.

an indication that in fact the very structure of reality is antinomical?[13] Hegel demythologizes thus the Kantian *noumena* by radicalizing Kant's skepticism. Perhaps there is nothing *more* out there to be known. The methodical doubt of Descartes is thus demoted from its hypothetical intelligible order and given concrete expression. As Küng has suggested, Hegel does not merely start with doubt, but consistently rests upon it.[14] The "existential" Hegel is, however, just a "moment" of the "absolute" Hegel, and doubt is merely the necessary passage towards certainty. Correlatively, this movement, or "coming to consciousness" is not merely a psychological or pedagogical experience but a movement of Being. This situation led some commentators to talk about an "objectification" of the categories (Kantian and Aristotelian). They are no longer mere instruments for thought, readily available to be applied to reality, but real entities, comparable to a certain extent to Plato's ideas.[15]

This suggests *a new understanding of knowledge.*[16] Since the Truth with capital T has its own rationality and mode of disclosure, the search for the right method cannot be done outside the truth. Method and content cannot be separated. "True scientific knowledge . . . demands abandonment to the very life of the object."[17] Hegel complains that Kantian Philosophy is a philosophy of *Verstand* (understanding) being thus condemned by its very nature to finitude. The kind of transcendence allowed by *Verstand* is what Hegel calls "bad infinity" (an infinite search without closure; a perpetual discovery of particulars without an accompanying integration within the Universal; a forever new certainty but without meaning). True Philosophy however, must rise beyond such a position, to a Philosophy of Reason (*Vernunft*) or of Spirit (*Geist*).

Nonetheless, Hegel uses the form-content distinction. Its meaning though, like the meaning of so many other terms in Hegel, is re-qualified. Content and form are not abstract categories expressing some method-content differentiation, but again, rather moments of the same movement

13. See Hegel, *Science of Logic*, trans. Wallace, 76–79.

14. Küng, *Does God Exist?*, 146.

15. See Weiss, "Dialectic and the Science of Logic," 86–91.

16. The *locus classicus* of Hegel's systematic critique of Kant is to be found in his *Lectures on the History of Philosophy*. For a detailed evaluation of Hegel's critique of Kant's epistemology, see for instance Hartnack, "Categories and Things-in-Themselves," 77–86.

17. Hegel, *Phenomenology*, 112.

of consciousness, or better, Spirit.[18] They point towards *degrees of authenticity*, to use an existentialist expression, since the content is always the same. It is the extent of *identification* with this content, or appropriation of it that varies. The forms (perception, feeling, will, concept, etc.) point towards qualitative modes of identification. It is important to see that this is more than simply an epistemological distinction. In the final analysis, as a movement of being, as it is, it heralds nothing less than a journey from appearance to Truth, from nothingness to Being, from death to Life. The passage from form to content is not merely a theoretical exercise, no longer a mere problem of knowledge, but a problem of salvation.

Let me briefly sketch the more concrete implications of these general points:

- The concern for unity and wholeness marks a decisive move towards *Systematicity*. "The truth is the whole,"[19] and only the whole can express the truth. "The systematic development of truth in scientific form can alone be the true shape in which truth exists."[20]

- Hegel also moves from the Kantian *a priori* to a fundamentally *a posteriori* type of philosophizing. It is true that this formal allegiance to a retrospective view is notoriously ambiguous.[21] Nonetheless, as we shall see shortly, his fundamental theological concerns explicitly call for such an approach.

- *Realism.* If we are to attach some idealism to Hegel, then such idealism is clearly different from that of Kant (and Fichte and Schelling

18. For details, see Hegel, introduction to *Science of Logic*, trans. Wallace, 5ff, para. 3.

19. Hegel, *Phenomenology*, 81.

20. Ibid., 70.

21. Charles Taylor argues that the first three chapters of Phenomenology are an essay in transcendental argument (Taylor, "Opening Arguments of the Phenomenology," 151–87). To view Hegel's *Phenomenology* as an extended transcendental exercise somewhat reinforces the credibility of a speculative field belonging to both Kant and Hegel which, as we have argued in chapter 3, plays such a significant role in Ricoeur's post-Hegelian Kantianism. If we insist however on the referential claim of Hegel's discourse we must stress that Hegel wants us to believe that no standard of truth is substantially contained by the subject who does the investigation in *Phenomenology*. It is history which explains itself. The task of the philosopher is to recollect rather than to predict. "We are naïve if we fancy that a philosophy can transcend its contemporary world." Hegel, *Philosophy of Right*, 11. For analyses which stress this aspect, see also Hyppolite, *Genesis and Structure of the Phenomenology of Spirit*, 4, 21; Kaufmann, "Hegel's Myth and Its Method," 44; Findlay, *Hegel: A Re-examination*, 23.

alike). Hegel's concern is precisely to bring God back into the world and that is translated into a paramount interest for the historical and the concrete. Findlay rightly points out that Hegel is rather a realist.[22] Nevertheless, a whole cluster of terms and especially their meaning is important in such an assessment. As we shall see, the problem is not so much that Hegel suggests that reality is a "creation" of the mind, as it is often claimed. The more important problems are rather "whose Mind" and what "reality," and what is the nature of both.[23]

And finally, let me make a few preliminary remarks about the more generic way in which Hegel's philosophical method is discussed, namely, his famous *dialectic*. It is difficult to try to "explain" dialectic as it is equally difficult to find another generic term to describe it. We can make a start by referring to Hegel's extensive use of the rich German term *Aufhebung*. *Aufhebung*, rendered often "to sublate," means equally to discard, to take up afresh or to raise. First of all, dialectic implies movement, process. In more explicit metaphysical terms, such a movement is not a formal advance of external contingencies which "happen" to interact and issue forth new realities, but a fundamentally internal and teleologically oriented dynamic of *Geist*. It is a necessary movement of differentiation, of "death" and "resurrection," of going out and returning in, of continual configuration and advance. Dialectic is not simply a method of "arriving at the truth" (as the Dialectic of the Greeks and especially the Platonic dialogues have been usually understood[24]) but rather reflects the very nature of truth itself. Again, it is not the "yes" and "no" of the investigat-

---

22. Findlay, *Hegel: A Re-examination*, 22ff.

23. An interesting parallel with the modern phenomenon of "virtual reality" can be drawn at this point. The advance of technology can produce in principle a world which would be "real" in every empirical sense, that is to say, open to "verification" in respect to all the five senses (if we are optimistic in our scientific prognosis). This potential scenario only confirms that "reality" does not come to us "by careful observation" (Luke 17:21) and finds itself in need of a more fundamental grounding. In such a light, only a dynamic and relational criterion of reality may reveal the fundamental inadequacy of virtual reality as a mere product of a finite mind, where a space for the idea of freedom is hardly conceivable, for instance. Our discussion of freedom in the next chapter will enable a closer investigation of such problems.

24. As O'Regan remarks, late Platonism tended to understand dialectic "as the study and discourse not of the way towards the forms but of the relation between forms, which relation is, in significant part, constituted by otherness" (cf. O'Regan, *Heterodox Hegel*, 101). On the other hand, Gadamer suggests that in fact Hegel is the first to actually grasp the depth of Plato's dialectic. Gadamer, *Hegel's Dialectic*, 6–7.

ing subject, but the "yes" and "no" of Being itself. Such a radical claim has continued to puzzle interpreters of Hegel ever since. Attempts to arrive at milder versions of Hegel's dialectic are therefore not surprising.[25] Crosso and Petry[26] for instance suggest that contradiction and dialectic belong properly to the logical or discursive sphere respectively. Milder versions of dialectic are also to be found in Taylor and Findlay, arguably still too epistemological in character.[27]

Whilst concern with Hegel's *Logic* tended to produce a more descriptive account of Dialectic (as referring predominantly to the movement of thought), the emphasis upon the "historical" Hegel (the Hegel of *Phenomenology*) led to an understanding of Dialectic as movement of being within history, with a consequent strong view of agency.[28] The first perspective is more concerned with being, yet it comes up with a more epistemological rendering of Dialectic, having the tendency to formalize the movement of being. By contrast, the second approach (especially evident in left-wing, non-metaphysical interpretations), is more concerned with knowledge, yet its Dialectic is more ontological in character. Whereas it takes seriously the movement of being, its excessive stress upon social and empirical aspects issues in a too "externalist" interpretation of Dialectic.

As we have seen, for Hegel the method must necessarily reflect the content. Dialectic cannot remain at a merely critical or analytical function. The ideal of a "transparent" logic is anticipated in this way. True Logic must be Onto-Logic. An eloquent example of dialectical movement is offered by Hegel's own relation to both Enlightenment and Romanticism. Referring to *Aufklärung*, Hegel suggests that its glorious

25 We deliberately avoided using the well-known categories of thesis, antithesis and synthesis as representing a distortion of Hegel's fundamental intentions. It seems to be quite an unanimous consensus among scholars in this respect especially since Müller's convincing criticism of such an account. Cf. Müller, "Hegel Legend of 'Thesis, Antithesis and Synthesis,'" 411–14.

26. Cf. O'Regan, *Heterodox Hegel*, 141.

27. In Findlay for instance the contradictory element of yes and no is solved by pointing to the *use* such a combination is put (Findlay, *Hegel: A Re-examination*, 25ff.). Findlay describes Hegel's "categorial development" as a repeated meta-hermeneutical exercise (a move to ever-superior levels of discourse). See also Findlay, "Contemporary Relevance of Hegel," 1–20. To be sure, the argument is compelling and his illustrations brilliant. Yet, the emphasis on use seems closer to Wittgenstein than to Hegel. It has to be remembered that in Hegel the meaning is neither regional nor separated from Truth.

28. See also Kaufman's comment in Kaufmann, "Young Hegel and Religion," 61.

victory over dogma and superstition, is a defeat as well. And the "positive" religion, as he calls it, is the very expression of such a defeat.[29] Genuine advance must "sublate" its opponent rather than radically opposing it. Such a move requires an "intellectualization" of Romanticism and a "spiritualization" of Enlightenment.[30]

In the hope that some light has been thrown upon Hegel's thought, in the context of his own intellectual development, we shall now turn to a closer treatment of Hegel's relation to the Christian Religion.[31]

## Reforming Theology: Hegel as a Christian Thinker.

It was not only that Hegel was interested in religion. He considered himself a Christian thinker. Moreover, he was convinced that religion and philosophy have the same subject matter, the Truth. For Hegel, the search for truth, is not idle philosophical exercise. It involves the whole person and above all is religious in character.[32] Hegel talks about it, with high regard, almost with reverence. It is like entering the holy of holies, being allowed into the inner sanctuary of truth.

> The object of religion, like that of philosophy, is the eternal truth, God and nothing but God and the explication of God. Philosophy is only explicating itself when it explicates religion, and when it explicates itself it is explicating religion. For the *thinking* spirit is what penetrates this object, the truth; it is thinking that enjoys the truth and purifies the subjective consciousness. Thus religion and philosophy coincide in one. . . . But each of them, religion as well as philosophy, is the service of God in a way peculiar to it.[33]

29. Hegel, *Faith and Knowledge*, 56ff.

30. I paraphrase Kroner's famous assessment: "Hegel was called upon to intellectualise Romanticism and to spiritualise Enlightenment." Kroner, *Von Kant bis Hegel*, quoted by Kaufmann, "Young Hegel and Religion," 73.

31. There are many philosophers who acknowledge the crucial importance of Hegel's theology in understanding his system (e.g., Findlay, Fackenheim, Iwan Iljin, Claude Bruaire, etc.). What exactly counts as "theological" however and whether this theology really "opens" Hegel's philosophy usually depends on the particular commitments of the critic.

32. Religion is more than the experience of God as in the case of Schleiermacher, implying the self-Revelation of God in history. See for instance Hegel, *Lectures on the Philosophy of Religion*, 1:149–73.

33. Ibid., 1:152–53.

As Hegel himself is well aware, such synthesis is far from being new. The Church Fathers, and the medievals used philosophy extensively in developing their dogmatic teachings. Two fundamental intentions lie behind Hegel's endeavor.

First, he wants to address the ills of the traditional medieval approach. More precisely Hegel fights against an abstract and substantial view of divinity to which attributes were applied in an utterly unrelated and artificial way. To this end, Hegel is committed to articulating an authentic theology of the divine names.[34] And secondly, Hegel renders the Romantic reaction to rational theology even more misguided. And precisely here, in Hegel's view, lies the problem of the theology of his day. Schleiermacher is the best instance of such an approach. In his account, theology's task is not so much to illuminate the nature of the divine, but more to enlighten our Christian religious experience. Such a treatment of theology's task robs Christian dogmatic of its very content. There is indeed a case for saying that Hegel misreads Schleiermacher when he calls him an antirationalist,[35] yet if his target is the Kantian *Verstand*, he is probably not far off the mark. Schleiermacher, in Hegel's view, instead of leading the Kantian productive imagination (which he himself considered as having authentic speculative value) towards *Vernunft*, collapsed it back into finitude by ascribing ultimate transcendental value to feeling.

## Revelational Content: The Centrality of Trinity

Hegel's attitude does not stop at the level of a mere criticism, but is determined to suggest solutions as well. If theology failed to fulfil its task in giving dogmatic expression to the logos of God (Theo-Logos), it remains the task of philosophy to fill this gap. Hegel is surprisingly lucid when he notes the radical departure of Romantic Intuitionism from the traditional doctrines.

---

34. The science of Logic as the advance from *Sein* to *Begriff* (from Being to Concept), or the categorial development in a philosophical perspective can be regarded as *Logica Divina*, therefore as a theology of the Divine Names. For details, see O'Regan, *Heterodox Hegel*, 86ff.

35. See O'Regan, *Heterodox Hegel*, 36. Such a position is implicit in Gunton's rendering of Schleiermacher. He suggests that the beginning of systematization is to be found in Schleiermacher, who considered Revelation to be "suprarational" (the implication being that it is at least rational, conceptual in form). See Gunton, *Actuality of Atonement*, 11.

> In recent theology very few of the dogmas of the earlier system of ecclesiastical confessions have survived or at least retained the importance previously attributed to them, and others have not been set in their place.[36]

Hegel does not refrain from giving examples:

> For though Christ as reconciler and saviour is still constantly made the focus of faith, nevertheless what formerly was called in orthodox dogmatics the work of salvation has taken on a significance so strongly psychological and so very prosaic that only the semblance of the ancient doctrine of the church remains. . . . It must still seem that the most weighty doctrines have lost much of their interest, faith in the Trinity for example, or the miracles in the Old and New Testament, etc.[37]

Hence, Revelation means positive content for Hegel in which Trinity is foundational (against Schleiermacher) and it means meaningful content as well (against the abstract medieval depiction of God). Apophaticism must be fought in all its forms, whether implicit or explicit. This revelational theme comes back time and again, whether in implicit form in the *Science of Logic* or *Phenomenology* or in more explicit terms in *Philosophy of History* or *Lectures on the Philosophy of Religion*. Christianity is the Absolute, the Consummate religion, the last and the most superior form of the manifestation of the Spirit. The mystery has been revealed in Christianity (cf. Eph 1:9). Therefore the way in which Christianity's content is to be positively articulated, and the richness of the doctrine recaptured once again, is by bringing Trinity back to the center of the discourse about God. In criticizing the rational theology's inability to attribute meaning to the term God, Hegel writes:

> The result is that one only knows in general *that* God is; but otherwise this supreme being is inwardly empty and dead. It is not to be grasped as the living God, as concrete content; it is not to be grasped as Spirit. . . . Thus it is just this definition of God by the church as a Trinity that is the concrete determination and nature of God as spirit; and spirit is an empty word if it is not grasped in this determination.[38]

---

36. Hegel, *Lectures on the Philosophy of Religion*, 1:156.

37. Ibid., 156–57.

38. Ibid., 126–27.

In sum, this rather bold and confident tone appears to be a *prima facie* confirmation of our working hypothesis: Hegel's apparent loose and sometimes puzzling language gathers in itself both philosophical and theological concerns, and a theological reading not only adds richness and intelligibility to his overall project, but in the last resort, rescues such intelligibility. We need, however, to further test this hypothesis against the rather different tone of Hegel's early writings before attempting a preliminary thematization of the main features characterizing Hegel's system.

There has been a long tradition of denial of Hegel's real Christianity. Left-wing interpretation of Hegel tends to look more to the early writings of Hegel and to the *Phenomenology*. In such an interpretation the young, revolutionary Hegel, Hegel the admirer of Napoleon gradually gives up his enthusiasm and conforms to the acceptable *status quo*. While it is true that Hegel's sharp criticism is directed indeed, not only against Christian theology ("Enlightened" or Romantic) but against Christianity itself, (especially when compared to the Greek ideal),[39] it is quite clear that he revised his views about that.[40] All his mature works prove that there is no suggestion that the Greek ideal would be somewhat superior to Christianity, which is the Absolute Religion. After a theological disillusionment at Tübingen, and possibly under the influence of Herder, Hegel, indeed, opposed a Romantic version of philohellenism to the dry, historicist approach of his theology teachers. We witness, however, a gradual departure from both the revolt against the "positivity" of Christianity and the Kantian, exemplarist approach, towards a more ontological understanding of Christianity. Such an interpretation would in fact be consonant with Hegel's own dialectic method. A finite negation turns up as a subsequent affirmation. Moreover, since Hegel listens (and partially approves) almost anything as having some truth, it would be at least surprising to learn that he secretly professed a radical denial of Christianity all along.[41] Certainly, a hasty conclusion that formal allegiance to a series of traditional doctrines would unproblematically render Hegel's

39. See for instance Jesus contrasted to Socrates. Hegel, *Early Theological Writings*, 82ff.

40. There are numerous examples of explicit denials of his early views: i.e., that Jesus is not merely a teacher of the Idea, like Socrates (cf. Hegel, *Lectures on the Philosophy of Religion*, 3:244n215, 316, 368). A similar point is made by Pannenberg when he discusses Hegel's recourse to the Greek's conception of freedom in his early writings. Cf. Pannenberg, *Basic Questions in Theology*, 3:148.

41. Jacques D'Hondt seems to insinuate such a view. See D'Hondt, *Hegel Secret*. Of course, "the meaning" of Hegel's approval of Christianity is another question.

philosophy "Christian," is equally misleading. Words may indeed deceive at times, and the hermeneutic of suspicion is not to be discarded too easily. Yet, rather than "deciding" for a non-Christian stance from the outset and systematically "explaining it away" whenever it seems to surface, it would be wiser to contemplate the whole with a minimum set of presuppositions. To ignore or to explain away the theological dimension, is to run the risk of reductionism, of prematurely concluding that Hegel is after all, mistaken.[42]

A good illustration of this latter point is suggested by Hegel's departure from the mathematical physical paradigm which dominated Kant's critical philosophy. As we have already noted, this is not to say that he abandons his commitment to the empirical world. It rather points to his undeterred belief that such a framework cannot account for the complexity of life. In fact "life" has been, as Marcuse suggested,[43] more or less consistently an ontological concept until the writing of *Phenomenology*.[44] A further advance on the "ladder of being" would eventually instate Spirit as the supreme ontological category. In the last resort, it is the Trinitarian God of Christianity who provides the paradigm, the criteria and the content for speculative thought.

# Revelational Content:
## Theological Themes in Hegel's Terminology

In what follows, under the guidance of this framework of interpretation, we shall embark upon a preliminary analysis of a number of theological themes from Hegel's terminology. It has been repeatedly stressed that a somewhat Heraclitean theory of truth as change or process, implicit in Hegel's dialectic, makes its system able to assimilate opposing principles into ever higher syntheses. Such a procedure transforms every potential enemy into an ally, making any critique of Hegel at least doubly difficult. Hegel points at times to the fact that it is *the very nature of reality* which calls for such a procedure. But what is the ground of

42. Popper's harsh criticism of Hegel may fit well this description. Popper, *Open Society and Its Enemies*, 2:27ff.

43. Marcuse, *Hegel's Ontology and Theory of Historicity*, 201–18, quoted by O'Regan, *Heterodox Hegel*, 123.

44. See, e.g., his illustration of the dialectical advance in the preface of *Phenomenology*, by comparing it with the development of a fruit from its bud. Hegel, *Phenomenology*, 68.

differentiation for Hegel? Does history really invite the kind of "seamless" dialectic Hegel is proposing?

Hegel starts by closely examining the Dialectics of the Greeks.[45] He moves, however, beyond their understanding of Dialectic in the direction of a stronger emphasis upon the relations between the categories, questioning the accidental character present in the very practice of predication.[46] Differentiation must eventually reflect a fundamental unity and conversely, we have differentiation in nature, because there is differentiation in God himself. This is not to say that God is "deduced" from reality. Rather the structure of reality is seen as reflecting God in the light of Revelation. For Hegel, indeed, God is not outside, beyond or above the world. He remains infinite and transcendent, yet He manifests himself in the finite reality. Since God and only God is the truth, the truth of reality is necessarily bound to God. We have, therefore, an equal stress upon both the concrete constitutive force of the particular, and its radical dependence upon the universal. In itself, the particular is transient while the universal is empty. As we shall see in more detail below, this unusual contrast is structural to Hegel's system being explicitly connected to the being of God. This goes further than saying that the universal and the particular must be thought together. It ultimately means to relate the problem of the one and the many to the very being of God himself. But to unpack this dimension in relation to history is to touch upon another theological theme, that of *Reconciliation*. History can be rational for Hegel because the "death" of particularity performs an ontological function. In other words, reconciliation carries with it more than the anticipation of the whole, bringing to the scene the means and the grounds of such a unity. Agency and history are inextricably bound to redemption in Hegel, in which the *Good Friday* motif is a central symbol. There is a victory in every defeat and a latent defeat in every victory. The very power of speculative thought rests upon such motive.[47] This brings us to the richest concept from Hegel's proposal, the locus where reconciliation finds its ultimate expression, the concept of Spirit.

---

45. In the Jena Logic, as Gadamer notes, "difference" is even called "the many." Gadamer, *Hegel's Dialectic*, 12.

46. Gadamer, *Hegel's Dialectic*, 16–17.

47. This might have been one of the most powerful arguments for a basic continuity of Hegel's thought. Such a case is weakened, however, as Hegel "invests" so much in this symbol that eventually it may in principle reconcile everything (God and man, universal and particular theism and atheism, etc.).

Part II: The Absolute Self

Various proposals have been made in regard to the meaning and origin of *Geist*, from more or less direct identifications with the Holy Spirit or mystical versions of the traditional doctrine of the soul to the idea of universal subject understood either metaphysically or purely in sociological or historical terms. There have been suggestions that Hegel's starting point has been the Kantian "transcendental apperception."[48] As it is well known, the "I which accompanies me in all my representations," is for Kant a formal principle, a regulative idea which enables a synthetic unity of all representations. For Kant, this "I" is not a thinking thing as for Descartes, but rather a form of representation. That is to say, we can talk about it as a subject of experience, but never as an object. In fact, one of Kant's famous paralogisms, refers to the false assumption of rational psychology that the "soul" can be an object of investigation.[49] It is not difficult to see the theological overtones of Kant's distinctions. The very ideas of autonomous freedom and dignity as conceived by the Enlightenment ultimately cannot dispose of the Unconditioned, the idea of God.[50] That is why both, soul and God must remain *noumena*.[51] In this way, Kant may be situated in the line of Augustine as a modern exponent of a tradition molded by the image of God doctrine, where God was to be found within the depths of the human soul. In this sense, Hegel's attempt to dispel the myth of "*Ding an Sich*" meant indeed an improvement on the Kantian apperception. But Hegel does something more radical. Because in Christianity "the mystery has been revealed," a change of perspective is effected from individual consciousness to universal perspective. The move is absolutely rational, Hegel wants to say, yet is fundamentally theological in the sense in which it presupposes and is enabled by Revelation. In this way, the meaning of *Geist* goes beyond a mere explicitation of the Kantian self. Moreover, as we shall see, it aspires to more than a mere social consciousness and even more than some universal Mind. To be

---

48  So Findlay, *Hegel: A Re-examination*, 49ff; Solomon, "Hegel's Concept of Geist," 125–49.

49.  Kant, *Critique of Pure Reason*, 233ff.

50.  Arguably, even in the light of the famous "Was ist Aufklärung," with its stress upon maturity qua autonomy, Kant's idea of freedom and dignity are still tied to the image of God doctrine. For a theological (and positive) interpretation of Kant's autonomy as appropriation, see Hare's study, *God's Call*, 87–119.

51.  His critique of rational cosmology and rational psychology could perhaps be interpreted as the "space" left for a theology of creation. Obviously whether a theology of creation can "develop" in such a "space" is another question.

sure, *Geist* can be seen to gather all those meanings in itself. Nonetheless, in an important sense it remains beyond all of them.[52]

Therefore there appears to be little doubt that Hegel is a philosopher of Revelation. The question in need of an answer now is how is this Revelation conceived? What exactly happens in Hegel's promissory synthesis that such a wholehearted and radical acceptance of Revelation turns out to be suspected of its very denial? As we shall see, there is something both incredibly exciting and terribly frightening in Hegel's mastery of meta-discourse. In a paradoxical alternation of Faustian struggle and kenotic dispossession the self gradually moves from the historical and contingent to the Notion, or the Absolute. Towards this grandiose view of reconciliation we shall now turn.

---

52. See in this respect the unsatisfactory translations of either Mind or Spirit as an accurate rendering for *Geist*. Craig rightly comments that "Mind is not theological enough, Spirit is not intellectual enough." Craig, *Mind of God and the Works of Man*, 174.

*5*

# The Unfolding of God's Story

## Revelation, History, and Rationality in Hegel

It was Gadamer who suggested that Hegel may become more important for hermeneutics than Schleiermacher.[1] This may come as a surprise for those who know Hegel as the author of the absolute system, the "conceptual" Hegel, the philosopher who thought he could think God's thoughts "before the creation of nature and of finite mind."[2] As it is well known, immediately after his death, Hegel's disciples divided among themselves, and the division has continued ever since, as nobody has succeeded in showing convincingly how Hegel's system works in actual fact.

One of the ironies of Hegelian criticism is perhaps this unanticipated fruitfulness of what at first sight appears to be a closed system and a finished task. It is precisely the elusiveness of the Hegelian "middle," which notoriously leaves the interpreter with a choice between clarity and completeness, that makes the above claim less surprising. Hegel was interested not only in history and texts but in the totality of the real, giving thus a paramount and inclusive importance to the concept of experience so dear to Heidegger and subsequent philosophical hermeneutics. In the preface of *The Philosophy of Right* Hegel writes:

> When Philosophy paints its grey on grey, some shape of life has grown old and it cannot by this unrelieved grey be made young again, but only known. The Owl of Minerva takes wing only as the twilight falls.

1. Gadamer, *Truth and Method*, 164–69, 173–218.
2. Hegel, *Science of Logic*, trans. Miller, 49–50.

This famous passage arguably shows Hegel as a retrospective think-er (over against a speculative rationalist), in Findlay's words, a perspec-tival rationalist or a realist. When we read *The Phenomenology of Spirit* with this in mind, we may indeed, come to believe that the historical adventures of consciousness are nothing more than a hermeneutic of his-tory and culture. Many critics took such interpretation as representing the "living Hegel," what is of permanent importance in him. Mure, for instance, arguing along similar lines, suggests that in fact this tension between totality and perspective in Hegel is due to his old Protestant faith. Hegel ultimately owes his "finalist view" to the belief that "Prot-estant Christianity is as permanent as the human race."[4] At first sight, such a claim seems to encourage the simplistic view that faith necessarily advances an unequivocal view of the whole, over against history, which, by its very nature, is fragmentary and open-ended. Yet, the suggestion is more specific, talking as it does, about "Protestant Christianity," which reminds the reader that faith is a historical phenomenon as well, and that in the light of the Owl of Minerva passage, its claims (including its abso-lute claims) appear to be fundamentally dependent on this latter charac-terization. This observation also gives us a hint on why Mure's proposal is not (or at least not yet) an answer for Hegel's finalism. On the one hand, the study of history itself, needs a further elucidation of the transcen-dental status of its critical function. There are many readings of history which are in fact more or less "final," Hegel's being just one of them.[5] On the other hand, it may be argued that the meaning of Christianity as final and Absolute, is far from being necessarily attached to the idea of an absolute system. Therefore, the meaning of the Protestant faith as "final" and its alleged functioning as absolute standard, for Hegel's philosophy in general, his view of history in particular, needs a theological elucidation.

We shall undertake this task by approaching the problem from two directions: On the one hand we shall engage with the "retrospective" Hegel, trying to uncover the rationale behind his hermeneutics of his-tory. On the other, a theological interrogation into the nature of the criti-cal control exercised by his Christian faith will be attempted. This double inquiry aims at uncovering the structure of Hegel's ascent to the Absolute and the ground of his famous "middle." Our principal resource will be

3. Findlay, "Contemporary Relevance of Hegel," 4.

4. Mure, "Hegel, Luther and the Owl of Minerva," 127.

5. E.g., Marx, or more recently Fukuyama, "End of History?," 3–18.

Hegel's *Philosophy of History*. Whilst we are well aware that a proper treatment requires the close assistance of his other works, it will, nonetheless, be the grammar of Hegel's ascent within the framework described above, that will constitute our main concern, rather than a detailed engagement with the Hegelian doctrines.

## Rationality and Contingency: History as Philosophy

From the very outset, Hegel makes it clear that he is not interested in just *any* reflection upon history. His own particular undertaking is to be distinguished from a mere recounting of events (able to reproduce the spirit of an epoch—as in Thucydides for example), and also from a mere reflection upon history made from a particular standpoint. Hegel is interested in World history, by which he means philosophic history.[6]

But in history "our thinking is subordinated to the given, of what is,"[7] Hegel remarks, while philosophy "has thoughts of its own brought forth by speculation from within itself and without reference to what is."[8] Hegel's philosophy of history sets out to solve precisely this dilemma. A philosophy of history, if it is to deserve the name, must reconcile the necessary truths of science with the contingent truths of history.

## The Realist Demand

In the introduction of his *Philosophy of History* Hegel writes: "The only thought which philosophy brings with it, in regard to history, is the simple thought of Reason—the thought that Reason rules the world."[9] For the critic attempting to assess Hegel's realism, this may appear disconcerting. It is not only that Hegel's presupposition is enormous, but he appears to presuppose what he wants to prove. Yet, whereas Hegel contends that Reason in history may be seen as a presupposition brought there from philosophy, he also claims that such a belief is not necessarily

---

6. Philosophic history attempts not to impose a speculative logic upon the fullness of historical experience, but rather to give real flesh to such a logic (apart from which Logic itself would remain a mere "realm of shadows"). Cf. Hegel, *Science of Logic*, trans. Miller, 58.

7. Hegel, *Introduction to the Philosophy of History*, 10.

8. Ibid.

9. Ibid., 12.

required because history itself can and "must reveal its rational process."
The investigation therefore, must be done "historically, i.e., empirically."[10]

Hegel substantiates his determination to avoid any "flight from his
tory" by distancing his own account from both pantheism, like that of
Spinoza,[11] and absolute idealism, like that of Schelling.[12] Both alternatives
in their own different ways, eventually dissolve the contingent rather
than interacting with it. Hegel's aim, as we have seen, is to understand
and express the truth not only as Substance, but as Subject as well. This
calls for the authentication of the Subjective, through the labor of the
historical and the concrete.

But even so, one may rightly argue that there are various ways of
reading the "facts." Reflection can adopt different, and sometimes opposing points of view. The mere rejection of the *a priori* concerns does not
transform the historian into an "objective" observer. Hegel is obviously
well aware of that. Although he does not engage with such problems at
this juncture, he implicitly refers them to the more general problems of
Kantian epistemology. It is the historical experience itself that decides
its own truth. In other words, the very problem of the "right criterion" is
premature and abstract, to the extent that it remains "outside" or "in front
of" real history.

The radical nature of this exposure to the concrete and contingent
aspects of history is brilliantly depicted in the first chapters of *Phenomenology*. Hegel's gradual advance from sense certainty to perception and
finally to understanding, attempts to dispel both the Kantian *Ding-an-
Sich* and the myth of a science without presuppositions. Hegel believes
that the very distrust in science or the fear of error may well be "just the
initial error."[13] On the other hand, however, any beginning is contingent
and in this sense, "science itself is a phenomenon."[14] The presuppositions
are therefore not eliminated by some kind of meta-procedure, nor are
they denied, by considering reason a passive *organon*. If history in its

10. Ibid., 13. Hegel continues by warning his readers against those historians who
create "*a priori* fabrications in history."

11. For a repudiation of pantheism, see for instance Hegel, *Philosophy of Mind*,
332, para. 573; Hegel, *Lectures on the Philosophy of Religion*, 1:374ff.

12. Hegel, *Phenomenology*, 78–79. By rejecting a mere "abstract unity" which is
simply proclaimed, Hegel rejects Schelling's intuitionism. Similarly, there is no "ought"
in Reason. Any ideality remains outside reality.

13. Ibid., 132.

14. Ibid., 134.

ontological sense is considered through *its effects*, authentic knowledge can only appear in its development. This starts to uncover the concrete meaning of the substance of history, which is Reason, as *"infinite power" and "infinite content."*[15] Such a power is not only implicitly present in history, but explicitly[16] as well. This is in fact the ground of its affirmation. A historical "fact" is thus as important as its interpretation. Hegel emphasizes, for instance, that historical narration *must be contemporaneous* with the deeds and events.[17] A historical community in which "the Spirit moves," interprets itself. The authentic historical advance presupposes the passage from the implicit, unreflective, immediate experience of freedom to an explicit awareness of this passage. The historical documents are in this way, not only the material form of a self-conscious community, which attain a certain degree of freedom, but they also provide the material substance for its subsequent development. This connection between "content" and "force" in history as a dialectic of thought and action, endows it with concreteness and realism.

## The Substance of History: Community

Hegel not only claims that Reason rules the World. Reason is also the *content* of history, indeed its most concrete reality.[18] Had this not been so, the link between history and truth would have been impossible. Hegel conceives of this content as being embodied in a community of concrete individuals. The subjects of history are therefore, those concrete *Volkgeister*, which carry the destiny of history in themselves. The historical development follows, according to Hegel, an immanent pattern of internal necessity which takes place in stages. The succession of cultures and nations in history with their own aims, values and aspirations displays the actualization of the labor of Reason to attain its goal. All this takes place under the guidance of an underlying consciousness of freedom. Freedom as the sole truth of Spirit, constitutes in fact, the overriding concern of Hegel's *Philosophy of History*.

15. Hegel, *Introduction to the Philosophy of History*, 12.

16. The implicit-explicit distinction is crucial for Hegel, being closely linked with the dialectic of being and knowledge. Only an explicit presence of a reality signals its presence-to-mind (*für sich*), therefore both, authentic knowledge *and* authentic being.

17. Hegel, *Introduction to the Philosophy of History*, 60.

18. "Reason is the Substance of our historic world." Ibid., 12.

The "spiritual" community rises from mere "nature," and grasps the inner rational movement of Spirit, i.e., its aspiration to freedom. Hence, the freedom, which approximates the life of the Spirit, translates itself in oriented action. The spiritual community is an "ethical" community. That prompts Hegel to distinguish what is essential from what is non-essential in history.[19] To live "historically" means to carry the "burden" of the Spirit, to be caught up by its movement towards freedom. At times Hegel seems to equate World history itself with this historical conscious-ness. This is why most of Africa for instance, remains outside the con-cerns of World history. History travels from East to West, where "Europe is absolutely the end of History, [while] Asia [is] the beginning."[20] The modern Prussian State, (from Hegel's time), is in Hegel's opinion, but the outcome of this long succession of the figures of Spirit towards a fuller and more rational determination, towards genuine freedom. "The East knew . . . only that One is free; the Greek and Roman world that some are free; the German world knows that all are free."[21] Hegel uses the par-able of a blind man receiving sight, who gradually moves from the initial delight of contemplation and astonishment to a gradual realization of himself and the world in which he lives. Such a movement is the move-ment of freedom, a rise from contemplation to activity, from the external sun to the inner light of Spirit.

Yet, a number of problems are still unanswered. First, such an ac-count appears to be unacceptably selective.[22] It is not only that the idea of freedom is drawn dangerously close to that of a heteronomous concept of power, but also the only criterion for a meaningful action seems to be its historical success. History seems to witness sad, and at times, irrational losses. This situation seems to suggest either a partial rationality or a can-cellation of particularity. In the former case, Reason has indeed power but not infinite power, in the latter case, if infinite, such a power becomes morally questionable.[23] Two additional and interrelated problems must be further addressed if Hegel's restatement of theodicy is to be credible:

19. Ibid., 65.

20. Hegel, *Philosophy of History*, 103.

21. Ibid., 104.

22. One of the oft-noted accusations of Hegel is that he does not show that His-tory is rational, but rather spells out what is rational in history.

23. This is just a restatement of the old theodicy problem. As it is well known, Hegel believed in fact that his philosophy is also a theodicy. Cf. Hegel, *Lectures on the Philosophy of Religion*, 1:147.

the ground and logic of this expanded Reason and its concrete anchoring in the historical flux.

## Logic and "Theo-logic"

To claim that Reason rules the world means, therefore, not only to claim that the apparent chaotic and diverse historical process possesses its own immanent logic, but also that such a logic is necessarily grasped by thought. It is in fact this latter aspect that endows this logic with flesh and blood, enabling Hegel to talk about both differentiation and unity which is not only rational but also spiritual.[24] As we have seen in the previous chapter, such a unity cannot be arrived at by causal or mechanistic models of interpretation. This is why Hegel is interested not only in means and ends, but in the goal of history, its concrete content and actualization. Hence, according to Hegel, an authentic logic, a Logic which is onto-logic, grasps the movement of history as a movement of the Spirit. But is it possible to "read" such logic in the historical process?

The crucial observation to be made at this juncture is that Hegel does not claim that he just "found" or "made up" such a logic, which would amount to bridging the necessary and the eternal with the contingent and the temporal. What he says instead, is that such reconciliation is *already* present in history itself, in the Christian religion, more precisely, in the event of Incarnation. Thus, the difficulty is recast in theological terms. The rationality of history must be seen in the larger context of God's relationship with the world. In this way, Hegel succeeds in indicating the ontological structure of what appeared initially to be an epistemological puzzle. This seems to be the first major indication that history can be contemplated as science, without imposing an external standard to it, or an *a priori* structure upon it. That which created the problem in the first place, i.e., the nature of history, announces in itself the solution: God takes the contingent and finite upon himself becoming man. "Thus in this history the nature of God, namely, spirit, is accomplished, interpreted, explicated for the community. This is the crucial point, and the meaning of the story is that it is the story of God."[25] Human history is *reconciling history*.

24. In criticizing pantheism, Hegel opposes "abstract unity" which dissolves the particular things, to "spiritual unity" which includes them into itself. Cf. Hegel, *Lectures on the Philosophy of Religion*, 1:376–77.

25. Hegel, *Lectures on the Philosophy of Religion*, 3:220.

## Power through Weakness:
## The Reconciliation of Freedom and Necessity

Yet, perhaps the most difficult problem remains the problem of connecting this theological insight with the concrete contingencies of history. Is Hegel's unperturbed and necessary movement from the individual to the State and finally to World history, really substantiating a conception of freedom which is not only for the one, or for the few but for all? Can this apparent irreducible plurality of individual and national ideas of freedom, finally converge into an all inclusive view? Before addressing this question a number of preliminary considerations are necessary.

It is important to remember that Hegel never gave up the ideal of autonomy codified in the famous "*Sapere aude.*" A free act must represent one's innermost aspiration. *Philosophy of History* reinforces this idea. Hegel writes:

> Spirit, on the other hand, is that which has its centre in itself. Its unity is not outside itself; rather, it has found it in its own self . . . Spirit is autonomous and self-sufficient, a Being-by-itself (*Bei-sich-selbst-sein*). But this, precisely, is freedom—for when I am dependent, I relate myself to something else, something which I am not.[26]

However such stress upon autonomy does not tell the whole story. Hegel does not rely upon abstract imperatives. In fact his first enemy is Kant's formal ethics which made suspicion (through the world of motivations) the backdrop of any value judgment. Hegel's move is to recast the categorical imperative back into the world of desires, pointing to the fact that without the passage through the historically concrete, any moral imperative remains at best abstract and idle, at worst a form of hypocrisy. "Nothing great has been accomplished in the world without passion"[27] Hegel says, and again "There is the infinite right of the subjective individual to satisfy himself in his activity and work."[28] The driving force of history is constituted therefore by the passions of humans. Do we have here a concrete embodiment of the Spirit's movement?[29] Probably

26. Hegel, *Philosophy of History*, 20.

27. Ibid., 26.

28. Ibid. It is difficult to miss the quasi-cynical echo of Ecclesiastes in this passage (cf. Eccl 3:22).

29. It should be noted at this point that the Hegelian *Sittlichkeit* aims to recover the Aristotelian notion of *praxis* (where action and being come together) and *phronesis*

not, since the structure of passion remains ambiguous. Hegel believes that "Passion is primarily the subjective and thus the formal aspect of energy, of will and activity, so that the content or goal remains as yet undetermined."[30] In fact those human passions are merely "the tools and means of the World Spirit for achieving its goal,"[31] which nevertheless is higher, and greater.

This brings us to the more arduous question of how one can reconcile the subjective and quite diverse passions of humans, with the necessary advance towards the goal of history, which is freedom. Hegel claims that in order for that to happen, a union is required—a union between the general or objective will and the subjective will of the individual. Hegel was well aware of the conditioning of the human being and its dependence upon external constraints. When someone obeys an external law he or she is not free. That was, according to Hegel, the main problem of the Jewish religion. Genuine freedom requires the internalization of the law. In his early writings and in *The Science of Logic*,[32] Hegel seems to suggest that such reconciliation is only possible through love, because love is both free and necessary. (First, it is free in the sense of being what Hegel calls a "genuine" passion or desire, therefore not compelled or forced. And it is necessary, in a double sense: first in the sense that it springs from the being of the lover, and secondly, in the sense in which it expresses the inner necessity of the very historical substance, which is Reason and Spirit.) When a historical community reaches this stage, the objective historical will is identical with the subjective wills of the individuals who see the meaning of their lives, their innermost aspirations, fulfilled in the historical destiny of their community. This is what Hegel calls the "beautiful ethical life."

---

(where the deontological point of view is subordinated to the teleological perspective). A genuine philosophy of history must be concerned not only with the inner motivation but also with the means, and ends, of action. Without a concrete ethical community, the practice of virtue remains "outside" history. That is why the "beautiful soul" is for Hegel an empty abstraction. It is true that in the end, as Milbank shows, the notion of *phronesis* is depotentiated as Hegel's Trinitarian grammar is undermined by his negative dialectics. (Cf. Milbank, *Theology and Social Theory*, 170–73.) But as we shall see, this is just part of the more general "collapse" of the Hegelian middle.

30. Hegel, *Introduction to the Philosophy of History*, 27.

31. Ibid., 28.

32. See Hegel, *Science of Logic*, trans. Miller, 603. Cf. Pannenberg, *Basic Questions in Theology*, 175. See also Hegel, *Wissenschaft der Logik*, 242.

As is known however, the concept of love and life from his early period (very much under the influence of Schelling's *Philosophy of Nature*),
will be later on subsumed under the concept of *Geist*. Love tends to be
equated with feeling in Hegel, lacking therefore the compass and explanatory power of *Geist*. Love, as expression of desire is still insufficient,[33]
lacking the capacity to comprehend and articulate the whole. And this
is even more evident when we come to History and contemplate the
spectacle of human passions, greed, pride and wickedness. This is why,
in *Phenomenology*, love has little place. Yet, the fact that the recognition
of the other comes through struggle, rather than through love, tells us,
according to Hegel, that the Enlightenment concept of freedom *qua autonomy*, its opposition to God, is the necessary moment of negation in its
march towards freedom. Nothing is lost in World history.

Hegel introduces here the crucial concept of the "cunning of reason."
Perhaps most of the time humans do not know what they are doing. They
know indeed what they *want* to do, but the ultimate significance of their
actions remains hidden to most of them. In this way, the World-Spirit is
able to use even the evil actions of the individuals in reaching its goal.
The concept performs a double function. On the one hand it renders human action as finite and perspectival. On the other, however, it touches
upon the theological ground of the very reconciliation between history
and truth functioning as a hermeneutics of providence. When one does
something for the wrong motives, he or she is just an instrument in the
hands of the Spirit (cf. Acts 4:27–28; Phil 1:17–18; Rom 8:28, etc.).[34] It is
at this juncture that the transition from the particular to the universal is
effected. This does not mean that every action sprung from the individual
desire has equal value. Indeed, Hegel talks not only about the "use" of
human action by the World Spirit, but also about the inner arbitration
between rival passions.

33. Thus neither happiness nor unhappiness could approximate the movement of
the Spirit. The "beautiful ethical life" is still insufficient because it lacks differentiation,
or "the struggle of subjective freedom" (Hegel, *Philosophy of History*, 107). Likewise,
the World-historical individuals, do not know happiness (Hegel, *Introduction to the
Philosophy of History*, 29; 33).

34. Philosophical critiques have been eager to stress the first dimension and less
the second one. So Charles Taylor who suggests that this category is not "another incomprehensible, mystical, Hegelian, idea," but rather "indispensable for any theory of
history which wants to give a role to unconscious motivation." Cf. Taylor, *Hegel*, 393.

"What matters is always the content of my conviction, the aim of my passion and whether the one or the other is more genuine."[35]

Therefore, an individual is free to the extent to which he expresses his most genuine desire,[36] yet not free, in so far as he is not able to indwell fully and envision the work of the World-Spirit.[37] When Hegel contends that happiness has no place in World history he makes more than an existential comment. He implicitly endorses the ontological gap between finite consciousness and the World Spirit.

Thus, an institution can become evil and Hegel's articulation of *Sittlichkeit*[38] allows for such a possibility. When this happens, the institution starts to "lose" its reality. And this is what the left-Hegelians understood so well. When we are told that "only the will that is obedient to the law is free" announcing that "the antithesis between freedom and necessity disappears,"[39] Hegel is concerned not in preserving the *status quo*, but in spelling out the nature of the "actuality" and "concreteness" of such law which follows the logic of any historical truth. This is why, precisely by not obeying the law, a new and superior apprehension of freedom may be opened up in a new figure of the Spirit.[40] Hegel is convinced that "where

35. Hegel, *Introduction to the Philosophy of History*, 27. It is true that in the next passage Hegel somewhat depotentiates a non-necessitarian paradigm by claiming that the more genuine passion "will enter into existence and become actual."

36. Hegel gives up an abstract idea of the Good, being prepared to identify traces of it in the very dialectic of desire. See for example the following passage: "I shall therefore use the term 'passion' to signify the particular uniqueness of a person's character—to the extent that the uniqueness of will does not have a merely private content, but is also what drives and motivates actions of a universal scope" (Hegel, *Introduction*, 27).

37. At first Hegel seems to believe (with Kant) that the only alternative to the "laws of Nature" are the "laws of Reason." Therefore a free act must be grounded in nothing external to reason. (For an elaboration of this view see Schacht, "Hegel on Freedom," 289–327.) Yet Hegel does not simply transpose freedom from the Spinosistic substance to man's reason (as Schacht would have it). What he aims at instead, as we shall elaborate in more detail below, is a more fundamental reconciliation which would bring God and man together. How successful he is in such an attempt, is obviously another question.

38 *Sittlichkeit* means simply ethics in German, yet, as Charles Taylor remarks, "No translation can capture the sense of this term" (cf. Taylor, *Hegel*, 376). Hegel uses it to describe the ethical life as objective and "concrete," as opposed to the Kantian *Moralität*, based upon an abstract categorical imperative. Taylor writes: "The crucial characteristic of *Sittlickheit* is that it enjoins us to bring about what already is" (Taylor, *Hegel*, 376). This is just another way of saying that there is no gap between "ought" and "is."

39. Hegel, *Introduction to the Philosophy of History*, 42.

40. This actualist and concrete emphasis ("the Spirit *is* what he does"), stressing

the Spirit is, there is freedom." Freedom, very much like Truth, is always present and concrete, yet, its fullness awaits for the end of history.

To sum, Hegel's own epistemology attempts to articulate being and becoming together, in the same breath, so to speak. In this way, freedom and necessity may coexist at the same level, being both grounded in the same ontological principle which is Spirit. In other words, the dialectic of *Geist*, or God as Spirit, gathers in itself epistemological, ontological, soteriological and eschatological concerns. History is ultimately the unfolding of God's plan. To claim that history is rational is to claim that such a plan has been unveiled. Consequently, Hegel's designation of Reason in history as having infinite power ultimately reflects his insistence upon God's success in Revelation. God determined to be known as Immanuel, as the God-man. In this way, Hegel believes, historical contingency is taken into the very being of God. An immediate implication is that to recognize contingency means to accept death as the undeniable and yet constitutive principle of life. This is for Hegel one of the greatest paradoxes of Christianity.[41]

> "God himself is dead," it says in a Lutheran hymn, expressing
> the awareness that the human, the finite, the fragile, the weak,
> the negative are themselves a moment of the divine. . . . This
> involves the highest idea of spirit.[42]

---

the "is" rather than the "ought" of history, leads to a paramount importance being accorded to the human institution. Hegel makes the enormous claim that "the State is the divine Idea as it exists on earth," and that "the State is the precise Object of World History in General. . . . Here, the freedom attains its objectivity. . . . The Law of the State is the objectification of the Spirit"(Hegel, *Introduction to the Philosophy of History*, 42). Such and similar claims led Popper to label Hegel as "the official philosopher of the Prussian State," "the archenemy of the open society" (cf. Popper, *Open Society and Its Enemies*, 2:25ff). However, as Kaufmann and others have stressed, this is an unfair rendering of Hegel's text. What Hegel is trying to say is that an institution simply by its mere existence, implicitly carries with it a certain truth. The role of the institution is to actualize freedom, and to the extent it does that, it is genuine, and the World Spirit is actualized in it. When it fails to do that, it soon becomes an "empty shell" being sublated by more developed figures of the Spirit. (See also Avineri, *Hegel's Theory of the Modern State*, 115–31.)

41. According to Jüngel, Hegel's most significant achievement for theology was "the systematic *connection* of the Christological source of the idea of the death of God with the epistemological-metaphysical problematic of modern atheism." Cf. Jüngel, *God and the Mystery of the World*, 97.

42. Hegel, *Lectures on the Philosophy of Religion*, 3:326.

This claim may well be Hegel's most radical attempt to safeguard particularity. The link between history and truth has its final abode in God himself who became man. This is not just a problem of knowledge. If contingency is to be rescued, negativity, the death itself, must become constitutive of the very being of God. Such a logic which assumes the death and resurrection pattern endorses a fractured Rationality, a rationality which is able to regain its truth not in a smooth linear process, not relying upon an underlying eternal substance but through dying. This is perhaps its crucial and most controversial characteristic: crucial, because only in this way can it be faithful to *all* experience; controversial, because Reason remains Infinite power by taking weakness in itself. Reason as infinite power and infinite content maintains its own being in the midst of disruption because it is not only "result" but includes the whole process.

In short, Hegel claims that a philosophical approach to History is possible because the paradox of the reconciliation of the necessary with the contingent is referred back to the paradox of Incarnation. One is not called to solve this latter mystery, because, among other things, Incarnation itself presupposes that the mystery has been revealed. Yet, what one *is* called to do, Hegel believes and, indeed, must do, is to spell out this mystery, to make it explicit, to present its meaning in a rational manner. This rational reconciliation ultimately hangs upon the meaning of the theological truth of God's relationship with the world. History by itself does not possess enough resources to answer either the idea of freedom or that of necessity.

## The Absolute Mediation

### The Promise

Hegel is often accused of being the arch-rationalist, the greatest metaphysician of the modern period. Yet, this radical mediation appears at first highly commendable. One can hardly fail to recognize the promise latent in such an attempt.[43]

Hegel's *Vernunft*, which is Absolute Reason and Spirit at the same time, Subject and Substance, heralds a holistic Rationality enacted in a community which is Christologically grounded and empowered by the Spirit. Furthermore, by recasting the problem of history in Trinitarian

---

43. Barth's appraisal of Hegel is telling in this respect. Cf. Barth, *Protestant Theology in the Ninenteenth Century*, 384–421. I will return to Barth's take on Hegel below.

categories Hegel's mediation performs a theo-logical task, that is to say, an explicitation of God, departing from both the Abstract God of the medievals and the undifferentiated love of the Romantics. If both the epistemological and ontological key to knowledge is the Word become flesh, and if knowledge and being must be understood together, that means that history, as the *story of the relationship between God and humanity*, is also a statement about God's own being. Perhaps the principal upshot of Hegel's grand mediation between history and truth, between rationality and contingency, is the articulation of a *meaningful* history. This concern for meaning would place Hegel's Trinitarian proposal in a distinct light.

As we have seen, Hegel was deeply convinced that without a differentiated whole, our talk about the world, ourselves and God is empty. Unity without distinction cannot be rational, while distinction without final reconciliation cannot be meaningful. Truth and meaning cannot be separated. While in Kant's philosophy the desire for unity was just another way of pointing to one's synthetic judgment, the newness with Hegel is his anticipation of a de-centering of consciousness, (at least in intent) in the sense that it is not the finite mind which brings unity to the fragmented world. As we have seen, the principle of such unity is external and the finite human mind is rather invited to participate in it.[44] One of the most important implications of this collusion between meaning and truth is that history is restored to its genuine messianic dimension.

Human history is meaningful history because it is also the history of God, having an *arche* and a *telos*. In spite of the ambiguities of his Christology,[45] Hegel is aware that whilst it is true that Christ came "when the time was ripe," the "when" of Christ's appearance cannot be

---

44. This concern for meaning led Hegel to contest Kant's *das Schlecht Unendliche*, infinity as infinite regress of progress. Genuine infinity cannot be essentially opposed to the finite. See Mure, "Hegel, Luther and the Owl of Minerva," 130. See also Pannenberg, *Metaphysics and the Idea of God*, 35–36.

45. For the centrality of the Christological dimension in Hegel, see Yerkes and Küng (Yerkes, *Christology of Hegel*; Küng, *Incarnation of God*). For Yerkes, as for Tillich, Hegel's Christology remains significant by its capacity to disclose an ideal archetype of humanity. In such a reading, Hegel's assumption of a fundamental God-man unity is never genuinely questioned. Yerkes, *Christology of Hegel*, 166; 311ff; Tillich, *Systematic Theology*, 14ff. For a critique of such a view and of Yerkes's rendering of Hegel in particular, see Daniel P. Jamros, "Hegel on the Incarnation," 276–300. Fackenheim is right, I believe, to say that Hegel wanted to describe Incarnation as both fully contingent ("the most radical case of contingency"), and yet, expected and needed. Cf. Fackenheim, *Religious Dimension*, 138.

transcendentally deducted but it must be read off from history.[46] In fact, it was this serious consideration of history as the history of God that led Hegel to both reject and accept natural theology. As O'Regan notes, if the tone of *Phenomenology* is overtly critical of natural theology, Hegel would later reconcile his theological understanding of history as history of revelation with natural theology.[47] Thus, natural theology makes a return only in the light of God's self revelation. This reinforces the idea iterated in the first part, namely, that a genuine theology of nature can arise only in the light of God's revelation in three persons. Moreover, it is only in this light that this meaningful history can be seen as being more than a mere rationalist and necessary development. A crucial feature of Hegel's "finalism," therefore, is that it does not necessarily preclude hope by a detached summing up of all history in the eternal now. Yerkes is profoundly right I believe, to note that:

> Only those who have never known the thrill of believing deeply that in their time God was doing a "new thing" for the redemption of human sorrow and suffering, and that they could actively have a share in it by putting their own wills and wits at his disposal—only those will read Hegel's claims to philosophical "finality" solely as expressions of a megalomaniac mind.[48]

Nonetheless, as has been widely remarked, Hegel's ascent to the Absolute was not exactly an expression of "hope." Let us further enquire into the nature of this grand view of reconciliation, by examining the ground and specific articulation of this moment when "hope and history rhyme."

## Openness and Closure

We shall take as our point of departure O'Regan's neat summary of the tension between openness and closure characteristic of Hegel's mediation. As is well known, Hegel believed that his proposal finally solved the ancient dispute between Parmenides's Being and Heraclitus's Becoming. O'Regan writes:

46. "That God appeared in *this* human being, at *this* time and in *this* place . . . can be recognized only from the point of view of world history. It is written: 'When the time had come, God sent forth his Son' [Gal. 4:4]; and *that* the time had come can only be discerned from history" (italics his). Hegel, *Lectures on the Philosophy of History*, 3:215.

47. Cf. O'Regan, *Heterodox Hegel*, 75–77.

48. Yerkes, *Christology of Hegel*, 226.

If Parmenides fails to introduce the richness and dynamism of appearance into Being thereby leaving it impoverished (LIIP 1 P. 256), Heraclitus fails to provide Becoming with an underpinning of determinate form that would guarantee meaning and intelligibility. The complementary deficits of Parmenides and Heraclitus also might be understood as an excess of circularity (as with Schelling) in the case of the former and excess of linearity (as with Fichte) in the case of the latter.[49]

Critics of Hegel usually highlight Hegel's stress upon the power of the concept and his optimism about the capacity of such language to express reality, which is contrasted with his relative contempt for metaphorical, representational language. Yet, in the light of the above synthesis, Hegel's attempt to retain both narrativity and meaning, both the dynamism of life and the completeness and intelligibility of truth, renders the relation between *Vorstellung* and *Begriff* in a distinct light. According to O'Regan, this double requirement leads Hegel to an implicit recognition that the concept and the metaphor cannot be kept apart.[50] More importantly, ultimately, it is the specifically Christian narrative that shows this to be the case. Granted this connection, the very tension between openness and closure takes shape in Hegel's discourse in the light of this more fundamental taxis.

Following Michael Rosen, O'Regan conceives the relationship between *Vorstellung* and *Begriff* under the guidance of two models: the "transformational" model, in which the concept is conceived as correcting the inadequacies of representation (e.g., its lack of necessity and metaphoricity) and the generative approach, where the concept is thought to generate its own content.[51] Since there seems to be evidence of both tendencies in Hegel's writings, O'Regan proposes a synthesis between the two models.

What remains largely unsaid in O'Regan, however, is in what way this implicit defense of the Hegelian middle is connected with Hegel's referential intention. It is true that he notes, with Rosen, the ironic string attached to Hegel's claim that it is religion which announces the autonomy

---

49. O'Regan, *Heterodox Hegel*, 298.

50. As we have seen in the previous section, this was also Ricoeur's reading of Hegel. In fact, O'Regan appeals for support to both Ricoeur and Habermas. Cf. O'Regan, *Heterodox Hegel*, 359–60.

51. Ibid., 358.

of philosophy.[52] But this insight is not properly referred to its problematic theological ground. O'Regan summarizes his position by asserting that "conceptual discourse has the ability to recursively account for its own presupposition. And in this ability to account for its own genesis lies its autonomy. It is in Hegel therefore . . . that science breaks the vicious circle of the illusion of no-presupposition and the ghost of dependence and thus relativity."[53] But without a more fundamental grounding, this "dependence" which turns out to be a more radical autonomy remains unconvincing. Moreover, in the light of O'Regan's explicit denouncing of Hegel's narrative Trinitarian grammar and its filiation with Boehme, and Valentinian and Gnostic thought, such a claim turns out to be highly problematical, only because, as Fackenheim rightly suggests, the interanimation between representation and concept is fundamentally dependent upon the theological distinction between the immanent and the economic Trinity.[54] In the controversial # 163 of *Encyclopaedia* Hegel writes:

> It is not we who frame the notions. . . . It is a mistake to imagine that the objects which form the content of our mental ideas come first and that our subjective agency then supervenes. . . . Rather the notion is the genuine first; and things are what they are through the action of the notion, immanent in them, and revealing itself in them. In religious language we express this by saying that God created the world out of nothing. In other words, the world and finite things have issued from the fullness of the divine thoughts and the divine decrees. Thus religion recognizes thought and (more exactly) the notion to be the infinite form, or the free creative activity, which can realise itself without the help of a matter that exists outside it.[55]

52. Ibid., 360.

53. Ibid., 359.

54. It is true that O'Regan suggests in passing that "it may be the case that Hegel may not be entitled to have it both ways," but he never unpacks this insight. (359) On the other hand, Fackenheim contends that since representation is crucial in Hegel's ascent, Hegel eventually needs the preservation of the double Trinity. (Cf. Fackenheim, *Religious Dimension*, 218–19.) Fackenheim's bold (albeit incipient and brief) proposal constitutes a very interesting Trinitarian exploration of a hermeneutical reading of Hegel which wants to preserve both the "productive" dimension of the Notion and the necessity of representation. "The notion *produces* the Truth (this is subjective freedom) but at the same time *recognizes* its content as *not* produced" (italics his). Cf. Fackenheim, *Religious Dimension*, 219. As we have seen in the first part, Ricoeur reads Hegel in a similar way, without inquiring though into the theological roots of such a reading.

55. Hegel, *Science of Logic*, trans. Wallace, para. 163.

It is not enough to say, therefore, that the two "spaces" of metaphor and of concept respectively "are systemically impure, infected by each other."[56] The above passage suggests that *the collusion between metaphor and concept is grounded not only in the distinction between language and reality but ultimately in a conception of God and his relationship with the world.*[57] Moreover, I contend that it is ultimately in the light of *this* latter conception that Hegel's "middle" turns out to be most problematic. Especially in his *Logic*, Hegel stresses the fact that the ascent to the Notion is a grounding as well. The language—World relationship in Hegel is correlative with epistemology—ontology and the subject—object relation. Truth obtains when the distinction in each case is sublated. The fundamental concept of Hegel's system, the concept of *Geist*, is the final apotheosis of this ascending and all-inclusive process of signification. There is little doubt that Hegel intended it to be both subject and predicate, truth and meaning, being and knowledge, noun and verb. Yet, as we look back from the perspective of this lofty synthesis, two opposing alternatives open before us.

In the first reading, the only reality seems to be the reality of the Concept. There is really nothing "outside" this ultimate Word. If "things are what they are through the reality of the notion," human history and ultimately all created reality are a mere variation of "action." In the other possible reading, the notion as pure form remains indeed a "realm of shadows" which, in order to gain "actuality," needs to be infused with content.

## The Impossible Middle

Let us briefly sketch the main theological ramifications of these two radical alternatives. A very brute scenario of what happens in Hegel's system may run as follows: If we take *Begriff* as the realm of pure form which needs the "baptism" of actuality, both God and the world undergo significant changes. Hegel's peculiar rendering of Aquinas's *Actus Purus* (by which potentiality is allowed into God himself) dissolves the self sufficiency of God. The World as finite, as God's "other," tends to become

---

56. O'Regan, *Heterodox Hegel*, 363.

57. Hermeneutic philosophy has later explored this "aesthetic" or creative dimension in relation to experience. It was therefore Hegel, before Heidegger, who anticipated that "language helps reality to become itself" (cf. Heidegger, "Hegels Begriff der Erfahrung," in *Holzwege*, 105–92, quoted by Ricoeur, *Hermeneutics and the Human Sciences*, 115).

constitutive for the very being of God.[58] In the light of the infinite-finite dialectic there seems to be no room left for an *ex nihilo* creation, and similarly, no place for God's freedom. That would confirm indeed, Hegel's "realism" but it would also change everything. On the ethical plane, in spite of its historical concreteness and teleological orientation, the overall perspective would remain sombre: "Salvation" is excessively "ontologized," while Luther's *theologia crucis* loses its ethical import by being incorporated into a logic of distinction.[59] The incorporation of the logic of Redemption into the historical scenario had the chance to overcome the abstract justification of medieval theodicies. Unfortunately, since eventually everything is reconciled in Hegel, the cry for "justification" is dissolved rather than answered.

We may recall, however, that Hegel himself was at times less optimistic about his own Absolute. Hegel ends *Phenomenology* with a somewhat cryptic suggestion that it is in the very nature of the Spirit to suffer. Similar suggestions are made at the end of *Logic*. This confirms the problematic nature of Hegel's "middle." If the Spirit "returns," history is nothing but the endless effort to "win" the world. It is this effort which ultimately constitutes the "life" of the Spirit. This uncovers a tragic view of reality in which it is a somewhat Manichean process that moulds the self of both God and man in an unending process of return to history, to what is still unredeemed, finite and ultimately "evil."[60] In this

---

58. For a detailed defense of a fundamental "narrative" reading of Hegel's immanent Trinity, see O'Regan, *Heterodox Hegel*, 81–85; Following Iljin, O'Regan maintains that the immanent-economic language no longer applies in Hegel as narrativity penetrates the divinity itself. Instead, Hegel's Trinitarian structuration is conceived in three successive divine epochs.

59. For Hegel's relation to Luther's *theologia crucis*, see O'Regan, *Heterodox Hegel*, 195ff.

60. Hegel's critique of "abstract personality" rightly pointed to the need to devise personhood in a concrete community. Nonetheless, as O'Regan argues, under the model of *Bildungsroman*, personhood in Hegel ultimately necessitates antagonism and struggle (O'Regan, *Heterodox Hegel*, 110–11). Pannenberg on the other hand, uses the notion of Subject to defend Hegel's view of Creation against the charge of neo-Platonic emanationsim. Cf. Pannenberg, *Basic Questions in Theology*, 3:165. Nevertheless, if the constitution of personality remains tragic (assimilation of what is alien), we are ultimately left either with an impassible subject (in which case we would want to "rescue" an apophatic dimension of subjectivity), or with a constitution of subjectivity which remains ultimately unable to distinguish between its own freedom and the freedom of the world. In fact, (although he ends up taking it on board) Pannenberg himself recognizes the problematic implications of the infinite-finite dialectic which guides the very distinction between God and the world (Ibid., 168).

case, Hegel's "description" does not fly from the world, but rather stays too much with it. The Spirit as Victor does not appear really to solve the problems of history but rather to accumulate them in a process in which Reason is constantly reconciled with violence. The fact that the Ultimate figure retains all its previous appearances is the final blow of misery, since there is no possibility of forgetting. A god who cannot really create out of nothing, cannot either really conquer and bring to an end the human misery. In this case the Hegelian attempt to "ontologize" Kant remains, ironically, exemplarist in implications, to the extent that God and the self somehow share equal "burdens." Similarly the problem of meaning as "exterior," as given, as a sign of grace, loses its substance, as do faith and hope and human action. In such a view, Hegel does not seem to succeed in closing the "narrative."[61]

If we follow the other route, history itself tends to lose its substance. Spirit has to overcome "nature" which is against "the Spirit."[62] Indeed, in the light of infinite-finite dialectic, nature does seem to remain impotent and "conceptless" for Hegel.[63] Moreover, nature as finite is not only uncertain, but ultimately evil.[64] This is why Spirit must *transcend* nature. In *Introduction to the Philosophy of History* Hegel writes:

> World History in general is thus the unfolding of Spirit in time,
> as nature is the unfolding of the Idea in space.[65]

If we corroborate this claim with Hegel's celebrated claim that "the truth of nature is that nature has no truth,"[66] the above statement appears to have the rather odd meaning that ultimately the truth of "space"

---

61. The postmodern confusion in regard to the meaning of "real" is but a version of such an alternative—the "real fake" (Eco), or the concept of simulacrum (Baudrillard), signaling the poverty of a "truth" derived from the historical process.

62. Hegel, *Lectures on the Philosophy of Religion*, 3:226–27.

63. For an exposition of such a view, see Dostal, "End of Metaphysics," 38–42. For Hegel the question is not whether something can be proved historically, but whether it is true in-and-for-itself. (E.g., Hegel, *Lectures on the Philosophy of Religion*, 330–331.) Hegel's pneumatic exegesis (his filiation with Luther) may be understood along such lines.

64. See for instance Hegel's reinterpretation of Lucifer not as the first (other) "son" of God as in Boehme, but as the external world "which is outside the truth." Cf. Hegel, *Lectures on the Philosophy of Religion*, 3:293.

65. Hegel, *Introduction*, 75.

66. "Mind is the existent truth of matter—the truth that matter itself has no truth." Hegel, *Philosophy of Mind*, para. 389.

is "time." This temporalization of space in Hegel shows that "explaining away" historical narrativity amounts to a more fundamental narrativity being attributed to divinity itself. From this perspective, Hegel's "anti-naturalism" voices a rather Gnostic gospel signaling, as in Kant's case, it may be added, a "return" to interiority. What we are told is not only that nature must be "transcended," but also that it is "knowledge" that initiates this ascent. In such a light, Hegel's reading of the story of the Fall[67] and his predilection for the mystic and Gnostic thought comes as no surprise.[68]

In *Phenomenology* Hegel suggests that the emergence of philosophical thought is associated with disengagement and alienation. After changing the material world through labor, the Spirit realizes that he is in search for "a better country." But this "better country" (in opposition to Marx's communist society) is ultimately for Hegel the Spirit's own realm, its own substance, as no object can possibly fulfill it. This "redemptive" process of reading its own truth in its "other" is essentially a process of "signification" in which what is "retained" is ultimately its own truth. Thus, "to signify" history is to lose it as history. The final collapse into the One as the apotheosis of logocentrism, is just the last word of the ritual spell of the philosophical discourse.

But what is the meaning of this last Word? Commenting on Hegel's language Charles Taylor concludes that the climax of the ascent reveals the "unproblematic nature of the referring relation" which in turn "reflects the lack of question about subjectivity."[69] But does this herald the advent of pure subjectivity, the ideal referring relation? Is this ultimate synthesis, really, the last word about the meaning of the relationship between God and the world, between the Creator and the created, in which both perfect subjectivity and perfect correspondence between language and reality are finally achieved? We have reasons to doubt that . . .

"If the Absolute is inside me, it is not an absolute, if it is outside me I can never reach it." Hegel's lifetime effort to solve this puzzle in

---

67. The story of the Fall (abstractly termed so in Hegel's opinion), is for Hegel "not just a contingent history but the eternal and necessary history of humanity." Cf. Hegel, *Lectures on the Philosophy of Religion*, 2:527–29, 739–41, 3:207–11, 300–304.

68. Hegel appeals to Boehme to support his idea of human nature as implicitly divine. Cf. Hegel, *Lectures on the Philosophy of Religion*, 99. He also quotes approvingly Meister Eckhart's famous claim, "The eye with which God sees me is the eye with which I see him; my eye and his eye are one and the same." Cf. ibid., 347.

69. Taylor, *Hegel*, 566.

a systematic way produced what von Balthasar called *identitas entis*.[70] Both, von Balthasar and Barth, deplored the "philosophical necessity" that "binds God and his Revelation, man, one to the other."[71] Barth famously labeled the identity "between thinking and what is thought," or put differently, Hegel's assumption of a "complete presence" of the thing thought in his thinking, "the secret of his secret."[72]

It is instructive to take a closer look at Barth's reflections on Hegel at this juncture, as it will set the stage for our reevaluation of knowledge and truth in the next section.

While Barth is usually generous with his predecessors, Hegel seems to occupy a special place in his account, as Barth goes to great lengths in showing his admiration for him. Somewhat surprisingly, Barth takes his cue from one of the most provocative and perhaps most irritating features of Hegel's philosophy, namely, its self-confidence. He notes (rightly so, as we have seen above) that such confidence goes beyond the naive Enlightenment rationalism of his day, as it necessarily entails confidence in Mind or Spirit, which for Hegel is the same thing with confidence in God. And to claim that confidence in God equals self-confidence is, in Barth's reading, "Titanism to the highest degree and at the same time to the highest degree humility" (381). "Where is the man," asks Barth rhetorically, "who, with the blood of this modern man in his veins, would not listen to this and hear the finest and deepest echo of his own voice?" (383).

Barth seems to almost give in to Hegel's seductive voice . . . There is "force and splendour," and there is "dignity, strength and value" in his discourse, Barth asserts (393). Moreover, Barth thought that "Hegel said most things better than most theologians. . . . Only someone who does not understand Hegel's philosophy can miss its peculiar greatness" (382). Even when evaluating Hegel's system, Barth warns that we must not think of it as a rigid, stable edifice, as its center "moves with the thinker

---

70. Balthasar, *Glory of the Lord*, 549.

71. Ibid., 548. See also Barth, *Protestant Theology in the Nineteenth Century*, 370–407. To be sure, von Balthasar thought this was (more or less) a common feature of German idealism as a whole. This was what enabled Hegel "to reinterpret *agape* directly and freely in the direction of *gnosis*" (548). Von Balthasar goes on to say that "insofar as German Idealism begins with the *identitas entis*, the way back to Christianity is blocked" (549). I think it would be fair to say, however, that it was Hegel who accorded intellectual prestige to what was more or less an unsubstantiated Romantic assumption. I will briefly return to von Balthasar's project below.

72. Barth, *Protestant Theology in the Nineteenth Century*, 377. Further references to the book are included in the text above.

himself" (391). He is fully aware that Hegel's resounding yes, is, more often than not, also a resounding no. That is why Barth lauds (at least *prima facie*) Hegel's dialectic: "It is the task of logic to adapt itself to life, not the other way around." And again, "The truth can only be so menacing . . . so unstable . . . if truth is identical with God himself" (399). Not an unmovable God but a God *in actu*. In other words, Barth fully embraces Hegel's pathos for truth and welcomes his dialectic rendering of it, because he is convinced that Hegel's demands were legitimate, that they were "theological" in character.[73]

In sum, Barth admires both Hegel's bold affirmation that "truth might be history, event" (401), and that theological knowledge is only possible "in the form of strict obedience to the self movement of truth" (401). Equally significant for Barth is Hegel's affirmation of the Trinity and its centrality in Hegel's account of the reconciliation between Revelation and Reason.

But Hegel's proposal must be "vigorously translated and transformed," Barth warns, if his demands are to be acceptable for theology. Barth conceives this "translation and transformation" in three ways (neatly corresponding to the 3 positive aspects taken up earlier: truth, the moving cognition of truth and the dialectical character of this movement). That is to say, in a somewhat Hegelian fashion, Barth "sublates" his initial (triadic) "yes" with a more fundamental "no!" So, indeed, Barth's "dialectic," as opposed to Hegel's, seems to be "negative," or "broken," rather than "conclusive"!)

First, it is the concept of truth. Can we really accept Hegel's unproblematic anchoring of humanity in the truth? "Does not man always exist at the invisible intersection between thinking and willing?" asks Barth. Moreover, can a theory of truth be divorced from praxis (404)? Significantly, in questioning Hegel's ideal unity of man, Barth makes recourse to Kant's primacy of practical reason. If the Hegelian concept of truth is to do justice to theology, it must be protected, "from one sided theorizing" (403). There is an irreducible (ethical) gap between the human and the divine. That is why sin cannot be just "passed through in a moment or longer." And that is why reconciliation is not "a mere continuation of the one eventual course of truth" but "an incomprehensibly new beginning"

---

73. Such excessive admiration may be attributed perhaps (at least in part) to Barth's "Revelation as event" period. Indeed, Barth believed that Reason, as "Absolute Reason" in Hegel, is identical with the "*event* of reason. . . . And that, really, is the key to everything." Barth, *Protestant Theology*, 384 (italics his).

(404). A concept of truth acceptable to theology, Barth believes, cannot think beyond "the dual mystery, of both evil and salvation" (404).

Barth notes further that when it comes to Hegel's "moving cognition of truth," unfortunately, Hegel's doctrine of the Trinity becomes identical with the basic principles of Hegelian logic and eventually with Hegel's anthropology and his teaching of life (404).[74] The result is that, in spite of Hegel acknowledging the historical nature of Revelation and the uniqueness of Christ, (due to the imperturbable advance of philosophy from representation to "pure logical content,") Revelation proper is ultimately dissolved in general knowledge and thus "objectified," and "reduced." The implication again, is that "the ethical space" has vanished. There is no longer "speaking and listening." Just pure knowing. . . . Thus, "the living God" becomes "the living man" (405).

Lastly, Barth discusses Hegel's identification of God with the dialectical method (406) which, in Barth's evaluation, deprives God of his freedom. Creation, Reconciliation, man, Church, everything becomes necessary . . .

> I am necessary to God. That is the basis of Hegel's confidence in God and the reason why this confidence can immediately and without further ado be understood as self-confidence as well. . . . Hegel, in making the dialectical method of logic the essential nature of God, made impossible the knowledge of the actual dialectic of grace, which has its foundation in the freedom of God (406).

In other words, if such dialectic is both essential to God's own nature and always-already accessible to the human subject, we can no longer talk about grace. This constitutes the most serious problem for theology, according to Barth, "the weightiest and most significant of the doubts about him which might be raised from a theological point of view" (406). The previous two points ("the single track nature of his concept of truth and the confusion of human with the divine self-movement,") are also grounded in this (406). In the end, according to Barth, it all boils down to a failure from Hegel's part to recognize that God is free.

While I resonate with the general tone of Barth's critique, it is impossible not to note the thinly veiled parallelism between Barth's first and

74. This may seem to run against his earlier claim that Hegel's doctrine of the Trinity is *not* a retrospective adaptation of his philosophy (ibid., 400). However, Barth only meant that such adaptation was not meant to comply with the wishes of the theologians of his time.

third critical points (i.e., his critique of Hegel's account of truth [conceived in an "internalistic" way] and his rejection of Hegel's identification of his dialectical method with the very being of God).

Let me unpack this further. Although Barth notes the inadequacy of Hegel's Trinitarian deployment (including, as we have seen, its root in the subject), it is God's freedom that concerns Barth the most, making it the root of all the other problems in Hegel. Of course, Barth is right to note that there is more to God than knowledge, that God's being cannot be reduced to *nous*. Nonetheless, Barth's (ultimately) voluntaristic stance seems to merely transpose Hegel's dialectic of the subject in "theo-logical" register, while leaving the structure of knowledge itself virtually unchanged. In other words, if Hegel's concept of truth prompts Barth to make recourse to Kant's practical reason, truth itself (i.e., the "ontological" counterpart of such concept of truth) prompts him to turn to God's will. The problem is not so much the "absolute" point of contact itself (Barth never questions Hegel's ideal self-confidence which equals confidence in God), but rather the fact that this is available in a method upon which the human agent has control! Barth seems (implicitly) to take on board Kant's (quite limited) understanding of what counts as (scientific) knowledge. Knowledge entails power and control and having control, means having the last word . . . Like in Ricoeur's case, it is the, so called, "retrospective view" that bothers Barth. Thus, the affirmation of the (ethical) "distance" between God and man, the radical "non-objectivity" of Revelation and the (implicit) return to Kant's practical reason. In other words, knowledge is necessarily "instrumental," therefore it must be "limited" if talk of "freedom" is to remain meaningful.[75] It is not difficult to see the tribute Barth pays to the logic of German idealism. As we shall see later, more than a mediation between intellectualism and voluntarism/theory and praxis is required here. Talk of knowledge and truth demands a larger context.

Nonetheless, Barth is certainly right to note that by absorbing the Creator-Creation distinction into a more fundamental logic of identity, Hegel's "great promise" suddenly becomes the "great problem." Hegel's "middle" may well invite us to reconsider God's pathos who leads to sacrifice; the *aporetic* nature of love as free giving; the bold voice of a

---

75. Barth's (quite abrupt) suggestion that Hegel's failure to recognize that God is free is equivalent with a failure to recognize double predestination, is therefore not surprising. This is no longer a problem of knowledge but of God's will. Barth, *Protestant Theology*, 406.

self-giving spirit who "utters his claims" while he gives up his life . . ."[76]
But, as we have seen, in Hegel's account God's love is not really the deter-
mining link between the immanent and the economic Trinity.

Kierkegaard's powerful critique of Hegel's mediating philosophy
unveils his ascent not as a fulfillment of God's pathos but as its ultimate
dissipation. Indeed, his underlying attack of Hegel's logic of identity in
*Sickness unto Death*[77] reveals the struggle of recognition in *Phenomenology* as a play of the self with itself and depotentiating the very concept of
experience as experience of concrete reality or of personhood. The other
potential "reading" of this dialectic play is even more worrying as evil is
ultimately rendered just another form of "otherness."[78]

Since all distinctions are finally sublated in the Creator-Creation
identity, instrumentality "equals" participation and the call is collapsed
into the response. The end of the *Phenomenology* suggests that there is
just one voice left, in which, indeed, "referring" equals "expression." The
historical result of this, again in Balthasar's terms, has been no longer an
"aesthetics of glory but only one of beauty . . . aesthetics as science, which
was rampant in the nineteenth century."[79]

76. Hans Küng commends Hegel's attempt to achieve that. See Küng, *Incarnation
of God*, 430. See also Jüngel's appraisal of Hegel in Jüngel, *God and the Mystery of the
World*, 63–104.

77. Cf. Kierkegaard, *Sickness unto Death*. Kierkegaard's powerful exposition of the
limits of reflection has been brought to my attention by Smith's article on Hegel and
Kierkegaard (cf. Smith, "Hegel, Kierkegaard and the Problem of Finitude," 209–26).
Arguably, however, in spite of his powerful critique, Kierkegaard still operates within
the same framework. Hence his "individualism," the "gap" between faith and reason, etc.

78. For a critique of Hegel's concept of "otherness," see Grier, "Speculative Concrete: I. A. Il'in's Interpretation of Hegel," 169–93. Barth was right to note that it was
the career of this small word, sin, that made all the difference in the world, preventing Hegel from becoming "the Thomas Aquinas of Protestantism" (Barth, *Protestant
Theology in the Nineteenth Century*, 421). Even Pannenberg, who generally has a more
sympathetic reading of Hegel, acknowledges "the dubiousness" of Hegel's concept of
Spirit. Cf. Pannenberg, *Metaphysics and the Idea of God*, 40–41. For a brief critique of
Hegel's Christology, see also Gunton, *Yesterday and Today*, 40.

79. Balthasar, *Glory of the Lord*, 549. We may note here in passing that Balthasar
seems to offer more scope for a theological critique of knowledge. While, as we have
seen, Barth seems to take an early refuge in Kant's practical reason, Balthasar's critique
of Kant transfigures aesthetics from a mere theory of perception (grounded as it is in
the subject, in Kant's account) into a theological aesthetics, where the revelation of
God's glory sets the terms of the discussion. It is the Triune God, the supreme "Form,"
that "impresses" Being, enabling it to "reflect back" and "express" glory in turn. "Logic"
comes last, in Balthasar's deployment, after *Aesthetics* and *Dramatics*, making thus,
Balthasar's proposal more hospitable to an understanding of knowledge not only in

As we have seen, truth is possible for Hegel only in this panoramic view in which the goal and the process, the saying and the said are finally brought together. What is more, this coming together is not only made "present" to consciousness but identified as its own life and substance. Inevitably, in the process, the Creator-Creation distinction is left behind. The more traditional idea of participation (to contain in part of what the other contains fully) remains inadequate for Hegel. It is not enough to participate in the truth. One must inhabit it completely. In a scenario where temporality wins over, where "the truth of space is time," participation in the above sense can be at best provisional.[80]

This "return" of instrumentality reminds us once again that the knowledge of God expounded in Scripture, with its related concepts of "participation" and unity with God, never attempts to "transcend" the fundamental *diastasis* between Creator and Creation, between human and divine agency. Such unity, rather than "concluding language," unbinds instead our freedom to respond to a call which is never exhausted, to praise God for eternity. The "bold self," "the capable agent" is rather born in such a language of praise.

By contrast, for Hegel, "there is but one Reason. There is no second super-human Reason. Reason is the Divine in man."[81] It is only when we unmask the subliminal presupposition of this universal "I" to which reflection returns time and again, that we can genuinely dismantle the shadow of the projecting consciousness which would preoccupy the left wing Hegelians from Feuerbach to Nietzsche. *And it is only in this way that we can further dismantle the "logic of identity" which would continue*

---

the wider framework of God's Trinitarian action but also informed by both "vision"(of God's glory) and "obedience"("listening" to its summons).

80. As we have seen, not even God escapes this logic. That is why the Immanent Trinity remains fundamentally in want as lacking the labor of actuality. It may be also said in this connection that we must express caution to calls of "transcending" either space or time. The "spatialization" of time (a tendency, arguably, noticeable in Augustine) or the "temporalization" of space (as in Hegel), tells us at least that attempts to "explain" the eternal through the temporal or vice-versa are bound to lead either to a celebration of eternity in opposition to the finite, or to a celebration of finitude with the danger of an immanent "inverted metaphysics." It is tempting to suggest at this juncture that we should do well to preserve a balance between the spatial and the temporal metaphors in our language of God. While this may work in principle, we need to remember that such prescriptions remain empty if they are not grounded in the material concerns of God's self-donation in Christ and by the Spirit.

81. Hegel, *Vorlesungen über die Geschichte der Philosophie*, 123, quoted by Fackenheim, *Religious Dimension*, 223.

*to haunt the very critique of idealism in the aftermath of the dissolution of the Hegelian middle.*[82]

## Concluding Remarks

It is time now to summarize the main lessons of our encounter with Hegel. As already anticipated above, Hegel's paramount problem, which ultimately mars his promising start in Revelation and his bold appeal to the Trinitarian language of God's self disclosure, is his false ideal of knowledge. Ultimately, it is the dialectic of the subject within the horizon of Hegelian Logic that "explains" the dynamic movement of God's action as Father, Son and Spirit.

There is no doubt that by referring the connection between history and truth to God's relationship with the world, Hegel's proposal promised to reinforce the conclusion we had reached at the end of chapter 3, namely, the need to devise the empowering of human agency at the intersection between a theology of creation and a theology of the Word. Moreover, Hegel was right to stress that a successful movement from concept to reality needs to be a divinely assisted movement. To understand history as a hermeneutics of providence presupposes at least attentiveness to the thought that God came to us, that the Word became flesh, and that the relationship between language and reality presupposes both a designative and a transformative process. Nonetheless, it has been the ultimate return to the Aristotelian ideal of knowledge as *noesis noeseos noesis* which eventually renders the promising Trinitarianly mediated distinction between Creator and the created, futile.[83] In this light, we may perhaps say more

---

82. Smith is right to point out that a hermeneutical philosophy which bases its emancipatory power upon a speculative philosophy (such as Heidegger's or Gadamer's) "could never break the hold of reflection" (Smith, "Hegel, Kierkegaard and the Problem of Finitude," 211). In fact, Gadamer's ultimate recourse to speculation and his reliance upon a dialogical model reveal the problem of hermeneutic rather than its promise. Genuine otherness seems to slip between speculation (and a problematic concept of participation) and criticism. Perhaps the very concept of *Erfahrung* needs to be further explored in the light of the Creator—Creation distinction, and in the light of God's self-giving in Christ and by the Spirit. As we shall see in more detail later, however, it is not "speculation" as such (understood in a non-pejorative way) that is the problem, but rather the ultimate "object" of this speculation.

83. Following Mure, O'Regan contends that Hegelian reflection on the categories represents a synthesis of the Platonic theory of forms and the Aristotelian theological notion of *noesis noeseos noesis*. Cf. O'Regan, *Heterodox Hegel*, 100.

about the very dialectic of openness and closure. We noted earlier with O'Regan the necessity of both meaning and truth, openness and closure. But it is precisely because Hegel's ideal of knowledge fails to overcome the Greek framework that the illuminating dialectic of openness and closure remains structurally inadequate. In this respect, we should recall Torrance's insightful observation that the "openness" of concepts "is determined by what they are open toward."[84] The concepts of openness and closure cannot by themselves regulate either our understanding of God's Trinitarian action or the Creator-created distinction. In other words, our longing for meaning cannot be fulfilled in any other conceptuality. God's action in and towards the world must always function as the ultimate horizon for our inquiries into meaning. It is reflection on God's triune existence and action, as Father, Son and Spirit, that "gives rise to (meaningful theological) thought"! To apply such insights to Hegel's Geist, for instance, is to note that Hegel remains a modalist because his intellectualist understanding of Spirit as Geist, misconstrues the concrete and particularizing work of the Spirit that upholds the creature "as creature," in its finitude, yet without severing it from its relationship with God and without denying it participation in the life of God.[85]

Thus, the first thing to be taken up in the next section will be a fresh reconsideration of the Trinity in the context of contemporary Trinitarian debates. It is our wager that by reflecting anew upon the being and action of God as Father, Son and Spirit, our conceptions of knowledge and truth will be clarified and corrected. And this brings me to my second point.

Since knowledge in general, theological knowledge in particular, are fundamentally theological terms, what is equally worrying in claims to "absolute" or "total" knowledge is not only the "totalizing" compass of the first term but also *the "non-theological" understanding of the second!* We may note in passing here that had Christian eschatology not gone beyond a mere teleology understood within an Aristotelian framework, postmodern thought would be right to reject it as just another totalizing claim.[86] In other words, *to arrive at a genuine "theo-logical" concep-*

84. Torrance, *Theological Science*, 16.

85. See Gunton's critique of Hegel in Gunton, *Intellect and Action*, especially chapters 3 and 4. Gunton's critique of Barth's pneumatology in chapter 4, where he engages Hegel, arguably spells out one of the implications of Barth's continuing allegiance to the logic of German idealism.

86. Avineri claims that we have in Hegel an eschatological-teleological conferral of meaning (Avineri, *Hegel's Theory of the Modern State*, 206). It may be argued,

*tion of knowledge* entails more than "limiting knowledge." Theological knowledge doesn't need to take refuge in new forms of voluntarism or nominalism because the presence of the risen Christ through the spirit in the community of believers endows the Church with a vision of the end, yet without subsuming history into an eternal now. In this sense, the freedom to praise God for eternity remains "meaningful knowledge" beyond openness and closure.

It follows, more specifically, that a criticism of Hegel must not be content with a mere limiting of his hyperbolic claim. We reiterate in this way an earlier point. Since the very structure of emancipation is at stake here, an assessment of Hegel's problematic middle must point to its defective theological ground.[87] In this sense, Kierkegaard's protest against Hegel's concept of mediation is not a call to immediacy but an insight into the "internal" problems of Hegel's system.[88] Hegel's failure thus reinforces our suspicions towards the post-Hegelian Kantianism which animates the hermeneutical self. Indeed, a mere return to Kant not only that does not sufficiently address the underlying view of God as absolute subject but implicitly stifles Hegel's promise (rather than "correcting and transforming it")! We should recall that Hegel remains

---

however, that without a transcendental Spirit a genuine eschatological vision is impossible. It is doubtful that the successive *kenosis* of both Father and Son, followed by the immanentization of the Spirit in Hegel, allows for a genuine distinction between an immanent teleology and Christian eschatology. Christian eschatology presupposes more than apocalypse implying the presence of the end in the middle of history. Thus, knowledge as the figure of the end must be shown to be more fundamentally grounded in a doctrine of participation. In other words, this is not only a knowledge that would vanish away (1 Cor 13:8), but a knowledge grounded in the preeminence of the divine "*I* know you. . . . Well done good and faithful servant." Knowledge reveals itself here in its ethical dimension as a response in faith to the Divine Call, as faithful reply to God's self giving in Christ.

87. In this sense, Ricoeur's critique of Hegel remains insufficient in itself. In "Should We Renounce Hegel?," Ricoeur seems to make the problem of the "same" radically dependent upon time and sequence (which arguably amounts to accepting a form of modalism). It may be argued here that the problem of "otherness" is more fundamental than the logic of temporality. In other words, the idea of "presence" does not necessarily imply "sameness" (see Ricoeur, *Time and Narrative*, 3:202).

88. Kierkegaard's outrage at the virtual silencing of God's voice in Hegel's sovereign rational conquest—that is, taking with the left hand what he has given with the right (cf. Kierkegaard, *Concluding Unscientific Postscript*, 347–86), touches in this way upon a problem which, as we have seen in our engagement with Ricoeur, would continue to haunt the hermeneutical self. The suspicion of a relapse into "immediacy" in Kierkegaard's case is due, as alluded to above, to his continuing reliance on the consciousness model.

seductive precisely because it confronts us with both meaning and truth, universality and concern for the particular! Indeed, his vision is too appealing to be simply abandoned or forgotten! Contemporary left-wing Hegelians' critique of relativism and historicism, at least points to the continuing relevance of Hegel's plea for universality.[89] To be sure, in those proposals, Hegel's discourse is stripped of its metaphysical/theological referent and his overarching claims are somewhat tempered. But there is no return to Kant (at least not in the sense described in the last section). In Žižek, for instance, Kant's "ethical field," or the experience of "excess" or "overabundance," is recast once again in "the object," in a mythological "gap" between "humanity and its own inhuman excess."[90] Although such "immanent transcendence" of the subject refuses Hegel's panoramic perspective, or a "neutral ground," being at the same time, an affirmation of finitude/perspective, "a reflexive twist, by means of which I, myself am included in the picture constituted by me" (17), as in Hegel, finitude, is after all, implicitly left behind. Hence the "anti-naturalism," the bold affirmation of universality, the radical affirmation of "the exception" as the source and ground of political action.[91] Significantly, Žižek believes that "Kant is not unable to reach the infinite—he is unable to see he already has what he is looking for" (27).[92] Read in this way, Hegel's project is a grand "transcendental" exercise, an inquiry into the condition of the possibility of all experience . . . But Žižek is aware that such a reading "remains too modest" (28). Indeed, to "limit Hegel" in such a way, is to miss his greatness! Note the (ironic) filiations with Barth's reading! It is the speculative dimension of Hegel's dialectic itself, in this "parallax gap," that becomes the fuel for a new affirmation of the subject. As with Barth, Hegel's great promise sounds too good to be abandoned! In Žižek's account, only such "new concrete, universal" is able to rise from the ashes of "historicism/ relativism" into "historicism proper" (which is the same thing with "radical politics"). While the New Left is right to note the poverty of "historicism" and the (political) impotence of abstract critiques of totality that are all too popular in the typical discourse of liberal democracy today, it is through this speculative "ontological difference" that Hegel's "greatness"

89. Žižek and Badiou are two examples in this regard.

90. Žižek, *Parallax View*, 5. I will include references to this work in the text above.

91. See also Badiou, *Saint Paul*, esp. 98–106.

92. In the light of Hegel's defective theological vision, Žižek is right to read Hegel as not really overcoming Kant's parallax logic, but rather bringing it into full vision (from the "in-itself" to "for-itself."). Žižek, *Parallax View*, 25.

survives in these new quests for universality. New visions of "freedom" are unveiled (over against the empty projects/"negative freedom" of liberal democracy) and we are told once again, that the necessary this is the contingent, and that the particular reaches the universal in concepts like "absolute subjectivity," and the "infinite power of the subject." The difference this time, is that the philosophical discourse leaves no doubts about its "a-theological" commitments. If it is to be truly "great," it must necessarily include (and sublate religion); it must explicitly "instrumentalize" God (or "God talk," since the two are equivalent) and proudly affirm true philosophical discourse as (necessarily and explicitly) idolatrous "theological" talk. (I.e., using theological language and categories to point back to "the object," that is to say, to the created order and endowing it with mythical powers.)

Looking at the vision opened up by those proposals (and still having a vivid recollection of the painful (historical and personal) experience of a similar utopia, not too long ago[93]), we may exclaim indeed, with Morpheus (the fictional character of *The Matrix*), via Žižek: "Welcome to the desert of the real!"[94]

In the light of the high stakes of the present discussions, the most important part of our task is still situated before us. Ricoeur often repeats that genuine ontology "returns" to the world. At a formal level, Hegel's "Absolute" may be seen as "the ontological peak" of our journey. Accordingly, the next step might have been to thematize the "descent" from such an ontological option. Yet, as it has become abundantly clear, the "peak" proved to be a false absolute . . .

*If the journey "from meaning to Revelation" never genuinely reaches "the promised land of ontology," Hegel's "inverse" journey from "Revelation to meaning" ultimately dissolves the reality of the promised land into the subject's "wanderings in the desert."*

But, there have been a number of indications already, that, perhaps we don't really have to choose between a whole encompassing logic that settles one and for all the relationship between the infinite and the finite and an "ethically suspended" system. Perhaps all this is not really about a choice between "full vision" and "abstract obedience"; between the chimera of "full presence" (the illusion of getting that key that would unlock

---

93. I am referring to the historical career of Eastern European Marxist-Leninist Communism.

94. Allusion to Žižek's critique of (American) liberal democracy, in *Parallax View*, 367–75.

all doors) and the austere vision of a "discourse of limitation" (of the Kantian type). What is more, even if we were in the position to choose between such "ideal journeys" (as if the Subject would fully control his or her starting points), perhaps we should be better off if we "think those journeys together." But if we are to truly "think them together" we need to re-state the terms of the discussion . . .

Indeed, a number of things must be re-thought, if Hegel's promise of freedom is to become an authentic ontological option, genuinely grounded in a Trinitarian view of God. If our discourse is to genuinely refer to God, we need to unpack theologically the implications of Fackenheim's suggestion that Hegel needed both the immanent and the economic Trinity if a synthesis of the "generative" and "transformational" approach is to be possible. More importantly, this observation meets up and gives a broader theological scope to the incipient promise of mediation between a theology of the Word and a theology of Creation, suggested by our analysis of Ricoeur spelled out at the end of chapter 3. As will become apparent, the success of this mediation will reveal itself to be fundamentally dependent upon a Trinitarian understanding of God's action.

In this way, not only will a viable concept of knowledge and of participation become possible but the whole concept of concrete freedom in a community may receive a non-speculative dimension, being conceived this time as faithful response to God's self-donation in Christ. What is more, the theological discourse frees itself from the impossible requirement of having the "whole," from the burden of "absolute mediation" or "total explanation," finding instead its truthful fulfillment as an obedient and faithful response to God's action in Christ and by the Spirit. True knowledge is possible not because there is an identity between our "return to ourselves" and the "final station of the Spirit," but because we are granted, in Christ and by the Spirit, the privilege of participating in God's "coming" to us. If we are truly to "revive and transform" Hegel's promise, we must dismantle the ideal of this "return" to consciousness (with its "internalist" consequences), and start talking about theological rationality in this new framework. And when it is "God's coming to us" that sets the terms of the discussion, the very structure of the ethical field itself is construed differently, tracing the contours of a genuine "ethics of freedom" that takes shape at the intersection between vision and obedience.

Ultimately, therefore, as we shall see in more detail in the following chapters, we do not really "return" from ontology to the world of experience since *our chances of talking adequately about both God and the world cannot be substantiated outside of this coming!*

"God so loved the world that he gave his Son" . . . It is this radical claim of "having come" to us at the very heart of an, indeed, mysterious and elusive, yet nonetheless unrelenting presence of divine agency in the world in both its ethical and epistemic dimension, that will preoccupy us in the remainder of this book. The "bold self," the "responsive agent" cannot be conceived except in relation to this presence.

*Part III*

# The "Responsive" Self—Theological Rationality in Trinitarian Perspective

## 6

# Trinitarian Description between Metaphysics and Hermeneutics

For since, in the wisdom of God, the world did not know God through wisdom, it pleased God through the folly of what we preach to save those who believe. For Jews demand signs and Greeks seek wisdom, but we preach Christ crucified, a stumbling block to Jews and folly to Gentiles, but to those who are called, both Jews and Greeks, Christ the power of God and the wisdom of God. For the foolishness of God is wiser than men, and the weakness of God is stronger than men.

1 CORINTHIANS 1:21–25

OUR TIME MAY NOT be propitious for reopening epistemological discussions, because for good historical reasons, epistemology is still regarded in many theological quarters with skepticism still inextricably associated, in whatever indirect manner, with a particular form of justification and verification. It is perhaps felt that concern with epistemological issues necessarily revives the primacy of the *principium cognoscendi* in the structure of theological discourse with its consequent plethora of discredited concepts and assumptions.

Yet, the resurgence of interest in the Trinity from recent times, in its manifold forms, increasingly calls for the explicitly theological task of clarifying the nature of its Trinitarian description. This complex endeavor requires more than a detached analysis of language. As our previous analysis amply attested, the emergence of the new takes place at the intersection between language and reality, knowledge and being. Thus, in many ways, such an undertaking calls into question assumptions (both theological and anthropological) pertaining to theological method.

In other words, sustained concern with "content issues" has its own logic and inner discipline. Even scholars who proclaim the death of epistemology they make such claims using standards and criteria they consider reliable and trustworthy. That is to say, "God-talk" necessarily entails assumptions about the nature of theological language and about human rationality. And even the hard line Reformed theologian would acknowledge that God's action in and towards the world, not only that confronts and challenges patterns of human knowing, acting and being, but functions as the condition of their very possibility. It follows that inquiry into knowledge and justification may not be necessarily about human vanity, "objectification" or control. Instead, it may take its cue from our deep longing for truth, goodness and beauty, from our deep desire to live and act in the light of these ideals. Perhaps, it is the way this practice is conceived rather than the practice itself that is the problem. What is more, perhaps, epistemology considered in its proper theological dimension, in spite of its bad press, is not really a human invention.

In the remainder of this study I shall attempt to make a contribution to this discussion by contemplating one more time the ontological option opened to us in the context of contemporary Trinitarian discussions. In the light of our previous analysis, which may be perhaps encapsulated as a "hermeneutical" and a "speculative" journey, Trinitarian discourse may appear both as a promise and as a problem. As a promise, by virtue of its hermeneutical grammar, because its anticipated unity of being rests structurally upon the fundamental insight that at the heart of the Christian message stands the story of God's redemptive acts in history, manifested supremely in Jesus Christ. As a problem, to the extent to which Trinitarian discourse as a "second-order" discourse may betray its root and enclose itself in a false totality. This somewhat explains the "hermeneutical anxiety" about theological rationality prevalent in many theological circles today.

Nonetheless, while attentive to such concerns, my primary aim will be to show *that the basic grammar of the Trinitarian description considered in its ontological intention calls for "a return to the world."*[1] This "return"

---

1. This somewhat parallels Ricoeur's call for the return of ontology to the dialogue with the sciences. As I shall try to show however, this epistemological dimension is structural to God's being in three persons. Therefore, it is neither a desire for "relevance" nor mere attempt at mediation or dialogue that guides our proposal.

will be shown to unveil an irreducible epistemological dimension at the very heart of its ontological description.

To affirm the above is to affirm that our longing for truth, goodness and beauty is radically informed by the one man, Jesus Christ, who not only that successfully lived in the light of these ideals, but, through the Holy Spirit, enabled such authentic existence for the rest of us. But it is also to affirm that this fundamental Christological insight must be constantly referred back to its Trinitarian grammar. The upshot of this referral, as we shall see in more detail below, is an extended sense of theological epistemology that would go beyond a mere rational evaluation of criteria and warrant into a more general critique of human practices and institutions.

In *Canon and Criteria*, William Abraham expresses the "hermeneutical anxiety" towards theological rationality alluded to above by suggesting that epistemology (conceived as a "modern" endeavor with a quite restrictive set of assumptions and goals) is, if not harmful, of little use for the theologian.[2] More recently, however, Abraham has defended a version of theological epistemology acknowledging that the theologian cannot discard the practice altogether. Yet, it is "deepening the love of God and the neighbor" that remains the final goal. Knowledge is secondary and penultimate.[3] I wholeheartedly agree with Abraham on this score. I suggest, nonetheless, that the version of theological rationality we are aiming at here may be in fact a better fit for the Canonical Theism Abraham is proposing. Moreover, it may dispel some of the (arguably unnecessary) tension between canon and criteria.[4] As we shall see, it is precisely the way in which this "return to the world" is conceived that makes all the difference.

— —

Let me make two preliminary observations. The project of metaphysics has been traditionally conceived as the attempt to understand the basic structures of reality in terms of first cause or principle.[5] In this sense,

---

2. Abraham, *Canon and Criterion in Christian Theology*. See also Abraham, *Crossing the Threshold of Divine Revelation*.

3. Abraham, *Crossing the Threshold of Divine Revelation*, 188–89.

4. Canon certainly presupposes more than criteria but it is seldom, if ever, less than that. Moreover, as our analysis will show, often times, human practices and institutions function as criteria. I will return to Abraham's proposal below.

5. See Aristotle's definition of Metaphysics or first philosophy as the study of being *qua* being, in *Metaphysics*, 1026a 32. But perhaps, as Habermas suggests, this goes back, in spite of the differences between Plato and Aristotle, to Parmenides. See Habermas, *Postmetaphysical Thinking*, 13.

metaphysics is often conceived in close association with the project of natural theology, presupposing as it does the subsuming of all discourse about reality (including God) under the same category of being.[6]

In the modern period, since Kant, but most notably since Feuerbach and Nietzsche, the critique of metaphysics has been radicalized being transformed in a critique of foundations and/or of reason. Consequent upon their work, in some strands of postmodern thought, the critique of metaphysics had become synonymous with a critique of presence (in the sense of something being present to consciousness). While in the episte-mological form the two discourses still maintain a common problematic, to the extent to which the postmodern discourse does not abandon the project of reason but rather extends its critique to ontological and lin-guistic aspects, arguably, its critique of presence and the manifest concern for the proliferation of dualities and hierarchies, often gets entangled in empty logical considerations failing to address the questions which are of real interest for theology.[7] To be more specific, it is the problem of referring in relation to our God-discourse that really interests us. In this sense, of course, a "meta-physics" in the strong sense is presupposed. Nevertheless, to the extent that the problem of meaning remains open, the postmodern critique can be relevant, since, as will become apparent, the Christian conception of Revelation challenges the "metaphysical" way of conceiving God.[8] I shall use metaphysics mainly in its first sense,

---

6. I am also aware that efforts have been devoted in some quarters to retain the con-cept of metaphysics while rejecting naturalism. See Dieter Heinrich, "Die Grundstruktur der modernen Philosophie. Mit einer Nachschrift: Über Selbstbewußtsein und Selbster-haltung," in *Subjektivität und Selbsterhaltung*, ed. Hans Ebeling (Frankfurt: Suhrkamp, 1976), 114, quoted by Habermas, *Postmetaphysical Thinking*, 11.

7 There is little wonder that postmodern philosophers have been accusing one an-other of "metaphysical entrapment." What is significant here is not only the incapacity of such discourse to escape (Hegelian) speculation (see for instance Žižek's critique of Derrida in Žižek, *Did Somebody Say Totalitarianism?*, 154), but the deadlock entailed by the implicit subjectivism of this "critique of presence." We have already mentioned the more recent neo-Marxist concomitant call for both "universality" and radical sub-jectivity (Badiou, Žižek). As noted in the last section, the New Left is at least aware that such a position can never sustain (political) action.

8. Such a critique does not aim to suggest that various philosophical categories (the Platonic great kinds for instance), must be necessarily replaced by more "founda-tional categories" which would be "theological." Rather it is the case that an ontology conceived in traditional metaphysical language, will be always in want, always in need of theological elucidation in both its critical and constructive form.

as an attempt to envision totality, even though I shall be attentive to some of the concerns expressed in the latter.

The second point concerns the use of the term ontology. I would like to separate ontology from its traditional understanding as a neat description of what stands for the being of all being. I shall use ontology in a looser sense, as being that discourse which attempts to point or to refer to the unity of being, without necessarily endorsing a totalizing perspective. As will become apparent, such a usage (while reflecting a certain commitment to meaning, and perhaps "metaphysical" in some postmodern characterizations) will enable us to examine in due course the referential intention of the Trinitarian description in its ontological, epistemological and semantic ramifications.

## Faithfulness to the *Sache*:
## The Hermeneutical Grammar of the Trinity

In 1931 Barth could note the singularity of his own decision to put the doctrine of the Trinity at the head of his *Church Dogmatics*. "It is hard to see," writes Barth, "how in relation to Holy Scripture we can say what is distinctive for the holiness of this Scripture, if first we do not make it clear (naturally from Holy Scripture itself) who the God is whose revelation makes Scripture holy."[9]

Thus the exploration of the question "who" for Barth, not only precedes but is the absolute presupposition of all the other questions. It is because God revealed himself in three persons that talk about God, Scripture and the reality of the Church, in and for which Barth writes, is possible at all. Barth's paramount concern for safeguarding the preeminence of God enabled him to say, that the Trinity is not a doctrine among others, but encapsulates the fundamental grammar of Revelation. Whilst few would doubt Barth's crucial impetus in pioneering the resurgence of interest in Trinitarian thought, his revelational model has come under criticism in recent years. Following this line of inquiry, Trinitarian theology in the wake of Barth, may be seen as an attempt to articulate the full scope and implications of Barth's initial insight. Alan Torrance, for instance, suggests that Barth's determination to allow his discourse to be shaped by the object under investigation, opens in fact the possibility of transcending such a model in the later volumes of his *Church Dogmatics*.

9. Barth, *Church Dogmatics* I/1, 300 (further abbreviated as *CD*), 1936 ed.

Torrance argues that it is the communion model, which corrects, clarifies, explores further and fulfils in fact Barth's original insight. Of course the question may be raised whether such a development may in the end not only correct or expand on such an insight, but change it altogether.[10] But this is just one way of entering the contemporary Trinitarian debate. Christoph Schwöbel in an informative survey notes that the theological and the methodological background of today's Trinitarian reflections are in fact incredibly diverse and most surely divergent as well, ranging as they do, from liberation theology to new appropriations of Hegel's speculative model.[11] What is indeed remarkable is the way in which the doctrine of the Trinity succeeded in capturing the interest of such diverse ecclesial traditions, denominations and theological schools. How are we to understand this situation?

An immediate indication is the fact that the doctrine of the Trinity may be seen as the coagulating factor of all Christian claims. Irrespective of their particular concerns or doctrinal development, Christian claims do refer to the same reality. More specifically, the identifying reference of all Christian talk about God must in some way or other connect back to a particular historical event, when God intervened decisively in history in Jesus Christ. The Christian God became man, taking upon himself not only contingency and finitude, but also the burden of humankind. Thus, apart from bringing to the identity of God a unique relation to history and time, in his redemptive acts, the Christian God presents the human story in relation to himself, as meaningful story with an *arche* and a *telos*. Moreover, through the Spirit, this God brings the Church into existence making her by grace, both witness and co-partner with him in the work of reconciliation and perfection of Creation. Reference to God as triune has been in its initial form but a recognition of such a reality expressed not in detached theological descriptions but in living experience.

*Trinitarian discourse as confession stands therefore at the crossroad between witness and praise, between proclamation and the naming of God*

---

10. Pannenberg for instance claims that Barth did not succeed in meeting his own demand. The exact meaning of this for Pannenberg, is indicated by his immediate reference to Rahner's identification of the immanent and the economic Trinity which, in Pannenberg's opinion, sharpens Barth's call. Cf. Pannenberg, *Systematic Theology*, 1:300, 327–28. Recently, F. LeRon Shults has suggested that it is the "relational" model that imposes itself with necessity in the light of recent developments in science, philosophy and theology (Shults, *Reforming Theological Anthropology*, 11–38; also Shults, *Reforming the Doctrine of God*, 5–11).

11. Schwöbel, "Renaissance of Trinitarian Theology," 1.

*in liturgical form. It is both an invocation of and a witness to the one who, by revealing himself through the Son and in the Spirit, made us one in the body of Christ and partakers in the divine life.*

It was, above all, this richness of the Christian experience as a new way of being in the world, which deeply challenged the notion of God inherited from the Greeks. The traditional distinctions between the contingent and the necessary, the eternal and the temporal, *theoria* and *praxis* appeared to have been dislodged from their safe conceptual framework and recast in this new story. Karl Rahner's identification of the economic Trinity with the immanent Trinity has been just a way of voicing the radical possibility opened by Trinitarian thought. If God really became man, the Christian story is not just a novel description of God, but a liberative praxis that alters our very understanding of time and history, ontologically rooted precisely in this unique narrative identification.

Therefore this comprehensive witnessing dimension, in its double aspect as, on the one hand, a series of unique identifications of God in this story, and on the other, its unprecedented potential of anticipating a novel unity of being beyond Greek monism or dualism, is inextricably linked with an equally comprehensive doxological dimension, as an integral response which continues the story and co-determines its fulfillment. It was this inherent potential of Trinitarian discourse to refer, to express these things "in one breath," so to say, that transformed reflections upon Trinity into a meeting ground of such diverse Christian theological reflections and practices.

But if the Trinitarian discourse takes its cue from this narrative identification, is this narrative not, at least in some sense, epistemically more significant? Is it not its double role as both, precondition and unsurpassable limit, an indication that it is this "first level discourse," that really matters, after all?

In what follows, I shall attempt to press further my analysis not only in the light of these questions but also against them. It may be the case that our very way of questioning may be misguided. Let me make a start by taking a closer look at the complex referring dimension of the Trinitarian confession.

## Reference and the Promise of the Story

I shall attempt to expound this faithfulness to the story as this is expressed in some forms of contemporary narrative theology. Irrespective of their particular orientation, the narrative theologians are relatively united in the claim that "we cannot transcend the story in some way to find the real God."[12] This "first-level"[13] discourse functions as limit horizon within which the meaning of the text is discerned. We cannot found the referential intention of the discourse upon a "foundation" exterior to the discourse itself. If one is to refer to the real God, one must start from it and end with it.

I shall use Paul Ricoeur as my guide in the attempt to identify the limits of such a proposal. Ricoeur's case is particularly instructive because he speaks as an "insider." Narrative theology, for Ricoeur, does not seem to be just an option, but the necessary path. Nevertheless, he is supremely aware of its difficulties.[14]

Ricoeur opens his remarks on narrative theology by summarizing what he considers to be its main "refusals and suspicions." He lists here a purely speculative theology, a morally oriented theology, and an existential theology; all those options in their various ways, ultimately make history redundant. Against such options, narrative theology affirms a form of discourse which elaborates "the horizon of meaning implicit in the narratives and symbols constitutive of the Jewish and Christian traditions"(236).[15] But in spite of its decision to take history seriously, Ricoeur wants to separate the project of narrative theology from that of a theology of history (understood as a world-history in a Hegelian sense).

Consequently, one of the tasks of narrative theology, according to Ricoeur, would be to liberate the discourse into an "unresolved dialectic

---

12. I took here Jenson's claim from his essay "What Is the Point of Trinitarian Theology?," 38. Even though Jenson is not a typical representative of narrative theology, the claim itself does represent a fundamental commitment of narrative theology. For an informative summary of Narrative Theology's tasks and concerns, see Fackre, "Narrative Theology," 340–52.

13 It is very significant to note that for Jenson, Trinitarian discourse *is not* a second-level discourse. ("Initially, it is rather the first-level act of calling on God by the triune name." Jenson, "What Is the Point of Trinitarian Theology?," 31.)

14. See Ricoeur, "Towards a Narrative Theology," in *Figuring the Sacred*, 236–48. I will incorporate page references into the text above.

15. According to Ricoeur, the narrative dimension must take into account its historical grounding. In fact, it is the particular theory of history (whether implicit or explicit) which would eventually bring insurmountable problems for narrative theology.

of memory and hope" (238). Such a task becomes even more stringent in the light of what Ricoeur calls "the increase of forgetfulness" of our past Enlightenment of tradition, manifest in the general collapse of tradition and authority and the loss of trust in the practice of story-telling. Ricoeur expounds what he considers to be the resources of narrative theology under the rubric of narratology. He reiterates here a somewhat older conviction that the possibilities of narrative theology lie precisely in the fundamental continuity between narrative in general and biblical narrative. Ricoeur mentions four traits of narratology which in various degrees can be applied to biblical narrative.

First, is the art of emplotment. Through its concordant-discordant pattern, the art of emplotment points to the twofold structure of human time, as passing away, and as enduring. Second, is the epistemological status of the intelligibility of this configurational act. Appealing to Aristotle's concept of *phronesis*, Ricoeur portrays a particular type of intelligibility characteristic to a story which is more akin to practical wisdom or moral judgment. That is to say, while there is a kind of universality yielded by the plot, such universality does not come under the rubric of theoretical knowledge. They are "universals of a lower order appropriate to the configurational act at work in poetic composition" (240). The biblical narrative intensifies this trait in Ricoeur's opinion because it is especially here that the particular identity of God comes to us veiled in a story. The next trait, the role of tradition, with its complex dialectic between innovation and sedimentation, rounds the formation of this narrative identity. "Christianity is a community of story tellers . . . a community at table together" (241), in which we are gradually taken up in the story recounted; "the story and our story become one and the same" (242). With the fourth trait, the meaning of the narrative, we reach the peak of the argument, because here Ricoeur's contribution is most apparent. "Meaning," he states, "is not confined to the so-called inside of the text. It occurs at the intersection between the world of the text and the world of the readers" (240). Ricoeur sketches briefly here a view of language which rejects the methodological decision present in various semiotic and linguistic approaches of arbitrarily imposing an inside and an outside to the text. But, while Ricoeur pleads for a view of language that preserves referentiality, he acknowledges that the emergent reference in the case of the Biblical narrative remains somewhat elusive. Indeed, "the story of the partnership between God and Israel is not only open and ongoing but unfathomable and unspeakable" (243). Moreover, the inexhaustibility of history is joined to the ineffability of God's name through the paradigmatic nature of the episode at the burning bush.

It is precisely here that Ricoeur wants to substantiate the difference between narrative in general and biblical narrative. The observation is of utmost importance because the inference seems to be that a purely immanent story tends indeed towards a certain kind of totalization precisely because they have a beginning and an end in time (242). A limit situation is reached here: on the one hand Ricoeur deplores what he called "the Christian pattern" (238), that is, the tendency to freeze the narrative in a theological all-encompassing structure which emerged after the closing of the canon. On the other hand however, the guide of narratology does not seem eventually able genuinely to address the problem of closure. The biblical text remains elusive and the intensifying trait concealed and ambiguous, *precisely because it is special*.

Ricoeur develops this special function of the biblical text as sacred story, in terms of its special relation to tradition, its authoritative character or its canonical form and its liturgical dimension (243). In such a light, "no biblical narrative works merely as narrative" (245). Ricoeur wants to stress not only the complex network of relationships between various literary genres, between Law, wisdom literature, prophecy, psalms, gospel, etc, but also the crucial role of reference in its relation to history. The emerging pattern of images and symbols traces a contour of meaning which is "alien to ordinary storytelling" (245). This complex relationship between narrative and non-narrative modes of expression brings us to the crux of the problem, namely, the transition from narrative to explicit theological discourse. Unsurprisingly, Ricoeur alludes to the role of imagination as potentially being the vital clue in any attempt to elucidate such a passage. He welcomes in this connection Niebuhr's *The Meaning of Revelation* as one of the first attempts to conceive Revelation as narrative. However, Ricoeur eventually criticizes his implicit theory of history which appears to conceive the relation between the story recounted and our story as a mere passage from theoretical to practical reason. Such an account appears to follow Kant too closely, issuing as it does in a mere practical theology, with its exemplarist and moralist implications. Ricoeur believes that we have reasons to defend a conceptual theology precisely because this "second-order" discourse is grounded in the first. Thus, the confessions and doxologies are rooted (like exodus credo or resurrection credo) in the narratives themselves. Ricoeur concludes that ultimately, narrative itself never existed without embryonic theological thinking on the one hand, and praise as the context of the telling of the story, on the other. "Praise, doxology and regulative assertions constitute a progressive series from which theologizing emerges (248).

In sum, there are two slightly different problems to which Ricoeur draws our attention: first, it is precisely the complex structure of this referring dimension implicit in the text itself, that calls for the transcendence of an alleged logic immanent in the story. As O'Donovan puts it "When everything is story there is nothing for the story to be about."[16] It is precisely because the story is about something, that is to say, about a God acting on behalf of a real community in real history that the text points beyond itself. In point of fact, this "aboutness" of the story points to a complex notion of agency which is not limited to a historical community in its narrative configuration.

But Ricoeur also draws our attention to the fact that this referring dimension is a feature of language in general, and what makes the biblical text special is its quality of not lending itself easily into a theory of history. Ricoeur is supremely aware of the subliminal temptation present in various forms of narrative theologies to refer the taxis of discourse back to an immanent logic of the story. But as we have seen, this narrative logic ultimately draws its resources from non-narrative elements, pointing thus beyond itself to a more fundamental taxis and a more primordial meaning. When such a taxis is conceived in purely historical and immanent terms, the direction of predication is implicitly reversed: *the logic of the story* is the logic of God.[17] . . . When this happens, what was initially a precious resource now becomes a worrying limitation. That is why Ricoeur seems to resist the seduction of a temporal logic. What he would be prepared to say about time, resembles what Aristotle said about being: "Human time is said in many ways in the Bible" (246).[18] *Perhaps, in the end, human time cannot be frozen into an immanent logic because, as with any created reality, its meaning must be decided in the relationship with its Creator.*

16. O'Donovan, *Resurrection and Moral Order*, 60.

17. In this sense Jenson's recourse to Aristotle remains inadequate, too close to a rather temporal explicitation of God (cf. Jenson, "Point of Trinitarian Theology," 40–42). Barth's position was perhaps more balanced when he claimed that "pre-temporality, supra-temporality and post-temporality are equally God's eternity and therefore the living God himself." Barth, *CD* II/1, 638.

18. The exact quotation: "Human time is shaped in many ways . . ." (Ricoeur, *Figuring the Sacred*, 246).

We have seen, therefore, that the theologizing is somewhat implicit in the structure of narrative itself. There are always non-narrative elements at work in the emergence of conceptuality. More importantly, we have pointed out with Ricoeur that what keeps the discourse open is precisely its special character in its immediate context of praise and worship in a community united in one confession. So, the promise of the openness of our discourse receives a new dimension in the light of this special community, which in its confession, not only proclaims, but also lives out the referential intention of its discourse.

## Referring as an Ecclesial Event

In actual fact, if our story is God's story, it cannot be separated from a community. It is neither a mere historical accident nor an archaeological discovery. In a sense, this community is both the precondition of the right discourse about God and its very fulfillment. The epitome of Christ's victory over the world (John 16:33) is the birth of the Church. "The gates of Hades shall not prevail against her . . ." God made manifest in a new life, a new mode of existence. That is to say, to follow the referential intention of the biblical text is to be awakened to the profound ontological implications of what the text is about. It is important to note that the recognition of this dimension is not primarily an attempt to mediate between a speculative and a skeptical view of history. It is rather a theological point meant to acknowledge the enduring presence and action of God which made both text and community possible.

It has been especially the merit of the Eastern tradition to draw our attention to this problem. The Eastern tradition has stressed unrelentingly that genuine Christian experience as an ecclesial event rests upon a reality which continues and fulfils the Incarnation.[19] The interest in the doctrine of the Trinity reflected more than a mere intellectual attempt of the Church to unify the experience which brought her into being.

---

19. See for instance Khodre, "Church in Movement," 22; or Lossky, *In the Image and Likeness of God*, 169ff. One of the principal lessons of Eastern Orthodox Ecclesiology was its stress upon Pneumatology. See also the informative survey of Orthodox ecclesiological debate in Zizioulas, *Being As Communion*, 123–32. It was perhaps the overtly Christological treatment of ecclesiology in the West that led to a treatment of history at the same logical level with the being of God. This situation led to either a hypostatisation of the world as a more or less independent entity, or to the irresistible tendency to affirm the preeminence of God against history.

Instead, it arose as an expression of its very life, in its daily liturgy, sacraments and doxology. Words and presence were brought together in the act of invocation. Thus, the Trinitarian confession was not developed primarily for apologetic or missiological reasons, but it has always been the expression of the very nature of the theandric being of the Church. To conceive it otherwise, is to fall ineluctably into functionalist models, something which the West is found to be always guilty of.

The referring dimension in such a case is less associated with an explicit theory of history or to an epistemological position. It is felt that to engage in such discussions runs the risk of diverting from the real concerns and calling of the Church. Again, faithfulness to the content is spelled out primarily in doxological and practical terms.

But the critical dimension has been always present in the life of the Church, and the long doctrinal debates against heresies prove that the Church has been always concerned about the kind of totality envisaged by her ontological vision. Her concrete life, with her problems and questions, aspirations and anxieties, have shown the referring dimension of her text and confession to be not only an invaluable asset and promise, but also a source of discord.

## Referring as a Problem

An interesting outcome of the encounter with the Eastern tradition in modern Trinitarian discussions has been precisely the resurgence of interest in historical theology prompted by the new reference points of the discussion.[20] The filioque clause is perhaps a good example in this respect. It was Vladimir Lossky who drew the attention to the fact that this was more than a mere doctrinal difference contingent upon historical and political concerns.[21] The re-consideration of the filioque clause led to an increasing awareness that there were, after all, the different Trinitarian models employed by the two traditions that brought about the specific character of their own theology, liturgy and daily practice and relation to culture. As Schwöbel notes, such situation prompted in the Western tradition an internal critique of its prevalent psychological treatment. The lack of interest in the Trinity in the last century is thus traced

---

20. E.g., Gunton, *Promise of Trinitarian Theology*, 31–55; Schwöbel, "Renaissance of Trinitarian Theology," 3–5.

21. Lossky, *In the Image and Likeness of God*, 71–96.

back not only to the Enlightenment, but to Augustine. As it has been amply shown in recent Trinitarian discussions, in the modern period, the Trinity had become not just of no practical significance, but potentially harmful.[22] This growing incapacity of theological discourse to genuinely refer marked its gradual attachment to a different grammar, enclosing itself in an alien *Weltanschauung*. Schwöbel perceptively remarks that it was the confrontation of the Western Church with a different conceptuality and practice that provided new criteria for assessing its own history,[23] revitalizing its own capacity to express a genuine critical function.

Examples can be also offered from the Eastern tradition. I shall only mention here Dorothea Wendebourg's now classic criticism of the doctrine of energies. Wendebourg launches a serious theological attack on the whole theological tradition which enabled the distinction between essence and energies, a distinction which eventually made the Trinity soteriologically functionless.[24] The principal problem of this conceptuality, Wendebourg contends, is that the energies take over the function of the persons. The schema of the fulfillment of creation, human being included, through participation in the energies, tends to make the historical career of Jesus redundant. Such an attitude arguably encouraged a certain detachment of the community from history, and tended to forget precisely its Christological roots which brought her into being.[25]

Thus the quite legitimate concern of preserving both the meaning of divine grace as participation in the divine life, and the radical distinction between God and Creation, gave rise to an ever accentuated tendency to re-polarize the discussion in two opposites: God as *energeiai* and God as *ousia*.[26] Palamas insisted, according to Wendebourg, that the distinction is not simply an epistemological one, but is constitutive of the very being of God, on the same level with Father, Son and Spirit distinction. The implication is that the "*hypostaseis* do not enter the created world,

---

22. See for instance Kant's remarks (*Religion Within the Limits of Reason Alone*, 92).

23. Schwöbel, "Renaissance of Trinitarian Theology," 4.

24. Wendebourg, "From the Cappadocian Fathers to Gregory Palamas," 194–98.

25. For a somewhat similar argument, see Gunton, *Brief Theology of Revelation*, 42ff, where he emphasises how the adoption of the doctrine of the forms in the medieval theology of Creation led to the loss of the mediative role of Christology in this theology.

26. Wendebourg, "From the Cappadocian Fathers to Gregory Palamas," 195.

they simply are."[27] This severing of the being of God from any connection with the world and history thus renders *theologia* (in this rather restrictive sense) as the only genuine and liberative discourse. Needless to add, anything less becomes "functional" and "less ontological."

Now some defense has been produced in recent times from both sides. On the one hand, the negative repercussions of the Augustinian inheritance have been greatly exaggerated, it is claimed, and a new quest for a "proper reading" of Augustine has been launched.[28] Similarly, it has been argued that the Palamite position is not a philosophical theory but it is based upon a practice. Moreover, the distinction itself, does not necessarily imply an erasure of the significance of Trinity, but rather a clarification of it.[29] Be that as it may, the main question remains: How can a community avoid getting entangled in a false totality? What has become clear is that this concern with the referential dimension is not merely an abstract intellectual debate, but is profoundly rooted in praxis.

We have seen so far that there are theological reasons, which seem to support the view that the Trinitarian confession must be both the presupposition and the ultimate horizon of a genuine theological discourse. But what are the epistemological and the semantic implications of such a claim? Is that to suggest that the Trinitarian discourse, to the extent that it starts and ends in prayer and worship, rests unproblematically in "full presence"? Does this mean that the critical dimension and responsibility of accounting for its own discourse is made redundant? We have just indicated, following the historical career of such an intention, how its referential claim, in fact, often stumbles and falls short of its call. Moreover, is it proper to conceive the semantic correlate of this situation as an

27. Ibid., 196.

28. See for instance Ayers's recent study (*Augustine and the Trinity*) that is a representative of the "new canon" of interpreting Augustine.

29. One of the recent attempts to defend the Palamite position from a Western perspective is that of Duncan Reid (*Energies of the Spirit*). Yet, even when the above considerations are granted, we may still wonder: is not the *logos* "rational" enough to account for the logic of God's relationship with the world so that we need a more foundational conceptuality? Or is not the Christ through the Spirit and in relation to the Father "personal" enough to guide our discourse of freedom and love when we want to talk about God as presence, fulfillment or meaning? Is the category of essence more apt to achieve that? It may be objected that the questions themselves, like the alternative criticized, are speculative. Yet, I would reply that this manifests a purely *a posteriori* concern of accounting for the kind of presence depicted by Paul in some of his prayers (e.g., Ephesians 1; Colossians 1; etc.).

unproblematic dwelling in "the fullness of the concept"? Towards such problems we shall now turn.

## In the Shadow of Metaphysics?

I would like to explore two potential directions in which the theological discourse may enclose itself, and to point to their corresponding set of problems. I must say from the very beginning that my intention is not to indulge in sweeping generalizations but to follow the logic of emerging patterns and to trace the contours of potential closures. The appeal to history is therefore more illustrative than genetic, and not dependent for that matter, on the strict success of a certain historical scenario.[30]

## The Burden of "Sense"

Let me start with a disclaimer. I am aware that the pair "discourse of sense" and "discourse of freedom" has a certain philosophical currency. My usage has been inspired by Ricoeur's phenomenological mediations of various Kantian dichotomies (freedom and nature, fact and meaning, etc). I hope I can make a better use of this terminology by applying it to the referential intention of the Trinitarian discourse. The way I use the term "sense" must be understood as a reply to a usage which ascribes to it an ideal semantic content (whether this is situated between "psychologism" and "realism" as Frege would have it, or as in Ricoeur where it tends to function as a formal pattern or structure which lends itself unproblematically to "explanation.") Whilst I usually refer critically to what I shall term a "discourse of sense" (where "sense" is conceived in an

---

30. I do not want to make my discourse "invincible," i.e., to adopt a "no risk" solution by establishing a procedure which would be able to accommodate all alternatives. Rather, the point here is to devise a critique, which would situate itself at an equal distance from both a historical and a systematic critique. This ultimately means to explore the tension between the "historicity" of a theological claim (which makes reading history an ever new and enlightening enterprise) and its referential intention. That is why I am not only prepared to accept reevaluations of Augustine or Aquinas, for instance, but I welcome such studies to the extent that they bring to light new aspects of the tension between the dynamism of the Gospel and the totalizing tendency of a system of thought or other. Thus what is ultimately in view is the question: How the lessons of historical theology as a second order critique (that is interested not only in the "historicality" of various disputes, but in the "aboutness" of those disputes) functions as a critical tool for the more systematic discourse of theology?

unproblematic identity with "reference," or as a neat "system" of thought), my ultimate intention is to point to the theological horizon opened up by such language. It is therefore imperative to note that "sense" is emphatically not the correlate of "nature." Therefore, the pair "discourse of sense" and "discourse of freedom" far from reviving old distinctions between freedom and nature, quite the contrary, aims to uncover the rich dynamic of God's relationship with the world. We also hope that this language will aid our quest for a theological rationality which attempts to understand the epistemological dimension in the light of its ontological structure.

Duncan Reid in a recent book, encapsulates what he considers to be the fundamental structure of the Western theological approach under the rubric of the identity principle, which, he believes, finds its most eloquent expression in Karl Rahner's famous claim that the economic Trinity *is* the immanent Trinity.[31] Reid argues that the structure of such an approach is crucially dependent on Aristotle, who, by refusing to take up the Platonic distinction between the intelligible and the sensible establishes a different structure of the relation between *ousia*, *energeia* and *dunamis*. Thus, the chain of being is subsumed under one ontological stratum. *Ousia* no longer denotes a concrete being as in Plato, but tends to become the formal substructure of reality.

Reid argues that the Aristotelian identification of essence and energy in actual things would become part of the grammar of Western scholasticism, "which identifies God's essence or substance as pure actuality (*actus purus*)."[32] This favoring of actuality over possibility in Western thought is obviously a complex question and we shall not address it here in any detail.[33] Neither are we interested here to assess whether, and to what extent, it is true that the mystery of God has thus been effectively dispelled in the Western tradition, or how feasible is to apply such a generic pattern either to the whole Western tradition or to such diverse theologians as Barth and Rahner, for instance. In spite of its potential problems, however, the analysis rightly uncovers the tendency in the

---

31. Of course, everything depends on how the copula "is" of this relation is interpreted. As we have seen in the previous chapter, the identity principle becomes worrying when the above relation between the immanent and the economic Trinity is used to support a more or less explicit identity between Creator and creation.

32. Reid, *Energies of the Spirit*, 9.

33. See Jüngel, *Theological Essays*, 95ff, for a theological view which challenges this principle. For the relationship between *energeia* and *dunamis* in Aristotle, see *Metaphysics*, 1049b 24–26. For other treatments, see Brentano, *On the Several Senses of Being in Aristotle*, chapter 4.

West, to subsume the Christian story into a neat and ordered discourse of being.[34] In such a picture, the world is, more or less, a settled reality having God as its "unmoved mover."[35]

A somewhat similar diagnosis has been offered when the analysis followed the concrete way in which the doctrine of the Trinity has been outlined in the West. We have already mentioned the implications of Augustine's psychological model of the Trinity. The emphasis upon the unity of divine essence, and especially the way in which that was related to the unity of divine actions, encouraged a strong monistic tendency in which the unity of God was obvious, whilst the Trinity was in need of explanation. At the limit, the "substantialist" tradition may become immersed in a cosmological vision in which God's relationship with the world is more or less contained in a neat "discourse of sense." The taste of the Western world for such a discourse brought about a distinctive worldview rightly treated with contempt in Heidegger's famous essay "*Die Zeit des Weltbildes.*"[36]

In such a scheme, soteriology becomes just the correlate of such "discourse of sense." The logic of grace is simply re-cast into the strait-jacket of this cosmological order, translated into contractual views where the ethical view of the world prevails.[37]There have been, no

---

34. Saying that however, I do not intend to reduce, say, Aquinas's theology to what I called a "discourse of sense." I am convinced that, at close inspection, one can identify in Aquinas a consistent effort to talk about God as the "living God." See the classical study of Mascall, who defends a reading of Aquinas that gives priority to existence over essence by unpacking Aquinas's dispute with the essentialist movement of his day; cf. Mascall, *He Who Is.* See also the more recent study of Marion, who suggests that even if Aquinas *does* think God as *esse*, he nevertheless does not chain God to Being. Cf. Marion, *God without Being*, xxiii.

35 Abraham notes that it is in Aquinas that we witness the move to a comprehensive epistemology: "Nowhere is the move to construe the canonical heritage of the church in epistemic categories more visible than in the theology of Thomas Aquinas" (cf. *Canon and Criterion in Christian Theology*, 86). Thus, a "universal epistemology" may be seen to follow naturally from an undisputed doctrine of being. However, Abraham rightly notes that "being concise and clear" in pursuing the truths of Christian Theology is not something that the human subject imposes but must be derived from the subject matter ("as far as the subject permits" [ibid., 87]). That's why Aquinas, in Abraham's view, is not a classical foundationalist, as his epistemology cannot be divorced from his theology. I will return to this point below.

36. Heidegger, *Holzwege*, 80, quoted by Ricoeur, *Conflict of Interpretations*, 462.

37. The famous *ordo salutis* may be mentioned here. For a critique from the perspective of revelation, see Torrance, *Persons in Communion*, 59–63. See also Ricoeur's critique of the ethical view of the world in general and of the Reformed doctrine of

doubt, protests against such tendencies from Luther, Pascal and Kierkegaard to Karl Barth.

The Enlightenment radicalized such a perspective by cleansing it of
its "mythological" dimension yet, in the process, undoubtedly contributed decisively to its collapse. The so-called "humiliation of the subject"
(in its cosmological, biological and psychological dimension), brought to
light how dependent its meaning was on a defective metaphysical vision.
This also brought to full vision the rather unfortunate habit of theology
to inscribe itself uncritically into the problematic of the day, rather than
to challenge it. It is sufficient at this point to recall the intractable Christological crisis reaching perhaps its climax in the nineteenth century, well
summarized by Schwöbel.

Schwöbel describes the crisis as being generated by three sets of
causes. The first cause, well encapsulated in Lessing's thesis about the antinomy between the necessary truths of reason and the contingent truths
of history recapitulates all the problems inherited from the Platonic
thought (i.e., the unsolvable tensions contingent-necessary, eternal-tem-
poral, history-metaphysics). The second relates to the antinomy between
past and present, whilst the third, to the disjunction between being and
meaning. It is relatively easy to see that the second and the third cause, to
the extent that they make appeal to the same problematic of temporality
and presence, still rest upon a Greek problematic.[38] The conclusion to be
drawn from this analysis is that the problem of time and eternity, necessity and contingency, etc. became painfully acute, rather than addressed
Christologically, precisely because the Christological problem has come
too late to the discussion in a situation where the structure of the whole
had been already set. Schwöbel's comment is worth quoting in full:

> It is perhaps due to the incomplete Christianization of Hellenism
> that the philosophical theology of Christianity has sometimes
> more contributed to this dualism than to its overcoming.[39]

---

original sin in particular. Cf. Ricoeur, "Original Sin," in *Conflict of Interpretations*,
269–86.

38. Schwöbel, "Christology and Trinitarian Thought," 113–46, evaluates such a
situation as a divorce between Soteriology and Christology: "This antinomy, seems
to confront us with a choice between a non-soteriological ontology (being without
meaning), and a non-ontological soteriology (meaning without being)" (Ibid., 119).

39. Ibid., 116.

This points again to the fact that when theological discourse does not resonate Trinitarianly, so to say, it encloses itself in a false totality, getting itself entangled precisely in the problems that it was supposed to address. Historically, this brings us to one of the most significant upshots of the failure of the medieval synthesis, namely, the critique of traditional metaphysics manifest especially in the retreat of theology to epistemological discussions. Unsurprisingly, the name of Kant features prominently here. As it is well known, it has been Kant above all who dispelled the excessive claims of theoretical reason. With him, we witness the inauguration of the modern critique of metaphysics and naturalism. However, the radical denial of naturalism and of metaphysics did not advance the theological discussions but in fact accentuated the crisis alluded to above.[40] Kant only transferred the cosmological pattern of order to the human mind, mirroring the cosmological order in an epistemological guise. Thus, the philosophy of Kant, and the theologies that have followed closely in his steps, tended to move to a different form of enclosure, epistemologically conceived this time.

An example which I think illustrates eloquently the incapacity of contemporary philosophical attempts to redeem the credibility of epistemology as a foundational science or as a systematic discourse,[41] is Gellner's defense of foundationalism. Gellner is convinced that "the Enlightenment has codified the only seriously acceptable principles of valid knowledge" (91–92). While he rightly criticizes the "relativist hermeneutics," his own attempt to bring together a universal rationality with its strict ethics, and a pragmatic good will (94), ultimately fails to indicate the ontological structure of the alleged foundation.[42]

40. Kantianism encouraged atheism, precisely because its anti-metaphysical thrust was monolithic and undifferentiated. We reiterate here an earlier point, namely, that neither metaphysics nor its rejection (as neat theoretical positions) really address the theological concerns. This is why Barth never rejected *a priori* the attributes of God for instance, for allegedly belonging to a "metaphysical structure."

41. Gellner, *Postmodernism, Reason and Religion*, 80–96. I shall include references in the text above.

42. Gellner recognises that "it is not easy to formulate these [principles] with precision or to general satisfaction, and that it may be impossible to demonstrate their authority" (ibid., 92). But such a claim depotentiates his expressed "foundationalism," that is, his belief in an inner core of universal principles of valid knowledge allegedly codified by the Enlightenment. The recovery of such a core of principles becomes thus an ideal task both in its historical form (Gellner admits that the concrete representatives of the Enlightenment were in fact "naturalists" in one way or another, that is to say, they believed in an ontological foundation), and in its Kantian expression (to

Perhaps Habermas's transcendental pragmatism, as a post-metaphysical version of the same effort to restore the unity of reason and the power of *Selbstreflexion*, is hardly in a better position in this respect, in spite of its invaluable insights (its preference for the linguistic model, and his famous paradigm of communicative action). Whilst its critical function must be welcomed (its illuminative depiction of the complex structure of human communication in its linguistic and historical dimension) its positive proposals remain largely formal.[43] In what follows, my intention is to point to the fact that such a discourse of systematic limitation does not rescue theology from self-enclosure.

Before that, however, I must point out that it is difficult to summarize in just one paradigm, the theology influenced by Kant. The main reason for this is undoubtedly the complexity of Kant's own writings. In fact, there is hardly within the philosophical tradition an undisputed reading of Kant.[44] Thus, we should not be surprised to find that the theology inspired in one way or another by Kant, is even more diverse. My intention is not to identify "traces of Kant" in different theologies, *but to try to understand the structure of the critique of knowledge within a theology conceived of as a discourse of systematic limitation, and to point to some of the damage done to theology by the application of Kant's distinctions to its content.*

---

the extent the transcendental function of the mind is left unchallenged by the more fundamental dialectic of desire).

43. I am aware that Habermas links his concept of communicative Reason with Hegel (cf. Habermas, *Philosophical Discourse of Modernity*, 303). This obviously raises the question of the way in which one devises the nature and scope of the transcendental exercise. Here however, I am referring more specifically to his description of the ideal speech-situation. It is doubtful that by an increasing abstractization of such regulative language a genuine arbitration between competing language games can be achieved. I do not want to deny its usefulness as a critical tool in uncovering the distortions of human communication. The awareness of our sinful condition should indeed prompt us to consider it seriously. See also Taylor's powerful critique of procedural ethics in general and Habermas's position in particular. Taylor, *Sources of the Self*, 53–90, 510.

44. The analytical tradition has opted quite unsurprisingly for a rather categorial reading of Kant. It is in such a reading that Kant's philosophy as "discourse of sense" reigns supreme. The "continental" tradition gave more consideration to the transcendental Kant, that is to say, to anthropological aspects and to the more dynamic aspects of knowledge. See Ricoeur's comment about that in Ricoeur, *Critique and Conviction*, 50. Ricoeur identifies Strawson's *Within the Bounds of Sense* as a supreme example of a "categorial" reading of Kant.

As it is well know, the seeds of the hermeneutics of suspicion lie in Kant's critique of the illusions of transcendental reason.[45] It must be contended that this "destruction of the idols" has a certain affinity with the biblical concern for safeguarding the uniqueness and ultimately non-objectifying nature of God. Nevertheless, the question arises of how we are to speak about the mystery of God. It is not difficult to see that not all discourses of limitations are equally legitimate or illuminative. A number of observations are in order in this connection.

First of all, the criteria of such a limit must not be either our own finitude or our consciousness of sin. If knowledge of God is not an inherent human possibility, but an expression of God's grace in revealing himself to us, our chance of understanding God *as mystery* is bound to the same source, namely, his gracious revelation to us. Here we should retain Barth's insight that the mystery, in order to be a genuine mystery, must be a re-vealed mystery.[46] To know God as mystery and to conceive of our knowl-edge of him as limited, is not a transcendental exercise but an *a posteriori* reflection, enabled by the Spirit, upon God's decision to reveal himself, upon his act of making impossible things possible. A theory of knowledge in itself should not be allowed to dictate either the positive content or the mystery of God.[47] If our theological language is truly to refer, it must not be founded upon human possibility in whatever form, nor can it be made dependent upon human awareness of its own limitations.

I shall refer briefly to what I consider to be a most eloquent con-temporary example of theology done under the aegis of Kant, namely to Kaufman's constructive theology.[48] For Kaufman, the discourse about God begins with human practices and speech; "God is a human word and a human idea" (15). In such an understanding the theologian's task

---

45. Kant, *Critique of Pure Reason*, translated by Meiklejohn, 208ff.

46. "The capacity to know God is given by Revelation and is not identical with the limitation of our perception and discursive thinking." Cf. Barth, *CD* II/1, 183. For a detailed discussion, see Barth, *CD* II/1, 3ff. See also Jüngel's plea for a *positive* concept of mystery (*God as the Mystery of the World*, esp. 250–55). "Part of the structure of the positive concept of mystery is . . . that it does not cease being mystery when it has been grasped" (ibid., 250).

47. Karl Rahner is right in claiming that divine mystery "constitutes not a regret-table imperfection in theology but rather that which is most proper to it, of its very nature" (*Theological Investigations*, 101). Yet, as Jüngel notes, his concept of mystery as the "horizon of all understanding," remains fundamentally in want due to his tran-scendental approach (*God as the Mystery of the World*, 251).

48. Kaufman, *In Face of Mystery*. I shall include references in the text above.

is "to develop a conception of human life in which . . . talk about God
. . . is intelligible" (15), "to attempt to construct conceptions of God, humanity, and the world appropriate for the orientation of contemporary
human life" (31). We find out (with sadness) that the central question for
theology is not pre-eminently who or what God is, or how God is to be
distinguished from the idols, nor is it how humanity is. "It is not primarily a speculative question, a problem of knowledge at all," Kaufman contends. "Most fundamentally it is a practical question: How are we to live?"
(15–16). Unfortunately, the notions which try to articulate the answer to
this latter question remain largely "human creations" (31). Thus, "God"
is a symbol, a mere human construction, which may be changed or even
dropped" (40) and replaced with something better. In such a paradigm,
Trinity merely represents the highest conceptualization (i.e., construction) of the notion of God (412ff). Since we cannot talk about God in
an objectifying way, Trinitarian discourse is reduced to a functional role
(417). While Kant, arguably, remained in a significant sense a realist,
Kaufman adopts a radically constructive approach, which emerges as a
self-enclosed picture from which the living God seems to have disap-
peared and we are left with our own ideas about God. But of course, such
application of Kant's categorial structure to theology is not new. It belongs to a certain theological style born in the nineteenth century, with
Ritschl and the twentieth-century neo-Kantians as its most important
representatives.[49] In each case the content of the gospel, the knowledge of
God revealed in Jesus Christ has been re-molded within the procrustean
bed of such a systematic critique.

It must be also said that more often than not, such analyses deny
totality. Yet, their prescriptive flavor betrays the self-enclosing tendency
which rather than truly preventing totality, it merely transposes it into
a different register. This illustrates that a theology for which Trinitarian
thought is no longer configurative is not able to account for its own discourse of limitation.

Nonetheless, this critical task at least reminded us that in the light of
theology conceived as a specific human task, it is often difficult to establish
how, based on revelation, theology is to devise its self-limiting discourse.
It is perhaps interesting to note in this connection how Kant remains significant for theology not so much by his theory of knowledge as such, as a
positive proposal, but rather by his transcendental critique, that is to say, by

---

49. See Barth's forceful criticism of Ritschl in Barth, *Protestant Theology in the
Nineteenth Century*, 654ff.

his critique of a facile or naïve realism. The problem is that this legitimate intention often takes over, depriving the affirmative discourse of its force, preventing thus the content from really shaping the form.

Attempts to articulate apophaticism, especially in Western theology, often betray filiation with such a tendency. "Trinity has not a descriptive but a regulative function. It permanently reminds us that there is a fundamental difference between God and our conceptions of God," writes Dalferth.[50] Somewhat similarly, Williams, commenting upon Ricoeur's view of Revelation, contends that the hermeneutical grammar of God's revelation necessarily compels us to a "negative theology."[51] If the Trinity functions only as a reminder of a difference, the referential dimension is lost, and the language employed merely performative, of practical value, creating in us at best, an ethical awareness.[52]

In a well-documented study, McCormack showed how Barth remained attached to Kant in a significant respect. He argues that Barth never abandoned the revealing-concealing dialectic of the *Sache*.[53] In spite of his commitment to material considerations and his preference for ontology, his dependence upon Kant remains a constant mark of his theological journey. McCormack seems at times to suggest that this "post-critical" dimension in Barth, which incidentally makes him a modern theologian, is somehow invincible.[54] But of course, the question may be raised of how and to what extent, the dialectic of revealing and concealing in Barth might have been better grounded theologically or

50. Dalferth, "Eschatological Roots of the Doctrine of the Trinity," 170.

51. Williams, "Trinity and Revelation," 197, 209.

52 Another example is offered by Kevin Hart who argues that negative theology is the only possible theology (which would resist deconstruction.) Cf. Hart, *Trespass of the Sign*. Such a position can become virtually indistinguishable from, say, Žižek's explicit atheism. (See, for instance, Žižek, *Puppet and the Dwarf*, 24: "God fully coincides with the gap between God and man, that God is this gap.")

53. McCormack, *Karl Barth's Critically Realistic Dialectical Theology*, 371.

54. Ibid., 465–66; McCormack contends that "to the extent that Barth concerned himself with philosophical epistemology at all, he was an idealist (and more specifically a Kantian)" (ibid., 465). He does not seem to have many problems with Barth's allegiance to Kant (reflected especially in the dialectic of veiling and unveiling). We may however legitimately ask whether, and to what extent, the Kantian grammar is not at the root of his problematic theology of Creation or perhaps even at the root of his Christomonism. As we have seen, Barth's view of the subject as re-iteration shows his continual dependence upon a philosophy of consciousness, confirming thus that Barth's attempt "to overcome Kant through Kant," to use McCormack's words, is problematic, after all.

perhaps given a better linguistic expression, less dependent upon Kant's discourse of limitation.[55] It is true that Barth insists in equal measure upon both the possibility of our knowledge of God as genuine and truthful and upon its inexorable limitation. We cannot determine in advance how much we can know in this life if we believe that God's action in this world has not ceased. But we do know that there is a difference, and it has been revealed to us *as difference*. Otherwise, faith and hope would not have any meaning. Yet, it must be said that Barth's view of Revelation as re-iteration brings him at times dangerously close to the consciousness model.[56] Perhaps the most difficult theological task is to try to articulate in the light of Revelation, such a difference in a positive way.[57]

Trinitarian discourse must, therefore, guard its own language by an unrelenting effort to spell out the mystery of God, neither speculatively nor in terms of a systematic discourse of limitation, but by pointing constantly to its content. Although theology is effective precisely in its use

55. McCormack insists at the end of his book that what he calls "critical realism" is employed strictly in a theological sense. Barth "wanted" to do theology, etc. But precisely because it is the reference of discourse which is ultimately at stake, such voluntaristic language remains unconvincing. Philosophy may well have a different agenda, yet, its interest in what is "real," and the dialectic between ideal and real have a common problematic. As Gunton shows (e.g., Gunton, *One, the Three and the Many*, 28ff), more often than not, the problem of philosophy is not necessarily the absence of God discourse, but its subliminal reliance upon false absolutes. See also Gunton's critique of McCormack in Gunton, Review of *Karl Barth's Critically Realistic Dialectical Theology*, 483.

56. "We know . . . in an 'enigma,'" says Barth, "therefore in a form which declares by concealing and conceals by declaring" (Barth, *CD* II/1, 53). This dialectic of identity and difference (similar at times to that of Heidegger), is evident in Barth's exegesis of 1 Cor 13:12. What is disconcerting here is not the way Barth interprets the specific limitation of knowledge, but the identity principle which Barth employs in his reading. "I shall know face to face even as God knows me." Barth writes: "I do not yet know him here and now as he already, here and now, knows me. . . . Here and now we know by way of faith" (ibid.). The implication seems to be that Eckhart's claim ("The eye with which God sees me is the eye with which I see him; My eye and God's eye are the same.") would somewhat hold true in the *eschaton*. If the verse is read as an analogy not as an ontological identity the concept of genuine knowledge need not be read in a symmetrical manner, as a logic of self-differentiation. In fact the necessity of self-differentiation as the mark of genuine knowledge is a prevailing feature of Barth's doctrine of revelation. This connects with my critique of Barth's take on Hegel in part 2. For a somewhat similar criticism, see Torrance, *Persons in Communion*, 245, where he talks about Barth's "subliminal appeal to the reflection logic of German idealism." See also Roberts, *Theology on Its Way*, 59–79.

57. To be sure, this was emphatically Barth's paramount concern. E.g., Barth, *Humanity of God*, 57: "The sense and sound of our word must be fundamentally positive."

of common language, and indeed, there is no intrinsic reason why philosophy should not occasionally function as an *organon* for theology, no philosophical structure or method can be shown in advance to be better suited to fulfilling its referential intention. When such explanatory power is claimed, as we have suggested, the theological discourse is not enriched but rather crippled.

We shall briefly offer a second example to illustrate this latter point, by referring to the theological use of some of Wittgenstein's insights. Such a position may seem in many ways superior, as the critique of metaphysics is launched this time with the support of a philosophy which renounces Kant's model of consciousness and adopts the linguistic model. Kerr's influential book *Theology after Wittgenstein* had the great merit of bringing together the huge theological implications of Wittgenstein's powerful critique of the metaphysical assumptions of the modern self, and of intentionalistic theories of meaning.[58] Wittgenstein's famous adage that "meaning is use" not only dislodged the privileged position of the intentional subject, but uncovered the action character of language preparing the ground for speech-acts theory. Theology, indeed, would do well not to ignore or minimize Wittgenstein's contribution. The criticism of philosophical theism which he made possible should not be underestimated.[59]

Yet, it must not follow too closely in his footsteps either. Wittgenstein's (legitimate) insistence upon shared forms of life and upon the regulative role of human institutions and customs which precede and regulate the language use,[60] arguably, lead to inadequate theories of meaning and validation in post-Wittgensteinian thought.[61] The type of communitarian epistemology in the wake of Wittgenstein too hastily implies an immanent form of life, *not as the counterpart, but as the substitute for*

---

58. Kerr, *Theology after Wittgenstein*, 168–90.

59. See for instance Phillips, *Religion without Explanation*.

60. See for instance Wittgenstein, *Philosophical Investigations*, 80–82, para. 199–206.

61. For a critique of Wittgenstein, see Findlay, *Wittgenstein*, esp. 191ff. It is interesting to note how the theory of speech-acts (inaugurated by Austin's famous book *How to Do Things with Words*) reopened the interest in intentionality and subjectivity. "The use-theoretical approach," writes Habermas, "is based on an intuition that has been recognized in its full import only after Wittgenstein" (Habermas, *Postmetaphysical Thinking*, 64). In this light, while a theological use of Wittgenstein must be welcomed, (to the extent it de-centers the subject by pointing to the importance of community and our linguistic practice), it ultimately remains an unfinished step to the extent to which it fails to "return" to the subject.

a criterion of reason.[62] As such, it tends to become a philosophy of the status quo, failing to distinguish adequately between truth and success. In which case, the configurative power of the referential dimension of the "practice" under consideration remains largely unexplored.[63] Obviously, what may appear as "meaningful" is not always true. In the last resort, no human practice (including worship or doxology), can claim for itself the status of an ultimate regulative function. Theological discourse draws its force precisely by working out the ontological implications of its reference in both its practical and theoretical dimension.

But whilst the West manifested a predilection for such a "discourse of sense" whether in its ontological form tending to subsume the being of God under the more general category of being, or in its more epistemological forms, Kantian or post-Kantian, the Eastern tradition starting with the communion of the Three persons found not God, but the world most problematic.

## The "Dizziness" of Freedom

It must be pointed out from the very beginning, that in spite of its apparent Platonic or neo-Platonic overtones, this "problematization" of the world reflects an authentically biblical theme: a world in need of redemption, in Paul's words, a Creation that "has been groaning as in the pains of childbirth" (Rom 8:22).

---

62. An example may be suggested by Hauerwas (*Unleashing the Scripture*, esp. 19–38). Traces of Wittgenstein can be identified in expressions like, "The preaching helps us see that what is at stake is not the question of the 'meaning of Scripture' but the usefulness of Scripture" (ibid., 37). What is inferred here is that since epistemology must be eventually referred to ethics (the interpretative norm is a question of value), it is the Church as a concrete historical entity that ultimately decides those values. E.g., "Of course, the text has no 'real meaning' . . . the Church creates the meaning of Scripture" (ibid., 36). Such a claim tends to collapse Christology into Ecclesiology by stating that it is the practice alone that shapes the criterion of reason. (Of course this position does not need to be specifically associated with Wittgenstein, being present in other postmodern theological accounts.)

63. This is obviously not to say that Wittgenstein was not interested in reference. "We can avoid ineptness and emptiness in our assertions only by presenting the model as what it is, as an object of comparison—as, so to speak, a measuring-rod" (Wittgenstein, *Philosophical Investigations*, 51, para. 131). Rather, the problem is, of course, the structure of such a reference and its tendency to be reduced to merely "immanent" forms of life.

It has been most notably in the Eastern tradition, in the mystical and ascetic communities that this dimension has been notoriously prominent. As we already anticipated, we find here an emphatic stress upon theology as being fundamentally a response to God which finds its concrete expression in a particular lifestyle and practice. The Trinitarian discourse in such a case is fundamentally a form of confession, inextricably linked to doxology. It is the counterpart of a way of life anchored in a genuine experience of participation in the divine life, which claims to live under the aegis of freedom and full communion with God. Since the purpose of Creation is to return to its Creator, it is insisted that such a discourse must become normative for all reality, this ideal of participation and freedom being thus projected upon the whole experience.

In its ontological form, as for example in some forms of extreme Palamism, or mystical theology, theological discourse takes flight from the world into a realm of its own. Its claim of description or, as the case may be, inability to describe, becomes itself the unsurpassable norm. In such a scheme, the discourse of "freedom" tends to swallow up the discourse of "sense." While, for the sake of orthodoxy, a formal affirmation of the material world has been usually maintained, the concrete experience of the world tended to be derided, since its meaning always lies beyond or above itself. Nevertheless, at the limit, of course, such a "discourse of freedom" becomes a new "discourse of sense," emerging either in new forms of essentialism, or in a speculative logic of subjectivity. Traces of such features may be found in some contemporary theologies, arguably in Lossky's mystical theology,[64] or in Stăniloae's philocalic vision.[65] The notions of communion or personhood tend to

64. Zizioulas for instance rightly contests Lossky's synthesis of Christology and Pneumatology molded as it is by both his categories of freedom and nature and the subject—object distinction. (Cf. Zizioulas, *Being As Communion*, 124–25). By effectively circumscribing the freedom dimension to pneumatology (the "subjective" aspect of the Church), Lossky's preference for apophaticism and mysticism comes as no surprise. In this way, the rich dynamic of God's action in Christ and by the Spirit is "frozen" in pre-established categories.

65. See especially his treatment of space and time. In spite of his valuable insights (especially in regard to time and the relation finite—infinite), Stăniloae's discourse of "sense" tends to become so "mythological" at times, that it is hardly intelligible as a discourse about the real world. Staniloae tends to imply that ultimately both space and time approximate moral distances. Such a "spiritualization" of Creation is threatened either by a gnostic vision (which would be inconsistent with his explicit appreciation of Creation as fundamentally good) or by the idea of a "virtual history," close to the neo-Platonic vision of history as a fleeting image of eternity. See Staniloae, *Teologia Dogmatica Ortodoxa*, 1:139. See also Bielawski, *Philokalical Vision of the World*, 201–4.

be articulated here not so much by recourse to *oikonomia*, but by appealing to ideal constructions (logical or experiential).

As we have already seen, this doxological dimension received in the West a somewhat epistemological twist, where worship and doxology subliminally became a form of justification. I mention it again, because such a discourse can also be read as a move from "sense" to "freedom." Since the foundational position of reason has been discredited, it was felt that the resurgence of interest in ontological description, as well as the new prominence achieved by the philosophy of action and the primacy of *praxis* over *theoria*, made worship an apt category for incorporating into itself such a paradigm change. We have alluded here to a type of theological discourse that had filiations with the late Wittgenstein, trying as it does, to take refuge in notions like practice, community and "language games." When such a discourse re-emerges as a "discourse of sense," it "returns" indeed to the world, but the associated ontology reflects a suspect immanentist flavor. In spite of its valid critique of traditional forms of rationality, view of language and techniques of justification, its positive proposal, when present, tends to get enclosed within itself, depriving its language of the very dimension of referring.

What I contest in these latter developments therefore is not so much the move itself, but its specific articulation and the point of its insertion vis-a-vis its theological grounding and its hermeneutical structure. Regarding the former, it is God's action in Christ and by the Spirit that should have primacy rather than specific social practices; regarding the latter, by collapsing Christology into Ecclessiology the discourse ends up being dishonest about its epistemic dimension.

To summarize, I have tried to show that the description of God as Trinitarian, reflects principally its hermeneutic grammar expressed in the Christian experience of the Creator God who revealed himself supremely in Jesus Christ who after his atoning death and resurrection, sent the Spirit to establish his Church. We have further seen that it was precisely this narrative dimension which called for the articulation of the doctrine, both from a textual and from an ecclesial perspective. I have tried to examine afterwards the way in which the Trinitarian discourse appeared to be haunted by various forms of totality. I attempted thus to trace two potential closures of what I have called "the discourse of sense": as a form of cosmology in its ontological guise and as a regulative grid in its epistemological form. As a discourse of freedom, the theological discourse in general, and the Trinitarian discourse in particular, was shown to face the same potential problems. It its ontological form, it may become so enamored with itself as to take refuge in the realm of pure or hyper-essence or a speculative logic of personhood. We have further seen that such a discourse of freedom emerges as a new discourse of sense, but a "sense" which left the concrete world of experience behind, which took flight from history. In its epistemological form, we noted how the discourse of freedom in its doxological or/and apophatic intention may be re-baptized in a Wittgensteinian conceptuality tending to subvert rather than affirm the very heart of the doxological dynamic, namely, its referring dimension

To the extent that the old Greek pattern reemerges in one form or another, the critique of metaphysics in some of its postmodern forms hits, indeed, a genuine target. It was because the Gospel, in its double dimension as fully worldly and incarnational yet, as radically different, *in* the world but not *of* the world, has been deprived of its power, that the old "Greek problems" can be seen to reappear.

## 7

# Epiphanies of Presence
## *On the "Return to the World"*

THEOLOGICAL DISCOURSE, WHETHER IMPLICITLY or explicitly, is in search of some kind of justification. It was because of its contamination by various intellectual heresies, old and new, that often this justificatory practice rather than letting the discourse flow beyond itself, tended to lead it into the fortress of a regulatory concept, practice or institution or a contingent or illusory foundation. But as history so often witnesses, it is precisely when discourse guards itself most securely that it must face the most formidable objection because it loses its ecstatic character, ceasing thus to reflect the overriding feature of its source.

How are we then to recover that kind of wisdom which can afford to be foolish, and that strength which emerges out of weakness? How are we to maintain the fundamental belief in a community for which, it is true that "the gates of Hades will not prevail against it," yet recognizing its problems and inadequacies? I do not intend to offer an exhaustive answer to such a question. Nor do I intend to prescribe an unequivocal norm for the right balance between what I called a "discourse of sense" and a "discourse of freedom." *My hope is rather that by refocusing our attention to God's action in and toward the world, as we inquire into our standards of rationality and knowledge, both the framework and the terms of the discussion will gradually change, allowing us to speak about epistemology and knowledge differently.*

We have already seen in the previous chapter how the Christian conception of God, as a triune community of persons, in their dynamic inter-relationships, inscribes itself into a worldly problematic, and we noted the implicit and irreducible epistemological dimension of this move. This was the first indication that epistemology, considered in its theological dimension, is not primarily about human reflection and subjectivity but about the *taxis* of God's encounter with the world as Father, Son and Spirit. Our critical analysis has further shown how attachment to misguided ideals of "sense" and "freedom" betray the Trinitarian grammar of this encounter, and in the process, not only that project "false totalities," but also produce distorted versions of both what counts as "real" and what counts as "knowledge."

In what follows, I will try to make a more positive contribution to this discussion. We will continue to move "within the whole," that is to say, we will continue to talk about God's encounter with the world in both Creation and Redemption, in the same breath, so to say. As we shall see, as we do that, traditional questions and concerns that usually animates epistemological discussions may fade into the background while new aspects of our encounter with the world/our response to God's action, as rational and responsible human beings, may receive new prominence.

## The Contribution of the Doctrine of Creation: "Sense" and "Freedom"

We shall look first at the structure of this encounter with the world as a move from "sense" to "freedom." I shall begin by recalling briefly the impressive theological contribution of a modern representative of Eastern Orthodoxy, John Zizioulas. Zizioulas's contribution stands out perhaps most notably, in its unrivalled effort to show how Trinitarian theology enabled a view of ontology freed from Greek monism (i.e., from cosmology, a tragic view of history). It is precisely the gloomy picture of such an orderly and unperturbed structure of "sense" that Christian theology comes to address.

Zizioulas argues that the development of Trinitarian thought marked its climax in the theology of the Cappadocian Fathers. We witness here, in Zizioulas's opinion, an unsurpassable achievement: the full-blown emergence of "ontological thought." The distinction between nature and person applied to the being of God enables us to substantiate, on the one hand, the radical distinction between God and the world, and on the other to trace the emergence of an ontology which allows for freedom and alterity. Thus the Fathers, Zizioulas writes, not only "broke the circle of the closed ontology of the Greeks" but revealed the existence of the world as being a consequence of freedom. "The being of the world, which means necessity, now becomes freedom."[1]

What I would like to retain from this, and what is remarkable indeed, is the fact that it was the distinctively Christian discourse of "sense," that is to say its doctrine of Creation, that emerged as an authentic discourse of freedom. We are presented here with two competing accounts of "sense" that grow out of a fundamental dissimilarity, one out of necessity, the other out of freedom. It is precisely because God as Trinitarian and as personal allows us to conceive a different type of "causation," a causation which does not subsume all being in an amorphous structure of sense, that a genuine presence of freedom in our world is made possible.

Now I would like to press this insight further and try to apply it to a less optimistic view of community and history and manifestly skeptical of the potential of Trinitarian theology. I am referring here to Paul Ricoeur. Let me recall briefly the structure of Ricoeur's disquiet: Ricoeur suspects that Christian theology in the West took on a foreign conceptuality, mainly Greek, imposing thus a different grammar upon the Christian experience. In order to recover the authentic Christian meaning we should go back to the first expressions of faith. Ricoeur also wants to address a different problematic, namely, the suspicion that the remnants of our experience of God are mere representations, that is to say, in Kantian language, a construction of the mind, an "objectifying" gesture. The rise to the concept as a more or less ordering of such representations is thus contemporaneous with the erection of the idol. To defeat this Kantian assumption Ricoeur contends that the expressions of faith carry with them in their symbolic form, an irreducible surplus of meaning which configures history. Thanks to their backward relatedness, dependent as they are upon what Ricoeur calls "foundational events" they are able to carry a wealth of meaning which unfolds into the future. Thus we must both start and end in this primitive experience. Ricoeur is not prepared to take presence for granted. Such presence is always prevented from occupying the central stage by both a fragile and finite subject and by an unholy history. Nevertheless, Ricoeur is a confessed Christian. He is a humble listener to the faith, as he often insists. Yet when he engages with exegetical and theological issues he wants to speak as a philosopher. In this sense, while he acknowledges the implicit and necessary belonging

---

1. Zizioulas, *Being As Communion*, 39–40.

to a community, he speaks *to the Church*, launching a warning against its potential totalizing discourse, or her tendency to embrace worldly structures of power.

On the contrary, Zizioulas as we have seen, speaks from the Church. In fact there is no other place from which one can utter the truth. His discourse is a programmatic address to Western society, profoundly interested in its problems and ready to answer its malaise by addressing its false gods, worldviews, and totalizing discourses, and direct it towards an ontology of communion. Its refreshing flavor of hope and liberation outlines a different way of existence as love and freedom in the body of Christ.

In what follows, I would like to think the two perspectives together. More precisely, under the guide of such a discourse of freedom, I shall try to identify openings in the very discourse of "sense," openings that may affirm "freedom" at the very heart of "sense." In order to be able to see these openings, however, we need to lay bare the distortion of "nature" under the objectifying paradigm with its plethora of epistemological assumptions. I shall conduct my analysis by referring mainly to the discourse of sense as a discourse of self-limitation.

Let me recall briefly the main suspicions lying behind such a discourse. We have seen in the previous section that in epistemological guise, Trinity tends to be last, not first. In Kaufman's neo-Kantian proposal for instance,[2] Trinity is the apotheosis of human construction. Such a discourse is no longer a genuine description, but the labor of a constructive *Verstand*. Ricoeur may take Kaufman's case as an example of honesty and intellectual integrity, because as we have already hinted, Trinitarian discourse is perhaps necessarily speculative. But the basic structure of suspicion is not new. In many ways, the Lutheran *Sola Scriptura* incorporated in itself somewhat similar concerns. The loss of confidence in an infallible tradition and community called for the re-conceiving of the structure of authority. One possibility appeared to be the securing of such witnessing language pneumatologically, a tendency present in one form or other in Protestant theology from Luther to Barth. The language can be faithful only when it is commandeered by God. Unattended, the work of the concept necessarily drifts away. What guides conceptuality on a different path and makes it more than mere human construction is the different agency of the Spirit. But it has been precisely this psychologizing and individualist understanding of illumination and inspiration, that has

2. Kaufman, *In the Face of Mystery*, 412ff.

often led theology to oscillate between a pure experience and an absolute [...] Reintriated in such a way the work of the Son and the work of the Spirit were easily hypostasized into principles, and, under the false guidance of a metaphysical concept of the image of God, on the one hand, and a psychological understanding of the Trinity on the other, translated into mere attributes belonging to the knowing subject, the principle of reason and the principle of imagination.[3] The main implications of this development in its objectifying gesture connects with some of the concerns expressed in the postmodern criticism, namely, the erection of a subject over against the world.

But it may be argued that before trying to "re-enchant" the world, one may do well to recognize the benefits of its demystification in the modern period. Moreover, I am aware that it has been argued that Christianity, mainly by its doctrine of Creation, in fact contributed positively to such demystification.[4] The affirmation of a realist, objective and ordered structure of the world on the one hand and the authentically biblical theme of a responsible agent on the other, has been a paramount stimulus in the development of the modern scientific revolution. I am not going to challenge such an argument. I rather want to show how what I believe to be a valid insight may envelop itself in a false security, how the excessive zeal of the "discourse of sense" may undermine itself.

I shall offer just one example by referring to Kant's treatment of space and time. I have chosen Kant, not only because he is one of the most significant champions of the discourse of sense, but also because, as we shall see, he makes important assumptions about the structure of Creation itself, assumptions still pervasive in the Western mindset. Space and time are for Kant, at the crossroad of the intelligible and the sensible, mediating, as he wanted his position to do, between rationalism and empiricism. They are both, Kant says, empirically real and transcendentally ideal.[5] This formal character might not have prevented in principle a genuine encounter with reality. Nevertheless, as a necessary condition of

---

3. It may be noted in passing here that the success of the recent resurgence of interest in theological imagination may be significantly dependent upon its capacity to explore the full implications of its estrangement, of its loss of Trinitarian guidance.

4. See for instance Foster, "Christian Doctrine of Creation"; Hooykaas, *Religion and the Rise of Modern Science*; Jaki, *Cosmos and Creator*. I owe these references to Colin Gunton. Cf. Gunton, *One, the Three and the Many*, 109. See also Torrance, *Theological Science*, 64ff.

5. Kant, *Critique of Pure Reason*, translated by Meiklejohn, 44–54.

the unity of experience in the mind, reason has been in point of fact made the last court of appeal, enclosing knowledge in a systematic structure discernible *a priori*. It is on this basis that the categories of understanding are developed and the field of objectivity organized. In such a context, Kant's skepticism in regard to history in general and incarnation in particular, comes as no surprise. Thus, Kantian epistemology effectively closed the world in a "discourse of sense." Freedom is a limit idea, it can be thought but not known.[6] This anticipates Wittgenstein's later claim from *Tractatus's* preface: "What can be said at all can be said clearly and what we cannot talk about we must pass over in silence."[7]

Had space and time been considered more seriously not merely as limiting epistemological concepts, as conditions for experience, but as part of the structure of reality, they could have been regarded not only as ensuring a formal unity to experience, but having an irreducible particularity proper to them. Moreover, in such a light, the categories of understanding themselves could have been treated less as ideal and unchanging forms of the mind, and more as perfectible counterparts of our experience.[8] Arguably, more than one hundred years later, Einstein's theory of relativity recognized precisely that.[9] The fact that his discovery marked one of the greatest breakthroughs in modern physics is hardly debatable.[10] To what extent, however, this new "discourse of sense" enabled a genuine discourse of freedom is far less clear.

6. Freedom as an object in the world (in contradistinction to Hegel's concrete actualization of freedom) is part of Kant's paralogisms being thus subjected to the same critique of transcendental illusion.

7. Wittgenstein, *Tractatus Logico-Philosophicus*, 3.

8. For a critique of Kant's categories of understanding, see Torrance, *Theological Science*, 90–91. I attempt to relate here a somewhat classical criticism of the category of substance (as employed in the Western tradition from Aristotle to Kant) to a more general criticism which includes the categories of sensibility (*Sinnlichkeit*). My suggestion is simply that Kant's expressed commitment to experience might have enabled him at least to question the Newtonian paradigm. Such a move may have subsequently prompted him to alter the categories of understanding themselves. For a criticism of Kant's view of time see also Heidegger: "The Kantian account of time operates within the structures which Aristotle has set forth; this means that Kant's basic ontological orientation remains that of the Greeks" (Heidegger, *Being and Time*, 49). See also Ricoeur's assessment of Kant's view of time in *Time and Narrative*, 44–59.

9. Torrance notes how Einstein fought for twenty years with Newtonian and Kantian conceptions of space and time (*Theological Science*, 92).

10. I am not referring here to Einstein's own metaphysical commitments associated to his discoveries but rather to the discovery itself in its historical significance.

Even so, the lesson for theology is that it is precisely by acknowledging the particularity of space and time as created realities, that they may appear not only as limiting knowledge, but in some sense as enabling it.[11] As Gunton has suggested,[12] modern science has at least drawn our attention to the fact that the search for the fundamental bedrock of reality may well be misguided as modern quantum physics and theories of the universe seem to indicate. We can perhaps retain C. S. Lewis's insightful comment that "we cannot go on explaining away for ever," and his equally witty observation that "the whole point of seeing through something is to see something through it."[13] Yet, his conclusion that "it is no use trying to see through first principles is far less self-evident. Perhaps the problem lies precisely in the deep habit of our gaze to determine in advance the structure of such seeing.[14] Part of the damage done by the concept of

It may be perhaps argued that Einstein's own commitments may be understood as a stronger form of rationalism as he never stopped believing in a "uniform system of thought." See for instance Einstein, *Out of My Later Years*, 95, quoted in Torrance, *Theological Science*, 111.

11. This particularity does not imply the absence of rules for thought (science always needs such rules), but rather the displacement of such rules as belonging unproblematically to the mind via the categories of understanding. Einstein's theory of relativity did indeed uncover such particularity as being distinct from the mind's regulative function. Of course, the question eventually is to what extent can we always trace such rules to an ever-deeper rationality of the world. Our proposal suggests that the world's connection to God must be conceived neither regressively (in a causal way), nor substantially (as a structure of depth—I am referring here to the Aristotelian and Thomist *substantia*). To see the reality of God as distinct from, yet related to, the world implies at least to devise the two at different logical levels. It can also be mentioned here that to recognize such particularity of time as a created reality, gives some credit to Heidegger's treatment of "Dasein" as "care," that is to say, human projects are possible precisely because of the temporality of *Dasein* (Heidegger, *Being and Time*, 274ff). As we shall see, however, an excessive emphasis upon finitude is damaging for theology. Arguably, time is not the only ingredient, and more significantly, not the most important one in the configuration of an authentic human project.

12. See for instance Gunton's favorable quotation of Mario Bunge: "A definitely undesirable rationale sustaining the cult of simplicity is of a metaphysical nature. . . . This drive, which feeds metaphysical fundamentalism, is dangerous because it leads to postulating the final simplicity of some form of experience or some kind of substance thereby barring any inquiry into their structure" (Bunge, *Myth of Simplicity*, 86–87, quoted in Gunton, *One, the Three and the Many*, 44).

13. Lewis, *Abolition of Man*, 48.

14. Or as Heisenberg put it: "Whenever we proceed from the known into the unknown we may hope to understand but we may have to learn at the same time a new meaning of the word "understanding" (Heisenberg, *Physics and Philosophy*, 201, quoted by Torrance, *Theological Science*, 16).

substance as traditionally conceived, that is to say understood in the light of the absolutisation of space and/or time, has been precisely this closing of reality in a structure of depth and/or in a causal system respectively.[15]

We may perhaps say that the profound meaning of recognizing a theological dimension to our experience of the world consists in identifying and resisting the totalizing claim of cosmology. To see Creation, as *creatio ex nihilo*, as fundamentally "in debt" so to speak, means to acknowledge God's relationship with it, his sustaining and upholding it at the heart of its ordered and stable constitution. It does not mean to replace a scientific description with theological jargon, with a personalist or metaphysical vision, or to adopt some kind of "God of the gaps" paradigm, but to point to this dimension of "freedom" at the very heart of the description itself. If theology may do any service to science, that is emphatically not by engaging in the endeavor of filling the uncertain areas in the scientific knowledge, whether this is done in a triumphant way, or in a more "modest" guise of a "faith of the gaps." On the contrary, theology may do well to challenge the closure of "sense" precisely where science is most sure of itself. To say, therefore, that the world has an irreducible theological dimension is to claim at least two things.

15. We meet in this way some of the problems discussed in chapter 5 in relation to Hegel (his re-hypostatisation of process implicated by the temporalization of space). It may be also said in this connection that I welcome modern attempts to displace the categories of substance and causality from their privileged position. However, it must be noted that this does not necessarily imply the complete dismissal of the Aristotelian theory of categories. It has been rightly noted I believe that it was the privileged position of substance in his metaphysics that constituted the problem. (Recent engagements with Aristotle try to question even such a conclusion and attempt to give a new meaning to the *energeia—dunamis* dialectic. E.g., Ricoeur, *Oneself as Another*, 308ff.) It has been also argued that from a logical perspective, the "reality" can be in principle "reabsorbed" in any other class (cf. Noica, *Aristotel*, 83). That is why the modern operational or relational logic for instance, arguably only stripped the metaphysical elements and re-interpreted Aristotle's theory of categories rather than radically opposing it. The relationship between Aristotle's classes remains undoubtedly an unsettled problem. (This does not necessarily mean that we should institute "relation" as a "metacategory," a tendency found in some modern non-substantialist anthropological and theological accounts. We shall return to this problem below.) Nevertheless, it is precisely this awareness that we understand the categories "as they come to speech" which reminds us about the invincibility of the epistemological dimension. Consequently, the language of Creation and of God's relationship with the world rather than basing itself upon an already given and settled categorial configuration should do well to challenge its totalizing claim and preserve in this way the fundamental openness of Creation to its Creator.

Negatively, it means to engage in a critique of foundation; there is more to the world than a particular paradigm would allow. Recent philosophy of science has amply shown that. A time comes when a model can no longer account for experience, and a paradigm change imposes itself.[16] Kantian epistemology has reminded us that human mind has indeed a totalizing, constructive dimension that tends to become deaf to the idiosyncrasies of our encounter with the world.

And positively, enabled by this dimension of freedom, it means to find new ways of referring to the genuine "foundations"; new ways of talking about God's agency, about the Creator God who is active in the world through the Son and in the Spirit.

I have also tried to show that to recognize the particularity of space and time means to overcome the prejudice that they are merely *a priori* categories of perception. It is precisely as *particulars* that they may uncover deeper levels of rationality. It must be also said that the discourse of freedom enabled by such openings has an *analogical character*. This only reiterates my previous denial of a strict causal relation between the created order and divine agency. Perhaps an analogy of extrinsic attribution (that is to say, a is to b as c is to d) may be a good first approximation. But such an analogy would be designed to avoid not only a substantialist proportionality but also formalism (to which this type of analogy is prone). Quite in accord with the logic of the argument so far, I would like to suggest that the primary function of theological discourse here is not to suggest an immediate causal connection with an ultimate all-powerful personal agency. (That would be just another form of the "God of the gaps" paradigm). Obviously, this is not to deny that God can, and does in fact act "directly" in the world. Rather, it is to suggest that we have reasons to believe that God's presence in the world may be read off at the very heart of its ordered structure. As Barth put it, "God honors law as well as freedom. . . . Part of the revelation of his wisdom is the wonderful revelation particularly dear to his Holy Spirit that two and two make four and not five!"[17] Thus, the theological discourse of creation must be primarily critical in relation to the scientific paradigm, yet, without being "empty" (that is, mere "theological jargon" devoid of any meaningful connection with our experience of the world). Its capacity to substantiate an authentic "content," that is, to come up with a genuine "discourse of

16. See Kuhn's now classic work on paradigm shifts, *Structure of Scientific Revolutions*.

17. Barth, *CD* III/3, 161.

sense" is ensured, as we have suggested, by its privileged capacity to move between two notions of "sense," to point to the *telos* of Creation, to see the world in its temporality not only as a process but as a redemptive process.

In other words, we may identify patterns of creation theology, for instance, compatible with the emerging paradigms prompted by such openings. Nonetheless, these latter paradigms have at best a parabolic value. It does not, therefore, mean that, in this way, we can show unequivocally the "theological" meaning of time and space nor would that mark the advent of an unproblematic meeting of cosmic time with existential time.[18]

Hence our talk about freedom at the heart of sense, as may have already become apparent, performs, in fact, a critique of "sense." *Consequently, the properly epistemological dimension of the doctrine of Creation as "discourse of sense," uncovers its non-epistemological structure, that is to say, a redemptive and transforming dimension.* In this light, the meaning of Creation as "good" does not close the creation in a safe discourse of sense, but opens it towards a discourse of freedom.[19] Creation is good because it has a *telos*, because it is fundamentally open to its Creator. This is one of the great lessons of the recent emphasis on eschatology.

But it may be objected that to discover such a theological dimension remains, more often than not, a mere ideal. Moreover, it can be argued that to try to articulate such a view in a consistent way, may turn out to

18. For a discussion of their relation, see Ricoeur, *Time and Narrative*, vol. 3, esp. 11–98. Certainly, the theory of relativity did not help us to appropriate existentially the passing of time. Quantum physics on the other hand may seem to operate with a concept of indeterminacy which has some resemblance with human freedom. But again, such resemblance is at best analogical. In this respect, to "restore chance to its sovereign glory" does not necessarily effect a relevant "re-enchantment of the world" for reasons which will become apparent shortly. (For a brief analysis of the attempt of this type of science [embodied by Ilya Prigogine, for instance] to re-enchant the world, see Calinescu, *Five Faces of Modernity*, 70–71.)

19. This shows once again that there is no such thing as a pure epistemological discourse. While I believe it is important and necessary to separate epistemology from ontology it is also imperative not to rely too much upon such formal distinctions (as the analytic tradition tends to do), but to constantly indicate the non-epistemological elements in the very epistemic practice. Such a possibility is opened to us, as we have seen, by following the structure of God's encounter with the world as Father, Son and Spirit. Therefore, what should be mentioned here is not only the importance of Christology (as T. F. Torrance tends to do with the implication of "freezing" "sense" in an ideal concept of *homousion*), but also the work of the Spirit as the Perfecter of Creation. (See Gunton, *One, the Three and the Many*, 206–8, where he talks about "finite perfection," to stress both dimensions, that is, a "historical" expression of such a "goodness" and the promise of its eschatological fulfillment.)

be just another metaphysical construction, to the extent that such a theological dimension may always hover above our experience of the world. Does not modern science prove that a genuine encounter with the world is indeed possible, that we can talk confidently and truthfully about the world? Is not all truth "God's truth?"

Yet, perhaps this latter line of inquiry is based upon a mistaken assumption. It is certainly instructive to recall here how the reaction against the modern objectifying paradigm and instrumentalist rationality unveiled the deep presuppositions of such a view of "sense." The critique of the Laplacean cosmic time, for instance, from Heidegger to the neo-Marxists, as Charles Taylor showed, rightly uncovered the stripping of Event (*Er-eignis*), of its richness.[20] This exaggerated desire to explain leaves us eventually not with more but with less "sense."

We may also note how a similar problematic has been brought to light on the linguistic plane by the theory of speech-acts. One of the greatest benefits occasioned by such studies has undoubtedly been the dismantling of the deep habit of analytic thought of reducing language to its denotative dimension, by pointing to other ways in which language functions (illocutionary and perlocutionary). But what appears most interesting in this connection is how such discoveries also revealed the rich dynamic present in the very denotative aspect itself. Here the theory of speech-acts unveiled not only the poverty of the positivist tradition, which claimed precisely such "immediacy of sense" (present in one form or another from Carnap to Whitehead), but also the deep problems of a view of rationality which relies upon a direct vision of reality (a pure categorial structure) immediately present to the mind.

Nonetheless, a more thorough theological exploration of this "claim to sense" is required. In what follows I shall take a closer look at how, this time, the discourse of freedom emerges as a new discourse of sense. It would be very important to see that it does so precisely because the corresponding discourse of freedom has become possible not at a different level, neither "beyond" nor "behind" our experience of sense. *In other words, such discourse is in no way "metaphysical" in the modern sense. Instead, it reveals the same intimate connection between God and the world: God is at work in the world, through the Son and in the Spirit.* As we shall see, the above objection, suggesting as it does an immediate

20. Cf. Taylor, *Sources of the Self*, 464.

and unmediated "sense" is the mirror image of an equally immediate and unmediated "freedom" claimed in a pure ecclesial or mystical event.

## The Contribution of the Doctrine of the Word: "Freedom" and "Sense"

There are a number of questions that may have lurked in the background of our previous analysis. Why is it necessary to maintain a certain irreducibility between the discourse of sense and the discourse of freedom? Why this insistence upon the "parabolic" value of the scientific endeavor in relation to Creation theology? It is at this juncture that Creation theology needs the decisive reply of a theology of the Word. "And the Word became flesh, and dwelt among us, and we beheld His glory, glory as of the only begotten from the Father, full of grace and truth. . . . For of His fullness we have all received, and grace upon grace. For the Law was given through Moses; grace and truth were realized through Jesus Christ" (John 1:14, 16, 17 NAS).

It is because in Jesus Christ not only grace, but also truth has been revealed that Paul could say that "no man can lay a foundation other than the one which is laid, which is Jesus Christ" (1 Cor 3:11). Indeed, since "all things hold together in Christ" (Col 1:16), the truth of Creation cannot be other than Christological.[21] We cannot talk about truth and rationality apart from the divine Logos. Maximus's doctrine of *logoi*, in spite of its speculative tendency, at least reminded us that the truth of Creation is grounded in Christ.[22]

Contemplated from the perspective of a theology of the Word, the "discourse of freedom" that emerged at the end of our previous investigation as a critique of "sense" can be properly appreciated only in the light of a God who, to use one of Jüngel's expressions, "*came* to the world in Jesus Christ, and as such, does not cease to *come* to the world" (italics his).[23] It is in this coming that the profound justification of our insistence on particularity is to be found. In Christ and through the Spirit, every particular

---

21. See also 1 Cor 8:6; Heb 1:2; Eph 1. For a more detailed treatment, see Gunton, *Triune Creator*, 21–22.

22. For an appraisal of Maximus's contribution, see Thunberg, *Man and the Cosmos*.

23. Jüngel, *Theological Essays*, 59.

entity is enabled to be what it was designed to be.[24] The compelling force of such remarks consists in the fact that *"truth," the new emerging "sense,"* comes to the world through the Word. Let us take a closer look at Jüngel's impressive and original contribution to a Word theology.[25]

For Jüngel the Word is the *topos* where God is to be found. God's presence is supremely manifest in the Word. In fact theology itself, according to Jüngel, "is essentially the doctrine of the Word of God."[26] Jüngel combines an undisguised sympathy for a certain type of philosophy of language born in the aftermath of the rejection of the metaphysical tradition, with the old Protestant theme of the Word of God in general and with Luther's *teologia crucis* in particular. Theology must re-think its concept of God if it is truly to refer to God. This theme of referring is thematized in the essay "Metaphorical Truth. Reflections on Theological Metaphor as a Contribution to a Hermeneutics of Narrative Theology."[27] Like Ricoeur, Jüngel finds the traditional rhetorical approach to metaphor wanting, being, as Jüngel believes, not only irretrievably caught up in an actualistic language indebted to an Aristotelian conception of being but also "connected at a very deep level with the understanding of truth as *adequatio intellectus et rei*."[28]

The rejection of a nonliteral view of metaphor must not be understood however as a belief in some ideal sense of the words.[29] As for Heidegger and for Ricoeur, speech is understood by Jüngel as preceding thought. His plea for literality reflects in other words his concern for "reference." Nonetheless, this reference is not "worldly" in any sense since no worldly language can speak about God. According to his celebrated analogy of advent, in coming to the world, God "makes use of the obvious in this world in such a way that he proves himself to be that which is even more obvious over against it. . . . God conquers, so to speak, the worldly obviousness . . . and establishes himself in it and with its help as the one

---

24. For the significance of pneumatology in the understanding of particularity, see Gunton, *One, the Three and the Many*, 180–209.

25. John Webster, the leading English translator and interpreter of Jüngel's works, notes the centrality of the category of "the Word" for Jüngel's theology (*Eberhard Jüngel*, 39).

26. Jüngel, *God as the Mystery of the World*, 162.

27. Jüngel, "Metaphorische Wahrheit," 71–122.

28. Ibid., 78.

29. In fact quite the contrary is the case. Jüngel, unlike Ricoeur, seems to accept with Heidegger the thesis of the metaphoricity of all language. Ibid., 100–101.

who is more obvious."[30] Accordingly, "the analogy of advent is . . . the method which makes possible language about God that corresponds to God."[31] In this way, the coming of God is contemporaneous with the advent of the new (2 Cor 5:17). God's presence in the world is always an expression of grace, a miracle. The new emerging framework of the concept of God, suggesting as it does, a notion of being which includes in itself both actuality and possibility enables Jüngel to claim *that God is not necessary* ("God is necessary is a poor proposition. It is not worthy of God"[32]), *but more than necessary.*

Jüngel's criticism of "actuality" and his correlative preference for possibility may perhaps correspond to what we have called the critique of "sense" and the emergence of freedom at the very heart of "sense." Indeed, Christ's victory over sin and evil signifies the affirmation of the true "sense" of Creation, of Creation as good as it is brought to perfection in Christ by the Spirit. At the same time, however, Christ's suffering and the Church's suffering reveal the ongoing competition between two notions of "sense" which appear to be equally "real." The temporal structure of this non-coincidence is perhaps an indication that it may well function as the sanction of reality when the discourse of freedom claims too much.

Now it must be allowed that this sanction of sense presupposes more than accounting for the existence of evil in the world. It wants to express the authentically biblical theme expressed for instance in Paul's claim that God was in Christ reconciling the world with himself (2 Cor 5:19). The Gospel of John depicts this in a most powerful way with its mysterious suggestion that the raising of the Son on the cross somewhat coincides with his glorification. Jüngel is undoubtedly right to claim with Luther that "for responsible Christian usage of the word "God," the Crucified One is virtually the real definition of what is meant with the word "God." Christian theology is, therefore, fundamentally the theology of the Crucified One."[33] There are however at least two aspects of the problem which need to be further explored here.

The "sanction of sense" conceived in this way, aims first to address the failure to consider the world and history in its temporal significance. To insist on this dimension is to acknowledge our creaturely status and to

---

30. Jüngel, *God as the Mystery of the World*, 285–86.

31. Jüngel, *Theological Essays*, 11.

32. Jüngel, *God as the Mystery of the World*, 25.

33. Ibid., 13.

affirm redemption as redemption not from finitude but from sin. Christ revealed our full humanity by living in space and time. In this respect, a commitment to a full incarnational Christology must not only welcome a certain type of appreciation of finitude, but also attempt to spell out its concrete implications. Efforts to account for the meaning of time and space in the light of a God who became man and took history upon himself like the one found in Barth, Jüngel or Jenson are therefore welcomed in principle.[34] Equally welcomed is Pannenberg's effort to do justice to the empirical and historical aspects of our experience of the world.[35] Christ lived on this earth in perfect relationship with the Father through the Spirit in time and space. And we should perhaps learn to value time and space in their concrete determinations without either decrying too much the irreconcilable fallenness of existence, or jumping too quickly to hypostatizations of a-temporal presence.

But it is precisely because the recognition of our concrete particularity must not be allowed to emerge as a new universality, finitude must be understood *within the larger context of God's Trinitarian action.* Indeed, to celebrate finitude too much may amount to re-embracing "the identity principle"[36] in another form.

God *became* man in Jesus Christ, and did not merely unleash a potentiality within himself. The Bible takes pains to describe Jesus praying

---

34. I agree therefore in principle with Jüngel's attempt to disentangle the concept of perishability from its negative connotations. Cf. Jüngel, *God as the Mystery of the World*, 184ff.

35. See especially Pannenberg, *Anthropology in Theological Perspective.*

36. The affirmation of finitude presupposes indeed a rejection of any hint of identity between the divine and the human. Nonetheless, when finitude becomes an unproblematic transcendental (being justified Christologically), the identity principle returns in another form. Jüngel's theology of death, with its sovereign lack of concern with preservation (God is present to man in death), very similar to that of Kant and Ricoeur it may be noted, remains unconvincing not only because it is "theocentric" ("God is my beyond"), excluding thus any concern for the human subject as Webster notes (*Eberhard Jüngel*, 91–92), but also because it transforms finitude into an absolute. God's presence with humanity in death spells out only half of Paul's Christology which affirms not only our dying with Christ but also our coming to life with him (e.g., Rom 8:11; 1 Cor 15:21). Jüngel rightly claims that "God became man in Jesus Christ in order to distinguish definitively between God and man forever" (*God as the Mystery of the World*, 94). Yet, when such a claim is made to give such a Christological weight to finitude we may rightly question, I believe, not only the restrictive concept of finitude employed by Jüngel but, as we shall see in more detail below, the worrying return of a still unexorcized view of God as absolute Subject where Christology tends to be the "negative moment" in the divine life.

to the Father and being assisted by the Spirit. We are told that in his humanity he "was like us in every way" (Hebrews 5). Now the comparison loses its force if finitude becomes an unproblematic transcendental. We learned from Hegel that we cannot hope to solve the problem of God's relationship with the world either by appealing to the speculative principle that the infinite includes the finite, or by including negativity within God himself. To conceive God Trinitarianly is to acknowledge God's act as both transcendent and immanent, *in* the world and *towards* the world. Is this not the way in which we can let creation "be itself" and not subsume it within the being of God yet without allowing it an autonomous existence either?

This last observation brings us, in fact, to the second dimension of history which needs explicitation, namely its "ethical" structure. To insist upon this second dimension is to push "sense" to the limits. It means to uncover the dimension of freedom, the "is" at the heart of the "is not." Attending to this dimension entails vision and "critical seeing," requiring one to contemplate history in this fundamental "non-coincidence." It also means to acknowledge life as "journey towards a better country," as an alternation of "presence" and "absence" between memory and anticipation, as an unfinished passage from the conflict of Romans 7 to the peace of Romans 8.

It is, however, of paramount importance to note that genuinely to affirm this sanction of sense at the very heart of freedom as a fundamental non-coincidence, as a reality of a battle, requires one fully to acknowledge its non-epistemological structure. I would like to clarify this further: I have called it properly epistemological to the extent to which Revelation or God's action in the world is seen as a form of "re-iteration." That is to say, God entered our space and time and "justified" himself in his actions. As is often insisted this "becoming" is part of God's very being. This identity of God's being *pro se* and God's being *pro nobis* (irrespective of the way in which the relation of identity is understood) is not only at the heart of Christology but the very ground of theological knowledge. As has been suggested, it is *in this sense* that we must welcome the celebration of finitude. But it is precisely by not giving due cognizance to the non-epistemological structure of this dimension that some theologies tend, in one way or another, to subsume God under this logic of "justification." On the contrary, when redemption is seen as the compound act of the Trinity, this properly epistemological dimension is prevented from occupying the central stage, whether that is translated in an "ethical view of the world,"[37] or in a logic of being which includes negativity within itself. In fact it is precisely this constant recourse to its Trinitarian grammar that prevents theological discourse from conceiving its "sense" as a view of life as conflict or to succumb to the seduction of a temporal logic.

It must be said here that in spite of its theological penetration, Jüngel's acclaim of the "death of God" theology echoes at times precisely such problems.[38] We cannot but agree with the thesis that in order to think adequately the essence of God, lordship and love must be thought together (21–22). Indeed, "godly power and godly love are related to one another neither through subordination nor dialectically (22).

To be sure, there is in Jüngel a penetrating theological analysis of Hegel's reflections on the "death of God" concept. Moreover, Jüngel's critical appraisal of Hegel perceptively highlights the damaging effects of Hegel's logic of identity between the divine and the human. Consequently, as in Ricoeur, we must note a *prima facie* rejection of Hegel's logic of retrospection ("the owl of Minerva gives in to the dove of the Spirit" (285). The analogy of advent, indeed, proclaims the sovereignty of the Word (253) by sweeping away every direct connection with the world.

Yet, arguably there is a sense in which "Hegel's owl of Minerva" is very much alive and well in what may be called the "negative logic of the cross," which appears at times to subliminally guide Jüngel's hermeneutical and theological enterprise.[39] With Heidegger, Jüngel claims that "whatever must be necessarily thought can only possibly be thought in the historical context of thought" (200). It is true that he goes on to say, "That does not mean that the position of our thinking within the history of thought is ultimately decisive with regard to what can still be thought today. Thinking must, rather, defend itself constantly against the tyranny

37. In the sense in which it adopts the same logic of correspondence in a different discourse; one which restores an ideal order disturbed by sin.

38. I shall include references to Jüngel's book *God as the Mystery of the World* in the text above.

39. See also David Ford's suggestion that "Jüngel [fails to question Hegel] critically enough as regards this understanding of self and love" (*Self and Salvation*, 64). Ford also perceptively notes the implicit intimations of Jüngel's theology of death with the Heideggerian's "being-towards-death." In Ford's opinion, Jüngel "leaves death as a functioning ultimate, the irreducible differentiator even in the being of God" (63). Ford's ethical correction of Jüngel (inspired by Levinas), which aims to blossom in a theology in which "the face of Christ [would be] as integral to it as the death of Christ" (62) is in this way much more hospitable to a view of God as communion. As we shall see below, it is this irreducible ethical dimension that may give a better expression to an ontological vision grounded in God's Trinitarian action.

of the spirit of the age. . . . But it cannot do that by ignoring with seeming sovereignty the spirit of the age" (200). Significant for our concerns here is the "historical weight" Jüngel accords to "the truth of atheism" which configures in a significant way the gap between "non-necessity" and "more than necessary."[40] This leads to a tendency to operate with an undifferentiated concept of presence, which fails to do justice to the rich dynamic of God's Trinitarian action in the world.[41]

The mistaken concept of presence propounded by the metaphysical tradition (largely based upon the Kantian concept of representation as something being present to consciousness[42]) should not blind us to the fact that, as Gunton notes, "nothing is outside the providential activity of God."[43] Perhaps even the traditional talk of the hiddenness of God's action (as found, however inadequately, in Luther for instance),[44] may prove to be preferable to giving "absence" and "nothingness" the ontological weight suggested by Bonhoeffer and Jüngel.[45]

40. Jüngel rightly notes that necessity is a relational concept (*God as the Mystery of the World*, 26). But to conclude from here that the concept of necessity necessarily makes God dependent upon someone or "thought" is to rely too much upon a Kantian representationalist picture in which the theological statements are hopelessly anthropological. In this respect I agree with Webster that Jüngel often tends to conflate ontological and epistemological issues (cf. Webster, *Eberhard Jüngel*, 54).

41. Jüngel tends to accept uncritically Heidegger's dialectical tension (radical distinction, secret kinship) between poetry and thinking, between *mythos* and *logos* (cf. Jüngel, *Theological Essays*, 57.) Jüngel does not indicate his dependence on Heidegger at this point but the parallel is obvious. (Cf. Heidegger, *What Is Philosophy?*, 95.)

42. See also Wolterstorff's illuminating essay on Kant which examines the consequences of Kant's theory of knowledge (his account of intuitions and of concepts) for theology. Wolterstorff suggests that we have good reasons to reject the Kantian mental representationalist picture. Cf. Wolterstorff, "Is It Possible and Desirable for Theologians to Recover from Kant?," 1–18.

43. Gunton, *Triune Creator*, 192.

44. See Jüngel's criticism of Luther in "Revelation of the Hiddeness of God," in Jüngel, *Theological Essays II*, 120–44.

45. Cf. Bonhoeffer, *Letters and Papers from Prison*, 359ff. For Jüngel's treatment of Bonhoeffer, see Jüngel, *God as the Mystery of the World*, 57–63. Now it may of course be the case that, as David Ford argues, "Bonhoeffer does not allow death to play a role such as that in Jüngel" (cf. Ford, *Self and Salvation*, 69). In such a case, one may claim that Jüngel gives an excessive ontological and systematic weight to what in Bonhoeffer is, as Jüngel himself in fact notes, "put terribly clumsily and badly" (Jüngel, *God as the Mystery of the World*, 61). It must be also said that Jüngel deliberately avoids the language of God's hidden action (cf. Jüngel, *God as the Mystery of the World*, 104n210), believing perhaps that a theological rethinking of atheism does better justice to the concept of the "death of God."

*The general flavor of such a theological discourse uncovers, it seems to me, a tendency which the present study has constantly sought to overcome, namely, a theological reply to the Cartesian epistemology which tends to follow too closely the adventures of the modern subject (its rise and fall).*

Such a reply tends to be insufficiently attentive to God's Trinitarian action in history. If we conceive of God's being as a communion of persons, then we must affirm indeed that while God was in Christ reconciling the world to Himself (2 Cor 5:19), He nonetheless remains the Father and suffered *as* the Father.[46] The world did not collapse when Christ died, not because of its autonomous status, but because God never ceased to be the Creator and the preserver God. Moreover, it was the same Father who raised Jesus from the dead (Eph 1:19–20). Webster indirectly points to this problem in Jüngel when he notes R. D. Williams's critique of Barth's early tendency in the *Church Dogmatics* to rely upon a monolithic concept of revelation which tends to promote a self-expressing and self-unfolding view of subjectivity rather than being as communion of persons. While Webster notes a certain weakness in Jüngel's pneumatology, he opines however that Jüngel successfully overcomes most of Barth's shortcomings highlighted by Williams because "the main thrust of his doctrine of God pushes against any idea of God as absolute and self-identical subject, since God's being is viewed as 'a going beyond himself into nothingness.'"[47] But the problem of an "essence behind God's Trinitarian existence"[48] is not the only problem standing in need of address by an adequate Trinitarian description which attempts to be faithful to a view of God as communion of persons. Without expressing an *a priori* preference for a "social model" of the Trinity, my intention is only to point again to the fact that an excessive stress upon divine contingency (temporality, nothingness) depotentiates the richness of God's action in and towards the world.[49]

46. See also Moltmann's brief critique of both Barth and Jüngel in Moltmann, *Crucified God*, 203–4.

47. Webster, *Eberhard Jüngel*, 76.

48. Ibid. Webster suggests that Jüngel's stress upon love and relation answers the above charge.

49. "God's being *remains* in the process of coming, that God is indestructibly his own origin and irrevocably his own goal, . . . as Father and as Son, and thus does not cease to come from God to God—in short, that God himself is mediation—that is the third mode of being of God, God the Holy Spirit." Cf. Jüngel, *God as the Mystery of the World*, 387–88. It is not only that Jüngel employs uncritically Barth's use of "mode of being," but he seems to simply replace the more traditional "spatial" metaphor of God as communion of persons (which implies perhaps an unacceptable concept of

An example may illustrate better the drift of our concern. As we have noted, Jüngel affirms with Heidegger the disclosive power of metaphor. This fascination for the tensive relationship between language and reality leads him to speak about Jesus as the parable of God. Whilst certain similarities between God's relationship with the world, articulated in terms of God's self-giving in Christ and the language-world relation may be certainly drawn, the long term effect of the radical "is not" at the very heart of the "is" seems rather to depotentiate than to think further the traditional *taxis* of Jesus, the Son of God, fully God and yet fully man. Jüngel rightly acknowledges that "the correspondence of human talk to God is not a capacity of language itself."[50] Yet, when the relation is understood as a Christological statement, as "the fundamental proposition of a hermeneutics of the speakability of God,"[51] it must not lose sight of the fact that Christology is something more than a transcendental designed to address the *aporia* of a generic emergence of the new or the language-world relationship. In the same passage Jüngel notes the playful character of the parable. From a Christological perspective this is certainly fine in so far as it reiterates the idea of "superabundance," of Christ as the free gift of God. But here it is perhaps most apparent how close the idea of Jesus as the parable of God is to collapsing the non-necessity of the world into the non-necessity of the Son. If the career of the two concepts is to be adequately differentiated, we need, I believe, to affirm both *logos asarkos* and *logos ensarkos*[52] when we refer to the being of God. Ultimately this may only reinforce Jüngel's demand for a non-dialectical relationship between love and freedom within the being of God.[53]

---

presence), with a temporal metaphor. In this way the emerging concept of God retains, it seems to me, a too accentuated polemical flavor.

50. Jüngel, *God as the Mystery of the World*, 289.

51. Ibid., 288–89.

52. As is well known in spite of Barth's reluctance to maintain the *logos asarkos* in connection with the doctrine of Creation and Reconciliation, he nonetheless affirmed it in his doctrine of God (Trinity and Christology). Cf. Barth, *CD* III/1, 54; *CD* IV/1, 52; *CD* I/2, 168ff. Of course, what is important here is the referential intention of those terms, rather than their historical career. Shults may be right to note that the *anhypostasis-enhypostasis* formula may not be a "Patristic doctrine," after all, but that does not, in itself, compromise its theological usefulness. (See Shults, *Reforming Theological Anthropology*, esp. 156–60.)

53. It may be noted in this context that, when freed from its Kantian strictures, Ricoeur's project appears to be more open to a mediation of Word and Creation. As we have seen in chapter 2, Ricoeur, unlike Jüngel, ultimately rejects the metaphoricity of all language. To give a positive expression to this refusal invites precisely such a mediation.

Nonetheless, Jüngel's impressive engagement with the philosophical tradition stemming from Descartes rightly reminds us that the cross of Christ forbids us to take presence for granted. We should resist a way of conceiving sense and freedom together, fused in an undisturbed presence, whether this is conceived of as a pure ecclesial event or as a practice raised to the status of a supreme transcendental.

In what follows, I shall briefly refer to an interesting example offered by Pickstock's recent book *After Writing: On the Liturgical Consummation of Philosophy.*[54] The book is of interest because it engages extensively precisely with this dimension of referring criticized by various postmodern Continental thinkers, notably by Derrida. She conducts a rich and informative argument against Derrida's interpretation of Plato pleading for the primacy of presence (language as transcendentally oral [25ff]), which she shows to be recoverable in an alternative reading of Plato. She ultimately wants to defend an account of language as an expression of liturgy. She rightly maintains that the language of liturgy, as a gift from God and a sacrifice to God, is in several ways impossible, and such an *aporia* is only resolved in the person of Christ (176–77). She is also careful not to organize her insistence upon various "linguistic and structural preconditions" of such a discourse (216) in a network of conditions of possibility. Her aim is not to articulate the conditions of another type of "universalized presence" (216), but to transcend the dual logic upon which the Derridian argument is based by the concrete deployment of the grammar of the liturgy.

Her argument is particularly instructive for our question of how the Trinitarian grammar of Christianity must guide its discourse back to the world. I agree with her intention of establishing the primacy of a presence which both renders better, and ultimately genuinely fulfils, the Platonic ontological intention. Yet I am more reluctant to accept her somewhat unclear contention that in the Eucharist understood as a form of action, a third alternative beyond presence and absence is uncovered.[55] Her

54. Pickstock, *After Writing.* I shall include references to this book in the text above.

55. The suggestion echoes somewhat Jüngel's rather cryptic claim that his answer to the question "where is God?" "goes beyond the alternative presence and absence." Now it seems to me that it is one thing to claim that "Faith cannot speak of God's presence without conceiving at the same time of God's absence, just as it has never been certain of God's presence without experiencing his hiddenness" (cf. Jüngel, *God as the Mystery of the World,* 54–55), and quite another to claim to have transcended this alternative. The mere fact that in Jüngel this "beyond" (at least in *God as the Mystery of the World*) is more hospitable to "absence" while for Pickstock seems to denote a form

eagerness to respond to Derrida's *différance* combined with a somewhat excessive dependence upon such language, leads her to see the Eucharist, not as a transcendental but rather as *the* transcendental, the condition of the possibility of all meaning, in which all dualities are reconciled and metaphysics ultimately dissolved. However we may wonder whether the illuminative argument about the centrality of the Eucharist does not, in the end, impose an unnecessary restriction upon the grammar of the Trinity. It is not clear why the *Logos* would exhaust itself in a such a discourse of freedom without maintaining a critical and in this sense, non-apophantic dimension. Would it not be fairer to maintain that the presence of Christ in the Eucharist neither exhausts nor transcends the dialectic of absence and presence, but rather brings it into full vision? The fulfilment of language in worship at least on this side of eternity cannot function as an ultimate and all-encompassing transcendental. Not all tears are wiped away in the Eucharist. There are some still waiting for the second coming. Paul's recourse to *anamnesis* in the passage about the Eucharist (1 Cor 11:17ff) reminds us not only about presence in relation to problems of temporality and spatiality, about which Pickstock is supremely concerned, but also about human forgetfulness. Does not Paul, in fact, conclude the same passage on an ethical tone? Our praise is still an event in the world, in which the response is not unproblematically absorbed in the call. And as confession, as bringing judgement and salvation it emerges as a "two-edged sword" in the midst of worship.[56]

## Creation, Word, and Truth

In sum, against the view of an immediate, unmediated sense, we attempted to uncover a dimension of freedom at the very heart of sense. If time and space are created realities, they carry with them a certain particularity and consequently a freedom potential.[57] As I trust has become appar-

---

of presence (in the Eucharist understood as an all-embracing transcendental), gives us reasons to be skeptical of the genuine possibilities of such a "sublation."

56. If Christ is Lord of the Church, it is he "who will present the Church pure and unwrinkled in that day," and to this end, he is sovereign and willing to summon her time and again.

57. This freedom potential may to be spelled out in two related directions; a freedom of operation in its alloted particularity (as any created reality); but since this may suggest a form of compatibilism (which would perhaps include a certain form of undeterministic freedom), a second imagery is required: freedom in relation to other

cut, saying that, I do not intend to revive an undifferentiated optimistic vision of theological rationality. Indeed, we are finite and sinful. But as we have tried to show in our extended engagement with both Ricoeur and Hegel, it has been a false ideal of knowledge that tended to regulate creaturely knowledge. That is why truthful knowledge is to be conceived of neither as an ideal totality nor against the background of our finitude or sin but in spite of them.

Conversely, against an unmediated view of freedom, we pointed to the necessary "return to the world of experience." Creation must be allowed to play a configurative role *not only as an idea*, necessary in a redemptive scheme (or in a discourse of freedom), but as a concrete act of God in and towards history. In spite of our fallen condition or of our finitude, our knowledge of the world is not "tragic." Arguably, this tendency to articulate "freedom" against the background of a "tragic" view of experience may be discerned at times in Zizioulas's theological discourse. As I have already suggested, I wholeheartedly welcome his stress upon ontology and soteriology. Yet, the suggestion that ontology is freed from gnoseology remains ambiguous. Contemplated in the light of his insistence upon the "tragic" aspect of nature,[58] such a claim may appear to be a concession made to Greek ontology (as being an accurate description of "nature" but deprived of freedom). Moreover, that would seem to encourage an excessive "constructivist" paradigm in which "the ideas" unproblematically "change" the world.[59] Zizioulas rightly resists the objectifying paradigm and an instrumentalist understanding of rationality which was traditionally associated with epistemology. But as we have tried to argue, epistemology need not be understood as being necessarily connected with such a worldview. We suggested with Ricoeur that it is

---

particulars. Here the specifically Christian idea of freedom comes in, namely freedom for the other. In science we only began to explore this freedom in relation. (See also Gunton's employment of the concept of perichoresis in Gunton, *One, the Three and the Many*, 163–66.)

58. Cf. Zizioulas, *Being As Communion*, 52.

59. In the same context, he seems to distance himself from a "revelational paradigm" in his criticism of Yannaras's use of Heidegger (Zizioulas, *Being As Communion*, 44–45). As we have tried to argue earlier, the theological use of Heidegger is indeed problematical. However, his implicit preference for hyper-essence, that is, an ontology which is not structurally dependent upon Revelation remains unconvincing. I may only repeat here that the right insistence upon the freedom of God should not prevent us from acknowledging that this very freedom of God was not the abstract freedom of philosophical speculation but was itself revealed as freedom of love.

wrong to suppose that distanciation, as a necessary counterpart in epistemic practice, necessarily involves an attitude of domination of nature, objectifying and reductive.[60] In the light of our previous considerations, to claim freedom from epistemology altogether remains untenable to the extent that the discourse of freedom itself performs a critical function having, therefore, an epistemological significance.[61]

Indeed, theological discourse "speaks responsibly" precisely in the unrelenting move between epistemology and ontology. The referring dimension dies away when such a dynamic is frozen in an ultimate explanatory structure of a prescriptive liberative discourse. If theological discourse is genuinely to refer, it needs to conceive of Creation and Redemption together; it ought to aspire to that perspective where vision meets obedience, and faith is no longer opposed to knowledge.

Let me illustrate one more time the force of this proposal by looking anew at two different appropriations of the relation between God and the world configured by the concept of the will of God. Our first interlocutor is William of Ockham. I shall begin with a quite positive reading of Ockham's position in the history of Western thought. T. F. Torrance in his *Theological Science* praises Ockham for challenging a mere causal understanding of the world.[62] Torrance contends that "by denying the direct causal connections in nature, he launched an attack against the prevalent physics and metaphysics of his day" (64). Thus the critique of the Aristotelian notion of substance and causality, contributed decisively to the collapse of the medieval synthesis. Ockham advanced "a doctrine of nature appropriate to a free creation contingent upon the pure will and wisdom of God rather than one conceived as grounded upon the unchangeable essence of God" (63). Torrance also rightly notes that Ockham was not so much interested in denying order and causality as Hume later was, or in promoting an "interventionist" view of God, but rather in drawing attention to the necessity of a different type of rationality, and in bringing to light an order of a different kind, more akin to God's rela-

60 See Charles Taylor's somewhat similar observation when he admits a certain validity of such a view and attempts to disentangle it from the faulty anthropology with which it is usually associated. E.g., Taylor, *Sources of the Self*, 514.

61. In fairness to Zizioulas however, I must point out that he acknowledges that genuine science always coincides with a "theological view" of the world. Cf. "Towards an Eschatological Ontology" unpublished paper presented at King's College London Research Seminar.

62. Torrance, *Theological Science*, 67. I shall incorporate the references in the main text.

tionship with the world (64). From the perspective of Torrance's specific aim such a move must be saluted since it occasioned the unprecedented development of the sciences. But Torrance insists less upon the more unfortunate implications of nominalism and its voluntaristic tendency which it prompted.[63] In *The One, the Three and the Many*, Gunton pursues this latter failure by showing how Ockham's nominalism made in actuality the doctrine of Creation effectively redundant. The price of the destruction of the medieval synthesis was indeed high.

Now I would like to compare Ockham's suggestion of a creation dependent solely upon the free will of God, with a particular way of insisting upon the distinction between the idea of Creation in the mind of God and the act of Creation itself, characteristic of the Palamite tradition. As is well known, the aim of this distinction is to articulate the fundamental truth that the cosmos has its basis in the will of God, whilst the relation between the persons of the Trinity is a relation of essence. However, as has been already alluded to, in Palamite thought this important distinction gives rise to unacceptable demands. The heart of the matter is the rejection of a Trinitarian discourse which begins from God's action in the world, since, it is argued, God (the Holy Trinity) is the only necessary being. It is not difficult to see how Lessing's "big ugly ditch" re-emerges in the assumption that the necessary cannot be communicated by the contingent truth of history. This happens because a *prima facie* valid insight is placed in an alien conceptual framework which depotentiates the ontological implications of Revelation.

It is noteworthy that both the Ockhamist and the Palamite construal are based upon a valid insight. Both wanted to substantiate a radical distinction between God and the world. Both challenged the metaphysical structure of a discourse which subsumes God and the world in an unproblematic continuity. Ockham was undoubtedly right in attacking Platonism and the doctrine of the forms and Palamism was equally right in denying a relation of substance between God and the created order (and in the attempt to preserve the freedom of God in Creation). Yet, in both scenarios a genuine dynamic of "Creation" and "Word," "sense" and "freedom" fails to blossom. In the first case, the explanation of the world takes a career of its own, and God's relationship with the world is no longer allowed to configure its rationality. The Palamite version slides into a different kind of "deism." The concrete

63. Even though he does mention the potential dangers. See Torrance, *Theological Science*, 67.

content of the doctrine of Creation is deprived of its power to describe the actual world. History itself, in such a scenario tends to become redundant, being read off in the speculative distinction between essence and energies. This "sacramental" or "philocalic" vision prompts "*a looking through*" more than a "*looking at*" the world.

Both alternatives ultimately betray an incapacity to conceive concrete relationality. In the latter case, Jesus in his concrete relationship with the Father and the Spirit, and in the former, the relation between concrete particulars conceived as a coherent and unitary structure of sense yet open to its Creator.[64] In both cases, a certain form of immediacy was implicitly advanced: the ideal of a "pure" vision of God and the equally defective ideal of a "pure" vision of the world.[65] Indeed, we should be constantly reminded that we cannot either cast God out from the world (Ps 139), nor can we rest in a pure ecstatic vision without returning to the world of actual experience (2 Cor 12:5). In this sense Palamism never "returns to the world," while nominalism remains essentially an unfinished step, which instead of pursuing the new vision enabled by its critique, undermined it by recourse to the language of the will.

In *The Triune Creator* Gunton perceptively notes how the Fathers, in direct confrontation with Greek thought, made the crucial distinction between God's will and his being.[66] Without questioning the continuous relevance of this language we may nonetheless wonder what kind of affirmations and distinctions are especially required in the light of our contemporary problems. Looking at the bewilderment of the modern subject (whether expressed in dire skepticism or naïve confidence) we

64. We may perhaps wonder to what extent an adequate understanding of Creation which conceives its relation to God in Christ and by the Spirit may allow us to conceive a cosmology or a worldview. Barth, as is well known, was skeptical about that. While there are undoubtedly limitations in such an endeavor which are theologically grounded, it must be said that often our skepticism is triggered by a wrong type of expectation. Precisely because the idea of substance as foundational is so entrenched in our thought structures, we tend to conceive particularity as self-subsistent, autonomous and incommunicable. This is why a mere replacement of substance with relation does not significantly advance the discussion.

65. If we agree with Torrance that Ockham did not intend to deny causality as Hume later did, we are left with the idea of "local rationality" which "grows out" from the particular so to say. In spite of its potential, this idea (even in some of its "Christological" forms), which incidentally made an impressive philosophical carrier from Spinoza to contemporary appropriations of Kant's productive imagination (albeit in different forms), is still haunted by idea of rationality which is inherent in "nature."

66. Gunton, *Triune Creator*, 65ff.

may perhaps decry as Hegel once did a humanity which seems "so deeply rooted in the earthly"[67] Yet if we are to carry the task of turning away our contemporaries from their "worldly" concerns we should perhaps attempt to turn their attention not so much to the worldly non-necessity of God or to ecstatic experiences which leave the "worldly" behind, but rather to the "aesthetics of glory" to which their minds have been blinded by the "god of this world" (2 Cor 4:4). It is from the perspective of such an "aesthetics of glory" in which Creation and Redemption no longer belong to different paradigms of interpreting the world, that our historical experience may appear both intelligible and redemptive. It is now time to conclude our hermeneutical and theological explorations of the "responsible agent." What kind of truth is suggested by our proposal and what kind of "justification" may such reflections invite?

67. Hegel, *Phenomenology*, 73.

# 8

# Conclusions

## *Towards a Theological Epistemology Informed by a Trinitarian View of Agency*

WE HAVE SEEN IN the course of our argument that by following the adventures of the modern subject, within the framework created by a mere dispute between the "inside" and the "outside" one cannot adequately speak of the emergence of Truth. That is why neither the expressivist, "constructive" self nor its "receptive" counterpart configured by the "outside" is ultimately able to convey the full dimension of this emergence. I have suggested here that a theological reply to this epistemological decision must question the more general framework of its theological assumptions. My proposal has gradually emerged as a response to what may be roughly described as being two extreme alternatives.

The first temptation is to see the practice of discerning the truth as conforming to an immutable external standard which substantially resides in nature. In such a view, the "freedom" of the world is conceived, whether implicitly or explicitly as a freedom anchored in its own "truth."

The other extreme would be to take the acknowledgement of the creative dimension of the mind (or of the word) as the sole truth of knowledge. At the level of the human subject, because there is always a non-coincidence between "impression" and "expression," ultimately truth is, as Nietzsche had it, a mere construction.[1] I wanted to challenge here a Christian response to such a view which, in one way or another, simply "transfigures" this claim into a theological key by attributing

---

1. Nietzsche, "On Truth and Lie in an Extra-Moral Sense," 46.

such a creative agency to God. Such a response, as I put it, "follows too closely the adventures of the modern subject." This tends to be one of the underlying weaknesses of the hermeneutical theologies which took up, in one form or another, an "expressivist" reading of Hegel.[2]

Our effort to deconstruct theologically both the notion of a "re-enchanted" world without God and the notion of the "Absolute Subject" who ultimately finds itself at odds with the world, was ultimately aimed at articulating the necessary framework for the further task of thinking Creation and Redemption together. The fundamental link in this latter task was shown to be Christological and pneumatological. Here the notion of providence meets the idea of God's redemptive "coming" to the world. It is Christological because we cannot talk about truth and rationality apart from the divine *Logos*. But it is also pneumatological because it is the Spirit who leads us into *all* truth. (John 16:13) Particular attention has been paid here to the tendency to "secularize" the Spirit with its consequent crippling of our understanding of God's action.

In order to uncover the full ontological, epistemological and semantic ramifications of our proposal we have devised this latter task of thinking Creation and Redemption together as an irreducible dialectic of what we have called "discourse of sense" and "discourse of freedom." The principal aim of this double discourse has been to show that if our talk about God is neither to remain empty nor to fulfill itself in a false totality, it has no other alternative except to unpack its Trinitarian grammar. More importantly, this unpacking cannot take place in idle theological talk, in detached intellectualist views of truth, because the encounter with the world is inscribed in its very grammar. God became human taking history upon himself. What is more, since this "coming to the world" expresses the very life of God, theological discourse cannot fulfill itself *against* a scientific, personalist, cosmological or "existential" problematic. Instead, it must include and confront all these fields and ways of looking at the world. In doing so, theology has in fact the chance of restoring such questions and problematic to their true dignity. In the process, theology performs an epistemological function in a double sense, as both a critique of authenticity and as pointing to the real "foundation."

---

2. Charles Taylor locates the origin of the "expressivist" turn in Herder (*Sources of the Self*, 368–90), noting however the distinctive way in which the turn is taken up by Hegel. We have seen in chapter 5 that "expressivism" may be seen as a potential "reading" of Hegel that, as I have suggested, had made (in one form or other) a significant career in the hermeneutical philosophies of our century.

The two come together because abundant life always comes as genuine knowledge. God's action in the Spirit is genuine *logos* because it always witnesses to Christ. It is because God's action in and towards the world is always mediated through the Son and in the Spirit, that Creation is no longer seen as a static datum, a "naturally" or immediately accessible truth, nor is Reconciliation perceived as a radical re-creation in a helplessly fallen world. In what follows, I will thematize the main epistemological implications of this proposal.

## Truthful Response—Doxic Obedience

We may begin by saying that a proper view of truth and justification can be disputed only in the light of this great unfolding. Rather than expressing an *a priori* and uncritical preference for a particular theory of truth (be it correspondence, manifestation, coherence, etc.), we wanted to show that *it has been "God's story" which reveals the career of truth in our world!* It is customary for philosophers to construct their theories of truth upon their epistemic proposals. By contrast, a proper theo-logical reflection on knowledge must start "in the truth," i.e., by attending to the reality of God's encounter with the world, by following the career of "the Word made flesh" who lived among us "full of grace and truth."

Two main reasons stood behind our decision to postpone a direct confrontation with the question of truth.

First, I did not want to relate directly the notion of truth to our experience of reality. There is, I think, some justification for the claim that mathematical truth for instance or what we may call a "truthful" experience of reality under the guidance of the scientific paradigm does not immediately or directly connect us with the notion of personal truth.[3] And my second concern was the undeniable reality of evil.

Yet, the whole thrust of our argument was directed not only against abstract appeals to truth, but also against a skeptical (Kantian or otherwise) or "apophatic" view of truth. Indeed, in spite of the above difficulties, the emergence of truth is possible in our world. Moreover, in the light of the Incarnate *Logos*, of the One who could claim about himself, "I am the way the Truth and the Life," we attempted to show that the "truth" of the created is neither in contradiction nor unrelated to the "truth" of redemption.

---

3. Cf. Ricoeur, *Histoire et Vérité*, 183.

This suggests that an analysis which attempts to be faithful to the rich dynamic of God's action, *must embrace both "particularity" (i.e., a differentiated view of truth) and the "unity" of God's action in and toward the world.* While an exhaustive theory of truth is beyond the scope of the present analysis, it is significant for our argument to look at how such considerations may be used for addressing some of the problems, limitations and *aporias* to be found in different conceptions of truth. I shall consider here only by way of example, Audi's brief and very clear presentation of the interconnections between various theories of truth.[4] He shows for instance, how the correspondence theory of truth ultimately relies upon some form of coherence. That is to say, correspondence theory operates within a "public," "recognizable" world that presupposes a more or less coherent way of looking at it. And conversely, the coherence theory of truth, if it wants to avoid the suspicion that it effectively operates with an underlying equivalence between being and thought, needs a pragmatic view of truth.[5] Of course, if in a "pragmatic" theory we further specify the nature and scope of its guiding idea of the good, successfulness or "usefulness," one may arrive at a proper eschatological vision of truth. From the perspective of God's redemptive action, and in response to it, one may "recapitulate" in this way the career of truth in our world.[6] In spite of the Fall, the "shattered *taxis*" of God's good Creation is shown to have its *telos*, its profound criterion of meaning and coherence in the Incarnate *Logos* who, through the Spirit, brings Creation to perfection. As Jüngel reminds us, however, this historical "march" of truth is not a form of *theologia gloriae*. The glory of the Son ("we beheld his glory," John 1:14) is indeed supremely manifest in weakness and his strength is the strength of His love. If I were to use one of Milbank's expressions, God in Jesus certainly does not perpetuate "an ontology of violence," but brings

4. Cf. Audi, *Epistemology*, 239–44. For a more comprehensive overview of various theories of truth, see Kirkham, *Theories of Truth*.

5. As we have seen in chapter 5, this was one of the notorious problems in Hegel for whom "the systematic structure of things cannot differ from the structure of our systematic awareness of them" (cf. Inwood, "Kant and Hegel on Space and Time," 64).

6. This is not to suggest an uncritical amalgamation of theories in paradigms of complexity informed more by our cultural diversity than by God's redemptive action. In this sense David Tracy's "aesthetic" proposal (of a coming together of various forms of correspondence, coherence, experiential, disclosive, narrative, transformational, conversion and consensus theories of truth), while undoubtedly integrative, arguably lacks a proper appreciation of God's Trinitarian action. (Cf. Tracy, *Analogical Imagination*, 53ff).

to full vision the true nature of God's action in history which is power in love. By raising Jesus from the dead, God confirms this alternative logic. In sum, to spell out the profound statement that "in him [Christ] and through him all things were created" (Col 1:18), is to attend to a conception of truth informed by the rich meaning of God's redemptive action in and towards the world.

In this way, the parallel discourse of sense and of freedom helped us to conceive the "is" and "ought" together in a paradigm molded by the Creation-Creator distinction yet attentive to God's Trinitarian action. Such a vision was constantly guided by the double concern of, on the one hand, being faithful to our experience of reality (empirical and historical) and on the other, of being theologically grounded in both Creation and Redemption. As I have tried to suggest, this entails an ontological vision which does not rest in full presence (cosmology or speculative logic of personhood). Genuine communion is never an unproblematic given but always a gift and a miracle. It is in the light of Truth that we see the world in its full plight. And it is in the light of Truth that we understand the value of suffering (1 Peter 4). Nonetheless, it is in the light of the same Truth that we can taste the future glory (Romans 5).

*It follows that to attend to this vision is to acknowledge that truth does not reside unproblematically either in the mind* (as in Aristotle[7] or various forms of rationalism) *or in the things* (as in various forms of empirical construals). Ultimately, the "truth" of the created cannot be conceived apart from the Creator Father in his redemptive acts through the Son and in the Spirit. As Zizioulas never tires of reminding us, it is, indeed, "only through an identification with *communion* that truth can be reconciled with ontology."[8] Yet, as we have suggested, such a vision does not automatically place us in an undifferentiated view of presence.

Our dialectic of sense and freedom enabled us to see that as we move towards "frontiers," the "truth" of the created reality seems to be receding, requiring from us something more like a practice of discerning it. It would be perhaps better to say that knowledge obtains not so much in an "identity," (when a perfect tuning of our mind with the reality to be investigated is obtained), but rather when a "right relation" is envisaged.

---

7. "Falsity and truth are not in things but in thought." Cf. Aristotle, *Metaphysics* 1027b 18–24.

8. Zizioulas, *Being As Communion*, 92. Such a claim, of course, opens up the (philosophically complex) problem of the, so called "metaphysics" of truth. I will return to this point below.

It is precisely this notion of "adequate practice" that opens up the ethical sphere, the realm of action. This link between Creation and Redemption enables us to say a number of things.

First, it leads us to devise "truthful" human action as grounded in the divine action, as enabled and assisted by Christ in the Spirit (2 Cor 3:18); if the Creation is transformed and perfected by the Spirit, then the ultimate framework of our search for truth is not "a structure of depth," neither a "causal universe" but an eschatological vision. Reality is indeed grounded in the newness brought about by Christ through the Spirit (2 Cor 5:17; 2 Cor 4:16–18).

Secondly, it is important to remark that such a view of rationality which "meets" the ethical dimension in what we may call a *doxic obedience*,[9] attempts to construe will and imagination together.[10] In this light, faith no longer appears as opposed to knowledge but part of the same fundamental enabling act of God in Christ and through the Spirit. "Doxic obedience" presupposes a "vision," an "aesthetics" of glory that guides human action in both its ethical and epistemic concerns. In fact, both the notion of "free enquiry" in scientific research and an ethics of freedom, cannot be conceived apart from such a vision.

In relation to the first, the existence of "models" arguably always presupposes a holistic, meaningful structure. That is to say, any "model" has an implicit *telos* contained within the very idea of the "whole." Due to the prospective and anticipatory dimension of the inquirer, the metaphor of "wholeness" is never purely "spatial" always subliminally "loaded" with ideas of "order" and "goodness." In fact, our heuristic devices speak more about the way in which we "humanize" the world than about the "distance" we take from it in our "objectifying" attitude.

---

9. The term *doxic* is meant to convey the idea of an informed faith (i.e., neither absolute knowledge, nor simply opinion).

10. This is not to establish the primacy of praxis over theory as Macmurray does for instance (cf. Macmurray, *Self as Agent*, xix, 85). Rather it is an attempt to think *theoria* and *praxis* together. I have not used the term "doxastic practice," common to Reformed epistemology, because my intention was to articulate more clearly this irreducible ethical dimension, the *diastasis* between God and the human subject characterizing the God—human relation yet, at the same time, to describe it as an invitation to be part of a community of love and freedom. Such a participatory dimension cannot be conceived apart from knowledge as genuine knowledge is constitutive of both love and freedom.

The concept of indwelling which has made a remarkable career in Polanyi's post-critical philosophy,[11] is in many ways close to Ricoeur's "humanized world," having also (arguably) intimations with Heidegger's view of truth as manifestation.[12] In addition to this "personal" dimension of inhabiting the world which reveals knowledge not only as embodied and situated, but linguistically mediated, we want to place an equal stress, however, upon the active involvement of the human agent. To talk about will and imagination together, presupposes more than a mere re-iteration of a "Barthian anxiety."[13] Indeed, I do want to question the traditional subject—object distinction with its plethora of assumptions. But an evaluation that takes its cue from the more fundamental distinction between Creator and Creation, will not claim to have transcended it, but rather try to articulate it differently. We acknowledged that the structure of createdness presupposes an alternation of presence and absence. Our engagement with Ricoeur has indicated that perhaps distanciation is not necessarily objectifying, not necessarily the "negative" correlate of "belonging," which knowledge ought to transcend. To appreciate creaturely knowledge (i.e., space and time in their particularity) is to appreciate its configurative dimension. It is precisely this dialectic of distanciation and appropriation seen as a positive feature of our createdness, that enables us to articulate not only the "givens" of our finitude and the experience of "belonging" to a world, but also this responsive dimension. But it is of paramount importance to remark that this responsive dimension is not conceived along the lines of the Enlightenment's autonomy ideal. Nor is it necessary to conceive it in terms of a "natural" capacity. The rejection of the substantialist tradition entails also a rejection of a substantialist view of the image of God understood in an Aristotelian framework. Indeed, the concept of the image cannot be properly articulated except Christologically and relationally.[14] In this sense, the concept of "doxic

11. Cf. Polanyi, *Personal Knowledge*; see also Polanyi, *Tacit Dimension*.

12. Consider for instance the way in which Polanyi believed that he solved Meno's *aporia* of how it is possible to know something new (*Tacit Dimension*, 22ff).

13. I have used Cunningham's designation in his criticism of Alan Torrance's book *Persons in Communion* (cf. Cunningham, Review of *Persons in Communion*, 155–56). Even though Cunningham's review fails to appreciate Torrance's contribution of going beyond Barth's revelational model, he is partly right to note a certain anxiety in Torrance's attempt at grounding human action.

14. See for instance Gunton, *Triune Creator*, chapter 9. I must say here that I partly agree with Harris's criticism of McFadyen's account of personhood, which tends to hypostasise relations (Harris, "Should We Say that Personhood Is Relational?," 214–34;

obedience" remains Christologically grounded, thus enabling the birth of responsible agency and suggesting the concrete *topos* where vision meets conviction.[15] In such a vision, call and response no longer live "on the most distant mountains"[16] yet neither are they dialectically suffused in some superior synthesis.

I must also point out that this idea of a "right indwelling" can be shown to be compatible with some of the experience of modern science. It has been often noted that as we advance to the micro-level, "instrumentality" becomes extremely problematic. Consequently the experience of knowledge appears to be indeed, more like an art of indwelling. This is certainly true, but it is important to note the limits of such a discourse. That is, the idea of "personal knowledge" or that of "humanized world" which succeeds in surprising the subject and object in their inextricable relatedness, can in no way claim a "perfect description" or an "ideologically free" discourse about experience. (In fact such a claim would amount to a return to a pre-critical position). That is to say, the metaphor of "attending to the rationality of the object," does not answer all the problems nor can it unproblematically place us in the "realist" camp. Such "attendance" can be in fact seen (often justifiably so) as just a more refined technique of domination.[17] This is why the doctrine of Creation is ultimately not a re-iteration of the givenness of the world, a "natural" knowledge, but a theological truth. *What we want to suggest here is that*

---

cf. McFadyen, *Call to Personhood*). As we have remarked earlier, the answer is not to transform relationality into a new universal but rather to articulate this "whatness" theologically. Whilst the rejection of the Aristotelian *ousia* (the Western *substantia*), prompted a more hospitable reception of its Platonic understanding in recent times, we should be reminded that a proper theological vision of "whatness" should go beyond a choice between the two understandings. In this sense, Harris's virtual return to Aristotle remains of little significance for theology.

15. For the more general postmodern tendency to overstress situatedness and to diminish agency, see Thiselton, *Interpreting God and the Postmodern Self*, 121–26.

16. I am alluding to the way in which Heidegger conceived the advent of novelty (how he devised the relation between thinking and poetry).

17. The recent ethical discussions of "playing God" occasioned by the possibilities opened by genetic engineering are telling in this respect. What we must remember here is that genuine rationality cannot be conceived apart from freedom and love. Indeed, it is not always easy, in a fallen world like ours, to distinguish between perfect manipulation (when one succeeds not only in convincing someone to take a course of action, but also in making him/her believe that he/she did it freely) and a genuine liberative discourse.

*if the ethical dimension is irreducible, a "perfect description," may be the wrong sort of ideal, for a world in which God has not cease to act.*

Thus, to understand and evaluate the ethical dimension of a scientific practice does not ultimately mean to bring together two alien domains. Instead, it means to grasp "the discovery" of the world, the world revealing its patterns of rationality to us, in inextricable connection with God's action of sustaining and perfecting the Creation. Only thus, the "artificial world" of modern human "expression" in general and the scientific endeavor in particular, can be said to have a genuine *telos* and in this sense, to have found its true *ratio*. The chances of science of not perceiving the ethical questions as alien to itself are dependent indeed on its capacity to disentangle itself from its protological and "foundational" orientation.

It is this irreducible ethical dimension (which confronts us with the frightening possibility of destroying our world) that distinguishes between a mere freedom of choice ("negative" freedom) and the possibility of genuinely realizing our freedom, of being coworkers with God (1 Cor 3:9) who alone can "authenticate" our actions by allowing us to participate in His "future." This brings us to the second dimension.

The ethics of freedom which we have only seen anticipated in Hegel and of which Barth's is perhaps the paramount example,[18] is fundamentally based upon such a vision.

"No longer do I call you slaves, for the slave does not know what his master is doing; but I have called you friends, for all things that I have heard from My Father I have made known to you" (John 15:15 NAS). Again, this perspective dislodges the restricted view of a choice between reception and construction, or the problematic ideal of a logic of identity in its manifold guises by grafting the idea of freedom at the very heart of the *diastasis* between Creator and creature. This is because God in Jesus Christ not only differentiates between God and man but also brings us into fellowship with him in a community of vision and hope.

---

18. E.g., Barth, *Ethics*, esp. 461–516; See also Jüngel's illuminating essay "Invocation of God as the Ethical Ground of Christian Action," in Jüngel, *Theological Essays*, 154–72.

# Virtue Epistemology
## and the Problem of Method in Theology.

In order to appreciate fully both this link between epistemology and ethics and the "responsive" dimension of the agent, it may be instructive to look briefly at Zagzebski's recent attempt to ground the normative dimension of the epistemic practice in a virtue ethics.[19] Working within the Catholic tradition, Zagzebski applies the traditional virtue theory of morality "to identify the normative aspect of knowledge" (209). Since belief is a necessary component of knowledge and the phenomenology of belief is ultimately similar to that of action, we can safely apply to our epistemic practice what we know about virtue from moral theory. By exploring this connection, the proposal aims to answer some of the shortcomings of Reformed Epistemology, which in Zagzebski's opinion is "too externalist, insufficiently voluntarist and insufficiently social" (209).[20]

Without going into the details of the controversy, we shall be content to note some aspects relevant for our discussion. Chief amongst them is one of Zagzebski's premises for the collusion of virtue theory and epistemology, namely the homology between belief and action. In opposition to Plantinga for whom, as Zagzebski summarizes it, we are "more like machines in our cognitional processes but conscious and free agents in our actions," the asymmetry between processes leading to acts and processes leading to beliefs is rejected (222). Granted that, however, it may be argued that it does not necessarily follow, as Zagzebski further maintains, that "both processes are governed by habits that come under the category of the voluntary." On the contrary, according to Saint Paul for instance, it is not only faith that is a gift from God, but also

19. See Zagzebski, *Virtues of the Mind*, esp. 165–96; Zagzebski, "Religious Knowledge and the Virtues," 199–225; further references to this latter book shall be given in the text above.

20. I may remind the reader here that, roughly described, a theory is internalist if "the criteria of justification or warrant are accessible to the consciousness of the believer" (Zagzebski, "Religious Knowledge and the Virtues," 201). Externalist theories on the other hand, "define justification in terms of the relation between a belief and features of the world that typically are not accessible to consciousness" (ibid.). The internalist account places a crucial weight upon the consciousness and will of the believer. In order to be justified or warranted, a belief must be within the control of the believer. While externalism aspires to an ideal categorial structure which transcends the consciousness of the believer, internalism maintains the role of the human knower which situates it closer to the more traditional rationalist position ("We control justification and warrant rather than the reverse.") (ibid., 202).

our good works (Ephesians 2:8–10). A way to surmount this difficulty is suggested precisely by contemplating the dispute between internalism and externalism from the perspective of God's action. This may enable us to go beyond an abstract dispute between voluntariness and involuntariness by recognizing elements of both in the phenomenology of every human action. In such a light, Zagzebski's promising mediation between epistemology and ethics appeals too soon to the Aristotelian theory of virtues. To be sure, she rightly recognizes that the pursuit of truth is ultimately non-instrumental. Truth is, indeed, pursued for its own sake. Yet, it seems to me, that this latter point should rather prompt us to look at the ultimate source of this reliable practice of attaining to the truth. The "habit of discerning the truth" is not the ground of the epistemic practice but rather the implication of being animated and empowered by the Truth itself. It is because God encounters us in Jesus and through the Spirit in a community of persons, and it is because justification is followed by sanctification that we have both the model and the power to respond creatively and to develop the epistemic virtue of discerning the truth. The assumptions about humanity (human beings are knowing creatures, generally rational, social by nature and self-reflective [210]), must be constantly informed by God's redemptive action, and most importantly, by Christ's revelation of our true humanity.

In this way, "good procedure" is, in a fallen world like ours, first of all, a question of unrelenting listening and obeying. Responsibility cannot, therefore, be frozen into a formal technique. "Functioning" properly, according to a design plan if it is to go beyond both, the imagery of "a well oiled machine" (221), and an abstract protological framework, needs indeed, as Zagzebski suggests, a communitarian doxastic structure, that is, a concrete community, the Church. But because God is at work in the Church in Christ and through the Spirit sanctifying her and bringing her to perfection, the concept of *phronesis* receives a distinct theological flavor. Thus, love for truth and the pursuit of good life come together in a community of character which is no longer grounded in the performance of a "natural habit" but arises as a faithful response to God's action in Christ and through the Spirit, "in whom are hid all the treasures of wisdom and knowledge" (Col 2:3 KJV). It is only in this new framework that the underlying consciousness model of epistemology may be properly uncovered and challenged. In this way, the dispute between what is voluntary and what is involuntary, between internalism and externalism is referred back to what we may call a *situated responsibility*.[21] It is this community of character which gathers in itself both dying for the self and the gift of the new life in Christ, both responsibility and the realization of our frailty and finitude. Without the almost foundational weight that tends to be accorded to the internalist-externalist distinction, we may perhaps talk more freely about both a form of voluntariness (without which the concept of responsibility remains meaningless), and involuntariness (which implicitly deconstructs the notion of an "absolute" subject).

What becomes apparent from the above is how important it is to maintain the Trinitarian framework of God's action in and towards the world when we address such issues. Ultimately, it is about God's action, about a Christology, a soteriology and a pneumatology, rather than about a "theory of virtues," that the theologian may want to talk about. Without proper reference to this framework, concepts such as "particularity" or "practical wisdom" will never save the day by themselves.

It is instructive to engage Abraham's version of theological episte-mology at this juncture, as it will further highlight the importance of such a Trinitarian framework.

I shall mainly look at his more recent *Crossing the Threshold of Divine Revelation*,[22] where he tackles the subject of theological episte-mology head on. While his stance on epistemology as employed in the history of the Church has been decidedly critical in his previous *Canon and Criteria*, Abraham clarifies and sharpens the target of his critique here. It is not the practice in itself that is the problem. The subject is in fact, unavoidable. What is more, Abraham is prepared to acknowledge here that "rationality and justification are linked to practices that have a pivotal role in human welfare" (173). Rather, it is the habit of the Western theological tradition (after the great schism) of starting with a general

21. It is in the light of the importance accorded to the human subject that the Catholic epistemologists often associate the Reformed stress upon the lack of control with epistemic luck (202). The rejection of voluntarism however (I do not decide what to believe), anchored as it is in the importance accorded to both prevenient grace and a non-meritorious understanding of salvation rightly rejects an abstract notion of free choice either grounded in natural reason or as an expression of naked will. The outcome of this rejection may well be therefore not necessarily a form of epistemic luck but rather a more concrete notion of responsibility. In fact it is on this path that the individual belief may be grafted within a world and an environment in which the believer may "function properly" according to "a design plan" successfully aimed at truth. (See Plantinga, *Warrant and Proper*, esp. 3–47.)

22. Abraham, *Crossing the Threshold of Divine Revelation*. I will include references in the main text above.

theory of knowledge and then trying to apply that theory to theology, that must be challenged.[23]To this end, Abraham proposes the principle of appropriate epistemic fit (11), which rather than beginning with the "how" question, starts with "the actual subject matter that claims our allegiance and, starting afresh, see where that takes us" (11). In other words, "the wise theologian," the canonical theist, is a "particularist." This entails suspicion towards the primacy of method and suspicion towards epistemology's overarching claims. The Church should not canonize any specific epistemology; it should not have "a grand theory of knowledge," claims Abraham.

But what exactly does it mean to be a "particularist"? Abraham has a number of things to say in this regard. We learn for instance that there is place for logical rules and argumentation strategies like deductive inference, inductive or abductive arguments, cumulative case arguments and so on. More significantly, Abraham mentions a number of "common assumptions" (what he calls "epistemic platitudes"), like the general reliability of our perceptual beliefs, memory, testimony, etc. that the theologian may assume to be reliable and true, unless he or she has good reasons to believe otherwise. If this may look like a disguised return to "the old modern ways," Abraham is adamant to note that divine revelation has a crucial role in this endeavor, as we shall see in more detail below. Besides, "there is a difference," Abraham maintains, between "success in providing good arguments and having to hand a theory of good arguments" (19). Equally noteworthy is the observation that due to the polymorphous nature of Divine Revelation, to the diversity of divine action, theological epistemology is necessarily particular and specific.

I certainly admire Abraham's brilliant defense of particularity and I wholeheartedly agree with his critique of modern epistemology, or "methodism," as he calls it. He is certainly right to suggest that when epistemology is reduced to proof, deductive arguments and surefire guarantees, "epistemic anxiety becomes the order of the day" (109).

I also appreciate his lucid description of the phenomenology of conversion, his account of what happens when we cross the threshold of divine revelation, and of the new world that is unveiled before the believer with its implications for epistemology. The balance between

---

23. "The canonical heritage of the church has something better to offer than epistemology" (Abraham, *Canon and Criteria*, 390). Abraham further claims that when such explicit epistemic program has been affirmed and imposed, the life of the Church has been crippled rather than liberated.

"externalism" (God's prevenient grace and his providential control) and "internalism" (the voluntary aspect of faith and trust), is also promising. While God provides the conditions of possibility of knowledge, we are responsible for our actions. We have intellectual duties and obligations.

I would like, nonetheless, to express three interrelated concerns regarding his position. The first has to do with the dynamics of divine action and human response. What is less clear at times in Abraham's proposal is how, exactly, would a particularist go about his epistemological work? How would she or he move between epistemology and ontology? What exactly would be taken for granted and why? At times, Abraham seems to opt for a form of reliabilism when it comes to knowledge of the world, yet advocate a radical "internalism" when it comes to knowledge of God. Take for instance Abraham's early suggestion (21–22) that to think of an epistemology of theology given to us in a divine revelation is absurd, as the appeal to divine revelation is itself one more epistemological proposal. But if methodism is left behind why force revelation into this "internalist" dead end? Is not the concept of Revelation more than a mere "epistemic" concept? Arguably, the circularity that worries Abraham is really a problem only if one retains the demands of modern epistemology. In the explanatory footnote, Abraham admits that he, in fact, only rejects one (popular) way of thinking of epistemology, rather than epistemology itself, more specifically, "methodism" or foundationalism. But if that is the case, than, thinking of epistemology as, in some sense, given in divine revelation may not be as absurd, after all. The main insight of externalist/reliabilist accounts of justification is precisely this primacy of being and experience over method/consciousness. After all, Abraham's own "epistemic platitudes" may be read as a form of reliabilism. Why not extend this "ontological awareness" when it comes to the concept of Revelation? I guess Abraham wants to speak on the behalf of the philosopher at this juncture. This also explains the somewhat unsettling claim that his "epistemic platitudes" do not entail the acceptance of any theological premise (39). Is this to say that God doesn't really have a say in our epistemological pursuits? That epistemology is a human affair through and through? "Our" effort to prove and justify? Hardly so, in the light of Abraham's overall argument. In later chapters, Abraham goes on to explain that once the threshold of divine revelation is crossed, theism can and must make a difference to epistemology. "Theology will rule out certain options and underwrite others in robust and surprising ways" (30). Abraham is supremely aware that theological epistemology is more than a philosophical exercise meant to adjudicate the truth of a worldview. While criteria like explanatory power, simplicity, fit with the world, internal consistency, coherence, etc. undoubtedly help, Christianity often invites for a different kind of arguments and *"different modes of assent and believing"* (44, my italics).

Perhaps Abraham is suggesting that once we abandon methodism and the skeptic's obsession with certitude, the starting point does not really matter that much. Being in "the same boat,"[24] means that we all "start" with assumptions that we can safely consider to be reliable unless proven otherwise. In other words, those ad hoc epistemic practices cannot be "naturalized" into some kind of "universal tools." In fact, arguably, Abraham re-visits most of them in the light of the whole.

Take for example his engagement with Plantinga where he rightly criticizes his implicit and explicit theological commitments (his virtual bypassing of the concept of Revelation or the Trinity, etc.) The same may be said about Abraham's discussion of *"oculus contemplationis"* (71). When he favors the latter over the "evidentialist alternative," Abraham invokes "phenomenological reasons." That is to say, rather than "arguing

---

24. Wolterstorff rightly avers that Abraham's "platitudes" are deeply contested philosophical positions (Wolterstorff, Review of *Crossing the Threshold of Divine Revelation*, 102–8). Indeed, the view that the cosmological and anthropological assumptions undergirding those "platitudes" would be universally accepted as true is overly optimistic. Both, my (Cartesian) friend and our mutual (Buddhist) local dentist, to allude to some of Abraham's examples, may have misgivings with some core claims in Abraham's list. "Being in the same boat" can be taken to mean "inhabiting the same world," or having somewhat similar experiences. But this is different from making (the "externalist") claim that the world "functions" in a certain way according to a design plan, despite the Fall, etc. One can argue that, more often than not, such "platitudes" turn out to be significantly shaped by deep seated metaphysical commitments. But Wolterstorff's overall critique misses the target, in my opinion. There is nothing wrong in reflecting upon God's revelation of himself *while* He performs various salvific events or addresses people in illocutionary acts. There is grace in that, too, and some of us (mainly theologians, I guess) may be called to talk about that as well. This "internalist" dimension has a legitimate place in our theological discourse. Such reflections become troubling, of course, when they replace rather than accompany actual obedience. But the theologian knows that true theology cannot exist outside obedience and worship anyway. Wolterstorff's point that "speaking is not revealing" may be true in our casual human encounters, but of little theological use when it comes to God discourse. Theological epistemology cannot be either radically externalist, as arguably, Wolterstorff's position tends to be at times (as if we had some kind of direct access to "the way things are") or radically internalist (as if epistemology is entirely about human effort and achievement); from a theological perspective, both extremes are inadequate.

themselves into believing," most people find themselves responding to God's prior action. They "naturally,"[25] "perceive" God, so to say.

What I want to highlight here is that this is "externalist," "ontological talk." Abraham seems (rightly) to reject the "high access" requirement of internalism, yet, allowing place for evidence. Some of us may be called to do that after all. . . . The same is true in the case of "special revelation." It is God's action in the believer that has primacy. Confirmation is *a posteriori* and usually *ad hoc*. More importantly, the confirmation remains particular and specific. It does not operate in isolation. It does not constitute an independent source of confirmation (73). Yet, the agent can and usually does affect "the way things are." *Oculus contemplationis* is not an "automatic" occurrence. We can enable it or stifle it. Virtue and sin play a significant role.

I cannot agree more. . . . But why then, is Abraham insisting that "we must challenge the claim that theism is essential to secure our network of epistemic platitudes" (39)? Part of it, I believe is due to his desire to establish the "public" dimension of Christianity. We should reject attempts to shut down critical questions, or suggestions that faith is a leap in the dark. Yet, as we have seen, Abraham also maintains that crossing the threshold of divine revelation not only that enriches one's perspective but, in important ways, changes things altogether! How is the procedure consistent then? How is reason prevented from occupying a foundational role? Abraham explains:

> The crucial observation to make at this point is quite simple. It is one thing to come to believe we have divine revelation and challenge the content of that revelation. It is another thing entirely to challenge or ask questions about the claim that someone possesses a divine revelation. Adopting the former, will indeed seriously undermine the core of the argument to date; pursuing the latter does not (92).

For those schooled in the Barthian tradition that would be equivalent, perhaps, with "wanting to have the cake and eat it too"! There is no doubt in my mind that Barth's position poses serious difficulties and, as Abraham rightly maintains, his implicit epistemology (apparent in his doctrine of Revelation) is theologically problematic.[26] But is this "crucial

25. I.e., "natural" response to God's providential activity. Abraham specifically mentions that "this order of business" does not make one dependent on arguments from natural theology.

26. For Abraham's treatment of Barth, see Abraham, William *Canon and Criteria*, chapter 14.

observation" so clear-cut and simple? Are we now in the position to unequivocally confront competing claims to revelation? Is it really possible to detach so dramatically the conviction that one has indeed, divine revelation from the content of such revelation? Moreover, isn't challenging or asking questions about the claim that someone possesses divine revelation a matter of "content"? Abraham is certainly right to attack heteronomous claims to divine revelation in this context, and to reject "leaps in the dark," but what is the source of those unending critical questions? What guides the theologian in this, indeed, crucial enterprise?

Of course, these are largely rhetorical questions. It is not my intention to press for a "deeper" level of rationality or a "more solid" foundation. My point is to highlight the fact that such talk is "successful" only as "theo-logical" talk, irrespective whether at stake is my inner experience of God or someone else's claim to revelation. I am skeptical that by returning to the distinction self-other, our epistemological questions will be all sorted out. Freud rightly taught us (against Descartes) that our own experiences can be equally deceiving. In other words, human reason is never the ultimate standard since it is God who speaks, opens up new visions, enables "world-constituting experiences" and creates "the logical space to inquire" into the validity of divine revelation, as Abraham rightly maintains (93).

I tend to see this final recourse to the self-other distinction as a capitulation to the demands of modern epistemology. This, I believe leads Abraham to insist that Revelation as opposed to the Bible or canon is an exclusive epistemic concept. Does not Revelation feed on the (ontological) reality of God's action in history, and supremely in Jesus Christ?[27] If that is the case, revelation cannot be a mere problem of reflective consciousness (as we have noted earlier, infinite regression and circularity is only worrying when epistemology aspires to occupy a foundational role). Abraham would agree with that, I believe. Again, it is very significant that, for Abraham, "the logical space to inquire" into the validity of divine revelation is to be found only after one crossed the threshold.

I agree that problems abound in both contemporary Protestantism and Catholicism and the tendency to epistemize either the Scripture or

---

27. This would require, of course, a more comprehensive concept of Revelation, that would include the totality of God's action in and towards the world (for a detailed exposition of such a concept see Gunton, *Brief Theology of Revelation* or Webster, *Holy Scripture*, 16–17); but even a more limited concept like Abraham's would need to make recourse to its (ontological) source.

ecclesiastical authority is certainly there. But, arguably, both Revelation and Scripture tend to take a too accentuated epistemic and polemical tone in Abraham's discussion. He is right to point out that the relation between revelation and the doctrine of the incarnation and the Trinity is multidimensional, informal and indirect" (108). Nonetheless, the theologian needs to constantly return to the ontological source of those concepts rather than to retreat in second order reflections on conditions of possibilities. Genuine critical talk can only emerge in such an exercise.

To sum up, it is this movement between ontology and epistemology between divine action and human response that must constitute the background of any inquiry into the source of our epistemic anxieties. As I pointed out above, our critical talk can be successful only as "theo-logical" talk. Furthermore, such "theo-logical" talk is only possible as "obedient response." True "externalism" cannot be safeguarded otherwise. If we are truly to depart from the obsessions of modern epistemology we should leave behind its associated philosophy of consciousness with its series of distinctions, Kantian or otherwise. Abraham's position is at times ambiguous precisely because it doesn't spell out this constant move between epistemology and ontology, which in fact is demanded by the principle of epistemic fit.

This brings me to my second disquiet, namely, Abraham's plea for particularism. This is nothing wrong with that in itself, of course. Calls for respect of particularity and rejection of "totalities" abound in recent theology for good reasons, as we have seen. But how "prescriptive" can we be when it comes to "particularity" and what is the guiding light when engaged in such an endeavor?

Like Ricoeur and other continental thinkers, Abraham takes his queue from Aristotle. An *a priori* methodology always cripples and distorts the "content" to which it is applied. Instead, method must fit the content. Indeed, if "being is said in many ways," so should method. But the same is virtually true for any other field of knowledge. In other words, it is in the light of our experience of the world, so to say, that such a principle is adopted. Do things change in the aftermath of "crossing the threshold of divine revelation? Should the theologian be in the position to return, and perhaps, qualify further such a position?

I suppose she or he should. In fact, reflecting on particularity is always done in the light of some kind of totality. In other words, there is always a universal-particular dialectic in play. But, for the Christian, this "whole" has a slightly different "taxis" than, say, Aristotle's universe has.

Arguably, it is the (fundamentally *a posteriori*) rich present experience of the canonical theist, immersed as he or she is in the history of the church that provides the criteria for such a theological exercise. It may be argued that this, in turn, is just a reply to God's action in Christ and by the Spirit in redeeming and perfecting the world. If Abraham's *ad hoc* epistemology is not to become a theory of *ad hoc* epistemology, more needs to be said about the *taxis* of this particularity and about its specific resources and context which cannot be other than God's unifying action in Christ and by the Spirit. Yes, Christian epistemologists could be foundationlists, reliabilists or coherentists, and their accompanying philosophical support may be impeccable. Moreover, the theologian may agree with specific applications of such proposals. But, in the light of "the whole" a theological critique of specific instances of such proposals, as we have seen, is not only possible but desirable. So, rather than generic respect for particularity (whether prompted by empirical observation or (memory of) painful historical experience, it is the unity of God's action *ad extra* that provides "the whole" in the light of which particularity is evaluated. It is the grand drama of God's encounter with the world that furnishes the structure of our appreciation of particularity. As we have seen, epistemology has a hegemonic tendency, the tendency of becoming "opaque" and autonomous, ceasing to reflect the reality that brought her into being. . . . But if it is true that, epistemology is ultimately not a human invention, theological epistemology is not primarily a matter of reflective consciousness but about obedience and about following the trajectory of this grand movement. This brings me to my last point.

Sosa concludes his seminal essay "The Raft and the Pyramid" by suggesting that the dispute between the methodist and the particularist cannot be settled without recourse to other issues, notoriously neglected by epistemologists, namely, the field of ethics and the problem of virtue.[28]

This is something that the theologian always knew, of course. . . . We cannot settle the problem of knowledge (especially of God but also of the world) in abstraction of God's redemptive action/human response. One may object to such sweeping claims and point to the fact that knowledge of the world has done quite well, and at times, even better, when God

---

28. Sosa, "Raft and the Pyramid," 134–53. It is also very significant to note that, as Zagzebski and Fairweather contend, it was the desire to avoid skepticism that fuelled the dispute between foundationalism and coherentism. In other words, the whole problematic was put in motion by a modern anxiety. (Zagzebski and Fairweather, Introduction to *Virtue Epistemology*, 4.)

was left out of the equation. It is certainly true that the habit of working "within limits" works quite well for science. But this type of pragmatic criteria would never suffice. Genuine knowledge always meets ethics. Let me unpack this further.

In an illuminating study, Hetherington unmasks what he calls the two dogmas of (modern) epistemology, namely, epistemic absolutism and "justificationism."[29] For far too long, Hetherington asserts, epistemologists have claimed that we either know or we don't. Similarly, it has been long claimed that what can be deemed as knowledge must necessarily be connected with some kind of justification, that knowledge cannot exist outside justification.

Arguably, once these modern assumptions are left behind, once we acknowledge that there are always degrees of knowledge we can see better why knowledge can be hardly conceived in independence from ethics. To begin with, we can hardly have "full knowledge" of anything. As the Apostle Paul reminds us, now we know in part. . . . We can certainly "know" trivial truths like 2+2=4. And this may, indeed, look harmless and "neutral." But such "truths" are hardly satisfying. A "better" knowledge of such logical truths would connect them with the truth of the created order, which in turn, will reach the ethical, the aesthetic and the metaphysical dimension of reality. What is also apparent in this exercise is that denying "absolutism," does not stifle the ideal of unity and wholeness. Aspiring to such "totality" is not necessarily "totalizing"! The Christian can certainly agree with scientists who may be either atheists or may have a different view of the world. But in the end, their knowledge of the "whole" would be "worse off." This is a matter of theological principle. Of course, in what way a particular knowledge would be "better off," may remain ambiguous. Moreover, the theological exercise of identifying this unity, as we have seen in the history of the Church, is by no means, a simple and straightforward one. Quite the contrary, it is tenuous and at times may lead to "false totalities." But failures should not deter us from holding fast to this ideal. It is this larger vision that should be paramount when we defend one article of faith or another, when we criticize

---

29. Hetherington, *Good Knowledge, Bad Knowledge*. Epistemic absolutism claims that one either has knowledge or one doesn't (so it doesn't allow for degrees of knowledge); justificationism, on the other hand, claims that each instance of knowledge has to include justification which is either internalist or externalist. Significantly, Hetherington shows how, once these dogmas are refuted, the sorites-inspired problems and the Gettier cases are easily answered (ibid., 110).

ideologies or unmask alleged solutions for our present malaise. Yes, we may start with, or make use of versions of what Abraham calls "epistemic platitudes," but it is this larger vision that dictates both the specific starting point and the way those logical rules and assumptions are employed. To know the world, in independence of God's action in Christ and by the Spirit, is to know less well . . .[30]

To summarize, our plea for particularity when talking about method in theology is a plea to follow the Trinitarian grammar suggested above. The principle of the appropriate epistemic fit should be employed *sub ratione Dei,* i.e., within the larger vision of God's action and purpose. As it has become apparent, it is not "the unity" in itself that is the problem, but usually the route to unity and the way such unity is conceived. It is not the unity of an always-already established method, that would accommodate in advance all possible content that should be in view. Rather the unity of its content, the unity of God's action in Christ and in the Spirit, redeeming and reconciling the world to himself. And it is not the totalizing effort of the mind, but rather the glimpses of that eschatological vision we find in our experience as coworkers with Christ in this great drama. Revelation is indeed plural, but it points to a unity of purpose and action leading to the final coming of God, to a new heaven and a new earth. Consequently, theological epistemology needs to be particular and specific but it also needs to be faithful to such announcements.[31] . . . Abraham would agree, I believe, that this double demand (the demand of epistemic fit, that is, primacy of content and respect for particularity, and the demand for unity and wholeness that would reflect the rich ontology of God's encounter with the world) is implicit in, what he calls "canonical theism." It is my contention that an explicit Trinitarian grammar has a decisive contribution in this task. Furthermore, once deployed, it unveils an irreducible ethical dimension.

As it has become apparent, engaging with "justification" and warrant is also an existential practice that ultimately connects us back to our desire for wholeness, for truth, beauty and meaning. In the light of those

30. Quite in accord with Abraham's own procedure, one can be "successful" without mastering the criterion of success, i.e., without having a "theory of what counts as successful." One may reply that such "strong" talk has left "theological reflection" and delved into "proclamation" and "preaching." But, perhaps, true theology never left those fields . . .

31. This indeed should encourage a sympathetic hermeneutics of past theologies less focused, perhaps, on their totalizing tendencies. This is what Abraham suggests, too, in the concluding part of *Crossing the Threshold of Divine Revelation* (188).

high stakes, there is no wonder that such "second order" discourses were transfigured into "foundations." . . . Idolatry and the tendency to "curve in on oneself (*homo incurvatus in se*) have been the recurring problems of humanity. Walking within "the autonomy of responsible thought" has become so dear to us, so strongly attached to notions like dignity and respect that we can hardly accept the notion that responding to a prior call can be the enabling factor in reaching our true rational potential. But the theologian knows that we are not and could never be the masters of this pursuit.

To conclude, what our analysis has shown, is not so much that our justificatory practices, as such, have been made redundant by the new postmodern paradigm, or in need to be abandoned or replaced by a hermeneutical approach, but rather how inextricably bound they are to our theological discourse and practices. Justification is rarely, if ever, a mere intellectual gesture. It always has practical, ethical and aesthetic concerns. While there are, indeed, problems with the modern subject and modern epistemology, as has become apparent time and again in our analysis, theological discourse, whether implicitly or explicitly, is always in search of some kind of justification. As the modern subject becomes the source of truth and meaning, such search no longer "happens" *Coram Deo*. . . . It becomes autonomous. . . . As a consequence, certitude or avoidance of skepticism become ideals valuable in and of themselves and faith and trust are severed from reason and authentic knowledge. . . . The Apostle Paul's claim that it is "in God, that we "move and have our being" no longer configures the intellectual frame of mind of the modern subject. But if epistemology, in its true theological dimension is not a human invention, if God "proved" himself in his Son, if he decisively "returned"[32] to the world he created, so to speak, then, ultimately, such efforts are, ultimately, not really about ourselves and our petty projects. As Murray Rae asserts, the knowledge of God is not, first of all, the fruit of human industry.[33] It is part of the task of theology to uncover this "non-technical" dimension of justification and warrant. Beyond strict appeals to reason, experience, witness, testimony and the like, from a theological perspective, epistemology requires the whole plethora of modes of thought and ways of speaking and acting, from prayer and worship to proclamation

---

32. I use the term metaphorically to refer to the Incarnation and to press home the epistemic dimension entailed. Of course, God never really "left" the world. . . . Also, I do not mean to limit Revelation to a form of "reiteration." Revelation presupposes more than that.

33. Rae, "Incline Your Ear," 161.

and evangelism that have always been part and parcel of the life of the Church.[34] This is so, because the Church is called to follow and respond to, in Webster's words, "the fellowship-establishing trajectory of the acts of God in the election, creation, providential ordering, reconciliation, judgement and glorification of God's creatures."[35] It is only in such an exercise that her critical discourse can find its true justification.

## Theological Reason between Creation and Redemption— Illumination Revisited

It is certainly easier to accept such claims when our focus is knowledge of God. It is more difficult to allow that such talk may be relevant for knowledge in general. Yet, our attempt to think Creation and Word together has taught us, as we have seen, that the truth of Creation cannot be separated from the truth of Redemption and that, consequently, knowledge cannot be separated from ethics. Moreover, talking about knowledge of both God and the world "in the same step," so to say, allowed us to identify the radical interpenetration of "Creation" and "Word," of "sense" and "freedom." In other words, there are ways of talking "theo-logically" about knowledge in general, ways to characterize knowledge of both God and the world. It is the same God, through the Son and in the Spirit that sustains and "enlightens" the created intellect.

John Webster's recent account of illumination is instructive at this juncture in more than one respect, as we shall see. Taking its cue from Augustine, Webster reminds us that in the most general sense, "illumination refers to the ways in which the operation of creaturely intelligence is caused, preserved and directed by divine light, whose radiance makes

---

34 This bears a superficial similarity to what James Robert Brown and others call a *narrative* style of explanation in which "an event or condition is explained by telling a story in which the thing to be explained is embedded." In this way the explanandum is said to be rendered "intelligible"; from the story we see how the events in question are possible." Brown, *Smoke and Mirrors*, 21. Of course, the Christian story confronts us with a much richer ontology than, say, a mere "scientific" view of the world. In this sense, Brown's plea for realism, remains "Platonic" and "not realist" enough, an intellectualist account that hovers above a (forever inaccessible and mostly "static") "in-itself." By contrast, as we have seen, the Christian view of the world defended here describes history as a dialectic of divine and human action, as an eschatological movement from "the way things are" to "the way things and people are called to be." . . . Probably a form of "anti-realism" from Brown's perspective.

35. Webster, *Holy Scripture*, 17.

creatures to know." This is, Augustine says, "what enables [the soul] to understand whatever is within the range of its powers."[36] Webster takes time to explore what he considers to be the proper setting of an account of illumination, namely, "a theological meditation on the economy of the Spirit" (328).

Corresponding to the perfect and wholly sufficient work of the Son in the redemption of fallen creatures, there is a further mission of God in their regeneration and restoration to intelligent, consensual, affective and active fellowship with God (328–29).

This letter work in the believer must not be conceived, Webster insists, as a subjective principle, as a mere "stirring of created minds." Instead, it must be referred back to the deity and personhood of the Spirit, the third person of the Trinity who "is in himself infinite divine wisdom, light and radiance" (330). Equally important, Webster avers, is to note that "the work of the Spirit in the *opus gratiae* of regeneration accords with his work in the *opus naturae* of creation. The work of the Holy Spirit in the redeemed "repeats, confirms and completes his mode of operation on and in all creatures, especially rational creatures" (330). Of course, this in no way diminishes the role of human response. The Spirit cherishes and conserves created realities and powers, offering no violence to them but so moving them that their integrity and dignity are preserved (330).

Significantly, Webster recalls Aquinas's treatment of the matter in *Summa* pointing out that in countering the supposed "autonomy" of human mental acts, Aquinas made recourse to the same Augustinian insight: it is the teacher who moves the mind of the learner. It is God who teaches man knowledge. The more formal language of primary and secondary causes, was never intended to obscure the crucial role of illumination.

Unfortunately, the Western intellectual tradition after Aquinas recounted a different story. The language of "causation" appeared not only as more convenient for the emerging "scientific" view of the world but as "rationally superior" to such "theological talk." What followed was the "naturalization" of world processes and events. The language of God's action in and toward the world, through the Son and in the Spirit was no longer constitutive to our understanding of the created order.

---

36. Webster, "Illumination," 325. The last paragraph is a direct quotation from Augustine (*Literal Meaning of Genesis*). I will include further references to this article in the text above.

The peculiarly modern problem of "naturalization" is discussed at length in Webster's *Holy Scripture: A Dogmatic Sketch*.[37] Christian theories of interpretation and theological hermeneutics today spend a great deal of time with postmodern theories of texts, speech-act theories or discussion about language games and the role of communities in interpretation, Webster complains. Not that this would be bad in itself. But the practice tended to lead to the severing of Biblical interpretation from its "theo-logical" roots. By contrast, Webster refuses "to fold the Holy Scripture" into a generic theory of texts as a mere "natural" or "historical" entity, or as mere "cultural poiesis." Instead, Webster talks about "an ontology of the Holy Scripture," which has the language of the triune God's saving and revelatory action at its core. The upshot of such talk is that divine movement cannot be reduced to always-already available properties of a text. God's action cannot be "arrested" or "commodified" in things upon which we have control.

The subject of interpretation where the text allegedly "achieves its realization" has to undergo the same critique. It is not the "expresivist" dimension of the human mind that has priority. That is why "faithful reading" is to be preferred to "interpretation." "Exegetical reasoning," Webster asserts, must bear the mark of all Christian existence "which is dying and rising with Jesus Christ through the purging and quickening power of the Holy Spirit" (88–89).

While this is especially apparent when we read Scripture, arguably, this is true for human reasoning in general. In fact, in a different context, Webster suggests that to live the Christian life is to live in this "new mode of common human life, the life of the Church," in which "God's limitless power is unleashed and extends into the entirety of human life: moral, political, cultural, affective, intellectual. Reason, like everything else, is remade in the sphere of the Church."[38] In other words, to speak "Christianly" and "truthfully" not only about God, but about everything else, is "an exercise of holy reason." Webster goes on to note that it was the same fall into "naturalism" that severed human reason from the drama of God's saving work. But "to think of reason as 'natural' and 'transcendent' in this way is, by the standard of Christian confession, corrupt, because it isolates reason from the work of God as creator, reconciler and perfecter."[39]

---

37. Webster, *Holy Scripture*.

38. Webster, *Holiness*, 2.

39. Ibid., 11.

It may be tempting to think that such theological talk is largely irrelevant in the daily exercise of reason, or that, as alluded to earlier, our present technological advances prove that secular reason has been quite successful in its endeavors and that such language may be not only irrelevant but distractive or even harmful for "scientific reasoning." But this is to fail to see God's grace in both creation and redemption. Webster again:

> Yet such is treachery of creatures against the nature and calling which God's love has conferred on them that the creaturely coordinate to the divine light almost ceases to be. "Almost," because it is not in the power of creatures to destroy their nature. They may despise their condition and situation, may attempt independent exercise of their given powers and so diminish them; but creatures cannot not be creatures, who have their being and come to know by the light of God (334).[40]

As noted earlier, the Christian scientist may well agree with his or her atheist counterpart, but ultimately the latter's knowledge of the whole would be "worse off."

But there is another reason why Webster's reflections on holy reason may be relevant for our project. Webster ascribes to his account of the nature of Holy Scripture "only a modest role," "ancillary," as he puts it, "to the primary theological task, which is exegesis."[41] Such an undertaking cannot "replace or eclipse the work of exegesis."[42]

But why engage in such an exercise in the first place? Webster hints at some of the reasons that may prompt the theologian to talk about such things. Unfortunately, there are other, less fruitful influences that tend to mold the exegetical self-understanding of the theologian. Yet, more needs to be said here lest some may be tempted to consider such analysis as mere "prolegomena," preparing the way for "real" theology. In other words, a somewhat "formal" endeavor the role of which may be to "precede" or "found" the "material" deployment of theology. Of course, as Webster's analysis amply indicates, nothing would be further from the truth. . . . It is not difficult to see that it is still a modern anxiety that may give rise to such a suspicion. In this sense, Webster's reflections on the nature of Holy Scripture performs a critical task, (not unlike the one undertaken here), and accordingly, should be conceived neither "behind"

---

40. Webster, "Illumination," 334.
41. Webster, *Holy Scripture*, 3.
42. Ibid.

nor "before" the exegetical task itself. Rather it is *the necessary counterpart of all concern with "material" issues.*

We need a dogmatic account of Scripture because we have lost our ways; because in trying to answer the "how" of exegesis, instead of turning to the "how" of God's encounter with the world, we turned to "methods" and "procedures" no longer connected with God's specific action in history but rather grounded in "secure" intellectual frameworks promising to offer "generic" responses, always-already there for us to "manipulate" and "use." When such "methods" take hold, the language of call and response becomes redundant and eventually irrelevant. . . . In this sense such reflections are not really "second order" reflections; yet, *they do perform* a critical function and in this sense, they have an irreducible epistemological dimension.

As we have seen, concern with "content," whether ideas or practices, whether biblical exegesis or exposition of doctrine, not only that is never pure, that is, devoid of "form," but it is always susceptible to the perils of our finite and fallen condition. That is why true reasoning is always under "the sign of baptism," always a "spiritual discipline." True Reasoning is "godly reasoning," requiring us to "make every thought subject to the divine Logos" (2 Cor 11).

If all this is true, what are the more concrete implications for our reflections on knowledge in general and for the epistemology of theology in particular? Towards such concerns we shall now turn.

## Method in Theology and the Irreducibility of God's Trinitarian Action

As we have noted at the beginning of chapter 6, critique of method has become common place in recent theology. Rejection of modernity and of various types of "foundationalism" have taken at times more radical forms by either claiming complete "freedom" from method or proclaiming "non-foundationalist" approaches that would completely leave the "old modern ways" behind.[43]

---

43. Non-foundationalist theologians like Ronald Thiemann or Nancy Murphy have been often accused of crypto-foundationalism. See especially the "post-foundationalist" approach of theologians like van Huyssteen or F. LeRon Shults. Van Huyssteen, *Essays in Postfoundationalist Theology*; "Is the Postmodernist Always a Postfoundationalist?," 373–86. Shults, *Postfoundationalist Task of Theology*, 25ff.

In what follows, I would like to press further Abraham's insight that the church shouldn't really have one method, that, when it comes to Christian epistemology, a plurality of approaches is not only welcomed but perhaps the norm. While, as Abraham claims, the "particularist" is better situated, adopting an epistemology as *the* epistemology of the Christian faith, presumably even if it claims to be a "particularist" one, is always a bad idea. Why is this so? We have already touched upon a number of reasons. Part of the problem is certainly our notorious incapacity to conceive the "whole," due to our finite and fallen condition. We have also noted the irreducible plurality of experience and perhaps, most important of all, the "totalizing" and "hegemonic" tendency of a method (any method) upon which humans have control.

Here, our attempt to think Creation and Redemption together might provide language for further theological reflection in this direction.

A number of things can be said in this connection. I will start with a brief overview of two (very different) epistemological proposals and then attempt to bring things together with some final reflections on method, knowledge and truth in the light of God's Trinitarian action.

Very few theologians today would cling to the old, so called, "classical foundationalist" position. Since its famous rebuttal by Plantinga and Wolterstorff,[44] few theologians, if any, would claim allegiance to such epistemological foundation. Nonetheless, this is not to say that the "foundationalist" model has been completely abandoned. Even the Reformed Epistemology program explicitly employs a form of "foundationalism." There maybe some wisdom in that. Perhaps the "modern" theologians were right in some respects in spite of their apparent allegiance to the modern dogma. More importantly, beyond and above the philosophical reasons that led to the alleged demise of foundationalism in its classical form, theologians are (at least some of them) more interested in the theological and biblical roots of such constructs. But even if a certain form of mild or soft foundationalism may prove to have some theological viability would it be right to employ it as *the* epistemology of Christian theology *tout court*?

David Clark in his recent *To Know and Love God*[45] seems to suggest precisely that. While I have no doubts that Clark's version of soft foundationalism neither tells the whole story, nor does it exhaust the potential

44. Plantinga and Wolterstorff, *Faith and Rationality*.

45. Clark, *To Know and Love God*. Further quotations from this book will be included in the text above.

of such an approach, I believe, nonetheless, that his proposal exemplifies the theological problems that typically emerge in such an undertaking.

Clark acknowledges the problems of modernity. Yes, the Enlightenment hope for a "single, rational, objective *and secular* view of the world" (163, italics his) was misguided. Nonetheless, Clark believes that the postmodern reaction "against what is right about the modern quest for genuine knowledge" (163) is worse off and that the challenges we are presently facing are "greater than before." In fact, Clark spends most of his time rebutting what he calls "postmodern perspectivalism" which inevitably leads, in Clark's view, to epistemic relativism. To be sure, the "soft foundationalism" Clark is proposing, explicitly rejects the restrictive criteria of "hard foundationalism," while acknowledging the positive contributions of both coherence and pragmatic criteria. He is even prepared to accept "what is true about perspectivalism." Nonetheless those alternative accounts (coherentism, pragmatism) can never be sufficient in grounding an entire web of beliefs (161). There are promising elements in Clark's proposal. Besides the recognition of the complexity of our epistemic practices, we find a number of filiations with reliabilism that implicitly depotantiates the old consciousness model of modernity. What is worrying in his account however, is not so much the potential philosophical objections (how, for instance, coherence and pragmatic criteria would genuinely play a role in a fundamental one-way structure of argumentation), but rather the absence of any significant theological reflections on our belief forming practices. Questions like "How does the grand narrative of God's encounter with the world impact our understanding of what counts as 'basic beliefs'"? or "How does the story of redemption feature into our epistemic practice?" receives virtually no attention. Clark leaves no doubt regarding his preference for a specific epistemic program and it is quite clear that the modern anxiety of finding certitude significantly shapes his proposal. His later discussion of different senses of reason (300) not only that fails to ground his soft foundationalism theologically, but seems to reinforce his allegiance to the old objectivist dogma. Rationality, as such, transcends worldviews, asserts Clark (contra perspectivalism) (300). Of course, this may be true, in some sense, if the old concept of unaided human reason is left behind. But the discussion is largely conducted at the level of reason as a noetic principle with no reference to the history of redemption.

The same "naturalism"—"more neutral patterns of thinking" (302) is discernible here. No reference to God's action and human response but an implicit assumption of what is always-already available for all thinking subject is by virtue of creation. As we have seen, when the language of God's action becomes superfluous, the ghost of "substantial-ism" (with its implicit "deistic" universe) is not far behind. Knowledge tends to be deliberated between the mind and the world in an unper-turbed "structure of sense."

At the other end of the spectrum, a number of theologians have completely abandoned (or so they thought) the foundationalist mode of justification. It is coherentism, they claim, with its metaphor of a web of beliefs that should guide our epistemic practices as it does better jus-tice to both our experience of reality and our present cultural situation. Rather than relying on a one-way building structure that emerges from a number of foundational beliefs, coherentism claims that each belief is supported by its ties to its neighboring beliefs. Ultimately, it is the coher-ence of the entire "web of beliefs" that achieves justification. One of the leading advocates of a form of coherentism when it comes to theological method has been Nancey Murphy. In what follows, I will take a closer look at her "epistemological holism" as expounded in *Beyond Liberalism and Fundamentalism.*[46]

Murphy offers a brilliant critique of the foundationalist program highlighting the difficulties (both philosophical and theological) en-tailed by the metaphor of the building. Yet, she acknowledges that the metaphor of the web by itself does not suffice. Murphy is not content to say (with Quine) that all standards of rationality (including the laws of logic) are internal to traditions. Instead, by appealing to Imre Lakatos's "research programs" in philosophy of science, and (more significantly), to MacIntyre's concept of tradition, Murphy suggests that the way a tradi-tion changes over time when confronted with new models/empirical dis-coveries may provide the clue to our epistemic queries. The abandoning of the old consciousness model is, predictably, part of the answer here. Practices and tradition are socially embodied. Language and knowledge are part of the social world rather than being opposed to it (105). Murphy goes on to say that the new linguistic model necessarily erases the oppo-sition between Scripture and experience (understood in an extended his-torical sense) as different sources of theology. The task of the theologian is seen as "reweaving" this (undifferentiated) "ensemble of signs" in order to respond to the epistemological crisis of the moment. In the end it is a

---

46. Murphy, *Beyond Liberalism and Fundamentalism.* Further quotations from the book will be included in the text above.

form of "historical success" or "rational superiority" of one tradition over its competitors that answers the charge of relativism.

I certainly sympathize with Murphy's ambitious project of "changing the rules of the game" (85); But modernity is just one of our many problems and perhaps the theologian should by wise not to embrace too quickly "the rules" of "the new (postmodern) king."

In spite of its invaluable insights, what becomes apparent in Murphy's account is the same tendency to "naturalize" both textual and historical hermeneutics. Take the above point, for instance; while there is some truth in the claim that there should be no opposition between Scripture and experience, what is at stake for the theologian and what needs to guide his or her engagement with the present is not the epistemological crisis at hand, but rather the voice of the Lord of the church addressing and challenging her practices and traditions. If this is true, MacIntyre's criterion of "historical success" (a tradition may fail on its own terms) cannot have the last word. Such judgment cannot remain at the historical level, if we are, truly, to repudiate Hegel's (in)famous claim that "what is rational is real." If the theologian is to overcome the impasse of a choice between incommensurability and the specter of totality he or she must refer such language to the more fundamental dynamic of God action in and toward the world.

It is in this direction that talk about tradition is not "historicized" and talk about epistemology and justification is referred back to its proper source. Again, historical reason cannot really make ultimate judgments about the "rational superiority" of one tradition over the other. To refer specifically to one of MacIntyre's examples, used by Murphy, one may argue that what remains theologically relevant in the historic debate between Augustinianism and Thomism was less Thomas's "adoption" of an Aristotelian account of science that did not need divine illumination (that appeared "successful" at the time), and more his theological correction of such an account. One may further argue that the language of primary and secondary causes, in the long run, did more damage than good to our understanding of both God and the world.

To be sure, Murphy engages the language of divine action in her chapter on Metaphysical Holism. Yet, her eagerness to defend the common (modern) source of the liberal/fundamentalist divide with their respective series of distinctions (expressivist vs. propositionalism; inside-out vs. outside-in approach to knowledge, interventionism vs. immanentism) prevents a genuine encounter between the two fields. Murphy is more interested here to show the demise of reductionism, to defend her plea for "high pri ndent causal levels of reality and to substantiate her "nonreductive physicalism." All this is good, of course and an integration between scientific accounts of natural causation and theological accounts of divine action are not only desirable but necessary in the present context. Yet, in the final analysis, the theologian is hardly after the "causal joint" between God and the world, or after the "laws" of divine-human interaction (153). Murphy's discussion is still trapped in a framework in which the human mind needs to have the final word and the choice is still implicitly between relativism and certainty. Perhaps the ghosts of both Descartes and Hobbes are still there in a still unexorcized anxiety of having to "choose" between competing webs of beliefs . . .

In fairness to Murphy, I must point out that, in spite of her favoring of coherentism, she is careful to note that her historicist-holism proposal should not be conceived as "the" new (proper) theological method but rather as a resource to understand theological method in the present context. Moreover, she explicitly claims that her overview "does not prescribe epistemological moves in biblical criticism or theological reasoning" (105). After all, theories of knowledge are dependent on theories of human nature that "in many cases, are ultimately theological" and that "theology is needed to justify epistemology." This is, certainly refreshing! But, she spends little time elaborating on that. Instead, in the conclusion of the book she returns to her philosophical and apologetic concerns. Theology is responsible both to the Church and to the academy and as a consequence, "a theory of truth" needs to be articulated "appropriate to the new epistemology" (155).

Very much like Clark, Murphy doesn't really offer a proper theological analysis of why some knowledge claims may work better than others. Evaluations are largely based on philosophical interpretation of history, tradition, or the present experience of science. True, it is in the new register of linguistic philosophy that her evaluations are carried out. While such an exercise may fulfill an important critical theological function, theological reason should not draw its resources from the dynamics of changing paradigms and whatever may seem to "work better" in a given epoch but rather from God's action in and towards the world. What is more, even as a philosophical critique, Murphy's proposal, may turn out to be an unfinished step. As Zagzebski rightly notes, the dispute between foundationalism and coherentism is still haunted by the modern "certitude" anxiety. The appeal to history and tradition, should have marked the passage to the (more promising) internalist-externalist debate in a more decisive way. Perhaps what the subject "knows" at a certain point in time, does not matter that much . . . Perhaps, "the way things are," should take precedence in the quest for justification. What is more, perhaps, such quest (with its associated concern with virtues and vices) may turn out to be more important for epistemology than the old quest for certitude. But as alluded to above, the theologian should not stop at this level either. Again, while it is true that a tradition may collapse under the weight of its own demands, the notion of success can hardly be elucidated without proper reference to the larger scope of God's action in history, to God's perfection of Creation, to what is genuinely "successful" and "true" theologically. That is to say, without proper reference to "theo-logy." In this sense, the internalist-externalist debate in epistemology, if it is not to relapse into (abstract) disputes between epistemology and ontology (what we know vs. "the way things are"), must be referred to the more fundamental language of God's action in the world between Creation and Redemption.

To summarize, what we have witnessed in both cases was a failure to properly refer the epistemic practice to the larger framework of God's action in and towards the world. As a consequence, in both cases, in spite of their differences, the specter of the philosophy of consciousness is still there somewhat molding the grammar of the epistemic practice.

The lesson to be learned from this is twofold. First, the theologian should resist privileging (in an *a priori* manner) philosophical frameworks (whether "trendy" or "classical"), when it comes to interpreting or "explaining" doctrine. Of course, as we have seen, this is usually easier said than done. The more specific point I am trying to make here, however, is that the theologian should pay particular attention to "primitive" terms or "configurative" metaphors like "foundation" or "web of beliefs." If what makes "better" sense to our "experience of the world" is itself, at least to some degree, socially constituted, the theologian should all the more resist such claims to "primitivity" and instead let the grand story of God's Trinitarian encounter with the world have a final word on the matter.

Secondly, the doctrines themselves must be "thought" together, in the light of the same Triune God who elects, creates, preserves, redeems and glorifies his creation. In this sense, our attempt to think Creation and Redemption together intends indeed to imagine a common framework of understanding the two, yet, without suggesting a superior "transcendental" which would "explain away" God's Trinitarian action, functioning as an Archimedean point of arbitration between the two. Yet, perhaps

a view of knowledge which renounced the ideal of "identity" is less con-
tentiul to di<sub></sub> "behind" the meaning of *ex nihilo* creation or to settle the
meaning of God's relationship with the world into a speculative infinite-
finite logic (as arguably both process theology in its various forms and
Christian "baptisms" of non-realist views do.)⁴⁷

Whilst wanting to reject equally a view of history as flux (Creation
as a mere variation of divine action), and a substantialist view, we can
perhaps say less about the "middle" itself.⁴⁸

*Ultimately our knowledge of the world may prove to be genuine knowl-
edge not because such identities can be established but because the divine
action manifest in both sustaining and redeeming the world expresses itself
as grace, as constant invitation to be part of a truly creative agency, which
alone, can give a future to our actions.*

Genuine knowledge, which is also true knowledge, does not dispel the mystery of divine agency between Creation and Redemption,
but finds its fulfillment when it responds to it. This is a way of thinking
*theoria* and *praxis* together, yet, without suggesting the primacy of either
of them. As we have insisted, responsible agency is not contented with
a view of "passive situatedness," nor can it accept a pure "creative" reason which "re-invents" the world in every new action.⁴⁹ It presupposes

47. I also believe that neither the infinite-finite dialectic not even Christology by
itself can unequivocally elucidate this problem. In fact, the language of Incarnation
is crucially dependent upon Creation. While there may be problems with accepting
the abstract distinction between *logos asarkos* and *logos ensarkos* (see footnote 52 in
chapter 7) such a decision may at least leave the "*ex nihilo*" mystery intact. Again, it
is the same "movement within the whole" that is required. God's Trinitarian action
remains the ultimate horizon.

48. While there is a certain timeliness to our stress upon the underlying continuity
between knowledge of God and knowledge of the world, faith and reason, human
freedom and the more general "freedom" of the created order, that does not mean that
we implicitly adopted the new (expressivist, pragmatic) "postmodern speculation"
as constitutive to our critique. Milbank's (by now) classic work *Theology and Social
Theory*, in spite of its brilliant critique of secular reason, at times seems to do just that.
Take for example his critique of Ricoeur's "modern" distinctions (understanding and
explanation, "sense" and "reference," etc.). It is in the light of a "better speculation" that
Milbank thinks that such distinctions are unwarranted. When he defends the "realism" of his "instrumentalist"/operational account of science Milbank avers that "such
speculation is not just a contemplative luxury (not even merely 'regulative') but will
influence all our practice." Unfortunately, no theological reason is offered in defense of
such totalizing claim. Milbank, *Theology and Social Theory*, 271–72.

49. If we believe for instance that Adam's naming of the animals was a genuine
"creative" activity, this activity ought to be understood not as a mere convention, but in

instead a vision opened and sustained by God's address. Under the guidance of a Trinitarian view of agency, this address is also an invitation which encounters us as persons, body and mind, will and imagination. It is only when, in Christ and through the Spirit, we experience God as communion of persons that the profound meaning of our irreducibly social constitution is uncovered in its true dimension.

So, "method" in Theology is ultimately "plural" precisely because we cannot really "control" the structure of this great unfolding. Our role as "the hearing church," is to respond to it. Rationality "functioning properly" is never always-already there, something that we can manipulate or control. As Webster puts it, "Being the hearing church is never . . . a matter of routine, whether liturgical or doctrinal."[50]

It is also true, of course, that we cannot (on this side of eternity) envisage totality. We are, indeed, finite and fallible. But to remain at this level is to fail to see what is at stake here. The ideal is not an infinite and perfect "knowledge" finding itself in detached contemplation/control of a (static) whole. That would be demonic knowledge; a form of "absolute" instrumentalism, oppressive and deterministic. Such "knowledge" would find itself in competition with the living God, the Father of our Lord, Jesus Christ! By contrast, the freedom of the created is the freedom of the finite, redeemed mind that "reigns with Christ" (Rom 5:17), participating in the divine life and sharing in the divine freedom (2 Pet 1:4; Col 3:3). It is God's Trinitarian action that sets the stage for "success" when it comes to knowledge in general, theological knowledge in particular, rather than alleged inherent features of "world" or "human mind." It is only by participating in the divine light that we can "truly know." Indeed, as Aquinas maintains, "nothing is knowable except as it bears a likeness to the First Truth."[51]

---

"For this I have been born, and for this I have come into the world, to bear witness to the truth" (John 18:37). No one puts the light under the bushel . . . The light coming into the world enlightens and redeems, describes and heals.

---

the larger Christological framework , of a "right" indwelling in profound accord with the *telos* of Creation. In the same way, the "creative" activity of a redeemed rationality is not working alone in a hopelessly fallen environment. Instead it participates through Christ and in the Spirit in the more concerted effort of the "perfection" of Creation.

50. Webster, *Holy Scripture*, 47.

51. Aquinas, *De Veritate*, 22, 2, Ad 1.

"As you sent me into the world, I have sent them into the world"
(John 17:0). If theological discourse is not to live for itself, it has to work
out the ontological and epistemological implications of this sending. My
proposal attempts to situate itself at an equal distance from both an epistemological and an ontological closure. In regard to the second, it claims
that we do indeed need a foundation, but such a foundation has an invincible theological dimension. That is to say, it does not conceive presence
in terms of an immediacy of substance, tradition, experience or reason.
In regard to the first, my argument is ultimately that this theological dimension is not "a mere way of looking," is not content with the world of
"as if" but has a genuine ontological referent.[52] In other words, the move
between ontology and epistemology is no longer a mind-world game.
More specifically, within the epistemological practice itself, the dispute
between internalism and externalism must be referred back to the larger
framework of God's Trinitarian action and human response. Our attempt
to substantiate a dimension of freedom at the very heart of sense, and the
presence of "sense" in the midst of freedom aimed to show precisely that.

I used the categories of the discourses of freedom and of sense,
largely in a critical sense, that is to say, to identify problems and point
to solutions. My intention (as I hope it became apparent) was not in the
least to substantiate a separation but to suggest that a genuine discourse
of sense fulfils itself in the discourse of freedom and conversely genuine
freedom labors its way back to the world of "sense." The distinction, as we
have insisted, is not absolute but rather a way of expressing a tension.[53]

While theological epistemology has an irreducible ethical dimension,
as we have seen, *doxic obedience* grounds an ethics of virtues rather than
being grounded by it. Our "musts" are empty if they are not lived out as
witness and as good news. This is perhaps one of the great lessons of the

52. That is to say, Creation is more than a mere expression of the unity of the world.
In this sense, Dalferth's notion of style which attempts to mediate between explanation (imitation) and expression, does not really go beyond Kant's mediation between
reception and construction. Why should we accept the Kantian point that unity is necessarily an ideal concept, a feature of our synthetic judgment? ("All unity is therefore
purpose-related: . . . This is the case for all unities, but particularly for the world." Cf.
Dalferth, "Creation—Style of the World," 119–37.)

53. It must be noted in this sense that the fact that we sometimes used Creation
and Redemption almost interchangeably with a doctrine of Creation and doctrine of
the Word must not be understood as implying that the doctrine of Redemption may
be equated with the doctrine of the Word. In this sense, the choice of placing the epistemological significance of God's agency at the intersection of the doctrine of Creation
and a doctrine of the Word has undoubtedly a polemical dimension.

friends of Job. And ultimately it must be acknowledged that there is a sense in which our discourse remains fragile. As a discourse *from* the Church, its challenge is to fully accept the folly of the Cross, yet, to surmount the suspicion of a mere appeal to theological jargon, to work its intelligibility as both "sense" and "freedom," as good news, rather than strange news.[54]

As a discourse addressed *to* the Church, it may face the singularity of its prophetic voice, the impossibility of justifying its "transcendental" status, to account for its own ground. Yet, this is not to say that the "justificatory" dimension of the proposal ultimately collapses under the weight of its own demands. Indeed, the prophet reminds us that authentic prophecy does not have a different source. . . . It is born in worship (e.g., Isaiah 6) and in "its return to the world" it brings judgment *and* salvation, the sanction of "sense" and the advent of genuine freedom. To participate in this movement is ultimately "a living sacrifice pleasing to God" (Rom 12:2), it means to "fulfill" worship by faithfully responding to God's *ek-stasis*.[55] It is true that there is a sense in which "witnessing to the truth" is condemned to "eternal penultimacy" (in Ryle's terms), that is to say it cannot assess its own performance. Indeed, unless a kernel of wheat falls to the ground and dies, it remains alone. Only when it dies, does it produce many seeds . . .

This acknowledgement shares with both Ricoeur and Jüngel the reluctance to rely upon a Cartesian concept of certainty. In a sense, this is just a way of unveiling the incapacity of rationalism to exorcise its psychological ghost. (That is to say, its compulsion to prop its untenable picture of a disembodied reason, of a pure categorial structure or of an unproblematic access to reality immediately present to the mind.)

Nonetheless, to insist too much upon this dimension is to give excessive credit to the paradigms we have just criticized. Theological epistemology in the aftermath of Descartes and Kant should be able to overcome this defensive attitude. God's "justification" in Christ and by the Spirit by whom he "purified for Himself a people for His own possession, zealous for good deeds" (Titus 2:14), proves that indeed, God can and does "justify" himself through the fallen structures of world history and human subjectivity. This continuous "meeting" with God in his

---

54. It is precisely when we recognize that theology's faithfulness to its object fundamentally means to respond in obedience to the Good News, that we realize that we cannot either "defend" it or make it more radical than it is.

55. For a rich and original elaboration of this dimension, see Ford, *Self and Salvation*, 107ff.

promise is, therefore, not a mere "unobjectifiable" happening or language event but a real presence of God in the midst of his people.

One of the fascinating things in the Trial passage as depicted by John is this alternative authority no longer based upon violence, which is deployed at the least expected moment, the moment of the apparent triumph of evil. With unequalled rhetorical mastery, John reveals that the glory we were able to behold in Jesus' powerful inauguration of the Kingdom, did not come to a halt at the Cross. John's intricate rhetorical strategy subtly reveals Jesus in his confrontation with Pilate as virtually dominating the scene. He is shown to be the real Judge as the very embodiment of Truth. Moreover, he proves to be King as well, the One to whom the authority belongs. (John 18:35–37) And lastly, he is shown to be very God. John does not say this explicitly, but the reader feels the "sublime" insinuating itself upon the realm of the ordinary. The silence and the gaps in the text hint at the ineffable, pointing to an order of meaning which escapes the reader's scrutiny. Jesus' "discontinuous dialogue," calls for an identification of the transcendent.[56]

*This is the theological ground of the possibility of truth in our world (in spite of evil!) and this is the "identity" (between "call" and "response") that the Christian (through the Holy Spirit) should aim at![57]*

God can be present in our responses, however weak and historically irrelevant they may appear at times. Indeed, my actions can be *true and successful*, even when I am not able to hold the criteria of such success. Renouncing modern epistemology is to renounce this internalist requirement. The notion of doxic obedience was meant to suggest that it is when we respond in faith that new horizons of meaning are opened to us. It is in this "renewal of the mind" that internalism "returns" but never as an independent source of justification. True Reason is always assisted, sanctified Reason.

It is because we are animated by the same Spirit and "because the foolishness of God is wiser than men, and the weakness of God is stronger than men" (1 Cor 1:25), that we can confidently affirm that the career of truth in the world is ultimately non-tragic, in spite of our notorious inability to

56. Nuttall calls it "technique of deliberate transcendence." Cf. Werner, "Fourth Gospel's Art of Rational Persuasion," 168. For the trial of Jesus seen as an epiphany, see also Blank, *Verhandlung vor Pilatus*, 63, quoted by Pryor, *John Evangelist of the Covenant People*, 78.

57. This is not to deny the uniqueness of Christ's work, of course. He is the First Fruit, the Exemplar who made such things possible for the rest of us.

fully discern its historical "weight."[58] By meeting us in his promise he confirms time and again that he is the same, yesterday, today and forever (Heb 13:8).[59] God's action does not remain abstract and exterior, but it becomes a "worldly experience" in a community. "Our hope does not disappoint, because the love of God has been poured out within our hearts through the Holy Spirit who was given to us" (Rom 5:5).

Again, this is not to deny the "internalist" dimension of human response. A holistic conception of theological epistemology will, indeed, acknowledge that in an important sense truth as correspondence remains invincible. From a redemptive perspective, the advent of truth requires the "logical" moments of both the uncovering of our real state before God and of our status in Christ. From the perspective of the doctrine of Creation, our heuristic devices presuppose the "good order of Creation" which fundamentally enables our very understanding of both "order" and "process." Such an indwelling will not lack vision yet will never cease to "listen." Indeed, the concept of "doxic obedience" acknowledges that the "perfect correspondence" which would be homologous to an "ideal indwelling," remains an eschatological hope "when God will be all in all." It is certainly still the case that the gift of community and the privilege of existing as the body of Christ may often surprise us with glimpses of such a vision. But its full extent may be contemplated at best "as in a glass dimly." This is not only a reminder that knowledge is secondary, but also that it is the "metaphysical" structure of truth, so to say, that defines and sustains such a vision. From a theological perspective, this goes beyond a mere "realist" perspective (philosophically defined), and even beyond the concept of "personal" truth.[60] Jesus' famous "I am the Truth" claim, ties God and creation in a "metaphysics" that is neither about mere "worldly" things (correspondence with intrinsic standards contained by the created order) nor does it rest on a "metaphysical" vision that hovers "behind," "above" or "beyond" the world. Ultimately, to speak about truth and knowledge is to speak about the career of truth in our world, to point to

58. This point further supports our critique of a theological reply to modernity which follows in the steps of the modern adventures of the subject.

59. It must be said here that in spite of what may appear an excessive stress upon the "new," Jüngel acknowledges that "the old has another side to it." "The old is not necessarily hopeless, for it also belongs to the good order of creation." Cf. Jüngel, "Emergence of the New," in *Theological Essays II*, 58.

60. While I certainly appreciate Devitt's critique of deflationary theories, more needs to be said about the "metaphysics" of truth, from a theological perspective (Devitt, "Metaphysics of Truth," 579–611).

the Creator God who sends his Son, in whom "all treasures of wisdom and knowledge" are hidden (Col 2:3), to reconcile the world to himself and "to bring unity to all things in heaven and on earth under Christ." (Eph 1:10).To live genuinely "in the truth" ultimately means to respond to such a vision. Indeed, it is only in Christ and by the Spirit that the created order "co-responds" to him, who is the ultimate standard of reality, of meaning and of truth.

# Bibliography

Abraham, William J. *Canon and Criterion in Christian Theology.* Oxford: Oxford University Press, 1998.

———. *Crossing the Threshold of Divine Revelation.* Grand Rapids: Eerdmans, 2006.

Albano, Joseph. *Freedom, Truth, and Hope: The Relationship of Philosophy and Religion in the Thought of Paul Ricoeur.* Lanham, MD: University Press of America, 1987.

Anderson, Pamela. *Ricoeur and Kant: Philosophy of the Will.* Atlanta: Scholars, 1993.

Aristotle. *The Works of Aristotle.* Translated by W. D. Ross. 2nd ed. Oxford: Clarendon, 1908.

Audi, Robert. *Epistemology: A Contemporary Introduction to the Theory of Knowledge.* London: Routledge, 1998.

Avineri, Shlomo. *Hegel's Theory of the Modern State.* Cambridge: Cambridge University Press, 1972.

Ayres, Lewis. *Augustine and the Trinity.* Cambridge: Cambridge University Press, 2010.

Badiou, Alain. *Saint Paul: The Foundation of Universalism.* Translated by Ray Brassier. Stanford: Stanford University Press, 2003.

Balthasar, Hans Urs von. *The Glory of the Lord.* Vol. 5, *The Realm of Metaphysics in the Modern Age.* Translated by Oliver Davies et al. Edinburgh: T. & T. Clark, 1991.

Barth, Karl. *Church Dogmatics.* 2nd ed. Vols. 1–4. Edited by G. W. Bromiley and T. F. Torrance. Translated by G. W. Bromiley et al. Edinburgh: T. & T. Clark, 1957–1992.

———. *Church Dogmatics.* Vol. 1, *The Doctrine of the Word of God.* Part 1. Translated by G. T. Thompson and Harold Knight. Edinburgh: T. & T. Clark, 1936.

———. *Ethics.* Translated by Geoffrey W. Bromiley. Edinburgh: T. & T. Clark, 1981.

———. *The Humanity of God.* Translated by J. N. Thomas and T. Wieser. London: Collins, 1967.

———. *Protestant Theology in the Nineteenth Century: Its Background and History.* Translated by B. Cozens and J. Bowden. London: SCM, 1972.

Baudrillard, Jean. *Système des objets.* Paris: Gallimard, 1968.

Bielawski, Maciej. *The Philokalical Vision of the World in the Theology of Dumitru Stăniloae.* Bydgoszcz, Poland: Wydawnictwo, 1997.

Bonhoeffer, Dietrich. *Letters and Papers from Prison.* Translated by R. H. Fuller. New York: Macmillan, 1972.

Bourgeois, Patrick. *The Extension of Ricoeur's Hermeneutic.* The Hague: Martinus Nijhoff, 1975.

Brentano, Franz. *On the Several Senses of Being in Aristotle.* Berkeley: University of California Press, 1975.

Brown, James Robert. *Smoke and Mirrors.* Oxford: Routledge, 1994.

# Bibliography

Busch, Eberhard. *Karl Barth: His Life from Letters and Autobiographical Texts*. Philadelphia: Fortress, 1975.

Calinescu, Matei. *Five Faces of Modernity: Modernism, Avant-Garde, Decadence, Kitsch, Postmodernism*. Durham: Duke University Press, 1987.

Caputo, John D. *Demythologizing Heidegger*. Bloomington: Indiana University Press, 1993.

Clark, David K. *To Know and Love God: Method for Theology*. Wheaton, IL: Crossway, 2003.

Craig, Edward. *The Mind of God and the Works of Man*. Oxford: Clarendon, 1987.

Cunningham, David S. Review of *Persons in Communion*, by Alan J, Torrance. *Modern Theology* 14 (1998) 155–56.

Dalferth, Ingolf U. "Creation – Style of the World." Translated by Douglas Knight. *International Journal of Systematic Theology* 1 (1999) 119–37.

———. "The Eschatological Roots of the Doctrine of the Trinity." In *Trinitarian Theology Today: Essays on Divine Being and Act*, edited by Christoph Schwöbel, 147–70. Edinburgh: T. & T. Clark, 1995.

Descombes, Vincent. *Modern French Philosophy*. Translated by L. Scott-Fox and J. M. Harding. Cambridge: Cambridge University Press, 1994.

Detmer, David. "Ricoeur on Atheism: A Critique." In *The Philosophy of Paul Ricoeur*, edited by Lewis Edwin Hahn, 477–93. Library of Living Philosophers. Chicago: Open Court, 1995.

Devitt, Michael. "The Metaphysics of Truth." In *The Nature of Truth*, edited by Michael P. Lynch, 579–611. Cambridge: MIT Press, 2001.

D'Hondt, Jacques. *Hegel secret: Recherches sur les sources cachées de la pensée de Hegel*. Paris: Presses Universitaires de France, 1986.

DiCenso, James. *Hermeneutics and the Disclosure of Truth*. Charlottesville: University Press of Virginia, 1990.

Dostal, Robert J. "The End of Metaphysics and the Possibility of Non-Hegelian Speculative Thought." In *Hegel, History, and Interpretation*, edited by Shaun Gallagher, 33–42. Albany: State University of New York Press, 1997.

Fackenheim, Emil L. *The Religious Dimension in Hegel's Thought*. Bloomington: Indiana University Press, 1967.

Fackre, Gabriel. "Narrative Theology: An Overview." *Interpretation* 37 (1983) 340–52.

Findlay, J. N. "The Contemporary Relevance of Hegel." In *Hegel: A Collection of Critical Essays*, edited by Alisdair MacIntyre, 1–20. Notre Dame: University of Notre Dame Press, 1976.

———. Foreword to *Hegel: The Essential Writings*, edited by Frederick G. Weiss, ix-xiii. London: Harper & Row, 1974.

———. *Hegel: A Re-examination*. London: Allen & Unwin, 1958.

———. *Wittgenstein: A Critique*. London: Routledge & Kegan Paul, 1984.

Fodor, James. *Christian Hermeneutics: Paul Ricoeur and the Refiguring of Theology*. Oxford: Clarendon, 1995.

Ford, David, editor. *The Modern Theologians: An Introduction to Christian Theology in the Twentieth Century*. Vol. 1. Oxford: Blackwell, 1989.

———. *Self and Salvation: Being Transformed*. Cambridge: Cambridge University Press, 1999.

Frei, Hans. *The Eclipse of Biblical Narrative*. New Haven: Yale University Press, 1974.

———. *Types of Christian Theology*. New Haven: Yale University Press, 1992.

Fukuyama, Francis. "The End of History?" *National Interest* (1989) 3–18.

Gadamer, Hans-Georg. *Hegel's Dialectic, Five Hermeneutical Studies*. New Haven: Yale University Press, 1976.

———. *Truth and Method*. 2nd ed. Translation revised by Joel Weinsheimer and Donald G. Marshall. London: Sheed & Ward, 1989.

Gellner, Ernest. *Postmodernism, Reason and Religion*. London: Routledge, 1992.

Gilson, Etienne. *The Christian Philosophy of Saint Augustine*. Translated by L. E. Lynch. London: Gollancz, 1961.

Grier, T. Philip. "The Speculative Concrete: I. A. Il'in's Interpretation of Hegel." In *Hegel, History and Interpretation*, edited by Shaun Gallagher, 169–93. Albany: State University of New York Press, 1997.

Gunton, Colin E. *The Actuality of Atonement*. Edinburgh: T. & T. Clark, 1988.

———. *A Brief Theology of Revelation*. Edinburgh: T. & T. Clark, 1995.

———. *Intellect and Action: Elucidations on Christian Theology and the Life of Faith*. Edinburgh: T. & T. Clark, 2000.

———. *The One, the Three and the Many: God, Creation and the Culture of Modernity*. Cambridge: Cambridge University Press, 1993.

———. *The Promise of Trinitarian Theology*. Edinburgh: T. & T. Clark, 1991.

———. Review of *Karl Barth's Critically Realistic Dialectical Theology: Its Genesis and Development 1909–1936*, by Bruce McCormack. *Scottish Journal of Theology* 49 4 (1996) 483–91.

———. *The Triune Creator*. Edinburgh: Edinburgh University Press, 1998.

———. *Yesterday and Today: A Study of Continuities in Christology*. Grand Rapids: Eerdmans, 1983.

Habermas, Jürgen.. *The Philosophical Discourse of Modernity*. Translated by Frederick G. Lawrence. Cambridge: MIT Press, 1986.

———. *Postmetaphysical Thinking: Philosophical Essays*. Translated by W. M. Hohengarten. Cambridge: Polity, 1995.

Hare, John E. *God's Call: Moral Realism, God's Commands, and Human Autonomy*. Grand Rapids: Eerdmans, 2001.

Harris, Harriet A. "Should We Say that Personhood Is Relational?" *Scottish Journal of Theology* 51 (1998) 214–34.

Harrison, Carol. *Beauty and Revelation in the Thought of Saint Augustine*. Oxford: Clarendon, 1992.

Hart, Kevin. *The Trespass of the Sign: Deconstruction, Theology, and Philosophy*. Cambridge: Cambridge University Press, 1989.

Hartnack, Justus. "Categories and Things-In-Themselves." In *Hegel's Critique of Kant*, edited by Stephen Priest, 77–86. Oxford: Clarendon, 1987.

Hauerwas, Stanley. *Unleashing the Scripture: Freeing the Bible from Captivity to America*. Nashville: Abingdon, 1993.

Hegel, G. W. F. *Early Theological Writings*. Translated by T. M. Knox. Chicago: University of Chicago Press, 1948.

———. *Faith and Knowledge*. Translated by Walter Cerf and H. S. Harris. Albany: State University of New York Press, 1977.

———. *Introduction to the Philosophy of History*. Translated by Leo Rauch. Indianapolis: Hackett, 1988.

———. *Lectures on the Philosophy of Religion*. Vols. 1–3. Translated by R. F. Brown et al. Berkeley: University of California Press, 1984.

# Bibliography

———. *The Phenomenology of Spirit.* Translated by J. B. Baillie. London: Harper & Row, 1931.

———. *The Philosophy of History.* Translated by J. Sibree. New York: Prometheus, 1991.

———. *Philosophy of Mind.* Part 3 of *Encyclopaedia of the Philosophical Sciences.* Translated by William Wallace. Oxford: Clarendon, 1894.

———. *The Philosophy of Right.* Translated by T. M. Knox. Oxford: Clarendon, 1942.

———. *The Science of Logic.* Part 1 of *Encyclopaedia of the Philosophical Sciences.* Translated by William Wallace. Oxford: Clarendon, 1987.

———. *The Science of Logic.* Translated by A.V. Miller. London: Allen & Unwin, 1969.

———. *Wissenschaft der Logik.* Vol. 2, *Die subjektive Logik oder Lehre vom Begriff.* Berlin, 1841.

Heidegger, Martin. *Being and Time.* Translated by John Macquarrie and Edward Robinson. Oxford: Blackwell, 1995.

———. *What Is Philosophy?* Translated by William Kluback and Jean T. Wilde. New Haven, CT: College and University Press, 1956.

Hetherington, Stephen. *Good Knowledge, Bad Knowledge: On Two Dogmas of Epistemology.* Oxford: Clarendon, 2001.

Husserl, Edmund. *Cartesian Meditations.* Translated by Dorion Cairns. The Hague: Martinus Nijhoff, 1960.

———. *Logical Investigations.* 2 vols. Translated by J. N. Findlay. London: Routledge & Kegan Paul, 1970.

Hyppolite, Jean. *Genesis and Structure of Hegel's Phenomenology of Spirit.* Translated by S. Cherniak and J. Heckman. Evanston, IL: Northwestern University Press, 1974.

Imamichi, Tomonobu. *Betrachtungen uber das Eine.* Tokyo: University of Tokyo, 1968.

Ingraffia, Brian. *Postmodern Theory and Biblical Theology.* Cambridge: Cambridge University Press, 1995.

Inwood, Michael. "Kant and Hegel on Space and Time." In *Hegel's Critique of Kant,* edited by Stephen Priest, 49–64. Oxford: Clarendon, 1987.

Jamros, Daniel P. "Hegel on the Incarnation: Unique or Universal?" *Theological Studies* 56 (1995) 276–300.

Jenson, Robert W. "Karl Barth." In *The Modern Theologians: An Introduction to Christian Theology in the Twentieth Century,* edited by David Ford, 1:21–35. Oxford: Blackwell, 1989.

———. *Systematic Theology.* Vol. 1, *The Triune God.* Oxford: Oxford University Press, 1997.

———. "What Is the Point of Trinitarian Theology?" In *Trinitarian Theology Today: Essays on Divine Being and Act,* edited by Christoph Schwöbel, 31–43. Edinburgh: T. & T. Clark, 1995.

Jüngel, Eberhard. *God as the Mystery of the World: On the Foundations of the Theology of the Crucified One in the Dispute between Theism and Atheism.* Translated by Darrell L. Guder. Edinburgh: T. & T. Clark, 1983.

———. "Metaphorische Wahrheit: Erwägungen zur theologischen Relevanz der Metapher als Beitrag zur Hermeneutik einer narrativen Theologie." In *Metapher: Zur Hermeneutik religiöser Sprache,* by Paul Ricoeur and Eberhard Jüngel, 71–122. Munich: Kaiser, 1974.

———. *Theological Essays.* Translated by John B. Webster. Edinburgh: T. & T. Clark, 1989.

——— *Theological Essays II,* Translated by Arnold Neufeldt-Fast and John B. Webster. Edinburgh: T. & T. Clark, 1995.

Kant, Immanuel. "Beantwortung der Frage: Was ist Aufklärung?" *Berlinische Monatsschrift* (1784) 481–94.

———. *The Critique of Judgment.* Translated by J. H. Bernard. New York: Hafner, 1951.

———. *The Critique of Pure Reason.* Translated by J. M. D. Meiklejohn. London: Dent & Sons, 1934.

———. *The Critique of Pure Reason.* Translated by Norman Kemp Smith. London: Macmillan, 1987.

———. *Religion Within the Limits of Reason Alone.* Translated by Theodore M. Greene and Hoyt H. Hudson. London: Harper & Row, 1960.

Kaufman, Gordon D. *In Face of Mystery: A Constructive Theology.* Cambridge: Harvard University Press, 1993.

Kaufmann, Walter. "The Hegel Myth and Its Method." In *Hegel: A Collection of Critical Essays,* edited by Alisdair MacIntyre, 21–60. Notre Dame: University of Notre Dame Press, 1976.

———. "The Young Hegel and Religion." In *Hegel: A Collection of Critical Essays,* edited by Alisdair MacIntyre, 61–100. Notre Dame: University of Notre Dame Press, 1976.

Kemp, Peter. "Ricoeur between Heidegger and Levinas." In *Paul Ricoeur: The Hermeneutics of Action,* edited by Richard Kerney, 41–62. London: Sage, 1995.

Kerr, Fergus. *Theology after Wittgenstein.* Oxford: Blackwell, 1986.

Khodre, Georges. "The Church in Movement." In *Orthodox Synthesis: The Unity of Theological Thought,* edited by Joseph J. Allen, 19–31. Crestwood, NY: St. Vladimir's Seminary Press, 1981.

Kierkegaard, Søren. *Concluding Unscientific Postscript.* Translated by David F. Swenson. Princeton: Princeton University Press, 1968.

———. *Philosophical Fragments.* Translated and edited by Howard V. Hong and Edna H. Hong. Princeton: Princeton University Press, 1962.

———. *Sickness unto Death.* Translated by Howard V. Hong and Edna H. Hong. Princeton: Princeton University Press, 1980.

Kirkham, Richard L. *Theories of Truth: A Critical Introduction.* Cambridge: MIT Press, 2001.

Küng, Hans. *Does God Exist?* London: SCM, 1980.

———. *The Incarnation of God: An Introduction to Hegel's Theological Thought as a Prolegomena to a Future Christology.* Translated by J. R. Stephenson. Edinburgh: T. & T. Clark, 1987.

LaCocque, André, and Paul Ricoeur. *Thinking Biblically: Exegetical and Hermeneutical Studies.* Translated by David Pellauer. Chicago: University of Chicago Press, 1998.

Lewis, C. S. *The Abolition of Man.* Glasgow: Collins, 1978.

Lindbeck, George. *The Nature of Doctrine: Religion and Theology in a Post-Liberal Age.* London: SPCK, 1984.

Lossky, Vladimir. *In the Image and Likeness of God.* Crestwood, NY: St. Vladimir's Seminary Press, 1985.

Loughlin, Gerald, *Telling God's Story.* Cambridge: Cambridge University Press, 1996.

Lowe, Walter. *Mystery of the Unconscious: A Study in the Thought of Paul Ricoeur.* Metuchen, NJ: Scarecrow, 1977.

# Bibliography

MacIntyre, Alasdair, editor. *Hegel: A Collection of Critical Essays.* Notre Dame: University of Notre Dame Press, 1976.

Macmurray, John. *The Self as Agent.* London: Faber & Faber, 1991.

Marion, Jean-Luc. *God Without Being: Hors-Texte.* Translated by Thomas A. Carlson. Chicago: University of Chicago Press, 1991.

Marx, Karl. "Theses on Feuerbach." In *Karl Marx: Selected Writings,* edited by David McLellan, 156–58. Oxford: Oxford University Press, 1977.

Mascall, Eric L. *He Who Is: A Study of Traditional Theism.* London: Longmans, Green, 1943.

McCormack, Bruce. *Karl Barth's Critically Realistic Dialectical Theology: Its Genesis and Development, 1909–1936.* Oxford: Clarendon, 1995.

McFadyen, Alistair I. *The Call to Personhood. A Christian Theory of the Individual in Social Relationships.* Cambridge: Cambridge University Press, 1990.

Merleau-Ponty, Maurice. *Sens et Non-Sens.* Paris: Nagel, 1948.

Milbank, John. *Theology and Social Theory.* Oxford: Blackwell, 1990.

———. *Theology and Social Theory: Beyond Secular Reason.* 2nd ed. Oxford: Blackwell, 2006.

Molnar, Paul D. Review of *Systematic Theology, Volume I: The Triune God,* by Robert W. Jenson. *Scottish Journal of Theology* 52 (1999) 40–81.

Moltmann, Jürgen. *The Crucified God.* Translated by R. A. Wilson and John Bowden. London: SCM, 1974.

Montefiore, Alan, editor. *Philosophy in France Today.* Cambridge: Cambridge University Press, 1983.

Müller, G. E. "The Hegel Legend of 'Thesis, Antithesis and Synthesis.'" *Journal of the History of Ideas* 19 (1958) 411–14.

Mure, G. R. G. "Hegel, Luther and the Owl of Minerva." *Philosophy* 41 (1966) 127–39.

Murphy, Nancey. *Beyond Liberalism and Fundamentalism: How Modern and Postmodern Philosophy Set the Theological Agenda.* Harrisburg, PA: Trinity Press International, 1996.

Nabert, Jean. *Éléments pour une Éthique.* Paris: Montaigne, 1962.

Nietzsche, Friedrich. "On Truth and Lie in an Extra-Moral Sense." In *The Portable Nietzsche,* edited by Walter Kaufmann, 42–46. New York: Viking, 1968.

Noica, Constantin. *Aristotel: Categorii.* București: Editura Humanitas, 1992.

O'Donovan, Oliver. *Resurrection and Moral Order: An Outline for Evangelical Ethics.* Leicester, UK: InterVarsity, 1986.

Ogden, Schubert M. *Christ without Myth: A Study Based on the Theology of Rudolf Bultmann.* London: Collins, 1962.

O'Regan, Cyril. *The Heterodox Hegel.* Albany: State University of New York Press, 1994.

Pannenberg, Wolfhart. *Anthropology in Theological Perspective.* Translated by Matthew J. O'Connell. Edinburgh: T. & T. Clark, 1985.

———. *Basic Questions in Theology.* Vol. 3. Translated by R. A. Wilson. London: SCM, 1973.

———. *Metaphysics and the Idea of God.* Translated by Philip Clayton. Edinburgh: T. & T. Clark, 1990.

———. *Systematic Theology.* Vol. 1. Translated by Geoffrey W. Bromley. Grand Rapids: Eerdmans, 1991.

Phillips, D. Z. *Religion without Explanation.* Oxford: Blackwell, 1976.

Pickstock, Catherine. *After Writing: On the Liturgical Consummation of Philosophy.* Oxford: Blackwell, 1998.

Plantinga, Alvin. *Warrant and Proper Function.* Oxford: Oxford University Press, 1993

Plantinga, Alvin, and Nicholas Wolterstorff, editors. *Faith and Rationality: Reason and Belief in God.* Notre Dame: University of Notre Dame Press, 1983.

Plato. "Philebus." In *The Dialogues of Plato,* translated by B. Jowett, 3:127–221. Oxford: Clarendon, 1871.

Polanyi, Michael. *Personal Knowledge: Towards a Post-Critical Philosophy.* London: Routledge & Kegan Paul, 1958.

———. *The Tacit Dimension.* London: Routledge & Kegan Paul, 1967.

Popper, Karl R. *The Open Society and Its Enemies.* Vols. 1–2. London: Routledge & Kegan Paul, 1969.

Pryor, John W. *John: Evangelist of the Covenant People.* Downers Grove: InterVarsity, 1992.

Rae, Murray. "'Incline Your Ear So That You May Live': Principles of Biblical Epistemology." In *The Bible and Epistemology,* edited by Mary Healy and Robin Parry, 161–80. Milton Keynes, UK: Paternoster, 2007.

Rahner, Karl. *Theological Investigations.* Vol. 11. Translated by David Bourke. London: Darton, Longman & Todd, 1974.

Reid, Duncan. *The Energies of the Spirit: Trinitarian Models in Eastern Orthodox and Western Theology.* Atlanta: Scholars, 1997.

Ricoeur, Paul. "Biblical Hermeneutics." *Semeia* 4 (1975) 29–148.

———. *The Conflict of Interpretations: Essays in Hermeneutics.* Edited by Don Ihde. Translated by Kathleen McLaughlin et al. Evanston, IL: Northwestern University Press, 1974.

———. *The Contribution of French Historiography to the Theory of History.* Zaharoff Lecture 1978–9. Oxford: Clarendon, 1980.

———. *Critique and Conviction.* Translated by Kathleen Blamey. Cambridge: Polity, 1998.

———. *De l'interprétation: Essai sur Freud.* Paris: Éditions du Seuil, 1965.

———. *Du texte à l'action: Essais d'herméneutique, II.* Paris: Éditions du Seuil, 1986.

———. *Essays on Biblical Interpretation.* Edited by Lewis S. Mudge. London: SPSK, 1981.

———. *Exégèse et Herméneutique: Parole de Dieu.* Edited by Xavier Léon-Dufour. Paris: Éditions du Seuil, 1971.

———. "Expérience et langage dans le discours religieux." In *Phénoménologie et théologie,* edited by Jean-Louis Chrétien et al., 15–39. Paris: Criterion, 1992.

———. *Fallible Man.* Translated by Walter J. Lowe. Chicago: Regnery, 1965.

———. *Figuring the Sacred.* Translated by David Pellauer. Edited by Mark Wallace. Minneapolis: Fortress, 1995.

———. *From Text to Action: Essays in Hermeneutics, II.* Translated by Kathleen Blamey and John B. Thompson. Evanston, IL: Northwestern University Press, 1991.

———. *Hermeneutics and the Human Sciences.* Edited and translated by John B. Thompson. Cambridge: Cambridge University Press, 1981.

———. *The Hermeneutics of Action.* Edited by Richard Kerney. London: Sage, 1995.

———. *Histoire et Vérité.* Paris: Éditions de Seuil, 1955.

———. *Husserl: An Analysis of His Phenomenology.* Translated by E. G. Ballard and Lester E. Embree. Evanston, IL: Northwestern University Press, 1967.

# Bibliography

—. "Intellectual Autobiography." In *The Philosophy of Paul Ricoeur*, edited by Lewis Edwin Hahn, 1–54. Library of Living Philosophers. Chicago: Open Court, 1995.

—. *Interpretation Theory*. Fort Worth: Texas Christian University Press, 1976.

—. "Kierkegaard et le mal." *Revue de theologie et de philosophie* 13 (1963) 293–302.

—. "Le sujet convoqué: A l'école des récits de vocations prophetique." *Revue de L'Institut Catholique de Paris* 28 (1988) 83–99.

—. *Lectures II: La Contrée des philosophes*. Paris: Éditions de Seuil, 1992.

—. "L'Identité Narrative." *Esprit* 7–8 (1988) 295–304.

—. "On Interpretation." In *Philosophy in France Today*, edited by Alan Montefiore, 175–97. Cambridge: Cambridge University Press, 1983.

—. *Oneself as Another*. Translated by Kathleen Blamey. Chicago: University of Chicago Press, 1992.

—. "Philosopher après Kierkegaard." *Revue de theologie et de philosophie* 13 (1963) 303–316.

—. *The Reality of the Historical Past: The Aquinas Lecture*. Milwaukee: Marquette University Press, 1984.

—. "A Response." Response to essays by J. D. Crossan and others. *Biblical Research* 24–25 (1979–80) 70–80.

—. *The Rule of Metaphor*. Translated by Robert Czerny et al. London: Routledge & Kegan Paul, 1978.

—. "The Status of *Vorstellung* in Hegel's Philosophy of Religion." In *Meaning, Truth and God*, edited by Leroy S. Rouner, 70–88. Notre Dame: University of Notre Dame Press, 1982.

—. *The Symbolism of Evil*. Translated by Emerson Buchanan. Boston: Beacon, 1967.

—. *Time and Narrative*. 3 vols. Translated by Kathleen McLaughlin and David Pellauer. Chicago: University of Chicago Press, 1984–88.

Roberts, Richard H. *A Theology on Its Way? Essays on Karl Barth*. Edinburgh: T. & T. Clark, 1991.

Rouner, Leroy S., editor. *Meaning, Truth and God*. Notre Dame: University of Notre Dame Press, 1982.

Schacht, Richard L. "Hegel on Freedom." In *Hegel: A Collection of Critical Essays*, edited by Alisdair MacIntyre, 289–327. Notre Dame: University of Notre Dame Press, 1976.

Schelling, F. W. J. von. *System of Transcendental Idealism (1800)*. Translated by Peter Heath. Charlottesville: University of Virginia Press, 1978.

Schwöbel, Christoph. "Christology and Trinitarian Thought." In *Trinitarian Theology Today: Essays on Divine Being and Act*, edited by Christoph Schwöbel, 113–46. Edinburgh: T. & T. Clark, 1995.

—. "Rational Theology in Trinitarian Perspective: Wolfhart Pannenberg's Systematic Theology." *Journal of Theological Studies* 47 (1996) 498–527.

—. "The Renaissance of Trinitarian Theology: Reasons, Problems and Tasks." In *Trinitarian Theology Today: Essays on Divine Being and Act*, edited by Christoph Schwöbel, 1–30. Edinburgh: T. & T. Clark, 1995.

Shults, F. LeRon. *The Postfoundationalist Task of Theology*. Grand Rapids: Eerdmans, 1999.

—. *Reforming the Doctrine of God*. Grand Rapids: Eerdmans, 2005.

—. *Reforming Theological Anthropology*. Grand Rapids: Eerdmans, 2003.

Smith, P. Christopher. "Hegel, Kierkegaard, and the Problem of Finitude." In *Hegel, History and Interpretation*, edited by Shaun Gallagher, 209–26. Albany: State University of New York Press, 1997.

Solomon, Robert C. "Hegel's Concept of Geist." In *Hegel: A Collection of Critical Essays*, edited by Alisdair MacIntyre, 125–49. Notre Dame: University of Notre Dame Press, 1976.

Solomon, Robert C., and Kathleen M. Higgins, editors. *The Age of German Idealism*. Routledge History of Philosophy. London: Routledge, 1993.

Sosa, Ernest. "The Raft and the Pyramid." In *Epistemology: An Anthology*, edited by Ernest Sosa and Kim Jaegwon, 134–53. Oxford: Blackwell, 2000.

Stăniloae, Dumitru. *Teologia Dogmatica Ortodoxa*. Vol. 1. București: Editura Institutului Biblic și de Misiune al Bisericii Ortodoxe Române, 1996.

Taylor, Charles. *Hegel*. Cambridge: Cambridge University Press, 1975.

———. "The Opening Arguments of the Phenomenology." In *Hegel: A Collection of Critical Essays*, edited by Alisdair MacIntyre, 151–87. Notre Dame: University of Notre Dame Press, 1976.

———. *Sources of the Self*. Cambridge: Cambridge University Press, 1989.

Thiemann, Ronald. *Revelation and Theology: The Gospel as Narrated Promise*. Notre Dame: University of Notre Dame Press, 1985.

Thiselton, Anthony C. *Interpreting God and the Postmodern Self: On Meaning, Manipulation and Promise*. Edinburgh: T. & T. Clark, 1995.

———. *New Horizons in Hermeneutics*. London: HarperCollins, 1992.

———. *The Two Horizons: New Testament Hermeneutics and Philosophical Description*. Carlisle, PA: Paternoster, 1980.

Thunberg, Lars. *Man and the Cosmos: The Vision of St. Maximus the Confessor*. Crestwood, NY: St. Vladimir's Seminary Press, 1985.

Tillich, Paul. *Systematic Theology*. Vol. 2. Welwyn, UK: Nisbet, 1960.

Torrance, Alan J. *Persons in Communion: An Essay on Trinitarian Description and Human Participation*. Edinburgh: T. & T. Clark, 1996.

Torrance, Thomas F. *Theological Science*. Edinburgh: T. & T. Clark, 1996.

Tracy, David. *The Analogical Imagination: Christian Theology and the Culture of Pluralism*. London: SCM, 1981.

Van Den Hengel, John W. *The Home of Meaning: The Hermeneutics of the Subject of Paul Ricoeur*. Lanham, MD: University Press of America, 1982.

———. "Paul Ricoeur's *Oneself as Another* and Practical Theology." *Theological Studies* 55 (1994) 458–77.

Vanhoozer, Kevin J. *Biblical Narrative in the Philosophy of Paul Ricoeur*. Cambridge: Cambridge University Press, 1999.

———. *Is There a Meaning in This Text? The Bible, the Reader, and the Morality of Literary Knowledge*. Leicester, UK: Apollos, 1998.

Van Huyssteen, J. Wentzel. *Essays in Postfoundationalist Theology*. Grand Rapids: Eerdmans, 1997.

———. "Is the Postmodernist Always a Postfoundationalist?" *Theology Today* 50 (1993) 373–86.

Wallace, Mark. "The World of the Text: Theological Hermeneutics in the Thought of Paul Ricoeur and Karl Barth." PhD diss., University of Chicago, 1986.

Ward, Graham. *Theology and Contemporary Critical Theory*. New York: St. Martin's, 1996.

Webster, John B. *Eberhard Jüngel: An Introduction to His Theology*. Cambridge: Cambridge University Press, 1986.

———. *Holiness*. Grand Rapids: Eerdmans, 2003.

———. *Holy Scripture: A Dogmatic Sketch*. Cambridge: Cambridge University Press, 2003.

———. "Illumination." *Journal of Reformed Theology* 5 (2011) 325–40.

Weiss, Frederick G. "Dialectic and the Science of Logic." In *Hegel: The Essential Writings*, edited by Frederick G. Weiss, 86–91. London: Harper & Row, 1974.

Wendebourg, Dorothea. "From the Cappadocian Fathers to Gregory Palamas: The Defeat of Trinitarian Theology." *Studia Patristica* 17 (1982) 194–98.

Werner, Martin. "The Fourth Gospel's Art of Rational Persuasion." In *The Bible as Rhetoric: Studies in Biblical Persuasion and Credibility*, edited by Martin Werner, 153–77. London: Routledge, 1990.

Williams, Robert R. "Hegel and Schleiermacher on Theological Truth." *In Meaning, Truth and God*, edited by Leroy S. Rouner, 52–69. Notre Dame: University of Notre Dame Press, 1982.

Williams, Rowan D. "Trinity and Revelation." *Modern Theology* 2 (1986) 197–212.

Wittgenstein, Ludwig. *Philosophical Investigations*. Translated by G. E. M. Anscombe. Oxford: Blackwell, 1974.

———. *Tractatus Logico-Philosophicus*. Translated by D. F. Pears and B. F. McGuinness. London: Routledge & Kegan Paul, 1974.

Wolterstorff, Nicholas. *Divine Discourse*. Cambridge: Cambridge University Press, 1995.

———. "Is It Possible and Desirable for Theologians to Recover from Kant?" *Modern Theology* 4 (1998) 1–18.

———. Review of *Crossing the Threshold of Divine Revelation*, by William J. Abraham. *Faith and Philosophy* 28 (2011) 102–8.

Yerkes, James. *The Christology of Hegel*. Missoula, MT: Scholars, 1978.

Zagzebski, Linda. "Religious Knowledge and the Virtues." In *Rational Faith: Catholic Responses to Reformed Epistemology*, edited by Linda Zagzebski, 199–225. Notre Dame: University of Notre Dame Press, 1993.

———. *Virtues of the Mind: An Inquiry into the Nature of Virtue and the Ethical Foundations of Knowledge* Cambridge: Cambridge University Press, 1996.

Zagzebski, Linda, and Abrol Fairweather. Introduction to *Virtue Epistemology: Essays on Epistemic Virtue and Responsibility*, edited by Linda Zagzebski and Abrol Fairweather, 3–14. Oxford: Oxford University Press, 2001.

Zizek, Slavoj. *Did Somebody Say Totalitarianism? Five Interventions in the (Mis)Use of a Notion*. London: Verso, 2001.

———. *The Parallax View*. Cambridge: MIT Press, 2009.

———. *The Puppet and the Dwarf: The Perverse Core of Christianity*. Cambridge: MIT Press, 2003.

Zizioulas, John. *Being As Communion*. Crestwood, NY: St. Vladimir's Seminary Press, 1985.

# Names

# Subjects

www.ingramcontent.com/pod-product-compliance
Lightning Source LLC
Chambersburg PA
CBHW070910100426
42814CB00003B/116